PLACE-NAMES OF NORTHERN IRELAND

Volume One

COUNTY DOWN I

NEWRY AND SOUTH-WEST DOWN

D1477162

Published 1992
The Institute of Irish Studies
The Queen's University of Belfast
Belfast

Research and Publication funded by the
Central Community Relations Unit

Copyright 1992

ISBN 0 85389 432 9 (pb)
ISBN 0 85389 449 3 (hb)

Printed by W. & G. Baird Ltd, Antrim.

Place-Names of Northern Ireland

VOLUME ONE

County Down I
Newry and South-West Down

Gregory Toner and Mícheál B. Ó Mainnín

The Northern Ireland Place-Name Project
Department of Celtic
The Queen's University of Belfast

General Editor: Gerard Stockman

RESEARCH GROUP

Professor Gerard Stockman

R.J. Hannan MA
Dr A.J. Hughes
Dr Kay Muhr
Mícheál B. Ó Mainnín MA
Dr Gregory Toner
Eilís McDaniel BA, MSc (1987–1990)

LIST OF ILLUSTRATIONS

Cover: Newry in 1609, *Escheated County Maps* no. 26 (Orior) (with permission of the Deputy Keeper of the Records, Public Record Office of Northern Ireland)

The cover logo is the pattern on one face of a standing stone found at Derrykeighan, Co. Antrim. The art style is a local variant of the widespread "Celtic Art" of the European Iron Age and dates to about the 1st century AD. The opposite side of the stone is similarly decorated. (Drawing by Deirdre Crone, copyright Ulster Museum).

The townland maps have been prepared from OSNI digitized data by Kay Muhr. Based on the Ordnance Survey map with the sanction of the Controller of HM Stationery Office, Crown Copyright reserved (Permit no. 354).

ACKNOWLEDGEMENTS

In a multi-disciplinary field of study such as place-names, consultation with outside experts is of vital importance. We cannot thank by name all those who have given us of their time and knowledge, but among them we count the following:

Eilís McDaniel, formerly of the Northern Ireland Place-name Project, who initiated the computerization of the project, collected historical forms for the parishes of Newry, Drumgath and Donaghmore, and assisted in determining Irish forms for the toponyms in these parishes.

Dr Cathair Ó Dochartaigh, Dr Leslie Lucas, W.C. Kerr, J.F. Rankin, Canon R.E. Turner, Mrs Maeve Walker.

Dr Kieran Devine, Dr A. Sheehan, Dr M.T. Flanagan, Mary Kelly, Dr Hiram Morgan, Pamela Robinson, of Queen's University, Belfast.

Art Ó Maolfabhail, Dónall Mac Giolla Easpaig, Pádraig Ó Cearbhaill, and Dr Nollaig Ó Muraíle of the Place-Names Branch of the Ordnance Survey of Ireland.

Angélique Day and Patrick McWilliams, Ordnance Survey Memoir Project, Institute of Irish Studies QUB.

Members of the Steering Committee: Michael Brand, Professor Ronnie Buchanan, Dr Maurna Crozier, Dr Alan Gailey, Dr Ann Hamlin, Dr Maurice Hayes, Tony McCusker, Dr Brian Walker.

Claire Foley, Ann Given, Dr Chris Lynn of the Archaeological Survey of Northern Ireland.

Leonard Brown, John Buckley, Chris Davidson, Geoff Mahood, Larry Toolan of the Ordnance Survey of Northern Ireland.

Dr Bill Crawford, Clifford Harkness, of the Ulster Folk and Transport Museum.

Dr Brian Trainor of the Ulster Historical Foundation.

Richard Warner of the Ulster Museum.

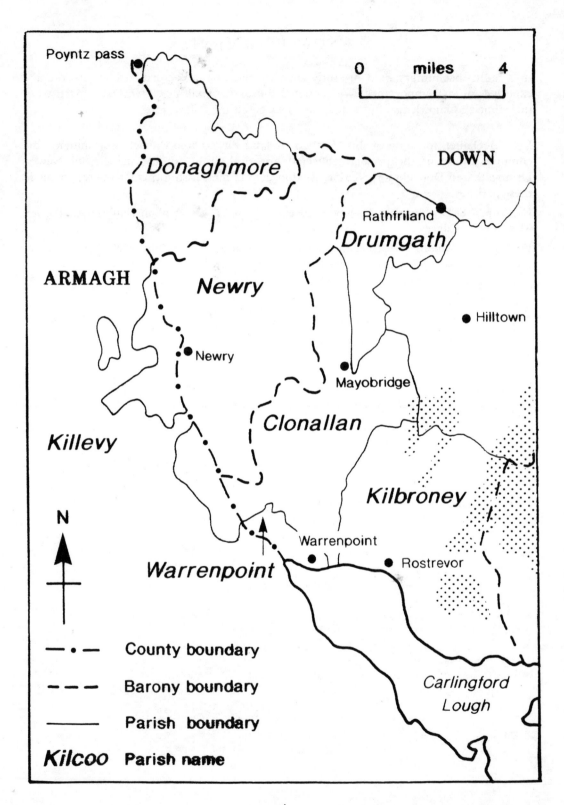

Poyntz pass

ARMAGH

DOWN

Donaghmore

Rathfriland

Drumgath

Newry

● Hilltown

● Newry

● Mayobridge

Clonallan

Killevy

Kilbroney

N

Warrenpoint ●

● Rostrevor

Warrenpoint

Carlingford Lough

0   miles   4

—·—·— County boundary

— — — Barony boundary

——— Parish boundary

Kilcoo Parish name

CONTENTS

GENERAL INTRODUCTION

BRIEF HISTORY OF PLACE-NAME STUDY IN IRELAND

Place-name lore or *dindsenchas* was a valued type of knowledge in early Ireland, to be learnt by students of secular learning in their eighth year of study. Stories about the origin of place-names appear regularly in early Irish literature. At the end of the epic "Cattle Raid of Cooley" the triumphal charge of the Brown Bull of Cooley around Ireland is said to have given rise to names such as Athlone (Irish *Áth Luain*), so called from the loin (*luan*) of the White-horned Bull slain by the Brown Bull. In the 10th, 11th and 12th centuries legends about the naming of famous places were gathered together into a number of great collections. Frequently, different explanations of the same name are offered in these legends, usually with no preference being expressed. In an entry on the naming of *Cleitech*, the royal palace of *Muirchertach mac Erca* on the Boyne, five separate explanations of the name are offered, none of which can be correct in modern scholarly terms. Place-name study was cultivated as a branch of literature.

Knowledge of Irish place-names was of practical importance during the English conquest and exploration of Ireland in the 16th century. Recurring elements in the place-names were noted by surveyors, and a table giving a few English equivalents appears on some maps of this period. There was concern that Irish names were "uncouth and unintelligible". William Petty, the great 17th-century surveyor and map-maker, commented that "it would not be amiss if the significant part of the Irish names were interpreted, where they are not nor cannot be abolished" (Petty 1672, 72–3). However, although the English-speaking settlers created many new names, they did not usually change the names of the lands they were granted, and the names of land units remained as they were, albeit in an anglicized form.

Interest in the meaning of Irish place-names developed further towards the end of the 18th century. The contributors to William Shaw Mason's *Parochial Survey of Ireland* often included a table explaining their local townland names, and this aspect was retained in the Statistical Reports compiled by the officers of the Royal Engineers on the parishes they surveyed for the first six-inch survey of Ireland in the early 1830s. Information on the spelling of place-names for the maps was collected in "name-books", and the Ordnance Survey was concerned to find that a variety of anglicized spellings was in use for many Irish place-names. The assistant director, Thomas Larcom, decided that the maps should use the anglicized spellings that most accurately represented the original Irish (Andrews 1975, 122) and he employed an Irish scholar, John O'Donovan, to comment on the name-books and recommend standard forms of names. O'Donovan was sent to the areas being surveyed to talk to local inhabitants, where possible Irish speakers, to find out the Irish forms. These were entered in the name-books, but were not intended for publication.

In 1855, a reader of *Ulster Journal of Archaeology* calling himself "De Campo" asked "that a list of all the townlands should be given in their Irish and English nomenclature, with an explanation of their Irish names" (*UJA* ser. 1, vol. iii, 251b). Meanwhile William Reeves, the Church of Ireland Bishop of Connor, had decided to compile a "monster Index" of all Irish townlands, which would eventually include the etymology of the names, "where attainable" (Reeves 1861, 486). Reeves' project was cited favourably by William Donnelly, the Registrar General, in his introduction to the first Topographical Index to the Census of Ireland: "It would greatly increase the value of a publication of this nature if it were accompanied by a glossary or explanation of the names, and an account of their origin" (*Census 1851* 1, 11–12).

However, it was left to another scholar, P. W. Joyce, to publish the first major work dealing exclusively with the interpretation of Irish place-names, and in his first chapter he acknowledges his debt to both O'Donovan and Reeves (*Joyce* i 7–8, 10). At this period the progress made by Irish place-name scholarship was envied in England (Taylor 1896, 205). The high standard of Joyce's work has made him an authority to the present day, but it is regrettable that most popular books published since on Irish place-names have drawn almost entirely on the selection and arrangement of names discussed by Joyce, ignoring the advances in place-name scholarship over the last hundred years (Flanagan D. 1979(f); 1981–2(b)).

Seosamh Laoide's *Post-Sheanchas*, published in 1905, provided an Irish-language form for modern post towns, districts and counties, and research on place-names found in early Irish texts resulted in Edmund Hogan's *Onomasticon Goedelicum* (1910). Local studies have been published by Alfred Moore Munn (Co. Derry, 1925), and P. M'Aleer (*Townland Names of County Tyrone*, c. 1920). The idea of a comprehensive official survey was taken up again by Risteard Ó Foghludha in the introduction to his *Log-ainmneacha* (1935). A Place-Names Commission was founded in Dublin in 1946 to advise on the correct forms of Irish place-names for official use and this was followed by the Place-Names Branch of the Ordnance Survey. They have published the Irish names for postal towns (*AGBP* 1969), a gazetteer covering many of the more important names in Ireland (*GÉ* 1989), a townland survey for Co. Limerick (1990), and most recently bilingual lists of the place-names of Cos Louth, Limerick and Waterford (1991).

John O'Donovan became the first professor of Celtic in Queen's University, Belfast, and in the 20th century members of the Celtic Department continued research on the place-names of the North of Ireland. The Ulster Place-Name Society was founded by the then head of department, Seán Mac Airt, in 1952 (Arthurs 1955–6, 80–82). Its primary aims were, (a) to undertake a survey of Ulster place-names; and (b) to issue periodically to members a bulletin devoted to aspects of place-name study, and ultimately to publish a series of volumes embodying the results of the survey. Several members undertook to do research on particular areas, much of which remains unpublished (Deirdre Flanagan on Lecale, and Dean Bernard Mooney on the names of the Diocese of Dromore).

The primary objective of the Ulster Place-Name Society was partly realized in 1987, when the Department of Celtic was commissioned by the Department for the Environment for Northern Ireland to do research into, "the origin of all names of settlements and physical features appearing on the 1:50,000 scale map; to indicate their meaning and to note any historical or other relevant information". In 1990, under the Central Community Relations Unit, the brief of the scheme was extended to include work on all townlands in Northern Ireland, and to bring the work to publication. Although individual articles have already been published by various scholars, the *Place-Names of Northern Ireland* series is the first attempt in the North at a complete survey based on original research into the historical sources.

METHOD OF PLACE-NAME RESEARCH

The method employed by the Project has been to gather early spellings of each name from a variety of historical records written mainly in Irish, Latin and English, and arrange them in chronological order. These, then, with due weight being given to those which are demonstrably the oldest and most accurate, provide the evidence necessary for deducing the etymology. The same name may be applied to different places, sometimes only a few miles apart, and all forms are checked to ensure that they are entered under the correct modern name. For example, there are a number of references to a place called *Crosgare* in 17th-century sources, none of which refer to the well-known town of Crossgar in Co. Down, but to a townland also called Crossgar a few miles away near Dromara. Identification of forms is most readily facilitated by those sources which list adjoining lands together or give the name of the landholder. Indeed, one of the greatest difficulties in using Irish sources and some early Latin or English documents is the lack of context which would enable firm location of the place-names which occur in them.

Fieldwork is an essential complement of research on earlier written sources and maps. Sometimes unrecorded features in local topography or land use are well-known to local inhabitants. More frequently the pronunciation represented by the early written forms is obscure, and, especially in areas where there has been little movement of people, the traditional local pronunciation provides valuable evidence. The members of the research team visited their respective areas of study, to interview and tape-record informants recommended by local historical societies etc., but many others met in the course of fieldwork kindly offered their assistance and we record here our gratitude. The local pronunciations have been transcribed in phonetic script and these are given at the end of each list of historical forms. The tapes themselves will become archive material for the future. The transcription used is based on the principles of the International Phonetic Alphabet, modified in accordance with the general practice in descriptions of Irish and Scottish Gaelic dialects. The following diagram illustrates the relative positions of the vowels used:

Front	Central	Back	
i		ʌ u	High
ɩ			
e	ï ö	o	High-mid
	ə		
ɛ		ǫ ɔ	Low-mid
a		ɑ	Low

Although this research was originally based on the names appearing on the 1:50,000 scale map, it soon became clear that many townland names, important in the past and still known to people today, were not given on the published version. Townlands form the smallest unit in the historical territorial administrative system of provinces, counties, baronies, parishes, and townlands. This system, which is that followed by the first Ordnance Survey of Ireland in its name-books, has been used in the organization of the books in this series. The names of all the relevant units are explained in Appendix B. Maps of the relevant barony and parish divisions within the county are supplied for the area covered in each book, to complement the published 1:50,000 series, and to make the historical context more accessible.

In the process of collecting and interpreting early forms for the *Place-Names of Northern Ireland* each researcher normally works on a group of 4 or 5 parishes. Since some books will contain 10 or more parishes, joint authorship will be the norm, and there may be differences of style and emphasis in the discussions within and between books. It seemed better to retain individuality rather than edit everything into committee prose. The suggested original Irish forms of the place-names were decided after group discussion with the general editor. The members of the group responsible for the text of each book will be distinguished by name on the contents page.

All the information in this book is also preserved in a computer database in Queen's University Belfast. It is hoped that this database will eventually become a permanent resource for scholars searching for examples of a particular type of name or name element. Modern map information, lists of the townlands making up historical parishes and baronies, historical sources and modern Irish forms are all available on separate files which can be searched and interrelated. The database was designed by Eilís McDaniel, and the Project gratefully acknowledges her continuing interest and assistance.

LANGUAGE

Since Ulster was almost wholly Irish-speaking until the 17th century, most names of town-lands are of Irish-language origin. Some early names were also given Latin equivalents for use in ecclesiastical and secular documents but few probably ever gained wide currency. Norse influence on northern place-names is surprisingly slight and is largely confined to coastal features such as **Strangford Lough** and **Carlingford Lough**. The arrival of the Anglo-Normans in the 12th century brought with it a new phase of naming and its influence is particularly strong in east Ulster, most notably in the Barony of Ards. Here, the names of many of their settlements were formed from a compound of the owner's name plus the English word *tūn* "settlement" which gives us Modern English "town". Names such as **Hogstown** and **Audleystown** have retained their original form, but a considerable number, such as **Ballyphilip** and **Ballyrolly**, derive from forms that were later gaelicized.

By the time of the Plantation of Ulster in the 17th century the system of townland units and their names already existed and this was adopted more or less wholesale by the English- and Scots-speaking settlers. These settlers have, nevertheless, left their mark on a sizeable body of names, particularly those of market towns, country houses, villages and farms which did not exist before the 17th century. What made the 17th-century Plantation different from the earlier ones was its extent and intensity, and it was the first time that the Irish language itself, rather than the Irish aristocracy, came under threat. The change from Irish to English speaking was a gradual one, and Irish survived into the 20th century in parts of Antrim and Tyrone. However, the language shift, assisted by an official policy that discriminated against Irish, eventually led to the anglicization of all names to the exclusion of Irish versions.

SPELLING AND PRONUNCIATION

Most of the historical sources used in this series were originally handwritten and this inevitably led to a considerable number of errors, both by contemporary copyists and by modern editors. Many of the documents, particularly grants, were copied time and again, while other sources sometimes only survive in late copies or published calendars. Mistakes could occur in any transcription but were particularly likely when the language or names being copied were unfamiliar. There is a long history of confusion in the Roman alphabet between letters of the type *i, u, n, m, w*. U and *n* are frequently confused, as are *m* and *w*. Where two or more of these letters occur together, the minims (vertical strokes) may be read in different combinations: the simple pair *ui* may be read as *iu, ni, in, m,* or *w*. Another common error is the confusion of long *s* (ʃ) and *f*. The name **Ballyhaft** (par. Newtownards, Dn) is frequently spelt in 17th-century sources with *s* instead of *f* and the modern form of the name may result from confusion of the written forms. In early sources, horizontal strokes (suspension strokes) could be written over a vowel as shorthand for a following *n* or *m*, but they were easily overlooked by scribes or editors. Spellings such as *Ballemulle* for **Ballymullan** (par. Bangor, Dn) may be explained in this way.

As well as taking account of spelling mistakes, there is sometimes difficulty in interpreting just what the spellings were intended to represent. For example, *gh*, which is usually silent in modern English dialects (e.g. night, fought) often retained its original value in the 17th century and was pronounced like the *ch* in Scots *loch* and *nicht*. Thus, *gh* was the obvious way to represent the Irish sound in words like *mullach* "summit", although both the English and Irish sounds were being weakened to [h] in certain positions at the time.

In Irish the spelling *th* was originally pronounced as in modern English *thick*, but in the 13th century it came to be pronounced [h]. The original Irish sound was anglicized as *th* or as *gh* at different periods but where the older form of the spelling has survived the sound *th* has often been restored by English speakers. In names such as **Rathmullen** and **Rathfriland**, where the initial element represents *ráth* "a ringfort", the *th* has almost invariably been re-established.

It is clear that some spellings used in place-names no longer signify what they did when first anglicized. The *-y* in the common elements "bally-" and "derry-" was selected to represent the final vowel in the corresponding Irish words *baile* and *doire* (the same sound as the *a* in "above") but this vowel is now usually pronounced as a short *ee* as in English words such as *happy, sorry*. In modern Ulster English, the vowel in words ending in *-ane*, such as *mane*, *crane*, is a diphthong, but in the 17th century it was pronounced as a long *a*. Thus, Irish *bán* "white" was usually represented in anglicized forms of names as *bane* as, for example, in the names **Kinbane** (Ant.) and **Carnbane** (Arm.) and this is frequently how the names are still pronounced locally.

SOURCES

The earliest representations of Irish place-names are found in a broad range of native material, written mostly in Irish although occasionally in Latin, beginning in the 7th or 8th centuries. The Irish annals, probably begun about 550 AD (Byrne 1973, 2) but preserved in manuscripts of much later date, contain a large number of place-names, particularly those of tribes, settlements, and topographical features. Tribal names and those of the areas they inhabited frequently appear among genealogical material, a substantial proportion of which is preserved in a 12th-century manuscript, Rawlinson B 502, but is probably much older. Ecclesiastical records include martyrologies or calendars giving saints' names, often with the names and locations of their churches. The Latin and Irish accounts of the life of St Patrick, which depict him travelling around Ireland founding a series of churches, contain the first lists of place-names which refer to places owned by a particular institution. Later Irish saints' lives also may list lands dedicated to the founder of a church. Medieval Irish narrative shows a great interest in places, often giving, for example, long lists of place-names passed through on journeys. Although many of these sources may date back to the 7th or 8th centuries, the copies we have often survive only in manuscripts of the 12th century and later, in which the spelling may have been modernized or later forms of names substituted.

The administrative records of the reformed Church of the 12th century are among the first to provide detailed grants of land. There are also records from the international Church, such as the papal taxation of 1302–06 (*Eccles. Tax.*). These records are more productive for place-name study, since the names are usually of the same type (either parishes or other land units owned by the church) and are usually geographically related, making them easier to identify with their modern counterparts. However, the place-names in these documents are not usually spelled as they would be in Irish.

Paradoxically, perhaps, the 17th-century Plantation provides a massive amount of evidence for the place-names of Ulster. Grants to and holdings by individuals were written down by government officials in fiants, patents and inquisitions (in the latter case, the lands held by an individual at death). A series of detailed surveys, such as the *Escheated Counties* maps of 1609, the *Civil Survey* of 1654–6, and Sir William Petty's Down Survey (*Hib. Del.* and *Hib. Reg.*), together with the records of the confiscation and redistribution of land found in the *Books of Survey and Distribution* (*BSD*) and the *Act of Settlement* (*ASE*), meant that, for the first time, almost all the names of smaller land units such as townlands were recorded. Unfortunately the richness of these resources has been depleted by two serious fires among the Irish public records, one in 1711 and the other in the Four Courts in Dublin in 1922. As a result, some of the original maps, and the Civil Survey covering the north-eastern counties, are lost, and the fiants, patents, inquisitions and Act of Settlement now only exist in abridged form in calendars made by the Irish Record Commission in the early 19th century. These calendars were criticized even at the time of publication for their degree of précis and for inaccurate transcription of names.

After the 17th century, little surveying of an official nature was carried out in Ireland, despite the clearance of woods and bogs and reclamation of waste land. The best sources for the 18th century, therefore, are family papers, leases, wills and sometimes estate maps, most of which remain unpublished. It became clear in the early 19th century that much of the taxation system was based on records that were out of date. The Ordnance Survey came to Ireland in 1824 and began in 1825 to do the first large-scale (six inches to the mile) survey of the country. Most of the variant spellings which they collected in their name-books were of the 18th or early 19th centuries, though in some cases local landowners or churchmen allowed access to earlier records, and these again provide a convenient and invaluable source of place-names. Minor names were also recorded in the descriptive remarks of the name-books, or in the fuller treatment of local names (water features, ancient monuments, church sites and other landmarks) in the associated Ordnance Survey Memoirs (*OSM*).

Early maps are an extremely valuable source, since they show the geographical relationship between names that is often crucial for identification purposes, and in many cases they are precise enough to locate lost townlands or to identify the older name of a townland. In parts of Ulster, maps by 16th-century surveyors may antedate texts recording place-names, thus providing the earliest attestation of the names in those areas.

However, maps have their own problems. Like other written texts they often copy from each other, borrowing names or outline or both. Inaccuracies are frequent, especially in the plotting of inland water features, whether due to seasonal flooding, or the lack of a vantage point for viewing the course of a river. Frequently the surveyor of the ground was not the person who drew or published the surviving map. The great continental and English map and atlas publishers, such as Ortelius, Mercator and Speed, all drew on earlier maps, and this custom undoubtedly led to the initiation and prolongation of errors of form and orthography. Sixteenth-century maps of Lough Neagh, for example, regularly show rivers entering the lake on the south between the Blackwater and the Bann where there are known to be none (Andrews 1978, plate 22). Unsurveyed territory was not always drawn to scale. Modern Co. Donegal, for example, is usually drawn too large on 16th-century maps, while Co. Derry is frequently shown too small. The *Escheated County* maps appear to have been partly drawn from verbal information and, in the map for the barony of Armagh, the draughtsman has produced a mirror image reversing east and west (Andrews 1974, 152).

William Petty's Down Survey provided the standard map of Ireland for the 17th century. In the 18th and early 19th centuries various individuals produced local county maps: Roque (1760) Co. Armagh; Lendrick (1780) Co. Antrim; Sampson (1814) Co. Derry; Sloane, Harris, Kennedy and Williamson (1739–1810) Co. Down; Knox and McCrea (1813) Co. Tyrone. These were consulted for the place-names on their own maps by the Ordnance Survey in the 1830s. Apart from published maps, a number of manuscript maps, some anonymous, others the original work of the 16th-century surveyors Lythe and Jobson, still exist. Richard Bartlett and Thomas Raven left important manuscript maps of Ulster from the early 17th century.

HOW TO USE THIS SERIES

Throughout the series, the editors have tried to adhere to the traditional territorial and administrative divisions used in Ireland, but this has not always proved possible. The convenient unit on which to base both research and publication has been the civil parish and all townland names and minor names are discussed under the relevant parish, regardless of whether they are in the same barony or county. Each book normally deals with the parishes in one or more barony, but where the barony is too large they are split into different books, some of which may contain material from geographically adjacent baronies. Every effort has been made to accommodate the historical system in a series of volumes of regular size. Each parish, barony and county is prefaced by an introduction which sets forth its location and history, and discusses some of the sources from which the older spellings of names have been extracted.

Within each parish, townland and other names are arranged in alphabetical order in separate sections following a discussion of the parish name. The first section deals with townland names. The second section deals with names of towns, villages, hills and water features which appear on the OS 1:50,000 map, but which are not classified as townlands. This section may also include a few names of historical importance which do not appear on the map but which may be of interest to the reader. Lesser names on the 1:50,000 are only treated if relevant material has been forthcoming. An index of all the names discussed in each book is given at the back of the relevant volume.

Each name to be discussed is given in bold print on the left-hand side of the page. Bold print is also used elsewhere in the text to cross-refer the reader to another name discussed in the series. The four-figure grid-reference given under each place-name should enable it to be located on modern Ordnance Survey maps.

Beneath the map name and its grid reference, all the pre-1700 spellings that have been found are listed, together with their source and date, followed by a selection of post-1700 forms. Early Irish-language forms are placed above anglicized or latinized spellings because of their importance in establishing the origin of the name. Irish forms suggested by 19th- and 20th-century scholars are listed below the historical spellings. Irish-language forms collected by O'Donovan in the last century, when Irish was still spoken in many parts of the North, require careful assessment. Some may be traditional, but there are many cases where the suggestion made by the local informant is contradicted by the earlier spellings, and it is clear that sometimes informants merely analysed the current form of the name. The current local pronunciation as collected by the editors appears below these Irish forms in phonetic script.

Spellings of names are cited exactly as they occur in the sources. Manuscript contractions have been expanded within square brackets, e.g. [ar]. Square brackets are also used to indicate other editorial readings: [...] indicates three letters in the name which could not be read, while a question mark in front of one or more letters enclosed in square brackets, e.g. [?agh], denotes obscure letters. A question mark in round brackets before a spelling indicates a form which cannot be safely identified as the name under discussion.

The dates of all historical spellings collected are given in the right-hand column, followed, where necessary, by *c* when the date is approximate. Here, we have departed from the normal practice, employed elsewhere in the books, because the database would otherwise have been unable to sort these dates in numeric order. In Latin and English sources a *circa* date usually indicates an uncertainty of a year or two. Irish language sources, however, rarely have exact dates and *circa* here represents a much longer time-span, perhaps of one or two centuries where the dating is based purely on the language of a text. Where no date has been established for a text, forms from that text are given the date of the earliest manuscript, in which they appear. Following normal practice, dates in the Irish annals are given as in the source, although this may give certain spellings an appearance of antiquity which they do not deserve. The Annals of the Four Masters, for example, were compiled in the early 17th century using earlier material, and many of the names in the text were modernized by its compilers. Moreover, annals were written later for dates before the mid-6th century, and the names, let alone the spellings, may not be that old. Another difficulty with dates concerns English administrative sources. The civil year in England and Ireland began on March 25th (Lady Day) until the year 1752, when the calendar was brought into line with changes made in the rest of Europe in 1582. Thus, the date of any document written between 1st of January and 24th of March inclusive has had to be adjusted to reconcile it with the current system by adding a year.

The original or most likely original Irish form of a name, where one is known to have existed, is given in italics on the top line to the right of the current spelling, with an English translation below. This includes Norse, Anglo-Norman and English names for which a Gaelic form once existed, as well as those of purely Irish origin. *Loch Cairlinn*, for example, was used by Irish-speakers for *Carlingford Lough* and this, rather than the original Norse, is printed on the top line. Although the name may have originally been coined at an early period of the language, standard modern Irish orthography is employed throughout, except in rare cases where this may obscure the meaning or origin of the name. The rules of modern Irish grammar are usually followed when not contradicted by the historical evidence. Where some doubt concerning the origin or form of a name may exist, or where alternatives may seem equally likely, plausible suggestions made by previous authorities, particularly the *OSNB* informants, are given preference and are printed at the top of the relevant entry. Nevertheless, where there is firm evidence of an origin other than that proposed by earlier scholars, the form suggested by our own research is given prominence.

Names for which no Irish original is proposed are described according to their appearance, that is, English, Scots, etc. The form and meaning is usually obvious, and there is no evidence that they replace or translate an original Irish name. Names which are composed of two elements, one originally Irish and the other English or Scots, are described as hybrid forms. An important exception to this rule is names of townlands which are compounded from a name derived from Irish and an English word such as "upper", "east", etc. In these cases, the original Irish elements are given on the right-hand side but the later English appendage is not translated.

In the discussion of each name, difficulties have not been ignored but the basic consideration has been to give a clear and readable explanation of the probable origin of the name, and its relationship to the place. Other relevant information, on the language of the name, on other similar names, on historical events, on past owners or inhabitants, on physical changes or local place-name legends, may also be included, to set the name more fully in context.

The townland maps which appear at the beginning of each parish show the layout of all the townlands in that parish. They are based on printouts from the Ordnance Survey's digitized version of the 1:50,000 map.

The rules of Irish grammar as they relate to place-names are discussed in Appendix A, and the historical system of land divisions in Ulster is described in Appendix B. The bibliography separates primary sources and secondary works (the latter being referred to by author and date of publication). This is followed by a glossary of technical terms used in this series. The place-name index, as well as providing page references, gives the 1:50,000 sheet numbers for all names on the published map, and sheet numbers for the 1:10,000 series and the earlier 6-inch county series for townland names. The index of Irish forms gives a semi-phonetic pronunciation for all names for which an Irish form has been postulated.

SUGGESTIONS FOR FURTHER INVESTIGATION

A work like this on individual names cannot give a clear picture of any area at a particular time in the past. Any source in the bibliography could be used, in conjunction with townland or other maps, to plot the references to a particular locality at that date, or to lands with a particular owner. Also the Public Record Office of Northern Ireland holds a considerable amount of unpublished material from the eighteenth century and later, which awaits investigation for information on place-names arising at that period.

Although fieldwork forms an integral part of place-name research, it is difficult for a library researcher to acquire the familiarity with an area that the local inhabitants have. Local people can walk the bounds of their townlands, or compare boundary features with those of the early 6-inch maps. Written or tape-recorded collections of local names (especially those of smaller features such as fields, rocks, streams, houses, bridges, etc.), where exactly they are to be found, how written and pronounced, and any stories about them or the people who lived there, would be a valuable resource for the future. The Place-Name Project will be happy to talk to anyone engaged on a venture of this kind.

Kay Muhr
Senior Research Fellow

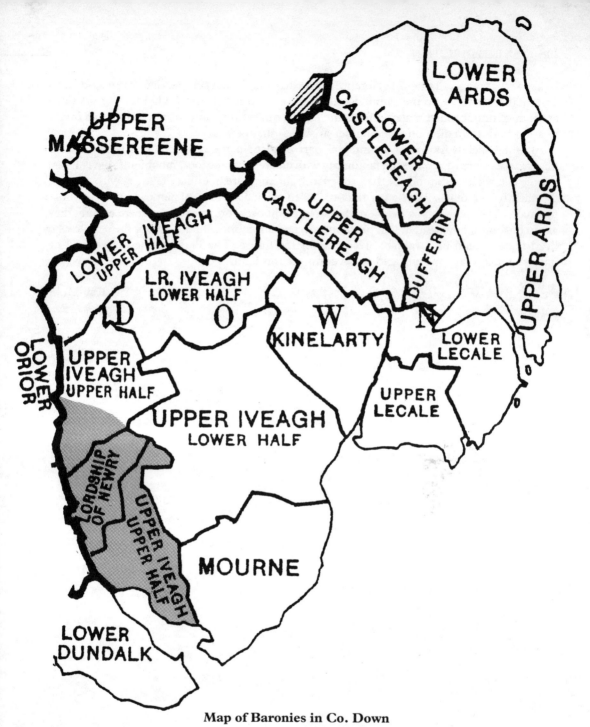

Map of Baronies in Co. Down

Ards Lower
Ards Upper
Castlereagh Lower
Castlereagh Upper
Dufferin
Iveagh Lower, Lower Half
Iveagh Lower, Upper Half
Iveagh Upper, Lower Half
Iveagh Upper, Upper Half
Kinelarty

Lecale Lower
Lecale Upper
Lordship of Newry
Mourne

Districts treated at one time as being in Co. Down are shown around the left-hand margin of the map. The area described in this volume, the Lordship of Newry and the Barony of Iveagh Upper, Upper Half (two sections), has been coloured to highlight its position.

INTRODUCTION TO COUNTY DOWN

The division of Ireland into counties was effected under English rule and is the most recent tier in the territorial administrative system of province, county, barony, parish and townland. The counties of Ulster as they now stand were established in the early 17th century, but were built up out of pre-existing smaller districts, some of which were preserved as baronies within the county. County Down is bounded by the sea to the south, east and north-east, but although some of its inland boundary markers are notable geographical features the area they delimit has partly been decided by historical events.

The *Ulaid* were once the most powerful tribal group in the north of Ireland and it is from them that the province of Ulster derives its name (Flanagan D. 1978(d)). However, in the 4th and 5th centuries they were driven eastwards into the modern counties of Antrim and Down under pressure from the *Uí Néill* and the *Airgialla*. In the south the new boundary between the Ulaid and the Airgialla may have been marked by the erection of the Danes' Cast along the marshes between the northern limit of the Newry River and the ford of the Bann at Banbridge. Of the chief Ulaid tribes, *Uí Echach Coba* were located along this borderland and *Dál nAraide* east of Lough Neagh and the lower Bann. A third tribe, *Dál Fiatach*, the "true Ulaid", settled in Lecale and in the vicinity of Strangford Lough. Their capital at *Dún dá Lethglas* (modern Downpatrick) was to become an important ecclesiastical centre. Other less important kingdoms within the reduced Ulster were the *Conaille Muirthemne* in north Louth (the Cooley peninsula) and *Dál Riata* in the Glens of Antrim.

From the 6th to 10th centuries the kingship of the Ulaid was shared by Dál Fiatach, Dál nAraide and Uí Echach Coba, but in the 8th century Dál Fiatach extended their influence northward over the area east of Lough Neagh. After the Anglo-Norman invasion the whole area east of the Upper and Lower Bann became the feudal Earldom of Ulster. However the influence of the local Dál Fiatach church was increased in 1186 when the Norman John de Courcy transferred the relics of three of the greatest Irish saints, Patrick, Brigid and Columcille, to Downpatrick cathedral. The diocese of Down, the boundaries of which were settled in the 12th century, was centred on this famous church and stretched as far north as the contemporary territorial limits of Dál Fiatach, though limited on the west by the Uí Echach diocese of Dromore. Through their ruling family of *Mac Duinnshléibhe* (MacDonlevy) Dál Fiatach retained some power as "king of the Irish of Ulidia" (*rex Hibernicorum Ulidiae*) until the late 13th century, though after their extinction the Gaelic title of *rí Ulad*, or "king of Ulster" (the province of the Ulaid), was claimed by the expanding O'Neills of *Cenél nEógain* to the west (Byrne 1973, 128–9).

Under the feudal Earldom of Ulster, English shire government was established in the territory of the Ulaid. It was divided into various native and other areas: the "bailiwicks of Antrim, Carrickfergus, Art, Blathewyc, Ladcathel" in 1226, the "counties of Cragfergus, Antrim, Blathewyc, Dun and Coulrath" in 1333 (*Inq. Earldom Ulster* i 31, ii 136, 141, iii 60, 63, iv 127). In 1549 the area was described as "the county of Ulster, that is to say the baronies of the Grenecastle, Dondalk, Lacayll, Arde, Differens, Gallagh, Bentry, Kroghfergous, Maulyn, Twscard and Glyns" (*Cal. Carew MSS* 1515–74, 223–4). In 1571 a commission was set up "to survey the countries of Lecale, the Duffrens, M'Carton's country, Slaighte M'Oneiles country, Kilvarlyn, Evaghe, M'Ghenes' country, Morne, the lands of the Nury, and O'Handlone's country, and to form them into one county, or to join them to any neighbouring counties or baronies" (*Fiants Eliz.* §1736). This led to the separation from Antrim of the modern county of Down, containing the baronies of Lecale, Dufferin, Kinelarty (McCarton's country), Castlereagh (part of the Clandeboy O'Neill country), Iveagh (Kilwarlin and Magennis' country), Mourne and Newry. However *O'Handlone's country* became part of Co. Armagh.

The county name, appearing as *Dun* in 1333, derives like that of the diocese from the Dál Fiatach capital *Dún dá Lethglas*. In the Norman and post-Norman period, Downpatrick usually appears in Latin and English documentation as *Dunum, Dun* or *Down(e)*, and in Irish writing of the medieval period the common form is *Dún*, never *Dún Pádraig* (Flanagan D. 1971, 89). In the *Ordnance Survey Memoirs* it is noted that Downpatrick was "more commonly called by the country people Down", and "even today *Down* rather than *Downpatrick* is the local usage" (*ibid.*). Thus, when the modern county was established at the end of the 16th century, Down was still the name of the shire town. The form *Downpatrick*, which had no currency before the early 17th century, became more popular from 1617 onwards, perhaps due to the creation in that year of the Manor of Downpatrick (*ibid.*). However it never influenced the county name.

The county boundaries were not settled all at once. Jobson's set of Ulster maps (c. 1590) and Norden's map of Ireland (1610) show the names and bounds of the three counties of Antrim, Down and Armagh. Both cartographers still include in Down the Cooley peninsula (now in Co. Louth) and also Loughgilly, O'Hanlon's chief seat in the barony of Orior (Co. Armagh). According to Jobson, Armagh extended across the outflow of the Bann into Lough Neagh to include Clanbrasil (later the barony of Oneilland East), and Down included Killultagh on the east bank of Lough Neagh (later the barony of Upper Massareene in Co. Antrim). A document in the state papers of 1603 refers to "Downe county alias Leycaile" (which includes *Cowley* and *Omethe* in modern Co. Louth), but gives *Kilulto* as a separate "country" (*Cal. Carew MSS* 1601–3, 451). In 1605 Killultagh was annexed to Co. Antrim (*CSP Ire.* 1603–6, 321). In the same year an inquisition on Clandeboy stated that the most noted boundary between the parts of it called Killultagh and Upper Clandeboy (later Castlereagh) was the river Lagan (*Inq. Ult.* §2 Jac. I), and the Lagan remains the boundary between Cos Antrim and Down to this day.

The land east of the Upper Bann on the shore of Lough Neagh, known as Clanbrasil, was traditionally Uí Echach Coba or Magennis territory. In 1605 *Clanbrassilagh* "which before lay doubtful between it and the county of Down" was formally annexed to the new county of *Ardmaghe* (*CSP Ire.* 1603–6, 318), becoming eventually the barony of Oneilland East. A dispute arose between John Brownlow and Capt. Edward Trevor in 1612 concerning the ownership of six townlands in Kilmore, a district between Clanbrasil and Killultagh. Brownlow had been granted the area as lying in Co. Armagh while Trevor had been granted exactly the same lands as lying in Co. Down (*Ulst. Plant. Paps.* 266, §60). The plantation commissioners found that the land was in Co. Armagh and awarded it to Brownlow, compensating Trevor with other lands. Sir Arthur Magennis then claimed the area from Brownlow as part of his own property in Co. Down, but the commissioners refused to recompense him unless he could prove title, and the lands remained in Brownlow's possession (*ibid.* 269, §61). Modern Co. Down has retained one townland still called Kilmore, a strip of land connecting it with Lough Neagh, although Kilmore is part of the civil parish of Shankill, all the rest of which is in Co. Armagh. The artificiality of the county boundary in this area continued to cause problems: Sir William Petty in his barony and county maps (*Hib. Reg.* c. 1657; *Hib. Del.* c. 1672) thought that the Bann formed the northern boundary between Cos Down and Armagh, and placed the Armagh parishes of Seagoe and Shankill to the west of the river instead of to the east. The diocese of Dromore, however, reflects the earlier boundary between Uí Echach Coba and Airgialla, in that it includes Seagoe and Shankill and follows the river Bann all the way to Lough Neagh (see **Iveagh** introduction p. 48).

The date at which the southern border of Co. Down was settled is difficult to ascertain from the sources. The ancient territory of the Ulaid had stretched as far south as the river

Boyne, and even after the Ulaid were driven east by the Uí Néill the Conaille tribe of north Louth remained part of the Ulaid confederation. The feudal Earldom of Ulster covered the same area, so that in 1549 the "county of Ulster" still extended from the north Antrim coast to Dundalk (*Cal. Carew MSS* 1515–74, 223–4, quoted above). In 1552 the royal grant of Newry, Mourne, Carlingford, Omeath and Cooley to Sir Nicholas Bagenal preserves the cohesion of the older territory, but already the first two areas are said to be in the county of Down or in *Ullestere*, and the others in the county of Louth (*CPR Ed. VI* iv, 387–90). The latest documentary reference to Cooley being part of Co. Down is in the Carew MSS for 1603, though it is shown on Jobson's and Norden's maps (all quoted above). However, in an earlier document in the Carew collection (1596) the northern limit of Co. Louth in the English Pale is given as "the fues and o'hanlon's country" i.e. Co. Armagh, as at present (Falkiner 1904, 141). By the time of the Plantation this is also the border of the re-established province of Ulster.

Barony of The Lordship of Newry
Barony of Orior Upper, Co. Armagh

Parish of Newry

Townlands

Altnaveigh (Orior Upper, Co. Armagh)
Ardarragh
Ballinlare (Orior Upper, Co. Armagh)
Ballyholland Lower
Ballyholland Upper
Ballynacraig
Benagh
Carnacally
Carnbane (Orior Upper, Co. Armagh)
Carneyhough
Carnmeen
Castle Enigan
Cloghanramer
Commons
Corcreeghy
Creeve
Crobane

Croreagh
Curley
Damolly
Derry Beg (Orior Upper, Co. Armagh)
Derry More (Orior Upper, Co. Armagh) (detached)
Derryboy
Derryleckagh
Desert
Drumalane (Orior Upper, Co. Armagh)
Drumcashellone
Edenmore
Fathom Lower (Orior Upper, Co. Armagh)
Fathom Upper (Orior Upper, Co. Armagh)
Finnard
Gransha
Greenan

Lisdrumgullion (Orior Upper, Co. Armagh)
Lisdrumliska (Orior Upper, Co. Armagh)
Lisduff
Lisnaree
Lisserboy
Loughorne
Newry Bridewell (Orior Upper, Co. Armagh)
Ouley
Ryan
Saval Beg
Saval More
Sheeptown
Shinn
Turmore

Town
Newry

The following detached townlands are too far away to be shown on the map:

Grange Lower (Barony of Oneilland West, Co. Armagh) (detached)
Grange Upper (Barony of Oneilland West, Co. Armagh) (detached)
Shannaghan (Barony of Iveagh Upper, Lower Half) (detached)

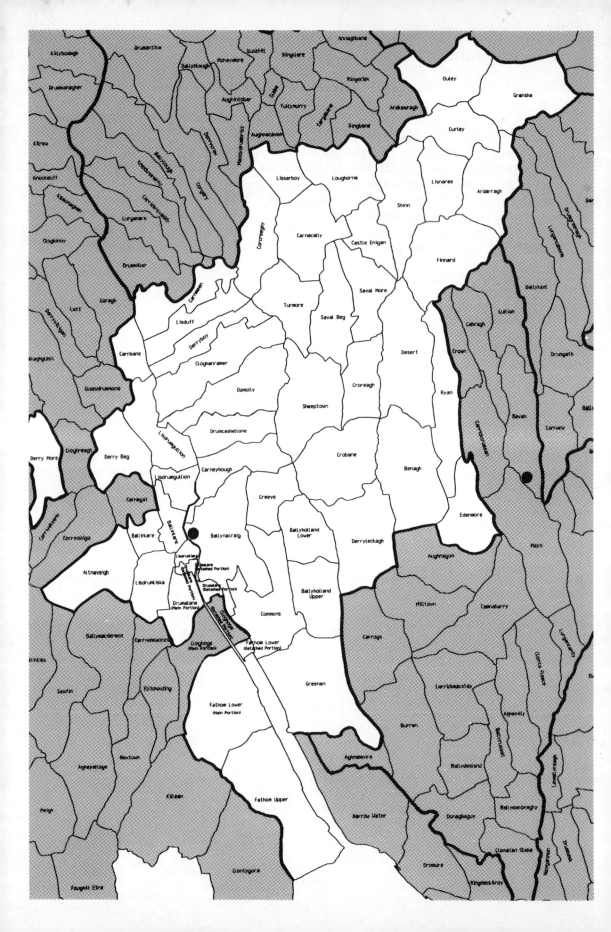

PARISH AND LORDSHIP OF NEWRY

According to the 17th-century historian, Geoffrey Keating, the Cistercian abbey at Newry was founded in 1144 by St Malachy (*Céitinn* iii 354). It was granted a charter, sometimes wrongly understood as a foundation charter (*Mon. Hib.* 285; cf. *EA* 117n) c.1157 confirming its lands and possessions by *Muirchertach mac Lochlainn*, king of the *Cenél nÉogain* and high-king of Ireland, in association with many of the kings and princes of south Ulster (*Newry Char. (Flanagan)*). Local tradition had it that the town took its name, in Irish *an tIúr* "the yew-tree", from two large yew trees which formerly grew in the grounds of the abbey (*Harris Hist.* 90) and the *Annals of the Four Masters* report that the monastery was destroyed by fire in 1162 "with all its equipment and books and even the yew tree which Patrick himself planted" (*AFM* ii 1146).

The monastery was converted into a secular college by Henry VIII in 1543 (*Fiants Hen. VIII* §366) and in 1552 the abbey and its lands were granted to Sir Nicholas Bagnall, Knight Marshall of Ireland (*CPR Ed. VI* iv 387). When Bagnall arrived in Ireland he found the lordships of Newry and Mourne "altogether waste, and Shane Oneil dwellinge within less than a mile to the Newrie, at a place called Fedom [Fathom] suffringe no subject to travell from Dundalk northward" (*Bagenal's Descr. Ulst.* 151). Newry was of great importance to the English as "it was a considerable Pass leading through the Bogs and Mountains between Dundalk and these Eastern Parts of Ulster, with which at that time there was no other Communication by Land" (*Harris Hist.* 88) and Bagnall immediately set about securing the town and surrounding area (*ibid.* 89).

The Newry Charter represents the earliest comprehensive source for the study of the place-names of Newry. The original does not survive but a copy was made in the early 17th century by Sir James Ware and this is now contained in a manuscript in the British Museum (Add. MS. 4792 fol. 155r–v). Reeves attempted to identify the names of the lands that were granted to the monastery and concluded that "they all belong to townlands in the Lordship of Newry" (*EA* 117n). However, many of his identifications have little or no foundation and it is virtually certain that the charter includes a small number of lands in the Kilkeel area. Indeed, less than half of the names mentioned in the charter can now be located in the lordship of Newry and these are wholly confined to the first part of the list, that is, from the mention of *Athcrathin* to *Fidglassayn* or, possibly, *Tirmorgonnean*. Reeves identified this latter as the townland of Turmore (*EA* 117n) but, apart from the difficulties in explaining the final element, the representation of the vowel in the first syllable is hard to reconcile with the historical spellings (see **Turmore**). Reeves also identified the names *Cimocul, Saolcean, Bile in Ledengan* and *Caractean* as the modern townlands of Carnacally, Ballyholland, Derryleckagh and Ryan but the 16th- and 17th-century forms offer no support for this conclusion. Similarly, his assertion that *Lisdorca* of the Charter represents the modern townland of Lisduff is without foundation. Reeves' view seems to be based on the belief that the second element in the name in the Charter probably represents Irish *dorcha* meaning "dark" and is thus more or less synonymous with the element *dubh* "black" in **Lisduff**. However, this hardly presents us with sufficient evidence for the identification of the two forms and it would appear that the townland of Lisduff was formerly known as *Lissenecrossne et var.* Finally, Reeves' identification of *Betheac* as the townland of Benagh must be questioned. The form in the Charter may represent Irish *Beitheach* meaning "a place abounding in birches" and, as such, may have been an earlier form of *Beitheanach* which gives us modern **Benagh**. However, *Betheac* is the last name to be listed in the Charter and so does not occur along with the other lands which can be safely identified as belonging to Newry. Indeed, there is a possibility that it is to be located in the parish of Kilkeel where there is also a townland called **Benagh** and this possibility is strengthened by the fact that other names from Kilkeel occur in this part of the list.

In August of 1549, two inquisitions were taken at Newry to establish the former properties of the collegiate church in the Newry and Carlingford areas (*Inq. (Mon. Hib.)* 286–288). A subsequent grant of 1552 to Nicholas Bagenal is very close in wording to these inquisitions, particularly the later one, and it is clearly copied, directly or indirectly, from there (*CPR Ed. VI* 388–9). All the grants and inquisitions relating to Newry in the late 16th and early 17th centuries are closely related, and there can be little doubt that they are all copied from one another. In particular, they invariably list the townlands of the parish in the same order, beginning usually with Moycarne (now lost) and following a direct path south through Carnmeen, Lisduff, Derryboy, etc. before veering north again. Even within this scheme, however, certain "families" of documents with an especially close relationship seem to emerge. Such, for example, are a grant of 1613 (*CPR Jas. I* 246b) and an inquisition of c. 1625 (*Inq. Ult. (Down)* §15 Jac. I); an inquisition taken at Newry on 23 May, 1638 (*Inq. Ult. (Down)* §84 Car. I) follows very closely a licence granted to Arthur Bagnall in 1606 (*CPR Jas. I* 86a) but with the addition of numerous aliases; and two documents dating from 1607 are virtually identical (*CPR Jas. I* 102b–103a, 494b–495a).

The *Bagenal Rental* of 1575 is very different from the other documents discussed here and, as such, is of considerable value. The Rental seems to have been compiled by someone with local knowledge and the spellings in it are often closer to the current form of the name than those of the 17th-century grants and inquisitions. As we have seen, the early grants and inquisitions are closely related, and it is clear that we are dealing with official documents which have been copied, time and again, from one another. This process facilitates the retention of more archaic spellings but it is also prone to the initiation and prolongation of errors (see **Ballyholland**). The Rental itself is not altogether free of mistakes for, although each part of the Rental is in the name of the respective "constable of the castle" (Randolph Brereton in the case of Newry), the document as it stands is in the same hand throughout (O'Sullivan 1985, 34). Not only is the spelling of the place-names occasionally inaccurate but also the spelling of the names of tenants, and many of the mathematical calculations are wrong (*ibid.*).

John O'Donovan met with considerable difficulties when he came to Newry to ascertain the origins of the local names for the Ordnance Survey. In a letter written in Newry on April 10th, 1834 he recounts some of his disappointments:

> Having heard that all the Roman Catholic clergy of Dromore were to be in Newry on the 9th of this month, I thought it advisable to remain here to see them, but in that I have been disappointed, although I had applied to Dr. Blake for that purpose on the evening before. However, when the time arrived, I found that I could not disturb them in their conviviality; and certainly although I was distressed at the disappointment, I am now convinced that it would have been very unpolite and obtrusive in me to interrupt so convivial and jovial a class of his Majesty's loyal subjects by my dry topographical and philological speculations. It has afforded me some consolation to learn that, with the exception of two, they could be of no assistance to me. (*OSL* 44–45)

He tried on numerous occasions to find a native of the area who could speak Irish or who understood the townland names but he was invariably told that there was no such person (*ibid.* 45). Finally, the Rev. Mr. Glenny, son of the proprietor of Glenville, took him to the oldest man in the parish, Old MacGilvoy (*ibid.* 46). He was 84 years of age but O'Donovan got him to pronounce the townland names in the Lordship of Newry as he had heard them in Irish and give their meanings (*ibid.* 46). O'Donovan expresses delight in the response he received from MacGilvoy and, indeed, his etymologies are often correct. However, he was, of course, working with no knowledge of the older spelling of the names and this sometimes led him into substantial errors. **Finnard**, for example, he takes to be derived from Irish *Fionnard* meaning "white height" but the earlier forms clearly show that it must have come from *Fionnúir*, an old name of obscure origin. **Benagh** is similarly misinterpreted as *Béanach* "pointed, peaked" and had he had access to the historical spellings he might have been able to suggest an Irish origin in *Beitheanach* "birch-abounding place".

The parish of Newry is not quite contiguous with the Lordship of Newry which is considerably smaller than the parish. Thirty-six of the parish's townlands are contained in the Lordship, but there are a further ten on the far side of the Newry River in the Barony of Orior Upper. The two detached townlands of Grange Upper and Grange Lower are situated in the Barony of Oneilland West in Co. Armagh, and the single townland of Shannaghan is sandwiched between the parishes of Drumgooland, Garvaghy, Annaclone, and Drumballyroney in the Barony of Iveagh Upper, Lower Half.

PARISH NAME

Newry   *An tIúr*
"the yew tree"

1. Iobhar Chind Trachta	AFM ii 936	1089
2. Iubhair Chind Trachta, abb manach	AFM ii 1136	1160
3. Iubhar Cinntrechta	AFM ii 1146	1162
4. co hIubhar Chinn Choiche	AFM iii 290	1236
5. co h-Iobhar Cinn Coice, mhic Neachtain, fris a raiter Iobhar Chinn Tragha an tan sa	CMR 276	1280c
6. ón Iobhraidh	Ad. Dána 85 §26	1439c
7. an Iubhair, abb manach	AFM v 1380	1526
8. an Iubhair, do mharasccál	AFM vi 1940	1593
9. go hIobhar Chinn Trágha	AFM vi 1966	1595
10. i nIubhar Cinntragha	AFM vi 1998	1596
11. don Iubhar	AFM vi 2024	1597
12. don Iubhar	AFM vi 2060	1598
13. an Iubhair, maruscál	AFM vi 2060	1598
14. go hIubhar Chinn Trágha	AFM vi 2110	1599
15. d'Iubhar Chinnchoidhce mic Neachtain risin abar Iubhar Cinn Trachta an tansa	C. Conghail Cláir. 30	1600c
16. isin Iubhar	AFM vi 2258	1601
17. ind Iobhar Cind Tragha	B. Aodha Ruaidh 128	1616c
18. co hIubhar Cind Tragha	B. Aodha Ruaidh 166	1616c
19. Iobhar Cinn Choiche mic Nechtain	B. Aodha Ruaidh 174	1616c
20. don Iobhar	B. Aodha Ruaidh 174	1616c
21. gusan Iobhar	B. Aodha Ruaidh 184	1616c
22. i nIubhur Cinn Tragha	Cín Lae Ó M. 10	1645c
23. an Iubhair, Captin	Cín Lae Ó M. 10	1645c
24. an Iubhair, maidhm	LCABuidhe 33 §42	1680c

3

25. ón Iubhar	LCABuidhe 50 §5	1680c
26. go hIobhar	LCABuidhe 246 §97	1680c
27. ó Iubhar na n-inbher nglan	LCABuidhe 246 §101	1680c
28. a. Nyvorcyntracta	Newry Char. (Flanagan)	1157c
b. Nivorc'yntracta	Newry Char. (Mon. Ang.) 1134	1157c
29. Viridi Ligno, Abbas de	Eccles. Tax. 116	1306c
30. de Viridi Ligno	Reg. Sweteman §43	1370
31. de Viridiligno	Cal. Papal Letters 421 et pass.	1414
32. (de) Viridi Ligno	Reg. Swayne 71 et pass.	1427c
33. Viride Lignum	Reg. Fleming §262	1454
34. Viridiligno	Annates Ulst. 290	1478
35. Viridi, Vicarius de Ligno	Reg. Dowdall §129 275	1542c
36. le Nyvorie (×2)	Fiants Hen. VIII §366	1543
37. Viridi Ligno, Vicarius de	Reg. Dowdall §113 81	1546
38. de Viridi ligno	Inq. (Mon. Hib.) 286	1549
39. Newry, the townland of	Inq. (Mon. Hib.) 286	1549
40. Newry, the town of	Inq. (Mon. Hib.) 286	1549
41. le Newery	CPR Ed. VI iv 387	1552
42. Newry	Gough's Map	1567
43. Ye Newry	Nowell's Ire. (1)	1570c
44. the Nury	Fiants Eliz. §1736	1571
45. Nowery (×2)	Fiants Eliz. §4327	1583c
46. the Newrye	Fiants Eliz. §4327	1583c
47. the Nury	Fiants Eliz. §5552	1591
48. the Newrye	Fiants Eliz. §6324	1599
49. Newry	Boazio's Map (BM)	1599
50. the Newerie	Fiants Eliz. §6557	1601
51. Newry	CPR Jas. I 28a	1603
52. Newrie	CPR Jas. I 10a,12a,30a	1603
53. Newrie	CPR Jas. I 35b	1603
54. Newrii	Bodley's Lecale 75	1603c
55. Newrie	CPR Jas. I 59a	1604
56. Newrie	CPR Jas. I 86a	1606
57. Newrie	CPR Jas. I 90b	1606
58. the Newrie	CPR Jas. I 96a	1606
59. Newry	CPR Jas. I 102b	1607
60. Newrie	Esch. Co. Map 5.26	1609
61. Newry	Speed's Antrim & Down	1610
62. Newrie	Inq. Ult. (Down) §§5,7,9,15 Jac. I	1620c
63. the Newrie (×2)	Ulster Visit. (Reeves) 29	1622
64. the Newry	Inq. Ult. (Down) §15 Jac. I	1625c
65. Newry	Inq. Ult. (Down) §6 Car. I	1627
66. Newry	Inq. Ult. (Down) §51 Car. I	1635
67. le Newry (×2)	Inq. Ult. (Down) §84 Car. I	1638
68. the Newry (×2)	Civ. Surv. x §77	1655c
69. the Newry (×2)	Inq. Down (Reeves 1) 101	1657
70. Nury, Lordshipp of	Hib. Reg. Up. Iveagh	1657c
71. Newry	Hib. Reg. Orior	1657c

72. Newry (Lordship & Parish)	BSD 130	1661
73. Newrye, Castle Towne & Manor of	BSD 130	1661
74. Nury Lordship	Hib. Del. (Down)	1672c
75. Nury (town)	Hib. Del. (Down)	1672c
76. Nury	Diary War Jas. II 24	1689
77. ye Newry (×2)	Diary War Jas. II 25	1689
78. Newry, Parish of	Bnd. Sur (OSNB) 99	1830c
79. Na Júr "of the Yew-Trees"	Harris Hist. 90	1744
80. Inbher Chinn Tragha "the River at the head of the Strand"	Stuart's Armagh 99	1819
81. Na Yur	Stuart's Armagh 99	1819
82. An t-iubhar "the Yew Tree"	J O'D (OSNB) 99	1834c
83. Iúbhar cínn tráighe "yew at head of the strand"	OSL 47	1835
84. Iubhar Chinn Trágha (an t-Iubhar)	Post-Sheanchas 102	1905
85. An tIúr	AGBP 118	1969
86. An tIúr	Éire Thuaidh	1988
87. An tIúr	GÉ 119	1989
88. 'nju:ri	Local pronunciation	1990

This name is particularly well-documented in native Irish sources where the earliest form seems to have been *Iubhar Cinn Tráchta* (modern *Iúr Cinn Tráchta*). Harris translates this as "the flourishing Head of a Yew-Tree" (*Harris Hist.* 90) but it is doubtless synonymous with the later form *Iubhar Cinn Trágha* (*Iúr Cinn Trá*) "the yew of the head of the strand". It was also called *an tIubhar* (*an tIúr*) "the yew".

The anglicized forms of the name must, however, come from *an Iubhraigh* (modern *an Iúraigh*), an oblique form of *an Iubhrach* (modern *an Iúrach*) "the grove of yew trees". This form, despite the fact that the anglicized form of the name derives from it, does not, with one possible exception, appear in Irish-language sources. In an early 15th-century poem by Tuathal Ó hUiginn, Niall Garbh Ó Domhnaill, Lord of Tír Chonaill, is portrayed as coming "*ón Iobhraidh*" (from *an Iúrach*) after a raid on *Baile Uí Bruin* (*Ad. Dána* 85 §26) but, unfortunately, this instance of the name cannot be certainly connected to Newry. Indeed, *an Iúrach* was the name of the stronghold of Rughraidhe mac Ardghail mac Mathghamhna who is probably the chieftain whose death is recorded in the *Annals of the Four Masters* under the year 1446, and it is very probably this house, rather than the settlement at Newry, which was attacked by Niall Garbh (*Gwynn Cat.* 208).

The form "Nova Ripa, alias Nieu Rie" cited by Lewis from the Royal Visitation Book of 1615 (*Lewis' Top. Dict.* 433) seems to represent an attempt to produce an etymology of the anglicized form of the name meaning "new bank (of a river)". According to Reeves, Newry was sometimes latinized *Ivorium* and *Nevoracum* but it is more frequently called *Viride Lignum* (*EA* 116n). Atkinson is doubtless correct in concluding that *Viride Lignum*, which he translates as "Green Tree", refers to the evergreen character of the yews associated with the monastery at Newry (*Atkinson's Dromore* 7). The Cistercians were fond of giving their monasteries clever, often paradoxical, Latin names such as (*de*) *Melle Fonte* "honey spring" (Mellifont) and *de Petra Fertile* "fertile rock" (Corcomroe), and *Viride Lignum* represents a further example of their ingenuity.

TOWNLAND NAMES

Altnaveigh	*Allt na bhFiach*	
J 0625	"the glen of the ravens"	
1. Ballaghan	CPR Jas. I 86a	1606
2. Altnaveagh	Esch. Co. Map 5.26	1609
3. Ballachan al' Altenfeagh	Inq. Ult. (Armagh) §2 Jac. I	1612
4. Ballachan orse Altenfeagh	CPR Jas. I 247b	1613
5. Ballaghane al' Ballaghowe	Inq. Ult. (Armagh) §27 Car. I	1638
6. Altnaveiagh	Inq. Arm. 228	1657
7. Alleviagh	BSD 10	1661
8. Altnaveagh	HMR Murray (1940) 134	1664
9. Aughnaveigh	Bnd. Sur (OSNB) 99	1830c
10. Alt na bhfiach "Ravens Glen"	OSNB Inf. 99	1835
11. Alt na bhFiach "Glen-side of the ravens"	J O'D (OSNB) 99	1835
12. ˌɔːknəˈveː	Local pronunciation	1990

The four townlands of Derrymore, Derrybeg, Ballinlare and Altnaveigh, which were once collectively known as "the four towns of Coghall" (*CPR Jas. I* 247b, *Inq. Ult.* (Armagh) §2 Jac. I), did not form part of the lands held by the old monastery at Newry but were purchased by Sir Nicholas Bagnall from the O'Hanlons (*Inq. Ult.* (Armagh) §2 Jac. I). The four townlands were the cause of some dispute in the early 17th century when the lands belonging to Oghy O'Hanlon became forfeit after he broke the conditions upon which they had been granted to him by Queen Elizabeth in 1587 (*Sur. Ulst.* 215; *Fiants Eliz.* §5090). An inquisition taken at Ballinlare on October 28, 1612, reports that Arthur Bagnall was seized of the townlands of Derrymore, Derrybeg, Ballinlare and Altnaveigh "all of which descended according to the course of common law, ever since the said sir Nicholas Bagnall purchased them from the O'Hanlons; but the said 4 towns were incerted by p[ar]ticular names in the late general survey, as escheated to his Ma[jes]tie by the forfeiture of sir Oghy O'Hanlon knt. and soe past to severall servitors and natives, by pattents in several parcells, whoe nowe claim the same." (*Inq. Ult.* (Armagh) §2 Jac. I).

The townland of Ballinlare was granted to a certain Callogh McDonnell in 1611 (*CPR Jas. I* 196b) and the townland of Derrymore was granted to Henry McShane O'Neill (*Ulst. Plant. Paps.* §65 272). The latter dispute was discussed by the Plantation Commissioners in 1612 (*Ulst. Plant. Paps.* §65 272) and was resolved in Bagnall's favour. On February 18 of the following year, the four towns of Coghall were granted to Arthur Bagnall along with other numerous possessions and rights (*CPR Jas. I* 247b).

The local pronunciation is noteworthy as it differs considerably from the modern spelling of the name. It is, nevertheless, supported by the spelling suggested by the Boundary Survey (9) and it must have some validity. As the two forms of the name are irreconcilable, they must represent different names. The standard form, as previously suggested (10–11), comes from Irish *Allt na bhFiach* "the glen of the ravens" and the local form probably derives from *Achadh na bhFiach* "field of the ravens".

Ardarragh	*Ard Darach*	
J 1433	"high place of the oak"	
1. Ardarre	Inq. (Mon. Hib.) 287	1549
2. Ardarre	CPR Ed. VI iv 388	1552

3. Ardaraghe (×2)	Bagenal Rental 124	1575
4. Ardagh	CPR Jas. I 86a	1606
5. Ardary	CPR Jas. I 103a	1607
6. Ardarii	CPR Jas. I 495a	1607
7. Ardarragh	CPR Jas. I 246b	1613
8. Ardaragh	Inq. Ult. (Down) §15 Jac. I	1625c
9. Ardagh	Inq. Ult. (Down) §84 Car. I	1638
10. Ardarragh	Civ. Surv. x §72	1655c
11. Ardarra	Census 82	1659c
12. Ardarre	BSD 130	1661
13. Ardarragh	Sub. Roll Down 280	1663
14. Ardarragh	Wm. Map (OSNB) 97	1810
15. Ardarragh	Bnd. Sur. (OSNB) 97	1830c
16. Ar-'dar-eagh	OSNB 97	1834c
17. Ard Darach "hill of the oak"	J O'D (OSNB) E42 no. 100	1834c
18. Ard darach "Altitudo Quercuum"	OSL 48	1834c
19. Árd Darach	Post-Sheanchas 21	1905
20. Ard Darach	AGBP 112	1969
21. Ard Darach	GÉ 7	1989
22. ‚ar'darə	Local pronunciation	1990

The name Ardarragh would appear to derive from a form *Ard Darach* (3, 7–8, 10, 13–16). However, a number of our sources show no trace of the final guttural spirant (1–2, 5–6, 12–13) and this might be taken as an indication that the second element was originally *dara*, an older form of the gen. sing. of *dair* "oak-tree". Nevertheless, the weakening of *ch* is characteristic of the Irish of east Ulster (O'Rahilly 1932, 210) and it is sometimes omitted from anglicized spellings. In the 17th century there are sporadic occurrences of the loss of final *-ach* in this area (**Ardkeeragh, Derrycraw**, in parish of Donaghmore) and in the name of the village of **Dromara**, Co. Down, which goes back to *Droim mBearach*, it is already absent in a form as early as 1306.

Ballinlare　　　　　　　　　　*Baile na Ladhaire*
J 0726　　　　　　　　　　　　　"townland of the fork/gap"

1. Ballaleyer	CPR Jas. I 86a	1606
2. Battaleire	CPR Jas. I 103a	1607
3. Ballinlare	Esch. Co. Map 5.26	1609
4. Ballinelare	CPR Jas. I 196b	1611
5. Ballylaer	Inq. Ult. (Armagh) §2 Jac. I	1612
6. Ballilayer al' Ballinlare	CPR Jas. I 247b	1613
7. (?)Ballynlare	Inq. Ult. (Armagh) §7 Jac. I	1621
8. Ballabeyer al' Ballaleier	Inq. Ult. (Armagh) §27 Car. I	1638
9. Bollinlare	Inq. Arm. 227	1657
10. Ballinlaer	BSD 10	1661
11. Ballinlare	HMR Murray (1941) 134	1664
12. Ballinlare	Reg. Free (OSNB) 99	1829
13. Ballinlare	Bnd. Sur (OSNB) 99	1830c

14. Baile an Láir "Middle town"	J O'D (OSNB) 99	1845
15. Baile-an-láir "middle town"	Joyce iii 64	1913
16. ˌbalən'eːr (?)	Local pronunciation	1990

O'Donovan (14) followed by Joyce (15) suggests that the townland of Ballinlare derives its name from Irish *Baile an Láir* meaning "middle town" but a number of early spellings clearly point to a pronunciation [bal'ə(n)'leːr]. This may suggest an Irish form *Baile na Ladhaire* "the townland of the gap", although the element *ladhar* is rare outside Cork, Kerry and Waterford (see Ó Maolfabhail 1987–8, 18–19). Ó Maolfabhail assigns only the meaning "gap" to *ladhar* but Dinneen gives a translation "a fork, esp. a natural fork or promontory, the land between two converging rivers or hills" (*Dinneen* sv. *ladhar*) which may also be applied to place-names. Joyce also notes this sense of the word and comments that there "are many rivers and places in the south called Lyre, and others in the north called Lear..." (*Joyce* i 530).

Ballyholland Lower
Ballyholland Upper
J 1124, 1025

Baile Uí Thuathaláin
"Toland's townland"

1. Letir Corcrach	Newry Char. (Flanagan)	1157c
2. Lyttelcorcagh and Tylaghtyry, two carucates in	Inq. (Mon. Hib.) 287	1549
3. Lytyllcorghe and Tyllaghterye, the two towns of	CPR Ed. VI iv 388	1552
4. Lyttell Corcaghe and Tyllaghtyrye, in the two townships of Hytowelan called	CPR Ed. VI iv 388	1552
5. little Coroge	Fiants Eliz. §4327	1583c
6. Little Coragh, Tylaghtery	CPR Jas. I 86a	1606
7. Little-Corragh, Tillaghterrie	CPR Jas. I 103a	1607
8. Littlecorragh, Tillaghtirrie	CPR Jas. I 495a	1607
9. Whollan al. Hitovalan al. Little-Corragh and Tillaghterry, 2 plowlands	CPR Jas. I 246b	1613
10. Whollan al. Hytowlan al' Littlecoragh and Tillaghtery, the 2 carewes or balliboes of	Inq. Ult. (Down) §15 Jac. I	1625c
11. parva Coraghe al' Carragh, Tilraghlery	Inq. Ult. (Down) §84 Car. I	1638
12. near Ballyhovenan	Inq. (Mon. Hib.) 287	1549
13. next Ballyhoveman	CPR Ed. VI iv 388	1552
14. next Ballihovenan	CPR Ed. VI iv 388	1552
15. Ballyhollanes	Bagenal Rental 126	1575
16. near Ballehaleman	CPR Jas. I 246b	1613
17. neere Balleholeman	Inq. Ult. (Down) §15 Jac. I	1625c
18. Ballyholand, Upper & Lower	Census 82	1659c
19. Ballyhollan, Upper & Lower	BSD 130	1661
20. Ballyholland	Sub. Roll Down 280	1663
21. Lower Ballywhollan	Wm. Map (OSNB) 97	1810
22. Upper Ballywhollan	Wm. Map (OSNB) 97	1810

23. Lower Ballyholand	Reg. Free. (OSNB) 97	1829
24. Upper Ballyholand	Reg. Free (OSNB) 97	1829
25. Ballyholand	County Warrant (OSNB) 97	1830
26. Lower Ballywhollan	Bnd. Sur. (OSNB) 97	1830c
27. Upper Ballywhollan	Bnd. Sur. (OSNB) 97	1830c
28. Lower Bal-ly-'ho-lan	OSNB 97	1834c
29. Upper-Bal-ly-'ho-lan	OSNB 97	1834c
30. Ballyholland	J O'D (OSNB) 97	1834c
31. Baile Uí Chualan[n] "O'Cuolan's town"	J O'D (OSNB) 97	1834c
32. Baile Chualann	OSL 47	1834c
33. Baile Uí Thuathaláin "O'Tolane's or Toland's Town"	Mooney 225	1950c
34. ‚balt'ho:ln	Local pronunciation	1990

The area around Ballyholland was once known by the tribal name of *Hytowlan* which probably comes from Irish *Uí Thuathaláin* (4, 9–11). This was divided into two townlands, the former of which can be identified with the *Letir Corcrach* of the Newry Charter (1) which Reeves mistakenly locates in the modern townland of Corcreeghy (*EA* 117n), and this points to an original Irish *Leitir Corcach* "hill-side of the marshes" or, less probably, *Leitir Corcrach* "purple hill-side". The final *r* in the first element (*leitir*) was early assimilated to the initial *l* and the whole re-analysed as English "little" (note particularly no. 11). The meaning of the name of the other townland, spelt *Tilaghtery* et var., is not immediately obvious.

The forms for Ballyholland show a large degree of confusion but, with the aid of the district name, we may suggest with some degree of certainty that it derives from the Irish *Baile Uí Thuathaláin*. *Ó Tuathaláin*, anglicized Toolan, Toland etc., was the name of an Ulster family originally from Inishowen, Co. Donegal (Woulfe 1923, 656). The majority of the later forms (12–30), as well as the local pronunciation, are reconcilable with this derivation and the initial *t* is clearly indicated in the district name (4, 9–10). The remaining spellings are extremely erratic and the problem seems to lie in the practice of copying early patents and grants from one another, thus compounding any errors that might arise (see p. 2 above). Reeves, identified the place called *Saolcean* in the Charter of Newry with this townland (*EA* 117n) but there seems to be little justification for this view. Apart from the difficulties in identifying it as the same place the phonetic development would be rather hard to explain.

Ballynacraig
J 0926

Baile na gCreag
"townland of the crags"

1. Ballyinecregg	Wars Co. Down 77	1641
2. Ballincrag	Census 82	1659c
3. Ballenecregge	BSD 130	1661
4. Ballincregg	Wm. Map (OSNB) 97	1810
5. Ballynacrag	Bnd. Sur. (OSNB) 97	1830c
6. Bal-li-na-'craig	OSNB 97	1834c
7. Ballynacraig	J O'D (OSNB) 97	1834c
8. Baile na g-creag "town of the rocks"	OSL 47	1834c

9. Baile na g-Creag
   "town of the rocks"   J O'D (OSNB) 97   1834c

10. ˌbalnəˈkrɛg   Local pronunciation   1990

Old Irish *e* followed by a non-palatal consonant became [a], spelt *ea*, in the majority of modern Irish dialects but in the Irish of east Ulster *ea* in stressed syllables frequently preserves its old sound of [e] (O'Rahilly 1932, 175–6). The second element in this name is obviously a form of *creag* "rock, crag", most probably the gen. pl., and in it we can see an example of this conservative feature of east Ulster Irish for the written and spoken forms clearly show [e] where we would expect [a] to have developed in other parts of the country. The absence of the mark of nasalization from the forms is hardly surprising as it is sometimes omitted from place-names as, for example, in the name Donegal (*Dún na nGall*).

The name Ballynacraig appears relatively late in our sources and it is possible that this area was formerly known as *Mabegge* which regularly appears in 16th- and 17th-century sources but which does not survive to the present day. Almost all these documents follow the same geographical progression beginning with *Cormyne* (Carnmeen) and proceeding through *Cornehoure* (Carneyhough), *Cravekynnewe* (Creeve), *Mabege*, *Lytelcorcagh* (part of Ballyholland), and *Tylaghtyry* (part of Ballyholland) so that the identification is virtually certain. *Mabege* probably goes back to an original Irish *Maigh Bheag* "little plain" although in the absence of a current pronunciation caution in suggesting an origin must be exercised.

Benagh   *Beitheanach*
J 1327   "place of birch trees"

1. Behanagh	Inq. (Mon. Hib.) 287	1549
2. Kehanaghe	CPR Ed. VI iv 388	1552
3. Behanagh	CPR Ed. VI iv 388	1552
4. Behany	Bagenal Rental 125	1575
5. (?)Behamye	Bagenal Rental 126	1575
6. Baynagh or Kehanagh	CPR Jas. I 246b	1613
7. Brynagh al' Kehannagh	Inq. Ult. (Down) §15 Jac. I	1625c
8. Beanagh	Civ. Surv. x §72	1655c
9. Benaghe	Census 82	1659c
10. Beannagh	BSD 130	1661
11. Benagh	Wm. Map (OSNB) 97	1810
12. Benagh	Bnd. Sur. (OSNB) 97	1830c
13. 'Be-nagh	OSNB 97	1834c
14. Béanach	OSL 48	1834c
15. Béanach "pointed, peaked"	J O'D (OSNB) 97	1834c
16. 'benək	Local pronunciation	1990

O'Donovan suggested that this name derives from the Irish *béanach* (recte *beannach*) "pointed, peaked" (15) but early forms with an internal *h* (1–7) almost certainly point to *beith* "a birch tree" followed by a suffix (the loss of internal *h* is a well-attested phenomenon in the Irish of east Ulster (O'Rahilly 1932, 207–8)). An adjectival suffix -*(e)anach*, which is largely interchangeable with the more usual -*ach*, has been identified by Ó Máille (1955(b)) in the well-attested name, *Muiceanach*, and this seems to best explain the origin of the termination here. However, we cannot reject out of hand a derivation from *beith* "birch tree" + the diminutive suffix *án* + adjectival suffix -*ach* which would be indistinguishable from the

PARISH AND LORDSHIP OF NEWRY

latter even in modern Ulster Irish, nor can we rule out the admittedly less likely possibility of an archaic formation such as *beith* "birch tree" + *eanach* "swamp, marsh".

Reeves identifies the name *Betheac* in the Newry Charter with this townland (*EA* 117n) but this is improbable, not only because of the differences in the forms, but also because it does not occur alongside those names in the charter which can be located in Newry (see, perhaps, **Benagh** in the parish of Kilkeel).

Carnacally	*Ceathrú Mhic Ceallaigh*	
J 1132	"MacKelly's quarter"	
1. Karemykallye	Inq. (Mon. Hib.) 287	1549
2. Karremykkale	CPR Ed. VI iv 388	1552
3. Carrickmikkall	CPR Ed. VI iv 388	1552
4. Karmakully	Bagenal Rental 125	1575
5. Carrickny, Cally	CPR Jas. I 86a	1606
6. Karemichally	CPR Jas. I 102b	1607
7. Karenchalle	CPR Jas. I 495a	1607
8. Carremickalle orse Tolliroddan	CPR Jas. I 246b	1613
9. Carrenichalle al' Tollytroddan	Inq. Ult. (Down) §15 Jac. I	1625c
10. Carricknically	Inq. Ult. (Down) §84 Car. I	1638
11. Cormakally	BSD 130	1661
12. Carrumacally	Sub. Roll Down 280	1663
13. Carrigvically	Wm. Map (OSNB) 97	1810
14. Carnacally	Bnd. Sur. (OSNB) 97	1830c
15. Carn Mhic Allaidh	OSL 47	1834
16. Carn Mhic Allaidh "Mac Ally's carn"	J O'D (OSNB) 97	1834c
17. Ceathreamha Mhic Eachmhilidh	Mooney 243	1950c
18. ˌkɑrnəˈkalʲə	Local pronunciation	1990

O'Donovan understood the first element in this name as *carn* "cairn, sepulchral heap" (15–16) but early forms suggest a more probable origin in Irish *ceathrú* "quarter" (1–2, 4, 6–9, 12). However, even in the earliest sources this seems to alternate with *carraig* "rock" (3, 5, 10, 13).

A number of early forms clearly indicate that the second element in this name is a surname beginning with *mac* (1–3, 6–7, 13) but a precise identification of the name is problematic. Several spellings show an *n* in the middle of the name (5, 7, 9–10) and this probably represents an error for *v* (from *mhic*) rather than the development from *m* to *n* which seems to occur later in the history of the name, for it is found after *Carrick-* as well as after *Kar-/Car-* (5, 10; cf. 13). O'Donovan criticizes the High Constable's practice of writing the name "Cairn-O'Kelly" and notes that it was called by the old inhabitants *Carn Mhic Allaidh* "which is undoubtedly a name of the most remote antiquity" (*OSL* 47). Mooney, however, suggests that the name was *Mac Eachmhilidh* (English MacCally) (17), a rare name found in east Ulster (Woulfe 1923 sv. *Mac Eachmhileadha*), but we might expect to see some trace of the internal consonants in our early documentation (see **Ballyagholy** in the parish of Clonallan). A number of other possibilities suggest themselves, but the most likely must be *Mac Ceallaigh*, anglicized "MacKelly", which occurs in the names of the townlands of **Ballykelly** in Seapatrick (*Baile Mhic Ceallaigh*) and **Ballyvicknakally** in Dromore (*Baile Mhic Ceallaigh*).

Carnbane
J 0729

Carn Bán
"white cairn"

1.	Carnebane	Esch. Co. Map 5.26	1609
2.	Carnebane	Inq. Ult. (Armagh) §2 Jac. I	1612
3.	Carnebane	CPR Jas. I 246b	1613
4.	Carnbanne	Civ. Surv. x §77	1655c
5.	Carreckbane	Inq. Arm. 229	1657
6.	Karne Bann	BSD 10	1661
7.	Carnebane	HMR Murray (1941) 137	1664
8.	Carnebane	Inq. Ult. (Armagh) §1 Will. III	1698
9.	Karnbane	Harris Hist. 203	1744
10.	Caranbawn	Bnd. Sur (OSNB) 99	1830c
11.	Cairn-bán	OSNB Inf. 99	1835
12.	kʲarnˈbaːn	Local pronunciation	1990

Harris, writing in 1744, describes a circular cairn on this site as being 180 yards in circumference and 10 yards high (*Harris Hist.* 203) and it is probably from this structure that Carnbane takes its name. A single spelling (5) apparently shows an alternative first element *carraig* but this does not necessarily reflect local usage and may simply be a scribal error.

The territory to the west of the Newry River comprising the townland of Carnbane and the lost townlands of Grange and Aghteeard was collectively known as Moycarne (*CPR Jas. I* 246b, *Inq. Ult.* (Armagh) §2 Jac. I, (Down) §15 Car. I) and this division is frequently used in grants and inquisitions of the 16th and 17th centuries (*Inq. (Mon. Hib.)* 287, *CPR Ed. VI* iv 387, *CPR Jas. I* 86a, 102b, 494b, *Inq. Ult.* (Down) §15 Car. I, §84 Car. I). In an inquisition of 1549, the "three carucates in Moycarne" were valued at 40s, and three years later Nicholas Bagnall was granted "the three 'lez carnes' [*recte* carues] of land, pasture, mountain and moor in the three towns of Moytarne [*recte* Moycarne]" (CPR Ed. VI iv 387). The name Moycarne clearly derives from Irish *Maigh Cairn* "plain of the cairn" where the cairn is probably the same as that referred to in the name Carnbane.

Carneyhough
J 0927

Of uncertain origin

1.	Cornehoure	Inq. (Mon. Hib.) 287	1549
2.	Cornehowre (×2)	CPR Ed. VI iv 388	1552
3.	Cornehooghe	Bagenal Rental 127	1575
4.	Cloghcornehore	CPR Jas. I 86a	1606
5.	Carnehore	CPR Jas. I 102b	1607
6.	Carnahore	CPR Jas. I 495a	1607
7.	Cornehowre	Inq. Ult. (Down) §15 Car. I	1625c
8.	Conehogh	Inq. Ult. (Down) §84 Car. I	1638
9.	Cornehough	Census 82	1659c
10.	Cornehough	BSD 130	1661
11.	Carrickhugh	Sub. Roll Down 280	1663
12.	Cornihogh	Wm. Map (OSNB) 97	1810
13.	Cornyhogh	Bnd. Sur. (OSNB) 97	1830c
14.	Cor-ny-'haugh	OSNB 97	1834c
15.	Carnyhough	J O'D (OSNB) 97	1834c

16.	Carn ui h-Eoch		
	"O'Haughey's carn"	J O'D (OSNB) 97	1834c
17.	Cárn Ui h-Eochadha		
	"O'Haughey['s] Carn"	OSL 47	1834c
18.	ˌkɑrnɪˈhɔx	Local pronunciation	1990

O'Donovan suggested that this name comes from an Irish form *Carn Uí hEoch* or *Cárn Ui h-Eochadha* (16–17) but a number of serious objections may be raised against such an etymology, not least the fact that the earliest forms may indicate that the final element originally ended in an *r*-sound (1–2, 4–7). Moreover, the genitive form of Ó hEochadha would lose its *h*-prefix, so that we would expect an Irish form *Carn Uí Eochadha* which might be anglicized Carnough or the like.

The development of an original final *r* into a velar fricative [x] is remarkable and cannot be explained in terms of the historical development of either English or Irish. The forms with *r* might, therefore, best be explained as the result of a scribal error. The documents in which they occur are all of the same type (grants and inquisitions) and it is possible that the corrupted form of the name was subsequently copied from one to another (cf. **Cloghanramer**). It is worth noting in this regard that the Bagenal Rental, which was compiled locally, is in agreement with the later forms. Nevertheless, the original Irish form and its meaning remain obscure.

Carnmeen   *Corr Mhín*
J 0830   "smooth hill"

1.	Enacratha	Newry Char. (Flanagan)	1157c
2.	Cormyne alias Enaghaynathreta	Inq. (Mon. Hib.) 287	1549
3.	Cormyne al' Enethaynaghreta	CPR Ed. VI iv 388	1552
4.	Cromyn(e)	CPR Ed. VI iv 388	1552
5.	Cromyne al' Enaghrenathreta	CPR Ed. VI iv 388	1552
6.	Cormyne	CPR Jas. I 86a	1606
7.	Cormine	CPR Jas. I 102b	1607
8.	Cormine	CPR Jas. I 494b	1607
9.	Cormyne orse Emthaynaghreta	CPR Jas. I 246b	1613
10.	Cormyne	Inq. Ult. (Down) §15 Jac. I	1625c
11.	Cormyne al' Knethayreaghreta	Inq. Ult. (Down) §15 Jac. I	1625c
12.	Cormynelargen	Inq. Ult. (Down) §84 Car. I	1638
13.	Cormyn ½ towne	Census 82	1659c
14.	Cormine	BSD 130	1661
15.	Cormeen	Sub. Roll Down 280	1663
16.	Carmeen	Wm. Map (OSNB) 97	1810
17.	Carnmeen	Newry Exam. (OSNB) 97	1830
18.	Carnmeen	Newry Tel. (OSNB) 97	1830
19.	Carmeen	Bnd. Sur. (OSNB) 97	1830c
20.	'Cor-meen	OSNB 97	1834c
21.	Carnmeen	J O'D (OSNB) 97	1834c
22.	Cárn Mín "smooth carn"	J O'D (OSNB) 97	1834c
23.	Cárn mín "fine carn"	OSL 47	1834c
24.	kʲarnˈmiːn	Local pronunciation	1990

O'Donovan's informant thought that the name Carnmeen came from Irish *Carn Mín* meaning "smooth cairn" (23) but earlier documents would point rather to *Corr Mhín* "smooth hill" or *Cor Mín* "smooth bend" (2–16, 19–20). The former seems more likely as there is a small hill in the eastern end of the townland (*OS 1:50,000* 29 J 0931). The first element has a broad range of meanings extending from "round hill" to "hollow" but it is probably used here in the former sense. In the name of Cormeen Hill in the townland of **Cormeen**, Co. Armagh, *corr* is obviously used in the sense of "hill" and the same sense is implied by the local etymology *Carn Mín* (22–3). While the other options must still be considered possible, these facts seem to weigh in favour of the sense "hill".

Castle Enigan

J 1232

Caiseal Fhlannagáin
"Flannagán's stone-fort"

1a.	Caselanagan	Newry Char. (Flanagan)	1157c
b.	Casellanagan	Newry Char. (EA) 117n. r	1157c
c.	Caselaragan	Newry Char. (Mon. Ang.) 1134	1157c
2.	Castellanegan	Inq. (Mon. Hib.) 287	1549
3.	Castellanegan (×2)	CPR Ed. VI iv 388	1552
4.	Castlelangan	CPR Jas. I 103a	1607
5.	Castlelonigan	CPR Jas. I 495a	1607
6.	Castlelonegan	CPR Jas. I 246b	1613
7.	Castalanagan	CPR Jas. I 246b	1613
8.	Castlelonegan	Inq. Ult. (Down) §15 Jac. I	1625c
9.	Castalanagan	Inq. Ult. (Down) §15 Jac. I	1625c
10.	Castlanegan	Inq. Ult. (Down) §84 Car. I	1638
11.	Castleneggan	Census 82	1659c
12.	Cisillannegan & Lissnerea	BSD 130	1661
13.	Castle Inigan	Sub. Roll Down 280	1663
14.	Castlenagan	Wm. Map (OSNB) 97	1810
15.	Castle-Enegan	Bnd. Sur. (OSNB) 97	1830c
16.	Castle-eni-'gan	OSNB 97	1834c
17.	Castle Enigan	J O'D (OSNB) 97	1834c
18.	Caiseal Eánagain	OSL 48	1834c
19.	Caiseal Eánagain "Flanigan's stone fort"	J O'D (OSNB) 97	1834c
20.	ˌkɛsļˈɛnəgən	Local pronunciation	1990

On the basis of 19th-century forms, O'Donovan concluded that Castle Enigan came from *Caiseal Eánagain* but a number of 16th- and 17th-century sources (4–6, 7–8) clearly point to an Irish form *Caiseal Fhlannagáin* "Flannagán's castle". The loss of the initial *f*- in the modern pronunciation results from the name's frequent use in the dative where the *f*- is lenited and disappears. The occurrence of the name in a pre-Norman document (1) and the use of an Irish name as a qualifying element clearly demonstrate that the first element does not refer to an English castle but rather to an Irish *caiseal* or "stone fort".

Cloghanramer

J 0929

Clochán Ramhar (?)
"thick stone structure/causeway"

1.	Cloghanrawyn	Inq. (Mon. Hib.) 287	1549

2. Cloghaurawyn	CPR Ed. VI iv 388	1552
3. Clough(hanramer)	Bagenal Rental 127	1575
4. Clochon-Rawyn	CPR Jas. I 86a	1606
5. Cloghane, Rawyne	CPR Jas. I 102b	1607
6. Clochane, Rawyne	CPR Jas. I 494b	1607
7. Cloghan-Rawen	CPR Jas. I 246b	1613
8. Cloghanrawen	Inq. Ult. (Down) §15 Jac. I	1625c
9. Cloghan al' Cloghyn, Rawyn	Inq. Ult. (Down) §84 Car. I	1638
10. Cloghanrawer halfe towne	Census 82	1659c
11. Clocanrawire	BSD 130	1661
12. Cloghanramer	Bnd. Sur. (OSNB) 97	1830c
13. Clochan ramhar "thick stony ford"	OSNB Inf. 97	1834c
14. Clachan Ramhar "large causeway"	OSL 47	1834c
15. Clochan-reamhar		
"thick stepping-stones"	Joyce iii 205	1913
16. ˌklɔxənˈramər	Local pronunciation	1990

Dinneen cites a noun *rabhán* (masc.) "the herb thrift, *armeria maritana*, growing in clusters on cliffs and used as fuel". On the basis of the earliest spellings which, with one exception, end in *n*, this might be taken as the original second element in this name (1–2, 4–9). However, *n* and *r* are sometimes confused in documents of this period and it is quite possible that the early forms, which are all taken from documents concerning grants of land, are based on a single scribal error. O'Donovan's local informant took the second element to be *ramhar* "thick" (13), and Joyce, who gives a similar interpretation of the name (15), notes that *ramhar* is used extensively in the formation of names, particularly of hills and rocks (*Joyce* ii 395). Joyce notes a tendency in the north for the *mh* of *ramhar* to become delenited and he cites a number of examples, including **Killyramer** in Co. Antrim, **Cullyramer** in Co. Derry and Kenramer on Rathlin Island (*ibid.* 396). *Bh*, on the other hand, is unlikely to become *m*. While one is loath to dismiss the evidence of the earliest spellings, the comparative view, coupled with the early but independent spelling in the Bagenal Rental (no. 3) and the etymology provided by the OSNB informant, argue strongly in favour of the element *ramhar*.

The first element is clearly *clochán*. This has a wide variety of meanings relating to stone structures such as "ruin", "heap of stones", "stone circle", "burying ground", or "causeway", and it is now impossible to determine the precise sense of the word in this name, although the presence of a bog in the townland (OS J 2909, 2910) perhaps indicates that it is used in the sense of "causeway" as suggested by previous authorities (13–15).

Commons   An English form
J 1024

1. Commons	Wm. Map (OSNB) 97	1810
2. Commons	Bnd. Sur. (OSNB) 97	1830c
3. ðə ˈkọmənz	Local pronunciation	1990

This is one of the very few townland names of purely English-language origin in the parish of Newry and its first appearance in Williamson's map of 1810 is understandably late (1).

Corcreeghy	*Corr Chríochach*	
J 1032	"boundary hill"	
1. Corkryghaghe	Inq. (Mon. Hib.) 287	1549
2. Corbrighaghe	CPR Ed. VI iv 388	1552
3. Corkreaghe	CPR Ed. VI iv 388	1552
4. Karkricagh	CPR Jas. I 86a	1606
5. Carkryghagh	CPR Jas. I 102b	1607
6. Carkrihatt	CPR Jas. I 495a	1607
7. Corchrechagh orse Corbrighagh	CPR Jas. I 246b	1613
8. Corcrechagh al' Corbrighagh	Inq. Ult. (Down) §15 Jac. I	1625c
9. Kearkrigagh	Inq. Ult. (Down) §84 Car. I	1638
10. Corkrighagh	Civ. Surv. x §72	1655c
11. Corcrighagh	Census 82	1659c
12. Corcrickee	Reg. Deeds abstracts i §214	1720
13. Corcreegagh	Wm. Map (OSNB) 97	1810
14. Carcreeghy	Bnd. Sur. (OSNB) 97	1830c
15. Cor-'creegh-hy	OSNB 97	1834c
16. Corcreeghy	J O'D (OSNB) 97	1834c
17. Cor críochach	OSL 48	1834c
18. Corr Críochach		
"round hill of the bushes"	J O'D (OSNB) 97	1834c
19. ‚kɔrˈkriːhi	Local pronunciation	1990

The letters *b* and *k* are frequently confused in documents of the 16th and 17th centuries and *b* has been substituted for *k* in a number of the forms for Corcreeghy (2, 7b, 8b). However, the preponderance of forms in *k* or *c*, coupled with the current pronunciation, leaves us in no doubt that this name comes from the Irish *Corr Chríochach* "boundary hill" which origi- nally may have referred to a hill in this townland which marked the boundary of Newry parish. Reeves sought to identify it with the *Corcragh* of the Newry Charter but the name there is properly *Letir Corcragh* and is undoubtedly the same as the *Lyttell Corcaghe* et var. of later documents which now forms part of **Ballyholland**. O'Donovan suggested that the original Irish form meant "round hill of the bushes" (18) but the meaning which he ascribes to the second element is unsubstantiated. Several other places in the north of the country were also known by the name *(An) C(h)orr Chríochach* including **Cookstown**, Co. Tyrone (*Gᴇ́* 77), and the townlands called Corcreeghagh in Cos. Louth, Cavan and Monaghan (*Joyce* iii 253–4).

Creeve	*Craobh*	
J 1026	"tree/bush"	
1. Cravekynnewe	Inq. (Mon. Hib.) 287	1549
2. Crebekynnew	CPR Ed. VI iv 388	1552
3. Crevekynewe	CPR Ed. VI iv 388	1552
4. Crewycknew	Bagenal Rental 126	1575
5. Cronekena	CPR Jas. I 86a	1606
6. Crebekynnew	CPR Jas. I 102b	1607
7. Crekekynnew	CPR Jas. I 495a	1607

16

8.	Crewe orse Crevekynnewe	CPR Jas. I 246b	1613
9.	Crew al' Crevellymewe	Inq. Ult. (Down) §15 Jac. I	1625c
10.	Cronekena al' Cronekenaw	Inq. Ult. (Down) §84 Car. I	1638
11.	Crine	Census 82	1659c
12.	Criue	BSD 130	1661
13.	Creeve	Wm. Map (OSNB) 97	1810
14.	Creeve	Bnd. Sur. (OSNB) 97	1830c
15.	Creeve	OSNB 97	1834c
16.	Craobh "a bush or wide-spreading tree"	J O'D (OSNB) 97	1834c
17.	Craobh "a bush or bushy place"	OSL 47	1834c
18.	kri:v	Local pronunciation	1990

According to Joyce, the name *craobh* was given to large trees "under whose shadows games or religious rites were celebrated, or chiefs inaugurated" (*Joyce* i 501) but, of course, this is not necessarily the case for every occurrence of the name and it may simply apply to any prominent tree. Historically, non-palatal *bh* was pronounced as bilabial [v] but in Ulster Irish it has gone to [u:] or [u] (O'Rahilly 1932, 77), a development which is witnessed in a number of our forms (4, 8–9). Those forms ending in [v] may preserve the older spelling of the name or they may simply represent the dative form, *Craoibh*.

Crobane
J 1227

Cró Bán
"white enclosure"

1.	Croa	Newry Char. (Flanagan)	1157c
2.	Croo	Inq. (Mon. Hib.) 287	1549
3.	Croo (×2)	CPR Ed. VI iv 388	1552
4.	Crowe	Bagenal Rental 125	1575
5.	Crove	CPR Jas. I 86a	1606
6.	Crooe	CPR Jas. I 102b	1607
7.	Crooe	CPR Jas. I 495a	1607
8.	Croore	CPR Jas. I 246b	1613
9.	Croor	Inq. Ult. (Down) §15 Jac. I	1625c
10.	Crocee	Inq. Ult. (Down) §84 Car. I	1638
11.	Ceo: bane	Census 82	1659c
12.	Crobane	BSD 130	1661
13.	Crebane	Sub. Roll Down 280	1663
14.	Crowbane (×2)	Forfeit. Estates 352b §32	1703
15.	Crobane	Harris Hist. 97	1744
16.	Crobane	Wm. Map (OSNB) 97	1810
17.	Crobane	Bnd. Sur. (OSNB) 97	1830c
18.	'Cro-bane	OSNB 97	1834c
19.	Cró bán "White shed or enclosure"	OSL 48	1834c
20.	Cro bán, "the white 'cro' or cattle fold"	J O'D (OSNB) 97	1834c
21.	kro'bɑ:n	Local pronunciation	1990

The qualifying element *bán* "white" is of relatively late occurrence in this name (11-20). Prior to this, the townland was known simply as *Cró* (1-10) and it is only when the neighbouring townland of *Droim Fornocht* comes to be called **Croreagh** (*Cró Riabhach*) that the adjective is added.

Croreagh
J 1229

Cró Riabhach
"dun/grey enclosure"

1.	Druimfornact	Newry Char. (Flanagan)	1157c
2.	Dromformott	Inq. (Mon. Hib.) 287	1549
3.	Dromfronot	CPR Ed. VI iv 388	1552
4.	Dromfernot	CPR Ed. VI iv 388	1552
5.	Dramfronett	CPR Jas. I 86a	1606
6.	Dramfronett	CPR Jas. I 102b	1607
7.	Dromfronnett	CPR Jas. I 495a	1607
8.	Dromfronett	CPR Jas. I 246b	1613
9.	Dromstronett	Inq. Ult. (Down) §15 Jac. I	1625c
10.	Drumfronett al' Drumfronett	Inq. Ult. (Down) §84 Car. I	1638
11.	Croreiaghe	Census 82	1659c
12.	Croriagh	BSD 130	1661
13.	Croreagh	Sub. Roll Down 280	1663
14.	Croreagh	Wm. Map (OSNB) 97	1810
15.	Croreagh	Bnd. Sur. (OSNB) 97	1830c
16.	Cro-reagh-'agh	OSNB 97	1834c
17.	Cró riach "grey cattle enclosure, fall or fold"	J O'D (OSNB) 97	1834c
18.	Cro riach	OSL 48	1834c
19.	kro're:	Local pronunciation	1990

The townland of Croreagh was earlier known as *Droim Fornocht* "bare ridge" (1–10), doubtless a reference to the exposed slopes of the north–south ridge which dominates the townland. The element *fornocht* frequently appears on its own in place-names and Joyce is no doubt correct in assigning it the sense "bare, naked or exposed hill" in such cases (*Joyce* i 400) but in this instance *fornocht* is probably adjectival (cf. *Druim Fornocht* in *AFM* i 320).

Curley
J 1434

Corrbhaile
"prominent townland"

1.	Tollaghnesowe	Inq. (Mon. Hib.) 287	1549
2.	Tullaghnesowe	CPR Ed. VI iv 388	1552
3.	Tullaghnesowre	CPR Ed. VI iv 388	1552
4.	Tolaghnesowe	CPR Jas. I 86a	1606
5.	Tollaghnesoive	CPR Jas. I 103a	1607
6.	Tollaghnesoiw	CPR Jas. I 495a	1607
7.	Tollensowe and Corbally, 1 plowland	CPR Jas. I 246b	1613
8.	Tullenesow, Corbally	Inq. Ult. (Down) §15 Jac. I	1625c
9.	Tullaghnesowe al' Tallaghsowe	Inq. Ult. (Down) §84 Car. I	1638
10.	Tullynesugh	Civ. Surv. x §72	1655c

11. (?)Corrobegg	Census 82	1659
12. Carrolly	BSD 130	1661
13. Corelly	Wm. Map (OSNB) 97	1810
14. Curley	County Warrant (OSNB) 97	1827
15. Curley	County Warrant (OSNB) 97	1830
16. Correlly	Bnd. Sur. (OSNB) 97	1830c
17. 'Cur-ley	OSNB 97	1834c
18. Cur Laoigh	OSL 48	1834c
19. Cor laoigh		
"round hill of the calf"	J O'D (OSNB) 97	1834c
20. 'körlı	Local pronunciation	1990

O'Donovan suggests this name comes from an Irish form *Cor Laoigh* "round hill of the calf" (18–19) but, quite apart from the fact that this would be expected to give stress on the second syllable, the earlier forms clearly point to an original *Corrbhaile* "prominent townland" (7b, 8b) and, indeed, there is a conspicuous hill here (OS J 1434). This type of name is very common throughout Ireland and normally occurs without any qualifying element, Corballybane in Co. Cork being one of the few exceptions. The internal *bh* became vocalized at an early date in our name producing trisyllabic forms (12–13) from which the current form developed through syncope.

According to one source, Arthur Bagnall was granted *Tollensowe* and *Corbally* in 1613 which, together, were reckoned as 1 plowland (*CPR Jas. I* 246b). The name *Tollensowe* et var., perhaps from Irish *Tulaigh na Subh* "mound of the berries", frequently occurs in our early documents where we would expect to find reference to *Corbally* (Curley) and it seems to have included those lands which the 1613 grant to Arthur Bagnall lumps together as 1 plowland.

Damolly
J 0928

Damh Maoile (?)
"house of the round hill"

1. Dammole	Inq. (Mon. Hib.) 287	1549
2. Damniole	CPR Ed. VI iv 388	1552
3. Dammole	CPR Ed. VI iv 388	1552
4. Damoyle	CPR Jas. I 86a	1606
5. Damoyle	CPR Jas. I 102b	1607
6. Damoyle	CPR Jas. I 495a	1607
7. Damwell orse Damole	CPR Jas. I 246b	1613
8. Damwell al' Damole	Inq. Ult. (Down) §15 Jac. I	1625c
9. Damoyle al' Damole	Inq. Ult. (Down) §84 Car. I	1638
10. Damolly ½ towne	Census 82	1659c
11. Damoley	BSD 130	1661
12. Damully	Reg. Deeds abstracts ii §201	1784
13. Demolly	Wm. Map (OSNB) 97	1810
14. Demolly	Bnd. Sur. (OSNB) 97	1830c
15. De-'mol-ly	OSNB 97	1834c
16. Damolly	J O'D (OSNB) 97	1834c
17. Da m-baile (sense not understood)	OSL 48	1834c

19

18. Dá mbaile, "two towns"	J O'D (OSNB) 97	1834c
19. Dón/Dún Mola (or Muil)	Mooney 233	1950c
20. Dún mhaolaoidh Mooney "The fort of the hilltop or eminence"	Mooney 233	1950c
21. də'molɪ	Local pronunciation	1990

The origin of this name is rather obscure. O'Donovan suggested Irish *Dá mbaile* "two town-lands" (17–18) but nasalization of a masc. noun would not be expected after *dá* except in the dat., in which case the numeral would take on the form *dib* (*GOI* 242). Mooney proposed an original *Dún Mola* "the fort of the hilltop" (19) and there is, indeed, a fort known as Springhill Fort here (*ASCD* 155) but there is no evidence of the long *u* or the final *n* and the first element might instead be interpreted as *damh* meaning "house". Several forms suggest that the second element may be from *maol* "hill" (4–6, 7a, 8a, 9) which has a variant gen. sing. *maoile* (*Dinneen* sv. *maol*), although the current form of the name favours an original *mullaigh*, gen. sing. of *mullach* "summit".

Derry Beg   *Doire Beag*
J 0727   "little oak-wood"

1. Derriebagg	Bagenal Rental 127	1575
2. Derybegg	CPR Jas. I 86a	1606
3. Derribegg	CPR Jas. I 103a	1607
4. Deribeg	Esch. Co. Map 5.26	1609
5. Derriveg	CPR Jas. I 190a	1610
6. Dirrybegg	Inq. Ult. (Armagh) §2 Jac. I	1612
7. Derrybegg	CPR Jas. I 247b	1613
8. Derrybegge	Inq. Ult. (Armagh) §27 Car. I	1638
9. Derybeg	Inq. Arm. 227	1657
10. Derribegg ½ Towne Waste	BSD 9	1661
11. Derrybegg	BSD 10	1661
12. Derrypegg	HMR Murray (1941) 134	1664
13. Derrybeg	Reg. Free. (OSNB) 99	1829
14. Derry-beg	Bnd. Sur. (OSNB) 99	1830c
15. Doire Beag "Roboretum parvum"	OSL 47	1834c
16. Doire Beag "Little derry or oak-wood"	J O'D (OSNB) 99	1835
17. ˌderɪ'beːg	Local pronunciation	1990

The oak-tree occupied a special place in early Irish thought and the word *doire* "oak-grove" is very common in Irish place-names (see McCracken 1971, 24–5 where there is a distribution map of townland names containing the element *derry*).

Derry More   *Doire Mór*
J 0527   "large oak-wood"

1. (?)Derremoghyr	Reg. Swayne 177	1438c
2. Derriemore	Bagenal Rental 127	1575
3. Derimore	CPR Jas. I 86a	1606

4. Derrmore	CPR Jas. I 103a	1607
5. Derrimore	Esch. Co. Map 5.26	1609
6. Dereymore	Ulst. Plant. Paps. §65 272	1612
7. Dirrymore	Inq. Ult. (Armagh) §2 Jac. I	1612
8. Derrymore	CPR Jas. I 247b	1613
9. Derrymore al' Derrymorris	Inq. Ult. (Armagh) §27 Car. I	1638
10. Dyrimore	Inq. Arm. 227	1657
11. Derymoore	Census 31	1659
12. Derrymore	BSD 10	1661
13. Derrymone	HMR Murray (1941) 134	1664
14. ˌderı'moːr	Local pronunciation	1990

This name is not as straightforward as might first appear for the earliest form, which can almost certainly be identified with this townland, cannot be reconciled with the most obvious interpretation (1). However, without further substantiating evidence, it would be extremely dangerous to postulate an origin on the basis of this single form and it is possible that it represents a mistranscription.

Derryboy

J 0930

Doire Átha Buí

"the oak-wood of the yellow ford"

1. Largen Dyrraughboy	CPR Ed. VI iv 388	1552
2. Largindirraghboy	CPR Ed. VI iv 388	1552
3. Durragh bowe	Bagenal Rental 127	1575
4. Largan, Daraghboy	CPR Jas. I 86a	1606
5. Largan, Darraghboy	CPR Jas. I 102b	1607
6. Largan, Darraghboy	CPR Jas. I 494b	1607
7. Lurgandaraghboye	CPR Jas. I 246b	1613
8. Lurgardarghboy	Inq. Ult. (Down) §15 Jac. I	1625c
9. Daraghboy	Inq. Ult. (Down) §84 Car. I	1638
10. Carrogboy (sic)	Census 82	1659c
11. Lurgandarraghboy	BSD 130	1661
12. Derraghboy	Reg. Free. (OSNB) 97	1829
13. Derryboy	Bnd. Sur. (OSNB) 97	1830c
14. Derraghboy	Newry Tel. (OSNB) 97	1834c
15. ˌderı'bɔːi	Local pronunciation	1990

Originally, the first element in this name appears to have been Irish *leargain* "a hill-slope" (1–2, 4–6) but this has since dropped out. Some of the forms seem to indicate that what is now the initial element was the gen. sing. of *dair* "oak", *darach* (4–8) but the quality of the vowel in the earliest sources (1–3), coupled with the fact that this element later stands in initial position, seems to indicate rather an original *doire* "oak-wood" followed by *áth* "a ford".

Derryleckagh

J 1125

Doire Leacach

"oak-wood abounding in flagstones"

1. Dyrreleragh, vill of	Inq. (Mon. Hib.) 287	1549
2. Dyrrelecagh	Inq. (Mon. Hib.) 287	1549

3. Dyrrelecaghe	CPR Ed. VI iv 388	1552
4. Dirrelacaghe	CPR Ed. VI iv 388	1552
5. Dirrelecaghe	CPR Ed. VI iv 388	1552
6. Darlackough	Bagenal Rental 126	1575
7. Dirlachogh	CPR Jas. I 86a	1606
8. Dirlekagh	CPR Jas. I 102b	1607
9. Derlecagh	CPR Jas. I 495a	1607
10. Dirrelecagh	CPR Jas. I 246b	1613
11. Derrylikagh	Inq. Ult. (Down) §15 Jac. I	1625c
12. Dirlachogh	Inq. Ult. (Down) §84 Car. I	1638
13. Dyrilakagh	Civ. Surv. x §72	1655c
14. Derrillackoghe	Census 82	1659c
15. Derrylarkaise	BSD 130	1661
16. Dirielarkagh	Sub. Roll Down 280	1663
17. Derylake als Derrylogh	Forfeit. Estates 352b §32	1703
18. Derrylake	Forfeit. Estates 352b §32	1703
19. Derileckagh	Harris Hist. 97	1744
20. Derrylackagh	Wm. Map (OSNB) 97	1810
21. Derrylackagh	Bnd. Sur. (OSNB) 97	1830c
22. Der-ry-'lack-agh	OSNB 97	1834c
23. Doire leaca	OSL 48	1834c
24. Doire leaca "oak wood of the flag stones"	J O'D (OSNB) 97	1834c
25. Doire leacach "Rocky oak-wood (of flagstones)"	Mooney 247	1950c
26. ˌdɛrə'leki	Local pronunciation	1990

The stones from which Derryleckagh takes its name are probably those near Derryleckagh Wood known as "The Long Stones" (OS J 2411). The site is said to be the remains of a "Giant's Grave" although no cairn is now traceable (*ASCD* 95).

Desert
J 1329

An Díseart
"the hermitage"

1. Dysart	Inq. (Mon. Hib.) 287	1549
2. Dysarte	CPR Ed. VI iv 388	1552
3. Desarte	CPR Ed. VI iv 388	1552
4. Dysert	Bagenal Rental 122	1575
5. Le Disart	CPR Jas. I 86a	1606
6. Le Disert	CPR Jas. I 102b	1607
7. the Dysert	CPR Jas. I 495a	1607
8. Disart	CPR Jas. I 246b	1613
9. Dysart	Inq. Ult. (Down) §15 Jac. I	1625c
10. Ryanledysert	Inq. Ult. (Down) §84 Car. I	1638
11. Dizarts	Census 82	1659c
12. Dissird, East & West	BSD 130	1661
13. Disart	Sub. Roll Down 280	1663
14. Desart	Wm. Map (OSNB) 97	1810

15. Dysarts	County Warrant (OSNB) 97	1827
16. Dysarts	Reg. Free. (OSNB) 97	1829
17. Desarts	Bnd. Sur. (OSNB) 97	1830c
18. 'Des-arts	OSNB 97	1834c
19. Desert	J O'D (OSNB) 97	1834c
20. Díseart	OSL 48	1834c
21. Díseart, "a desert or wilderness"	J O'D (OSNB) 97	1834c
22. An Díseart "The Wilderness or Secluded Place"	Mooney 249	1950c
23. 'dɛzərt	Local pronunciation	1990

John O'Donovan noted that this name was generally pronounced *Desarts* (18) and this is reflected in a number of later spellings (11, 15–17). This may represent an oblique form *Dísirt* of the Irish *Díseart* "a retreat, hermitage" or simply an English plural form of the name (see 12). There may be a connection between this name and the spread of the Culdee movement in the 8th and 9th centuries but some instances of this element in place-names are, apparently, older still. Deirdre Flanagan has suggested that the use of *díseart* in place-names may have begun as early as the 6th century with the meaning "hermitage" and that by the 8th and 9th centuries it had developed a more specialized meaning "a place apart: a monastic house observing a stricter rule" (1981–2(c), 72). Of course, because of the nature of a hermitage, we often have no record of the retreat, and frequently its existence becomes apparent only if it gave its name to the place (see also *Joyce* i 324–6).

Drumalane   *Droim Leathan*
J 0824   "broad ridge"

1. Ballibrindrumloughan	CPR Jas. I 86a	1606
2. Dromlogane	CPR Jas. I 103a	1607
3. Dromlahan	CPR Jas. I 133b	1609
4. Dromhahan	Esch. Co. Map 5.26	1609
5. Dromlaghan	Inq. Ult. (Armagh) §2 Jas. I	1610
6. Dromloghan	Inq. Ult. (Armagh) §27 Car. I	1638
7. Drumleane	Inq. Arm. 227	1657
8. Drumalane	Reg. Free (OSNB) 99	1830
9. Drummalane	Bnd. Sur (OSNB) 99	1830c
10. Druim leathan "wide ridge or hill"	J O'D (OSNB) 99	1835
11. ˌdrọMə'le:n	Local pronunciation	1990

A number of early forms ending in *-lo(u)ghan* et var. (1–2, 5–6) may indicate that this name comes from the Irish *Droim Locháin* "the ridge of the small lake" but the subsequent development would be rather difficult to explain. It is true that short *o* tends to *a* and *ch* is reduced to *h* in the Irish of east Ulster but this still would not produce the current pronunciation (11), unless by analogy with another name. Thus, it seems preferable to interpret the second element as *leathan* "broad" which would give a final syllable [lehən], later becoming [le:n]. In the earlier forms, which may have been influenced by names containing the element *loch* and *lochán*, the *-gh-* should probably be taken to represent *h*.

Drumcashellone   *Droim Caisil Eoghain* (?)
J 0928   "the ridge of Eoghan's cashel"

1. Haghirnecloghe (Aghirnecloghe)	CPR Ed. VI iv 388	1552
2. Aghernecloghe	CPR Ed. VI iv 388	1552
3. Atherne Cloghcornehore	CPR Jas. I 86a	1606
4. Agherneclogh	CPR Jas. I 102b	1607
5. Agherneclagh	CPR Jas. I 495a	1607
6. Agherneclogh	CPR Jas. I 246b	1613
7. Agherneclogh	Inq. Ult. (Down) §15 Jac. I	1625c
8. Atherne al' Arthern, Cloghcornehore al' Cloghcornehare	Inq. Ult. (Down) §84 Car. I	1638
9. Drumcassellowen	Census 82	1659c
10. Aghnecley	BSD 130	1661
11. Drumcassloan	Sub. Roll Down 280	1663
12. Drumcashelhone	Wm. Map (OSNB) 97	1810
13. Drumcashellone	Bnd. Sur. (OSNB) 97	1830c
14. Drum Caisel Luan "ridge of Luan's stone fort"	J O'D (OSNB) 97	1834c
15. Drum Caisil Luain "the ridge of cashel or fort of Luanus"	OSL 47	1834c
16. ˈdrọmˌkaʃˈloːn	Local pronunciation	1990

O'Donovan derived this name from *Druim Caisel Luan* "ridge of Luan's stone fort" (14–15) but it may come from *Droim Caisil Eoghain* "the ridge of Owen's fort" or, perhaps, *Droim Caisil Abhann* "the ridge of the cashel of the river" for a river passes nearby to both the east and west of the townland. Settlement features, such as *dún*, *ráth* and *caiseal*, are more commonly qualified by personal names and *abhainn* is perhaps less likely an origin than the personal names cited here. *Luan* is a rare and obscure name and so *Eoghan* may be more likely. Drumcashellone appears at a relatively late date in our sources but it may, in fact, be of much older date than this.

Edenmore   *Éadan Mór*
J 1426   "large hill-face"

1. Edenmore	Inq. (Mon. Hib.) 287	1549
2. Edenmore	CPR Ed. VI iv 388	1552
3. Eddanmore	Bagenal Rental 124	1575
4. Edenmore	CPR Jas. I 86a	1606
5. Edenmore	CPR Jas. I 102b	1607
6. Edenmore	CPR Jas. I 495a	1607
7. Edenmore	CPR Jas. I 246b	1613
8. Eddenmore	Inq. Ult. (Down) §15 Jac. I	1625c
9. Edenmore	Inq. Ult. (Down) §84 Car. I	1638
10. Edenmore	Civ. Surv. x §72	1655c
11. Edenmore	Census 82	1659c
12. Eddenmore	BSD 130	1661
13. Edenmore	Sub. Roll Down 280	1663

14. Edenmore	Wm. Map (OSNB) 97	1810
15. Edenmore	Bnd. Sur. (OSNB) 97	1830c
16. 'Eden-more	OSNB 97	1834c
17. Éudan mór		
*"great brae, or brow of a hill"	J O'D (OSNB) 97	1834c
18. Eudan Mór "large brow of a hill"	OSL 48	1834c
19. i:dn̥'mo:r	Local pronunciation	1990

The word *éadan* as a place-name element is found almost exclusively in Ulster where there are 14 Edenmores (ó Maolfabhail 1987–8, 80). Our Edenmore is situated on a large hill-face overlooking Derryleckagh Lake (OS J 1426, J 1425).

Fathom Lower   *An Feadán*
Fathom Upper   "the stream/gully"
J 0922, J 1020

1. Fedan	Boazio's Map (BM)	1599
2. Ffaddam, 4 vill' de	Ex. Inq. 2 Jac. I 45	1605
3. Feddan,		
the fishing of the waters of	CPR Jas. I 86a	1606
4. Fedan and Clanree, the waters of	CPR Jas. I 102b	1607
5. Fedane or Ragaffa	CPR Jas. I 103a	1607
6. Magaffa orse Fedan	CPR Jas. I 133b	1609
7. Fadan	Esch. Co. Map 5.26	1609
8. Fedan	Norden's Map	1610c
9. Moygaffa al' Feddan	Inq. Ult. (Armagh) §2 Jac. I	1612
10. Glanreemagaffee al' Faddam	Inq. Ult. (Armagh) §27 Car. I	1638
11. Feddans, two towns of	Inq. Arm. 228	1657
12. Athefindom	BSD 10	1661
13. (?)Bothsodams	HMR Murray (1941) 134	1664
14. Upper & Lower Fathom Mt.	Rocque's Map (Coote)	1760
15. Fathom	Taylor & Skinner 11	1777
16. Upper/Lower Fathom	Bnd. Sur (OSNB) 99	1830c
17. Feadan "watch tower"	OSNB Inf. 99	1835
18. Feadan "a brook, rill,		
rumell, a streamlet"	J O'D (OSNB) 99	1835
19. an Feadán	Post-Sheanchas 67	1905
20. Feadan "a streamlet"	Joyce iii 351	1913
21. Fiodha-dun "forest castle"	Canavan 1989, 40	1989
22. 'fadəm	Local pronunciation	1990

The editor of *Marshal Bagenal's Description of Ulster*, in a note to the text, derives the name Fathom from *fiodh* "a wood" and observes that "the surrounding country is delineated on Blaeu's map as a forest" (*Bagenal's Descr. Ulst.* 151n). However, the internal *dh* would have become vocalized or gone to [γ] at an early date and this clearly did not happen. Moreover, the earliest spellings show no trace of the *-th-* we find in later forms (1–11, 13). Tony Canavan (1989, 40) cites a view that Fathom derives from *fiodha-dun* (*recte fiodh-dún*) meaning "forest castle" (21) but the earliest forms all show a clear *a* in the last syllable (1–11) so that such an origin, while not impossible, is unlikely.

The most probable origin of the name, therefore, would seem to be from *feadán* meaning "water-course, gully". The final *n* seems have been confused with *m* at a fairly early stage (2, 10, 12–16) and this may have resulted in the name being reformed by analogy with English "fathom" (14–16). The townland was divided into two parts, Upper and Lower Fathom, and this may explain the curious form *Bothsodams* in the *Hearth Money Rolls* of 1664 (13) which, if we correct the common error of *s* for *f*, may be rendered "both Fadams". Although there is no evidence of the article in any of the above spellings, the Irish name for **Flag Staff**, *Barr an Fheadáin*, clearly shows that it did form, at least at a later date, part of the name.

Finnard
J 1331

Fionnúir
meaning uncertain

1. Fynor	Inq. (Mon. Hib.) 287	1549
2. Fynnor	CPR Ed. VI iv 388	1552
3. Fenor	Bagenal Rental 126	1575
4. Fennor	CPR Jas. I 86a	1606
5. Fennor	CPR Jas. I 103a	1607
6. Fennor	CPR Jas. I 495a	1607
7. Fennor	CPR Jas. I 246b	1613
8. Fennor	Inq. Ult. (Down) §15 Jac. I	1625c
9. Fennor	Inq. Ult. (Down) §84 Car. I	1638
10. Fenone	Civ. Surv. x §72	1655c
11. Fennare	Civ. Surv. x §72	1655c
12. Finer and halfe Finer	Census 82	1659c
13. ffennor, East & West	BSD 130	1661
14. (?)Finis	Sub. Roll Down 280	1663
15. Finors	Wm. Map (OSNB) 97	1810
16. Finniards	County Warrant (OSNB) 97	1827
17. Finard	Newry Tel. (OSNB) 97	1830
18. Finnard	Reg. Free. (OSNB) 97	1830
19. Finors	Bnd. Sur. (OSNB) 97	1830c
20. Fin-nars	OSNB 97	1834c
21. Finnard	J O'D (OSNB) 97	1834c
22. Fionn ard "white height"	OSL 48	1834c
23. Fion[n] árd "white height or hill"	J O'D (OSNB) 97	1834c
24. Fionnabhar "White Plain"	Mooney 251	1950c
25. ˈfinərd	Local pronunciation	1990

Older documents show that the final *-d* in Finnard is not original so that this name cannot mean "the fair height" and Mooney is probably correct in suggesting that it comes from Irish *Fionnabhar* (recte *Fionnabhair*), modern *Fionnúir*. This name is given to a variety of places in early texts but its meaning remains obscure. In Jocelyn's *Life of St Patrick*, it is translated as *Campus Albus* "white plain" (cited *Joyce* ii 267), but some doubt has been expressed about this interpretation by modern scholars (*ibid.*). *Finnabhair* is also found as a personal name and in this usage O'Curry proffered the translation "fair-browed" (1861, iii 10) but Joyce dismissed this interpretation on the grounds that the personal name *Finnabhair* is inflected as a k-stem giving a gen. sing. *Fionnabhrach* whereas *abhair* "brow" is a dental stem with a gen. sing. *abhrat* (*Joyce* ii 267). T. F. O'Rahilly suggested that the second element in the name is connected with Celtic *dubron* (Irish *dobhar*, Welsh *dwfr*, *dwr*) and postulated a Celtic origin *Vindo-dubris* meaning "a place on (or near) white water" (O'Rahilly 1933, 210).

Grange Lower	An Anglo-Norman form	
Grange Upper		
J 9454, J 9353		

1. Grange	Esch. Co. Map 5.28	1609
2. the Grange, parcel of land	Inq. Ult. (Armagh) §2 Jas. I	1610
3. the Grange, the precinct or territory of	CPR Jas. I 246b	1613
4. Grange ONeland	Civ. Surv. x 77	1655c
5. Granges of O'Neillan otherwise The Grange of O'Neilland otherwise the Grange of Oneland	Reg. Deeds abstracts ii	1764
6. Grange O'Neill	Lewis' Top. Dict. i 671	1837

This detached portion of the Lordship of Newry, situated in the barony of Oneilland in Co. Armagh is occasionally called Grange Oneilland *et var.* in our early sources to distinguish it from other places of the same name. It was formerly a large tract of land variously styled as "precinct", "territory" and "parcel of land" in the early sources where it is subdivided into smaller units or half-towns (*CPR Jas. I* 103a, 246b, *Inq. Ult.* (Armagh) §2 Jas. I). On the element *grange*, see **Gransha** below.

Gransha	*An Ghráinseach*	
J 1535	"the grange/granary"	

1. Grange	Inq. (Mon. Hib.) 287	1549
2. Graunge	CPR Ed. VI iv 388	1552
3. Grange	CPR Ed. VI iv 388	1552
4. Graunge	Bagenal Rental 126	1575
5. Grang	CPR Jas. I 86a	1606
6. Grange	CPR Jas. I 103a	1607
7. Grange	CPR Jas. I 495a	1607
8. Grange	CPR Jas. I 246b	1613
9. Grange	Inq. Ult. (Down) §15 Jac. I	1625c
10. Grange	Inq. Ult. (Down) §84 Car. I	1638
11. Grange	Civ. Surv. x §72	1655c
12. Grange	Census 82	1659c
13. Grange & Oully	BSD 130	1661
14. Grange-owly	Sub. Roll Down 280	1663
15. Granshagh	Wm. Map (OSNB) 97	1810
16. Gransha	Bnd. Sur. (OSNB) 97	1830c
17. 'Gran-shaw	OSNB 97	1834c
18. Gráinseach "a Grange"	OSL 48	1834c
19. Gráinseach "a grange or monastic farm"	J O'D (OSNB) 97	1834c

20. Gráinseach	Mooney 251	1950c
21. 'granʃə	Local pronunciation	1990

The word *gráinseach*, from which Gransha takes its name, is derived from the Norman–French *grange* and, indeed, in 16th- and 17th-century sources Gransha is invariably called *Grange* (1–14). A grange was a unit of land held as farm-land by a monastic house of the 12th- or post-12th-century period, frequently of Anglo-Norman foundation (Flanagan 1981–2(c), 75). It was not always adjacent to the monastery and could be, as in this particular case, some distance away. Gransha was one of the townlands formerly held by the church of St Mary and St Patrick at Newry which were granted to Nicholas Bagnall in 1552 (*CPR Ed. VI* iv 387–8).

Greenan *Grianán*
J 1122 "eminent place"

1. Grenan, alias Borenymy	Inq. (Mon. Hib.) 287	1549
2. Grenan alias Borenymygan	CPR Ed. VI iv 388	1552
3. Brenan alias Borenemygan	CPR Ed. VI iv 388	1552
4. Gremen	Bagenal Rental 126	1575
5. Greenan	CPR Jas. I 86a	1606
6. Grenan al. Borenemygan	CPR Jas. I 102b	1607
7. Grenan orse Borenygan	CPR Jas. I 495a	1607
8. Greenam orse Brenam orse		
Borenymigan	CPR Jas. I 246b	1613
9. Greenan al' Brenan al'		
Borerynugan	Inq. Ult. (Down) §15 Jac. I	1625c
10. Greenen al' Greenan	Inq. Ult. (Down) §84 Car. I	1638
11. Greenan	Civ. Surv. x §72	1655c
12. grenan	Civ. Surv. x §72	1655c
13. Grenan	Census 82	1659c
14. Greenane	BSD 130	1661
15. Granan	Sub. Roll Down 280	1663
16. Grenan	Wm. Map (OSNB) 97	1810
17. Grinan	County Warrant (OSNB) 97	1827
18. Grianan	Carlisle (OSNB) 97	1834c
19. 'Gri-nan	OSNB 97	1834c
20. Grianán "a Sunny place"	OSL 47	1834c
21. Grianán "solarium,		
a fort on a hill"	J O'D (OSNB) 97	1834c
22. Grianán	Mooney 237	1950c
23. 'gri:nən	Local pronunciation	1990

Greenan is the anglicized form of Irish *Grianán* and, although this element is found in names of places throughout Ireland, its meaning remains rather obscure. It is a derivative of *grian* "sun" and is used in medieval literary texts with the sense "a sunny chamber, a bower, a soller, an open balcony exposed to the sun, an upper room" (*DIL* sv. *grianán*). Clearly, this cannot be the meaning of the word in names of places and Art Ó Maolfabhail ventured the suggestion that it was applied to places of some importance, regularly used by the public

28

(ó Maolfabhail 1974). However, despite a thorough examination of the literature and of many of the individual sites which bear the name Greenan, Ó Maolfabhail produces no evidence in support of his proposed translation and it certainly cannot be applied to our Greenan which must always have been overshadowed by the monastic settlement at Newry. A quite different interpretation of the word is given in the *Leabhar Breac* version of *Cormac's Glossary* (c. 1395) where *Temair* (Tara) is glossed *grianán nó tulach* "a greenan or a hill" (*San. Corm. (LB)* 42) and in his dictionary of Scottish Gaelic, Dwelly attributes the meaning "peak of a mountain" to *grianan*. Of the sites visited by Ó Maolfabhail, most had a good view (*op. cit.* 61) so that the primary meaning of *grianán* in place-names may be "hill, mound" and, indeed, our Greenan commands an excellent view of Carlingford Lough. Ó Maolfabhail, probably correctly, has pointed to another series of Greenans where the name seems to mean "sunny spot, a place which is good for drying things" (*ibid.* 69). One informant, Dan McArdle of Greenan, explained the name as "something to do with the setting sun" but the element *grian* is all too obvious in the name for this etymology to be taken too seriously.

Lisdrumgullion
J 0728

Lios Droim gCuillinn
"fort of the ridge of the steep slope"

1. Lisdromgallin	Census 31	1659
2. Lisdrumgullion	Taylor & Skinner 22	1777
3. Lisdrumgullion	Reg. Free (OSNB) 99	1829
4. Lisdrumgullion	Bnd. Sur (OSNB) 99	1830c
5. Lios Droma Cuillin[n] "fort of the holly ridge"	J O'D (OSNB) 99	1835
6. Lios Drom cCuleann "fort of the hill of hollies"	OSNB Inf. 99	1835
7. ˌlɪsdrɒmˈgölʲən	Local pronunciation	1990

Occurrences of this name are very rare in early documents but it must be very old as it preserves nasalization after the old neut. *droim*, a feature which disappeared from Irish c. 1000 AD. Nasalization would not be normally expected after a gen. sing. noun as in **Lios Droma Cuillinn* so that the first element, from the Irish *lios* meaning "fort", must have been added to a pre-existent name *Droim gCuillinn* "ridge of the steep slope", perhaps without the expected inflection of *droim*. The element *gullion* (et var.) is often translated as if it were from *cuileann* "holly-tree" but T. S. Ó Máille has convincingly argued that in many cases it actually comes from *cuilleann* (gen. *cuillinn*) "a steep slope" (Ó Máille 1960).

Lisdrumliska
J 0725

Lios Droim Loiscthe
"fort of the scorched ridge"

1. Dromliskin	CPR Jas. I 86a	1606
2. Dromliskine	CPR Jas. I 103a	1607
3. Dromlesken	CPR Jas. I 133b	1609
4. Dromleshagh	Esch. Co. Map 5.26	1609
5. Dromleskin	Inq. Ult. (Armagh) §2 Jac. I	1612
6. Dromliskin	Inq. Ult. (Armagh) §27 Car. I	1638
7. Lysdrumlesgagh	Inq. Arm. 228	1657

8. Lissumseska	BSD 10	1661
9. Lisdrumliscagh	Reg. Deeds abstracts i §214	1720
10. Lisdrumliska	Reg. Free (OSNB) 99	1829
11. Lisdrumliskagh	Bnd. Sur (OSNB) 99	1830c
12. Lios droma liseaic "Fort of the Ridge of the Sluggard"	J O'D (OSNB) 99	1835
13. Lios-droma-leisgidh "fort of the ridge of the lazy fellow"	Joyce iii 475	1913
14. ˌlɪsdrọmˈlɪskə	Local pronunciation	1990

Many of the early forms of this name, in contrast to the later spellings and the current pronunciation, show a final *n(e)* (1–3, 5–6). However, they all appear in closely related grants and inquisitions, and, as the development of *n* to an *agh*-sound would be impossible, it seems likely that they are based on a scribal error. The interpretation of the final element by O'Donovan and Joyce (12–13) as "a lazy fellow, a sluggard", while imaginative, is not very probable, and we might rather suggest an origin in *loiscthe* "burnt, scorched". Joyce notes that land burnt for agricultural purposes (as, for instance, when heath was burnt to encourage the growth of grass) was designated in Irish by this word (*Joyce* i 238). It is attested as an element in a number of place-names, and Stockman (1991) notes its application to topographical features such as *achadh* "a field", *má* "a plain" and *machaire* "a plain". The first element in the current form of the name, from Irish *lios* "fort", is a comparatively late addition and may refer to the enclosure known as Watson's Fort (*NISMR* Armagh sheet 26 §13).

Lisduff
J 0830

An Lios Dubh
"the black fort"

1. Lyssene Crasne	CPR Ed. VI iv 388	1552
2. Lysnecrasse	CPR Ed. VI iv 388	1552
3. Lessenecrassane	Bagenal Rental 127	1575
4. Lissenegrossen	CPR Jas. I 86a	1606
5. Lissennecrossne	CPR Jas. I 102b	1607
6. Lissenecrassne	CPR Jas. I 494b	1607
7. Lisnecrosse or Lissenecrosne	CPR Jas. I 246b	1613
8. Lisnecrosse al' Lisnecrasue	Inq. Ult. (Down) §15 Jac. I	1625c
9. Lissengrossen	Inq. Ult. (Down) §84 Car. I	1638
10. Lisduffe	Census 82	1659c
11. Lisseduffe	Sub. Roll Down 280	1663
12. Lisduff	Bnd. Sur. (OSNB) 97	1830c
13. Lios dubh "Black fort"	OSL 47	1834c
14. Lios dubh "black fort"	J O'D (OSNB) 97	1834c
15. lɪsˈdọf	Local pronunciation	1990

There is no evidence now of a fort in this area but Lisduff clearly derives its name from the Irish *An Lios Dubh* "the black fort". It is evidently the same place as the *Lissnecrossne* et var. of earlier documents (1–9) which, in the grant to Nicholas Bagnall of 1552 (1), is said to be next to *Cormyne* (modern **Carnmeen**).

Lisnaree	*Lios na Rí*	
J 1433	"the fort of the kings"	

1. Lisnerye	Inq. (Mon. Hib.) 287	1549
2. Bysnerye	CPR Ed. VI iv 388	1552
3. Lysnerye	CPR Ed. VI iv 388	1552
4. Lysnery	CPR Ed. VI iv 388	1552
5. Lesnerye	Bagenal Rental 124	1575
6. (?)Lise-ne Ree	Bartlett Maps (Esch. Co. Maps) 2	1603
7. Lisnery	CPR Jas. I 86a	1606
8. Lisnerrye	CPR Jas. I 103a	1607
9. Lisnerrie	CPR Jas. I 495a	1607
10. Lisneree	CPR Jas. I 246b	1613
11. Lisnery	Inq. Ult. (Down) §84 Car. I	1638
12. Lissvery al' Lisnery	Inq. Ult. (Down) §84 Car. I	1638
13. Lissnerea & Cisillannegan	BSD 130	1661
14. Lisnaree	Wm. Map (OSNB) 97	1810
15. Lisnaree	Bnd. Sur. (OSNB) 97	1830c
16. Lis-na-'ree	OSNB 97	1834c
17. Lios na ríogh "fort of the kings"	J O'D (OSNB) 97	1834c
18. Lios na ríogh "Munito regum"	OSL 48	1834c
19. ˌlisnəˈriː	Local pronunciation	1990

There is a rath here (J 1433) from which the townland may have been named. No evidence has yet come to light to substantiate its claim to be "the fort of the kings" save for a note on Bartlett's map of South-East Ulster which names it as the place "where the McGenis is made" (*Bartlett Maps (Esch. Co. Maps)* 2). However, Bartlett places it several miles north of its actual location at a prominent hill called Knock Iveagh and this, rather than our Lisnaree, may have been the site which he had in mind. Standard Modern Irish would be expected to yield a form *Lios na Ríthe* but the older gen. pl. form, formerly spelt *rí(o)gh*, now *rí*, has been adopted here in accordance with the evidence of the historical spellings.

Lisserboy	*Liosar Buí*	
J 1033	"yellow fort"	

1. Lisarboy	CPR Jas. I 86a	1606
2. Lisarboy	CPR Jas. I 102b	1607
3. Lisarboy	CPR Jas. I 495a	1607
4. Lassarboy	CPR Jas. I 246b	1613
5. Liscarboy	Inq. Ult. (Down) §15 Jac. I	1625c
6. Carkachaghelishorby	Inq. Ult. (Down) §84 Car. I	1638
7. Shyn al' Lysharby	Inq. Ult. (Down) §84 Car. I	1638
8. Lissardley	Civ. Surv. x §72	1655c
9. Lizard boy	Census 82	1659c
10. Lisardboy	Wm. Map (OSNB) 97	1810
11. Lisardboy	Bnd. Sur. (OSNB) 97	1830c
12. Lisserboy	J O'D (OSNB) 97	1834c
13. Lisear Buidhe	OSNB Inf. 97	1834c

14.	Lisear buidhe "yellow fort"	OSL 48	1834c
15.	Lios ard buidhe		
	"fort of the yellow height"	J O'D (OSNB) 97	1834c
16.	ˌlisərˈbɔi	Local pronunciation	1990

O'Donovan disregarded his informant's etymology of this name (13–14) and proposed an Irish form *Lios Ard Buidhe* "fort of the yellow height" (15) but the earliest forms tend to support the informant's suggestion (1–7, 12). *Liosar* is a compound of the element *lios* "fort" and the suffix *ar* which is frequently misunderstood as a collective. T. S. Ó Máille has argued that whatever collectivity was formerly attached to the suffix *ar* in Irish has long since disappeared and that it is now used, especially in toponymy, merely to add point to the meaning already conveyed in the root word (Ó Máille 1987). Ó Máille, therefore, would translate *liosar*, not as "forts", but as "fort-thing" or, more simply, "fort" (*ibid.* 35).

The *Ordnance Survey Memoirs* note that there are two forts in this townland, the larger one being called Leister's Fort "in consequence of a man being interred in it who commited suicide" and the other called Traymount (*OSM* iii 106).

Loughorne
J 1233

Loch Eorna
"lake of barley"

1.	Loghorn, the island of	CPR Jas. I 102b	1607
2.	Loghorne, the island of	CPR Jas. I 495a	1607
3.	Loughorne island	CPR Jas. I 246b	1613
4.	Loughorne, island of	Inq. Ult. (Down) §15 Jac. I	1625c
5.	Loghorne	Census 82	1659c
6.	Loughown	Sub. Roll Down 280	1663
7.	Loughorn	Reg. Deeds abstracts i §214	1720
8.	Loughorn	Wm. Map (OSNB) 97	1810
9.	Loughorn	Bnd. Sur. (OSNB) 97	1830c
10.	'Lough-orne	OSNB 97	1834c
11.	Loughorne	J O'D (OSNB) 97	1834c
12.	Loch orna "Barley Lake"	OSL 48	1834c
13.	Loch eórna "barley lake"	J O'D (OSNB) 97	1834c
14.	Loch Eorna "Barley Lake"	Mooney 255	1950c
15.	lɔxˈoːrn	Local pronunciation	1990

John O'Donovan recounts a local tradition that the lake from which Loughorne takes its name was once inhabited by a monster and that this beast destroyed all the barley in the neighbourhood, so that the lake was named *Loch Eorna* "lake of barley" (*OSL* 48). Whereas the tradition may be somewhat fanciful the explanation of the origin of the name seems plausible.

Ouley
J 1435

Uanlaigh (?)
"place of lambs"

1.	Ballyownley	Inq. (Mon. Hib.) 287	1549
2.	Balliownley	CPR Ed. VI iv 388	1552

3.	Ballyownley	CPR Ed. VI iv 388	1552
4.	Ballrownely	CPR Jas. I 86a	1606
5.	Balleowullie	CPR Jas. I 103a	1607
6.	Balleowullie	CPR Jas. I 495a	1607
7.	Ownlye	CPR Jas. I 246b	1613
8.	Ownly	Inq. Ult. (Down) §15 Jac. I	1625c
9.	Balleownely	Inq. Ult. (Down) §84 Car. I	1638
10.	Owlye	Civ. Surv. x §72	1655c
11.	Oully & Grange	BSD 130	1661
12.	Grange-owly	Sub. Roll Down 280	1663
13.	Owley	Wm. Map (OSNB) 97	1810
14.	Ouley	Bnd. Sur. (OSNB) 97	1830c
15.	'Oo-ley	OSNB 97	1834c
16.	Umhlaidh	OSL 48	1834c
17.	Abhlaidhe		
	"apple trees or orchards"	J O'D (OSNB) 97	1834c
18.	Ubhallach/Abhallach	Mooney 255	1950c
19.	Uaigh or Uamhan + -lach		
	"Place of caves or kilns"	Mooney 255	1950c
20.	'u:lt	Local pronunciation	1990

The majority of the 16th- and 17th-century forms contain an internal *n* (1–4, 7–9; the *u* in forms 5–6 is probably to be read as *n*) but it is tempting to dismiss these as based on an error in an early grant or inquisition (see p. 2 above). Thus, O'Donovan's suggested origin in Irish *Abhlaidhe* "apple trees or orchards" (17), or *Umhlaidh* (16), and Mooney's proposed *Ubhallach* "place abounding in apples" (18), and *Uaighleach* "place abounding in caves" (19), are attractive possibilities. However, the absence of the *n* from the modern forms can be explained as a normal sound change (assimilation to the following *l*). Moreover, the absence of the prefix *Bally-* in two early forms which also contain the *n* may be adduced as independent evidence of the presence of [n] in the name, and we may dismiss the suggestions made by O'Donovan and Mooney. Mooney's suggestion of *Uamhanlach* "abounding in caves or kilns" is, however, plausible, save that there is no archaeological or historical evidence to support such an origin. We might, therefore, tentatively suggest a derivation from *Uanlach*, meaning perhaps, "a place for lambing" with which we may compare *muclach* "a piggery" and *broclach* "a place frequented by badgers", both of which occur in other place-names (*Joyce* ii 5).

Ryan
J 1428

Rian
"path/track"

1.	Ryan	Inq. (Mon. Hib.) 287	1549
2.	Ryan	CPR Ed. VI iv 388	1552
3.	Ryan	Bagenal Rental 122	1575
4.	Ryen	CPR Jas. I 86a	1606
5.	Rien	CPR Jas. I 102b	1607
6.	Ryen	CPR Jas. I 495a	1607
7.	Rian	CPR Jas. I 246b	1613
8.	Ryan	Inq. Ult. (Down) §15 Jac. I	1625c

9. Rawyn	Inq. Ult. (Down) §84 Car. I	1638
10. Ryenledysart	Inq. Ult. (Down) §84 Car. I	1638
11. Ryan	Civ. Surv. x §72	1655c
12. Ryan	Census 82	1659c
13. Rian	BSD 130	1661
14. Reyan	Wm. Map (OSNB) 97	1810
15. Reyan	Bnd. Sur. (OSNB) 97	1830c
16. Ryan	J O'D (OSNB) 97	1834c
17. Regan	OSM iii 109	1834c
18. Rian "a road or track"	OSL 48	1834c
19. Rián "a track"	J O'D (OSNB) 97	1834c
20. Raon "track, path"	Mooney 257	1950c
21. Ráithín "Little Fort"	Mooney 257	1950c
22. raiən	Local pronunciation	1990

Ryan comes from the Irish *Rian* "road, path" and was probably named after a track that ran through this long narrow townland. *Rian* was probably represented reasonably faithfully by the earliest English-speaking settlers in the area but some time in the 15th century Middle English [i:] was diphthongized to [ai] (Barber 1976, 290–2) giving us a current pronunciation which differs somewhat from the original Irish form (22).

Saval Beg
J 1130

Sabhall Beag
"small barn"

1. Savellbegg	Census 82	1659c
2. Sawillbegg	BSD 130	1661
3. Savellbeg	Wm. Map (OSNB) 97	1810
4. Savelbeg	Bnd. Sur. (OSNB) 97	1830c
5. 'Sa-vel-beg	OSNB 97	1834c
6. Savalbeg	J O'D (OSNB) 97	1834c
7. Sabhal beag "the small barn"	J O'D (OSNB) 97	1834c
8. ˌsavəl 'bɛg	Local pronunciation	1990

This name appears only in the later half of the 17th century and previous to that date it seems to have formed part of **Saval More**.

Saval More
J 1230

Sabhall Mór
"large barn"

1. Savelmore	Inq. (Mon. Hib.) 287	1549
2. Savelmore, the two towns of	CPR Ed. VI iv 388	1552
3. Savelmore, the two towns of	CPR Ed. VI iv 388	1552
4. Sawllomore	Bagenal Rental 126	1575
5. Savellmore, the two towns of	CPR Jas. I 86a	1606
6. Savellmore	CPR Jas. I 102b	1607
7. Savelmore, the 2 townes of	CPR Jas. I 495a	1607
8. Savellmore	CPR Jas. I 246b	1613
9. Samellmoore	Inq. Ult. (Down) §15 Jac. I	1625c
10. Savillmore	Inq. Ult. (Down) §84 Car. I	1638

11. Savelmore	Inq. Ult. (Down) §84 Car. I	1638
12. Savellmore	Census 82	1659c
13. Sauillmore and Sonne	BSD 130	1661
14. Savellmore	Sub. Roll Down 280	1663
15. Savellmore	Wm. Map (OSNB) 97	1810
16. Savelmore	Bnd. Sur. (OSNB) 97	1830c
17. 'Sa-vel-more	OSNB 97	1834c
18. Savalmore	J O'D (OSNB) 97	1834c
19. Sabhal	OSL 48	1834c
20. Sabhal mór "the great barn or granary"	J O'D (OSNB) 97	1834c
21. ˌsavəl ˈmoːr	Local pronunciation	1990

The earliest reference to the neighbouring townland of **Saval Beg** occurs only in the latter half of the 17th century and it would appear that, prior to this, the two townlands of Saval More and Saval Beg were collectively known as Saval More or "the two towns of Saval More" (2–3, 5, 7).

The word *sabhall* "a barn" is very rare in Irish place-names and occurs only in a few names in the north of Ireland, most notably the parish and townland of **Saul** in Co. Down, and the townland of **Sawelabeg** in Co. Tyrone. **Sawel** is also the name of a mountain in Co. Tyrone and *sabhall* forms the second element in the name Drumsaul in the parish of Ematris, Co. Monaghan.

There was also a church at Armagh called *Sabhall* which was burnt in 916 (*AU Mac Airt*) and again in 1020 (*AU Mac Airt*). Muirchú describes an incident according to which St Patrick, after founding his church at Armagh, came across a hind and her calf "in the place where the altar of the transverse church [that is, a church along a north–south rather than the more usual east–west line] at Armagh now stands" (*in loco in quo nunc altare est sinistralis aeclessiae in Ardd Machae* (*Trip. Life Stokes* i 292.6–8). In the *Vita Tripartita* the place where Patrick finds the deer is called *Saball* (*ibid.* i 230) and it is clearly the same as the *Saball* at Armagh which is mentioned in the annals. According to Colgan's Third Life, the church founded at Saul on Strangford Lough by St Patrick was also a transverse one (*Trias. Thaum.* 21–34) and this has led some commentators to assert that the word *saball* became an ecclesiastical term used to denote a transverse church (Mac Airt 1958, 70–71; *EA* 220). Joyce suggests that several transverse churches were erected in other districts in imitation of the church at Saul and called by the same name and postulates as possible sites Saval More and Saval Beg in Newry, Drumsaul in the parish of Ematris, Co. Monaghan, and Sawel in Tyrone (*Joyce* i 114–5). However, the word continued to be used in the lexicon in the sense "barn" and this is its exclusive application in the collected examples (*DIL* sv. *saball*) so that it is more probably in this sense that the word became attached to the majority of place-names. In particular, we should note that the name of St Patrick's church at Saul is usually rendered into Latin as *Sabulla Patricii* or *Horreum Patricii*, "Patrick's Barn" so that even in the most illustrious of the sites bearing this name *sabhall* was still understood as "barn", not church.

Shannaghan
J 2141

Seanáthán (?)
"old ford"

1. Shanaghan	CPR Jas. I 86a	1606
2. Shannaghan	CPR Jas. I 103a	1607

3. Shanaghan	CPR Jas. I 495a	1607
4. L. Shanaghan	Speed's Antrim & Down	1610
5. Shannaghan	CPR Jas. I 246b	1613
6. Shannaghan	Inq. Ult. (Down) §84 Car. I	1638
7. Shanaghan	Wars Co. Down 79	1641
8. Shanachan	Inq. Down (Reeves 1) 101	1657
9. Shanahan	Hib. Reg. Up. Iveagh	1657c
10. Sancanbegg & Sancanmore	BSD 130	1661
11. Shanachans	Sub. Roll Down 280	1663
12. Shanachons	Wm. Map (OSNB) 97	1810
13. Shanaghans	Bnd. Sur. (OSNB)	1830
14. 'Shan-agh-an	OSNB 97	1834c
15. Shannaghan	J O'D (OSNB) 97	1834c
16. Seanachán	OSL 48	1834c
17. Sean[n]achán "fox-covers"	J O'D (OSNB) 97	1834c
18. Seanachán	Post-Sheanchas 78	1905
19. Sean Athan "old ford"	Mooney 35	1950c
20. 'ʃanəhən	Local pronunciation	1992

The townland of Shannaghan is part of the parish of Newry even though it is some distance away in the barony of Iveagh Upper where it stands between the parishes of Drumgooland, Garvaghy, Annaclone and Drumballyroney. O'Donovan (16–17) derives the name from Irish *Seanachán* for which he suggests the meaning "fox-covers" but, while there is a variant form of *sionnach* "fox", *seannach*, O'Donovan's postulated form is otherwise unattested. Mooney's suggestion (recte *Seanáthán* "old ford") is more plausible. *Áthán*, a compound of *áth* "a ford" and the diminutive suffix *án*, is found in a number of place-names, although these appear to be confined mainly to the south of the country (*Onom. Goed.* 52 sv. *athán*; *L. Log. P. Láirge* 4). Nevertheless, the name suits the local topography and may have originally referred to a crossing over the Bann where Katesbridge now stands.

Sheeptown
J 1028

An English form

1. Shepetown	Inq. (Mon. Hib.) 287	1549
2. Shepetoune	CPR Ed. VI iv 388	1552
3. Shepetowne	CPR Ed. VI iv 388	1552
4. Sheepstowne	CPR Jas. I 102b	1607
5. Sheepstown	CPR Jas. I 495a	1607
6. Sheepeston	CPR Jas. I 246b	1613
7. Sheepestowne	Inq. Ult. (Down) §15 Jac. I	1625c
8. Sheepestowne	Inq. Ult. (Down) §84 Car. I	1638
9. Sheepstowne	Census 82	1659c
10. Sheepestowne, Upper & Lower	BSD 130	1661
11. Sheepstowne	Forfeit. Estates 352b §32	1703
12. Sheepstown	Forfeit. Estates 352b §32	1703
13. Sheeptown	Wm. Map (OSNB) 97	1810
14. Sheeptown	Bnd. Sur. (OSNB) 97	1830c
15. 'Sheep-town	OSNB 97	1834c

16. Baile na g-Caorach	OSL 48	1834c
17. 'ʃi.ptaun	Local pronunciation	1990

The name Sheeptown is clearly of English origin despite the fact that the Census of 1659 records that all twenty-one persons living in "Savellbegg Sheepstowne & ½ Sheepstowne" were Irish (*Census* 82). The annals record an attack on the castle (*caislén*) of *Ath Cruithne*, a subdivision of Sheeptown (see below), and the "slaughter of the English who inhabited it" (*do marbhadh na nGall do bí ann, Miscell. Ann.* 1213.4). In 1237, Hugh de Lacy confirmed the grant of "the castle of *Athcruthain* with all its islands and appurtenances" (*castellum de Athcruthain cum tota insula et pertinentiis suis*) which had been made to the monastery of Newry by Muirchertach mac Lochlainn and other Irish nobles "before the coming of the English to Ireland" (*ante adventum Anglicorum ad Hyberniam, de Lacy Char.* 257). The castle mentioned here would appear to have been an Anglo-Norman construction for, although there is now no trace of it, it is described as a *castellum* in Latin and *caisleán* in Irish and it is closely associated with the Anglo-Norman invaders. In any case, the references cited here clearly indicate, despite the assertion of the *Census*, that there was a strong English presence in Sheeptown extending as far back possibly as the Anglo-Norman invasion. The motte and bailey overlooking the Newry River known as **Crown Mound** may have been the original site of this castle as its name would seem to be derived from *Cruithen*.

The strategic importance of *Athcruthain* is attested prior even to the Anglo-Norman invasion. It is reported in the Annals of Ulster that a group of Norsemen from Strangford Lough led by Alpthann son of Gothfrith landed at *Linn Duachaill* on September 4, 926. They were routed by Muirchertach mac Néill at the bridge of *Cluain na Cruimther* during which Alpthann fell and his army was slaughtered, and the survivors were beseiged at *Áth Cruithne* for a week until Gothfrith, king of the foreigners, arrived from Dublin to relieve them (*AU (Mac Airt)* 926).

Sheeptown is divided into two parts in many of our sources and the spellings of these name are listed below:

1. occ Ath Cruithne	AFM	924
2. oc Ath Cruithne	AU (Mac Airt)	926
3. caislein Atha Cruitne	Miscell. Ann.	1213
4. d'Áth Mór risin abar Áth Cruithne	C. Conghail Cláir. 30	1600c
5. Athcrathin	Newry Char. (Flanagan)	1157c
6. castellum de Athcruthain	De Lacy Chart. 257	1237
7. two carucates in Shepetown, one called Athiruthyn, the other Lyssennellagh	Inq. (Mon. Hib.) 287	1549
8. in the two towns of Shepetoune whereof the one is called Athyrnayn and the other Lessynnelleth	CPR Ed. VI iv 388	1552
9. the two towns of Shepetowne called Athtruham and Lyssenelleth	CPR Ed. VI iv 388	1552
10. Shepstowne	CPR Jas. I 86a	1606
11. the two carues of Sheepstowne	CPR Jas. I 102b	1607
12. the 2 carnes of Sheepstown	CPR Jas. I 495a	1607

13. Sheepeston, 2 plowlands, viz.
    Athername otherwise Athtruthin
    and Lessimelleth   CPR Jas. I 246b   1613
14. the 2 carewes or balliboes of
    Sheepestowne, viz. Athername al'
    Athtruth, and Lyssymelleth   Inq. Ult. (Down) §15 Jac. I   1625c

Athcruthain was known in Irish as *Áth Cruithne* "ford of the Cruithin" (1–4) but the later spellings in English documents are hopelessly incorrect (7–9, 13–14). Thus, it would be hazardous to postulate an origin for the name of the other part of Sheeptown which is variously spelt *Lyssennellagh, Lyssenelleth* etc. (7–9, 13–14). The author of the earliest extant recension of the epic Cattle-Raid of Cooley implies that *Áth Cruithne* was named after a warrior called Cruthen who was slain there "on his ford" by Cú Chulainn (*TBC Rec. I* 1524) but there can be little doubt that it owes its name to the tribe of the Cruithin (see **Crown Mound**).

Shinn   Of uncertain origin
J 1332

1.	Ballesthyne	Inq. (Mon. Hib.) 287	1549
2.	Ballyshyne	CPR Ed. VI iv 388	1552
3.	Ballyshyn	CPR Ed. VI iv 388	1552
4.	Shenoo	Bagenal Rental 125	1575
5.	Shynne	CPR Jas. I 86a	1606
6.	Shynne	CPR Jas. I 102b	1607
7.	Shyme	CPR Jas. I 495a	1607
8.	Shine	CPR Jas. I 246b	1613
9.	Shyne	Inq. Ult. (Down) §15 Jac. I	1625c
10.	Shynne	Inq. Ult. (Down) §84 Car. I	1638
11.	Shyn al' Lysharby	Inq. Ult. (Down) §84 Car. I	1638
12.	Shynn	Civ. Surv. x §72	1655c
13.	Sheine	Census 82	1659c
14.	Shin	Reg. Deeds abstracts i §214	1720
15.	Shinn	Wm. Map (OSNB) 97	1810
16.	Shinn	Bnd. Sur. (OSNB) 97	1830c
17.	Shin	OSM iii 109	1834c
18.	Sionnaigh "foxes"	OSL 48	1834c
19.	Sionnaigh "foxes"	J O'D (OSNB) 97	1834c
20.	Síodhan	Mooney 259	1950c
21.	ʃɪn	Local pronunciation	1990

O'Donovan (18–19) thought that this name might come from Irish *Sionnaigh* "foxes" but it is unlikely that an animal name would stand on its own as a place-name. Mooney's suggestion of an original *Síodhán* (modern *Sián*) "fairy-mound" is more likely, but the modern pronunciation suggests a short vowel. An original long vowel might be argued on the basis of the earlier forms but some doubt must remain given the ambiguity of the majority of the spellings. We might also suggest *sine* "teat" but *ballán* seems to have been the only word in use for teat in recent times in Ulster (*LASID* i 18), although it does not necessarily follow that *sine* was never known here. Nevertheless, the lack of a qualifying element tends to militate against such a derivation for parts of the body in place-names are usually qualified by an adjective, noun or personal name.

A similar name is found as a river and lough name in Sutherland in Scotland, and it also forms the second part of the place-name Invershin at the junction of the rivers Shin and Oykell (Nicolaisen 1958, 189). Nicolaisen dismisses the suggestion that it is related to *sin*, gen. sing. of *sean* (ibid. 190–1) and he suggests an alternative derivation from Indo-European *Sindh-nā* which is identical with Sinn (Germany) and cognate with the Shannon (Ireland), Sinnius (Italy) and Senne (Brabant), and means simply "river" or "water-course" (*ibid.* 191–2). However, there is hardly enough evidence to conclude with any certainty that this is the origin of our Shinn. Indeed, the evidence as a whole is so ambiguous that any postulated original should be treated with extreme caution.

| **Turmore** | *An Tuar Mór* (?) | |
| J 1030 | "the large field/pasture" | |

1. Ballytoyrremore	Inq. (Mon. Hib.) 287	1549
2. Ballyntoyrremore	CPR Ed. VI iv 388	1552
3. Ballyntorre More	CPR Ed. VI iv 388	1552
4. Towermore	Bagenal Rental 125	1575
5. Tarmore	CPR Jas. I 86a	1606
6. Ball, Twyermore	CPR Jas. I 102b	1607
7. Balletwyermore	CPR Jas. I 495a	1607
8. Toyremore	CPR Jas. I 246b	1613
9. Toyrmore	Inq. Ult. (Down) §15 Jac. I	1625c
10. Terrmore	Inq. Ult. (Down) §84 Car. I	1638
11. Termore	Inq. Ult. (Down) §84 Car. I	1638
12. Toremore	Census 82	1659c
13. Tooremore	Sub. Roll Down 280	1663
14. Turmore	Wm. Map (OSNB) 97	1810
15. Turrmore	Bnd. Sur. (OSNB) 97	1830c
16. Turmore	J O'D (OSNB) 97	1834c
17. Tuar mór, anciently Srath mór	OSL 48	1834c
18. Tuar mór		
"great bleach or green field"	J O'D (OSNB) 97	1834c
19. tər 'mo:r	Local pronunciation	1990

O'Donovan (*OSL* 48) suggests that Turmore was anciently called *Srath Mór* "large river meadow" but, although this origin suits the description of the terrain, I have been unable to substantiate the claim. The current form, according to O'Donovan (*ibid.*) comes from *Tuar Mór* ("large field, pasture") and this seems to best explain some of the early spellings, although a derivation from Irish *Teamhair Mhór* "great elevated place" remains a distinct possibility (cf. **Tamary** in the parish of Clonduff). As the stress fell on the final syllable, the vowel of the weakly-stressed first syllable was shortened giving the indistinct vowel of the later forms (5, 10–12, 14–16).

OTHER NAMES

Ballybot	*An Baile Bocht*
J 0727	"the poor townland"

The district of Ballybot on the far side of the Newry River was settled by people from the neighbouring countryside as the town grew because there was little or no room in the old town (Canavan 1989, 79). Initially, the people who established themselves in Ballybot were poor people who had come to Newry seeking employment as labourers, dockers and servants and this gave rise to the name *An Baile Bocht* "the poor townland" (*ibid.*)

Bernish Rock	A hybrid form	
J 0724		
1. ðə ˈbarnəʃ	Local pronunciation	1990

Despite the lack of any early spellings we can be reasonably sure that the first element in this name derives from Irish *Bearnas* meaning "a gap" (cf. *Joyce* ii 13; Ó Máille 1989–90, 128; **Ballybarnes**, parish of Newtownards).

Clanrye River	*An Rí*	
J 1030, 1229, 1126	meaning uncertain	
1. fri Gleann roglach Rige (:Mide)	AU (Mac Airt) 212	759
2. hi Rig	IB 47	850c
3. go Glent [recte Glend] Righe	AFM ii 734	995
4. go Glend Ríghe	AFM ii 994	1113
5. co Glenn Rigi	CGH 142b27	1125c
6. Glinne, Ciaran	Mart. Gorm. Feb 4 p30	1170c
7. i nGlionn Righe	AFM iii 38	1178
8. o Glind Rige	CMR 142	1280c
9. Glenn Rigi	Fél. Óeng. Feb 8 p70n	1400c
10. co Glendrighe	AFM iv 1124	1483
11. go Gleann Righe	Céitinn ii 364.5660	1600c
12. ó Ghlionn Ríogh	Céitinn iii 302.4728	1600c
13. i nGlinn Righe	Mart. Gorm. Feb 4 p30n	1630c
14. Glenn Rigi	Mart. Gorm. Feb 9 p70n	1630c
15. fo Ghlenn Righe	LCABuidhe 10 §8	1680c
16. do Ghleann Righe	LCABuidhe 50 §5	1680c
17. Glenna Righe, tórainn	LCABuidhe 50 §5	1680c
18. Glanrye, the river of	Inq. (Mon. Hib.) 286	1549
19. Glanry	CPR Ed. VI iv 387	1552
20. Glan Ree	Boazio's Map (BM)	1599
21. Owen Glin Ree Fl:	Bartlett Maps (Esch. Co. Map) 2	1603
22. Glin Ree	Bartlett Maps (Esch. Co. Map) 2	1603
23. Glanree, the river of	Inq. Ult. (Armagh) §2 Jac. I	1604
24. Glanrie, the river of	Inq. Ult. (Armagh) §2 Jac. I	1604
25. Glanree, the waters of	CPR Jas. I 86a	1606
26. Clanree, the waters of Fedan and	CPR Jas. I 102b	1607
27. Clanree, the fishings of Fedam and	CPR Jas. I 494b	1607
28. Glanry, the river of	Inq. Ult. (Down) §15 Car. I	1625c
29. Glenry, the towne of	Inq. Ult. (Down) §15 Car. I	1625c
30. Glanreemagaffee	Inq. Ult. (Armagh) §27 Car. I	1638
31. Glanry, in rivul' de	Inq. Ult. (Armagh) §27 Car. I	1638
32. Glanrye, river of	Civ. Surv. x §72	1655c
33. Glinn, the river of	Civ. Surv. x §74	1655c

34. Nury fl.	Lamb Maps (Down)	1690c
35. the River of Newry	Harris Hist. 141	1744
36. The River of Newry	Harris Hist. 144	1744
37. (?)Newry River	Rocque's Map (Coote)	1760
38. Newry river	Statist. Sur. Dn. 17 et pass.	1802
39. the Newry river	OSM iii 61	1834c
40. the Clanrye ... afterwards the Newry water	Lewis' Top. Dict. 432	1837
41. An Rí (Newry River)	GÉ 150	1989
42. ðe 'klɑn'rəi 'rivər	Local pronunciation	1990

The river on which Newry is built used to be called the *Glanrye River* but in the 18th century it came to be known as the Newry River (34ff.) although Clanrye, a corruption of *Glanrye*, is still applied to the river's upper reaches. There is no shortage of Irish forms for Clanrye and the original Irish was undoubtedly *Gleann Righe* (modern *Gleann Rí*) "valley of the *Righ*" where *Righ* was the name of the river which ran through the valley (1, 3–17; 2). The majority of references in the early literature are to the valley (*Gleann Righe*) rather than to the river but the name *Righ* is found in a 9th-century tale concerning Mongán mac Fiachna and Fionn mac Cumhaill (form 2; see also Arthurs 1952–3(d) 39). The river was apparently later renamed *Abhainn Glinne Righe* "the river of *Gleann Righe*" for it appears on Bartlett's map as "Owen Glenree fluvius" (21).

There is a tradition that part of the Boyne was called *Rig Mná Nuadat* "the fore-arm of Nuada's wife" (*Met. Dinds.* iii 26), and the eruption of nine rivers called *Righ* (*naoi Righe*) in Leinster is recorded in *AFM* (i 30–32), the best known of which is the Rye on the borders of Meath and Kildare (*ibid.* n.). Thus, it would appear that *righ* was a relatively common river-name and it may have meant something like "river". J. B. Arthurs has suggested that the river-name goes back to a root **reg-/*req* the primary meaning of which is related to water (*loc. cit.* 39) but it may rather derive from the Indo-European root **reg-* in the sense "stretch, extend". Arthurs dismisses this latter possibility on the grounds that the primary meaning of the verb is "to stretch in a straight line", a sense which is hardly suitable for a river-name (*ibid.*), but this narrow meaning is not preserved in the Old Irish reflex *rigid* "stretches, distends".

The development of *Glanrye* to Clanrye (26–7, 40) would appear to be a relatively late phenomenon and, as we shall see, it may well have occurred solely within the written tradition. The element *gleann* "valley" is much more common in Irish place-names than *clann* "family" and it would be rather peculiar to find it replaced by the latter in common usage so that we must suspect that we are dealing here with a scribal error. The name seems to have fallen into disuse in the 18th century and Harris invariably refers to the river which runs through Newry as the Newry River (*Harris Hist.* 35–6). This point is made most clearly by Lewis who states that the river was "anciently called the Clanrye, but afterwards the Newry water" (*Lewis' Top. Dict.* 40). No mention is made of *Glanrye* or Clanrye by the Ordnance Survey (see *OSNB* and *OSM*) and the river is again called the Newry River (39). O'Donovan, in his edition of *AFM*, anglicizes the Irish *Gleann Righe* as *Glenree* and states that its exact location was unknown until he identified it during his work for the Ordnance Survey (*AFM* iii 40n).

Reeves states that the Clanrye "extended northwards, beyond Scarva, in the parish of Aghaderg" (*EA* 253n) but this claim is based on the rather dubious conclusion that the parish church of Aghaderg was situated in *Glenree* (*ibid.*) He identifies the church of

Tamhlacht Gliad i nGlinn Righe (*Mart. Gorm.* Feb. 4 (n); *Mart. Don.* 39) with the *Hacyglid* of the *Ecclesiastical Taxation of Pope Nicholas III* (*EA* 253n) which he elsewhere identifies as Aghaderg (*EA* 112–113n). However, his identification can be dismissed on two accounts. First of all, there is no connection between *Tamhlacht Gliadh* and the place called *Tamhlact Mennann* which Reeves, probably correctly, locates in the parish of Aghaderg (ibid. 113n). *Tamhlacht Gliadh* is associated with a saint *Colmán* (*Mart. Tal.* p. 84, Feb. 4) or *Ciarán* (*Mart. Gorm.* p. 30, Feb. 4; *Mart. Don.* 39) whose feast is celebrated on Feb. 4 whereas *Tamhlacht Mennann* is associated with three British saints, *Nasad, Beoan* and *Mellan* whose feast-day falls on Oct. 26 (*Fél. Óeng.* pp. 226–8, Oct. 26; *Mart. Don.* p. 285). Secondly, it is doubtful whether the *Hacyglid* of the Taxation is to be taken as Aghaderg. The differences between the spelling from the Taxation and the name Aghaderg are too great to be dismissed as scribal errors as Reeves claims (*EA* 112n). Moreover, *Hacyglid* appears in the Taxation among the names of other parishes from Upper Iveagh the order of which follows a geographical pattern which would indicate that *Hacyglid* is to be located somewhere in and around the modern parish of Drumgath (*EA* 110–116). Thus, it is sandwiched between *Donnachmore* (Donaghmore) and *Clondalan* (Clonallan) which is followed by the names of *Clondyme* (Clonduff), *Glentegys* (Kilbroney) and *Viridi Ligno* (Newry).

The location and course of the Clanrye is clearly identified in the description of the barony bounds in the *Civil Survey* of 1654–6. According to this survey, the Barony of Upper Iveagh proceeds "along the glin flush [Glin Flush] unto the river of Glanrye meering betwixt the lordshipp of the Newry and the lands of Clarenagan [Clanagan in Donaghmore] to a bogg called Fuoladuffy meering betwixt Dirycragh and Corkrighagh..." (*Civ. Surv.* x §72). The inaccuracy of early maps is immediately obvious to anyone who looks at them in detail and a number of these appear to show the Clanrye flowing into or near to Lough Neagh (*Bartlett, Boazio*). This confusion may be partially due to the fact that the river which runs into the Newry river through Donaghmore was known as the *Glenwater* or *Glin Flush*. As we have seen, the *Civil Survey* reports that the *Glin Flush* runs into the river of *Glanrye* at the boundary between the parishes of Donaghmore and Newry and elsewhere in the *Survey* the boundary of the Barony of Orier is traced "by the said river [Bann] and the Glenwater to Carnbanne, and soe through the bridge of Newry" (*Civ. Surv.* x §77).

The confusion is also, perhaps, due in part to the fact that the *Glenn Rige* was, from a very early date, conceived of as the boundary between Down and Armagh. In early Irish documents it is frequently referred to as the westernmost limit of the territory of the *Ulaid*. Tradition has it that, after the three Collas had defeated the *Ulaid* and driven them into the east of Ulster, they drew a boundary between them and the *Ulaid* along *Glenn Righe* from Newry (*LCABuidhe* 50; *CGH* 142b27). The borders of the dioceses of Ireland were determined by the Synod of *Ráth Breasail* c. 1118 and were recorded by Keating who copied them from the Book of Clonenagh. Keating notes that the boundary of the diocese of Down is not found in his exemplar but the editor of his *History of Ireland* rightly adverts to a scribal error which resulted in the boundaries of the diocese of Down being confused with those of Connor (*Céitinn* v 269). The emended text gives *Ollorbha* (Larne Water) and *Cuan Snámha hAidhne* (Carlingford Lough) as the northern and southern limits of the diocese and the western and eastern limits are defined by *Glenn Ríogh* (showing re-analysis of the name as "valley of the kings") and *Colbha nGearmainn* (unidentified) (*Céitinn* v 269, emended reading).

1. fl. Coche	Hondius' Map	1591
2. (?)Cothe flu.	Mercator's Ulst.	1595
3. Flu Coety	Boazio's Map (BM)	1599

4. Coyitie	Bartlett Maps (Esch. Co. Map) 2	1603
5. Cociti flu	Speed's Antrim and Down	1610
6. Cociti	Speed's Ulster	1610

A river called *Coety* et var. appears on a number of early maps (1–6) and Mooney identifies this as the Newry River (Mooney 1952–3(c) 38). However, the exact location of the river is uncertain and Mooney's suggestion that the name originates in the Irish *caodh-dae* "swampy" must also be treated with caution (*ibid.*, and see note by J. B. Arthurs, *ibid.*). Moreover, *Iubhar Cinn Choiche* (modern *Iúr Cinn Choiche*) is given as an ancient name for Newry in a number of Irish documents (see **Newry** 4–5, 15, 19) and it might be suggested that here the final element represents the same river name ("the yew at the head of the *Coiche*) as is represented in the later (corrupted) spellings on the maps. It is true that the map spellings bear little resemblance to the name *Coiche*, but the earliest form is remarkably close to the Irish (1) and the spelling on Mercator's map of Ulster (2) conforms well with that if one takes into account the frequent scribal confusion of *t* and *c*. Indeed, all the forms may be explained as the gradual deterioration due to the compounding of scribal errors.

Craigmore Viaduct
J 0628

A hybrid form

The first element in this hybrid name very probably derives from Irish *An Chreig Mhór* "the large rock or crag".

Crown Bridge
J 1027

see **Crown Mound**

1. Crown-bridge	Harris Hist. 88	1744
2. Crown-Bridge	Harris Hist. 144	1744
3. Crown-bridge	Harris Hist. 218	1744
4. ˈkraun ˈbrɪdʒ	Local pronunciation	1990

According to Harris, Crown Bridge was so called from the neighbouring earthwork known as **Crown Mound** (*Harris Hist.* 88).

Crown Mound
J 1028

Ráth Cruithne
"rath of the Cruithin"

1. Crown-Rath	Harris Hist. 218	1744

Situated on high ground overlooking the Clanrye River in the townland of Sheeptown stands a motte and bailey known as Crown Mound (*ASCD* 206). Aodh Úa Dubhgeanáin of Mayobridge, Co. Down, suggests in a reply to a query made in an early number of the *Journal of the Co. Louth Archaeological Society* that Crown Mound means "the mound of the Picts" (*Cruithen*) (*UJA* i (1906) 96). **Duncrun** in Co. Derry, is known in the annals as *Dún Cruithne* (*Joyce* i 100) and Joyce derives the names **Drumcroon** in Co. Derry and **Drumcroohen** in Co. Fermanagh from a name meaning "the Pict's ridge" (*ibid.* 101).

An old name for part of the townland of **Sheeptown** in which Crown Mound is situated was *Áth Cruithne* "ford of the Cruithin" and so it is distinctly possible that the element *crown* in the name of the mound, like *crun* and *croon* in the names mentioned above, is derived from *Cruithne*. The diphthongization of *ū* in English, as in Mod. Eng. "town" from Mid. Eng. *tūn*, probably occurred quite early in the 15th century (Barber 1976, 291–2) and in several Irish place-names the element *dún* "a fort" has been anglicized *down* (cf. **Downpatrick**, Co. Down; Downings, Co. Donegal).

Harris relates two local traditions concerning the mound which he calls "Crown-Rath", the first of which has it that the rath took its name "from some Resemblance it bears to a Crown" (*Harris Hist.* 218). The other tells how the rath was raised to perpetuate the memory of a combat between two royal warriors over the possession of a crown which was supposedly fought on an artificial platform on the west side of the rath (*Harris Hist.* 218–19). This latter tale is clearly fanciful but some credit may be given to the first. However, the association of the townland in which the rath stands with the name *Áth Cruithne* seems to point to a different origin and even this tradition may be dismissed as a later folk etymology.

Flag Staff	*Barr an Fheadáin*	
J 1020	"top of the water-course"	
1. Barr an Fheadáin	L.antS. 98	1905
2. Barr an Fheadain	Tempest's Louth 88	1952
3. Barr an Fheadáin	Local Inf.	1962

According to Peadar Ó Sluagháin, a native of Omeath in Co. Louth, a flag used to be raised on Flagstaff Hill to inform the pilot in Warrenpoint or Omeath of the approach of a ship. The Irish form, apparently current among native speakers in Omeath until the demise of Irish in that region, means "the top of the *Feadán*" or "the top of the little stream" (*Feadán* being the hill or the townland – anglicized **Fathom** – in which the hill is situated). A similar story is related about the city of Flagstaff in Arizona, USA, which tells how lumberjacks celebrating the 4th of July, 1876, nailed a US flag to the top of a tall ponderosa pine and called the previously unnamed settlement Flagstaff (*Enc. Brit.* iv 814).

Glenny's Bridge	An English form	
J 1228		
1. Glenny-Bridge	Harris Hist. 144	1744

The Clanrye River is spanned between Croreagh and Desert by Glenny's Bridge. The Glennys were a prominent family in the nearby parish of Donaghmore but it was probably from the family of that name living at Glenville that the bridge was named (cf. Canavan 1989, 113; *Prerog. Wills Index* 195 (1770)).

Hawkins Bridge	An English form
J 1230	

The name Hawkins has a long association with the Newry area. Certain lands formerly belonging to Maginnis, Lord Iveagh, were granted to William Hawkins of London after the rebellion of 1641 (*Harris Hist.* 80) and it was doubtless from a member of this family that Hawkins Bridge was named.

Pollnagrasta	*Poll na nGrásta*
J 0920	"the hole of the graces"

Pollnagrasta probably comes from the Irish *Poll na nGrásta* "hole of the graces", perhaps referring to a holy well.

Sheep Bridge   An English form
J 0931

1. Sheep Bridge	Harris Hist. 144	1744
2. Sheep Bridge	Taylor & Skinner 4	1777

In **Sheeptown**.

THE BARONY OF IVEAGH
Iveagh Upper, Upper Half

1. nepotes Ecach	AU (Mac Airt) 214	761
2. H. Echoch Cobho	AU (Mac Airt) 228	776
3. nepotes Echdach Cobho	AU (Mac Airt) 256	801
4. la Hu Echach	AU (Mac Airt) 300	842
5. Hu Echach, for Ultu 7	AU (Mac Airt) 434	1005
6. ria nUib Eachach	AU (Mac Airt) 490	1054
7. hUa Echach, itir Ulto 7	TBC Rec. I l. 4154	1100c
8. Hūi Echdach	CGH 140b23	1125c
9. Hūa nEchach, de forslointib	CGH 157,15	1125c
10. Hūi Echach Ulad	CGH 157,40	1125c
11. hūa nEchach, Genelach	CGH 161bc47	1125c
12. Hūi Echach Coba	CGH 162a43	1125c
13. Hūi Echach	CGH 162a56	1125c
14. hūa nEchach Coba, Genelach	CGH 162b13	1125c
15. h. nEchach, ri	A. Conn. 300	1347
16. Ó nEachach Cobha, Uirríogha	Topog. Poems. 383	1350c
17. i n-Uib Echach Ulad	Fél. Óeng. Feb 18 p76n	1400c
18. h. nEchach, ri	A. Conn. 400	1407
19. h. nEchach, ri	A. Conn. 438	1418
20. h. nEchach, adbar rig	A. Conn. 474	1434
21. i n-Uaib Echach Ulad	Fél. Óeng. May 22 p134n	1453
22. de Oneach (×2)	Newry Char. (Flanagan)	1157c
23. Oneac, regis	Newry Char. (Flanagan)	1157c
24. Oneachulad, dux Claneda	Newry Char. (Flanagan)	1157c
25. Oueh	Cartae Dun. 422 §10	1227c
26. Oweagh	Reg. Swayne 103	1500c
27. Evaghe	Fiants Eliz. §1736	1571
28. Iveaghe, alias the country of Magnisse	Fiants Eliz. §4327	1584
29. Iveaghe, the country of	Fiants Eliz. §4327	1584
30. Iveagh (×2)	Fiants Eliz. §4327	1584
31. Iveaghe	Fiants Eliz. §4327	1584
32. Iveagh, country of	CPR Jas. I 394b	1609
33. Iveagh	CPR Jas. I 188b	1611
34. Iveagh Territory	CPR Jas. I 235a	1612
35. Iveagh	Inq. Ult. §13 Car. I	1629
36. Iveagh	Inq. Ult. §85 Car. I	1639
37. Upper Iveagh	Civ. Surv. x §§72–3	1655c
38. Lower Iveagh	Civ. Surv. x §§72–3	1655c
39. Lower Eveagh	Civ. Surv. x §72	1655c
40. Iveagh	Civ. Surv. x §73	1655c
41. Vpper Eveagh, The Barony of	Hib. Reg. Up. Iveagh	1657c
42. Upper Iveagh Barony	Census 72	1659c
43. Lower Evagh Barony	Census 78	1659c
44. Lower Evagh Bar.	BSD 68ff.	1661

45. Lower Euagh Bar.	BSD 81f.	1661
46. Upper Evagh Bar.	BSD 104ff.	1661
47. Upper Evagh	Hib. Del. Down	1672c
48. Lower Evagh	Hib. Del. Down	1672c

Iveagh is the largest barony in Co. Down, stretching from Lough Neagh to Rosstrevor, and from Poyntzpass to Newcastle. It was divided in the 17th century into Lower (northern) and Upper (southern) Iveagh by a line running east to west between Dromara and Banbridge. Since then each part has also been divided into Upper and Lower halves, the northern part by another roughly east to west line, dividing Hillsborough from Dromore; the southern part by a line roughly running north to south, and passing through Katesbridge and Rathfriland (see the barony map of Co. Down facing the county introduction). Iveagh has also had to be divided up in the books of the place-name series. The following parishes are all in Upper Iveagh, Upper Half.

The bounds of Iveagh are largely determined by physical features. To the west lies the Newry River, extending northwards along the line of bogs through which the Newry Canal now runs. Part of this boundary was marked in ancient times by an earthwork now known as the Danes' Cast. The northern limit followed the river Lagan, as far east as its tributary now called the Ravernet River, which forms the north-eastern boundary of the barony. Slieve Croob is also on the eastern boundary, and south of it the Ballybunion River. Iveagh reaches the sea at Newcastle and Rosstrevor, with the barony of Mourne in between, the dividing line marked by some of the western peaks, such as Slieve Bearnagh, Slieve Meelmore, Slieve Muck, Pigeon Rock Mountain and Shanlieve. The Lordship of Newry forms an independent barony dividing the upper part of Upper Iveagh into two distinct halves. The bounds of Iveagh are described in 1584 (*Fiants Eliz.* §4327), and again in the Civil Survey of 1654–6 where the division between Upper and Lower Iveagh is outlined in detail (*Civ. Surv.* x §§72, 73).

The name Iveagh derives from *Uíb Echach* (later spelled *Uíbh Eachach*), the dative or locative form of the tribal name *Uí Echach* "grandsons/descendants of *Echu*". Uí Echach were one of the tribes of the confederation of the *Ulaid* "Ulstermen", after whom the province of Ulster is named (Flanagan 1978d). They shared the kingship of east Ulster with *Dál Fiatach*, the historic Ulaid, and with *Dál nAraide* of south Antrim, who like them belonged to the ethnic group called *Cruthin*. The Echu from whom they claimed descent is reputed to have been either father or son of *Crund Ba Druí*, a descendant of *Fiacha Araide*, ancestor of *Dál nAraide* (O'Rahilly 1946, 499). The *Uí Echach* were also known as *Uí Echach Coba* to distinguish them from similarly named tribes, to the east in the Ards peninsula (*Uí Echach Arda*), and to the west in Airgialla. The epithet was taken from the area they inhabited, known in Irish as *Mag Coba* and appearing in Anglo-Norman documents as the castle of *Moycove* (*Pipe Rolls John* 56, 60). It is also attested as part of the original name of the Iveagh parish of Donaghmore: *Domnach Mór Maige Coba*.

As with other early tribes Uí Echach subdivided into various septs. The dominant group in medieval times were the Magennises, from *Mac Óengusa* "son of Angus". The Uí Echach genealogies (*CGH* 161 bc 55) list an Óengus as son of *Aitíd mac Laigne*, who, according to the annals, was king of Ulster when killed in AD 898 (*AU (Mac Airt)* i 349), and Óengus mac Aitíd is given by Keating as the ancestor of the family (*Céitinn* iv 24, 94). Their chief seat was at Rathfriland, near the hill of Knock Iveagh which provides a view of the whole barony. The 16th-century cartographer, Richard Bartlett, who was interested in the inauguration sites of Irish chieftains, wrote beside Knock Iveagh on one of his maps: "Lisenree where the Magenis is made" (*Bartlett Maps (Esch. Co. Maps)* 2). It seems likely that Lisenree derives from an original Irish *Lios na Rí* "fort of the kings", but of the two modern places called **Lisnaree** in or near the barony, the closer is in the Lordship of Newry several miles further south, while the other is near Banbridge. As well as being tribal rulers, and patrons of Gaelic poets, many Magennises also became important churchmen, either in the local diocese of Dromore or further afield. The family maintained its importance in the 16th and early 17th centuries, keeping their lands together by submitting to the English policy of surrender and regrant[1], but several members, including Arthur Viscount Magennis, were implicated in the rebellion of 1641 (*Wars Co. Down* 75, 77–81) and their lands confiscated.

Both the older tribal name Iveagh and the contemporary chieftain's surname of Magennis were used to refer to the area in 16th- and early 17th-century maps and written sources: *McGenis* on Goghe's map, *Yveage* on Ortelius', *Mac Gynis lande called Iveache* on a map of south-east Ulster c. 1580, *Euagh or McGennys contry* on Norden's map, 1610, *Evagh al. Magenis's countrie* (*Inq. Ult.* §2 Jac. I col.e, 1605).

The area covered by the diocese of Dromore is similar to but larger than the barony of Iveagh, and reflects the earlier extent of Uí Echach Coba influence to the south and north. The north-western boundary of the diocese follows the river Bann from Knock Bridge (on the modern boundary with Co. Armagh) all the way to Lough Neagh, and includes the district of Clanbrasil, now the barony of Oneilland East. Clanbrasil was traditionally part of *Uí Echach* but was annexed to the new county of Armagh in 1605. At the south-eastern corner of Lough Neagh, on the southern edge of Killultagh, was a district called Kilmore. This territory was lost by the Magennises in 1612 and, with the exception of the townland of Kilmore (see **Down** introduction), is no longer in Iveagh. It remains, however, in the diocese of Dromore. North of Kilmore is the parish of Aghalee which is also in the diocese. It was part of Iveagh in 1584 but was annexed in 1605, with the rest of Killultagh, to Co. Antrim (barony of Upper Massereene). In the south, Mourne was disputed between the dioceses of Down and Dromore throughout much of the medieval period, while Newry was included in Dromore until the 16th century. By the 18th century, however, the Lordship of Newry and the barony of Mourne had come to be regarded as forming an "exempt jurisdiction" as far as the established church was concerned (see *PNI, County Down, vol. iii: The Mournes*). In 1869 both were restored to the Anglican diocese of Dromore, although in the Roman Catholic administrative system Mourne is now in the diocese of Down.

---

[1] *Fiants Eliz.* §4218, §4327 (all Iveagh); §4649, §4650; *CPR Jas I* 181b, 396a (separating Kilwarlin from southern Iveagh).

PARISH OF CLONALLAN

The civil parish of Clonallan is situated in the barony of Upper Iveagh and is comprised of just over 11,560 acres (*Census* 1871). It is bounded by the parishes of Newry, Drumgath, Clonduff, Kilbroney and Warrenpoint. The latter, a tiny parish of just over 1,125 acres (*Census* 1871), contains only three townlands: Dromore, Narrow-water and Ringmackilroy. Historically it was included in both the Anglican and Roman Catholic parishes of Clonallan. In the organization of the Church of Ireland, however, it was separated from Clonallan in 1825 (*OSM* iii 115) although it remained "in the gift of the Chancellor of the diocese, as incumbent of Clonallan" (*Lewis' Top. Dict.* ii 675). In 17th-century documents of a civil and administrative character **Warrenpoint** is also closely bound up with Clonallan, so much so that they are best considered here together.

Although Clonallan is believed to derive its name from *Dallán Forgaill*, famous for his eulogy in Irish of the illustrious Saint Columba, it is with another saint, *Conall mac Aedha*, that it is associated in early Irish documentation. This Conall is commemorated in the martyrologies on April 2 which, interestingly enough, is also the feast day of Saint *Brónach*, from whom neighbouring **Kilbroney** derives its name (*Mart. Gorm.* 68). Little trace of the ancient church of Clonallan appears to survive; the *Northern Ireland Sites and Monuments Record* merely notes that the Anglican church in Clonallan Glebe "occupies [an] early site" (*NISMR* sheet 51 §61). There are many references to it, however, in medieval ecclesiastical documentation and it seems that it was a comparatively prosperous benefice. In the *Ecclesiastical Taxation* of 1302–6 the church of Clonallan was valued at four marks, which contrasts favourably with the larger neighbouring parishes of Clonduff, two marks, and Kilbroney, one mark (*Eccles Tax.* 112–4).

In the middle ages the parish was normally held by a canon of Dromore who, strictly speaking, was appointed directly by the pope. When in 1422–3, for example, Clonallan fell vacant through the resignation of Patrick Okeallaych, Pope Martin V decreed in a papal bull that the abbot of Newry should look into the matter and appoint, if suitable, one Peter Maguryn as a canon of Dromore and priest of the parish (*Annates Ulst.* 295). The income of Clonallan was estimated at eight marks sterling at that date (*Annates Ulst.* 289). In 1500, however, the prebend of Clonallan was recorded as having an income of just six marks and as such was exempt from the *annates*, the tax levied by the pope on any ecclesiastic directly collated by him to a particular benefice (*Annates Ulst.* 291). By 1546 Clonallan had regained its prosperity for, in a "taxation of all benefices in the diocese of Dromore" dating to that year, "the prebend of Clondallan" was valued at nine marks (*Reg. Dowdall* §113). After the reformation the crown appropriated the right of collation and in 1604 (*CPR Jas. I* 63b) and again in 1607 (*CPR Jas. I* 104b) James I appointed William Cornewall and William Webb respectively to the benefice. Two years later the king appointed Webb chancellor to the cathedral chapter of Dromore and granted him not only "the whole rectory or prebend" but also "the vicarage of Clonallan with all that pertained to it" (*Jas. I to Dromore Cath.* 314). This, presumably, is why, in the Church of Ireland, the prebend of Clonallan was subsequently associated with the chancellorship of Dromore cathedral (*Lewis' Top. Dict.* i 348). It is interesting that in 1629 Arthur, Viscount Magennis, was seized of the advowson of the parish church of Clonallan (*Inq. Ult.* §13 Car. I); the right to present to the benefice had passed from the pope through the king to the local landlord.

Historically, all of Warrenpoint and much of southern Clonallan formed part of the old district of the *Legan* (see **Kilbroney**). In the 1570 grant of the area to John Sanky, the townlands of Narrow-water, Dromore, Ringmackilroy, Aghnamoira, Burren, Carrogs, Carrickmacstay, Ballydesland, Donaghaguy, Ballymaconaghy, Ballyrussell, and Tamna-

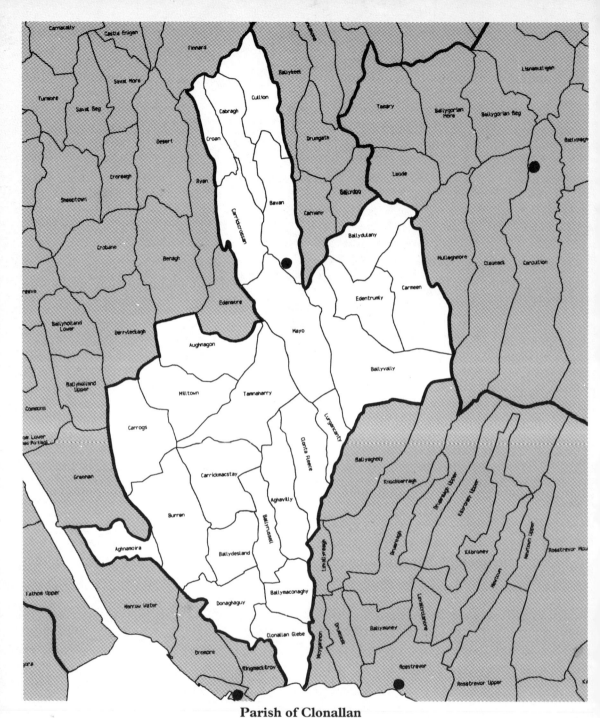

Parish of Clonallan

Barony of Iveagh Upper, Upper Half

Townlands	Ballyrussell	Carrickmacstay	Edentrumly
Aghavilly	Ballyvally	Carrogs	Lurgancanty
Aghnamoira	Bavan	Clonallan Glebe	Mayo
Aughnagon	Burren	Clontafleece	Milltown
Ballydesland	Cabragh	Croan	Tamnaharry
Ballydulany	Carmeen	Cullion	
Ballymaconaghy	Carrickcrossan	Donaghaguy	*Town:* Mayobridge

Based upon Ordnance Survey 1:50,000 mapping, with permission of the Director of the Ordnance Survey of Northern Ireland, Crown copyright reserved.

harry are all recorded (*Fiants Eliz.* §1609). In an inquisition dating to 1629, however, the contiguous townlands of Aghavilly, Clontafleece and Lurgancanty are also said to be in the *Lyegan* (*Inq. Ult.* §13 Car. I) and presumably Clonallan Glebe, which being church land was not included in any of these documents, was also considered part of the district. We have seen that the 1570 grant to John Sanky came to nothing and that in 1583 the *Legan* was regranted to Hugh Magennis (see **Kilbroney**). In 1609 all these lands (with the exception of Carrogs and Aghnamoira) were found to be in the possession of Hugh's son Arthur (*CPR Jas. I* 395b–396a) and in 1612 they were officially granted to him (*CPR Jas. I* 235a). These two documents are closely related, although the transcriptions in one may sometimes be more or less accurate than transcriptions in the other. On Arthur's death in 1629 his possessions passed to his son Hugh (*Inq. Ult.* §13 Car. I) who still held the same lands in 1639 (*Inq. Ult.* §85 Car. I). These 1629 and 1639 inquisitions also resemble each other, although the latter document has omitted a number of townlands towards the end of the list. Only occasionally do spellings vary significantly but the 1639 inquisition is clearly the poorer copy. It is also important to note that the 1609 and 1612 grants, and 1629 and 1639 inquisitions, reproduce most of the townlands in exactly the same order and only seem to diverge towards the end of the lists. It is reasonable to assume, therefore, that all four documents ultimately derive from a single source.

It is interesting that all the *Legan* townlands are marked on the *Hibernia Regnum* map of c. 1657, the purpose of which was to record all lands available for confiscation. In the *Book of Survey and Distribution* (*BSD*) Carrickmacstay, Ballymaconaghy, Ringmackilroy, Lurgancanty, Aghavilly, Clontafleece and Tamnaharry are specifically stated to have been in the possession of the Lord of Iveagh and his wife *Sorcha* (anglicized Saragh) in 1640, whereas Corrogs and Aghnamoira were held by one Edmond Magennis, presumably a near relative of the John Magennis who held them in 1609 (*CPR Jas. I* 394b). The remaining *Legan* townlands of Narrow Water, Dromore, Burren, Ballydesland, Ballyrussell and Donaghaguy are also recorded in *BSD* and, although they are not associated with anyone in particular, they were almost certainly held by the Magennises. By 1661, however, all these lands had been acquired by mainly three owners, Joseph Deane, William Baker and William Hawkins (*BSD* 107–8, 111–2), the last of whom was also in possession of most of the *Legan* townlands in **Kilbroney**.

Clanawly, like the other old territorial name the *Legan*, extends beyond the borders of present-day Clonallan, for it embraces the townlands of Ballykeel and Lurgancahone in neighbouring Drumgath and Ballyagholy in Kilbroney. Within Clonallan it consists of the townlands of Croan, Cabragh, Cullion, Carrickcrossan, Bavan, Ballydulany, Edentrumly, Carmeen, Ballyvally, Mayo, Aughnagon, Milltown and *Tawnaghhenrie* (see **Tamnaharry** below). *Clanawly* derives from *Cinéal nAmhalghaidh* in Irish, i.e. the territory held by the tribe or kindred of *Amhalghadh*, and appears to have formed part of the ancient patrimony of the *Méig Dhuibh Eamhna* family (*Topog. Poems* ll. 399–400). The remote origins of this particular family are unknown but it is familiar to us in the persons of Donald and James McYawne who alienated the seven townlands of Killowen in neighbouring Kilbroney to Nicholas Bagenal in 1568 (see p. 131). MacCana, writing c. 1700, spells the name *MacDuibhne* and claims that they had been prominent in the area before being dispossessed by the Magennises and almost wiped out in the Confederate wars (*MacCana's Itinerary* 46–7).[1] The earliest townland lists for *Clanawly* corroborate what MacCana has to say, for the Magennises are the prominent landowners and there is no mention of the Méig Dhuibh Eamhna. There appear to have been two major groupings within the district. In the schedule of Iveagh freeholders dating to 1609 John Magennis is recorded as possessing Corrocks and Aghnamoira in the *Legan,* and Croan, Cabragh, Cullion, Ballykeel, Lurgancahone,

Ballyvally and Carmeen in *Clanawly* whereas Hugh McCon McGlassny Magennis held the remaining townlands of Milltown, Aughnagon, Mayo, Carrickcrossan, Bavan, Tamnaharry, Edentrumly, Ballydulany and Ballyagholy (*CPR Jas. I* 394b). In 1610 both surrendered their lands to the king (*CPR Jas. I* 195b) but were regranted them in 1611 (*CPR Jas. I* 190a). These documents are clearly related although there are some significant differences in spelling.

Only a short period of time seems to have elapsed before Hugh alienated Ballydulany and what appears to have been only half of Bavan to George Sexton of Dublin (*CPR Jas. I* 194b). When Sexton died in 1632 these lands were inherited by his daughter Mabel, and her husband Michael Doyne of *Tullerouse* in Co. Antrim[2] (*Inq. Ult.* §30 Car. I), and in an inquisition dating to 1636 Doyne is stated to have alienated them to Arthur Hill and John Walsh (*Inq. Ult.* §71 Car. I). In *BSD*, however, both Ballydulany and Bavan are said to have been in the possession of his wife in 1640 and would seem to have been still held in the family in 1661 (*BSD* 111, 112). As regards the rest of Hugh McCon's lands we know that he alienated Edentrumly, Ballyagholy and other "divers lands" in *Clanawly* to Edward Trevor by deeds dated the 4th and 10th March 1611 (*CPR Jas. I* 373b). These other "divers lands" were undoubtedly Milltown, Aughnagon, Mayo, Carrickcrossan, Tamnaharry and the other half of Bavan; an inquisition dating to 1635 (which resembles the 1609 schedule and the 1611 Magennis grant) informs us that Trevor had acquired them some time in the reign of James I (*Inq. Ult.* §51 Car. I). According to this inquisition Trevor had let these back to Magennis but only for the duration of "his natural life". Fortunately Mooney has discovered a "deed" which allows us to be more specific.[3] The latter document tells us that the lands of Aughnagon, Carrickcrossan, Mayo, Milltown and Tamnaharry were legally acquired by Edward Trevor on 23rd June 1618; Bavan does not appear to be mentioned. As none of these lands remained in Magennis hands we would not expect them to be marked on the *Hibernia Regnum* map of c. 1657. Strangely enough, Ballyagholy and Edentrumly are marked on that map, but they are also designated "Protestant" and it is clear that both these and the other townlands acquired by Trevor were still in his family's possession in 1661 (*BSD* 107, 112).

When we turn to consider the rest of *Clanawly* we see that John Magennis did not dispose of his property as rapidly as Hugh. According to an inquisition dating to 1632 (which also resembles the lists of 1609 and 1611) six of the seven townlands which were found to be in his possession in 1609 were still held by Magennis on the occasion of his death earlier that year. He had, however, set ¾ of Cabragh to Coconaght Bannon for a period of 21 years and there is no mention of Croan (*Inq. Ult.* §32 Car. I). The estate passed to his son Hugh but by 1640 it was in the possession of one Edmond Magennis, presumably another member of that family. By now the estate had been considerably reduced for Lurgancahone and Ballykeel are recorded in the possession of Arthur Hill and Cullion in the possession of Mabel Sexton (*BSD* 111, 112). Again there is no record of Croan, or indeed of Carmeen, although the fact that the latter is marked on the *Hibernia Regnum* map suggests that it was still in the hands of the Magennises. The remaining townlands, Ballyvally and Cabragh, are also marked on Petty's map, but at least part of Ballyvally is designated "Protestant" (*Hib. Reg.* Up. Iveagh). By 1661 Ballyvally had come into the hands of William Baker and Cabragh was held by William Hawkins (*BSD* 112).

After 1661 the transfer of land seems to have ceased, at least for the time being. Joseph Deane's lands in the *Legan* are again enumerated in 1666 in the *Acts of Settlement and Explanation*, as are his lands in Meath, Kilkenny and Tipperary (*ASE* 107b §9). William Baker is called William Barker in the same source, and his lands are also recorded in 1667 as are his other estates in the south (*ASE* 91a §4). By the time the lands of William Hawkins are listed in 1681 William himself had died and had been succeeded by his son John, who successfully requested the king to create all his estates in Iveagh into the manor of Rathfryland (*ASE* 273b–274a §29). These three lists appear again in the *Rent Roll* of 1692 but, whereas the lands are listed in exactly the same order, the transcriptions in the latter are often very inaccurate (*Rent Roll Down* 8, 10). Another document pertaining to the second half of this century is also worthy of mention: the *Subsidy Roll* of 1663. Only six townlands in Clonallan and two in Warrenpoint are named, but the names of the individuals associated with them, presumably people who rented the land from the likes of Deane, are interesting. Some of these appear to be English: John Vaughan of Narrow Water, William Wallace of Ringmackilroy, Richard Babe of Aghnamoira, John Reignolds of Edentrumly. However, there are others: Phelemmy Magines of Carrickmacstay, Cohonat M'Mahon of Ballymaconaghy, Patrick oge O'Margan of Aghavilly and Manus O'Fegan of Cullion (*Sub. Roll* 276, 277), the last two of which are stated to be among the most common native surnames in the barony of Upper Iveagh in the *Census* of c. 1659 (*Census* 77). In the later 18th and 19th centuries the most prominent name in the parish was that of the Hall family and the survey of their estates in 1800 (*Map Hall Estates*) is one of the latest sources used in tracing the history of the names of Clonallan and Warrenpoint.

It remains to mention the latest of all our sources: the *Ordnance Survey Name Books* (*OSNB*), compiled by John O'Donovan in the course of the first Ordnance Survey of Ireland in 1834. The chief value of this source is in the Irish forms provided by some old and local informants. In the name books for Clonallan O'Donovan consistently refers to "Oyne McStay and others", but we know as little about McStay as we do about John Morgan, O'Donovan's informant for Kilbroney parish.[4] Neither Clonallan nor Warrenpoint was considered to be in the "Irish district", that part of the county in which Irish was most widely spoken at the beginning of the 19th century (*OSL* 50, 79). Nonetheless, McStay was undoubtedly an Irish speaker with a knowledge of the native place-names. Only such a man could have known that the Irish name for Narrow-water was *Caol* for example. As against that one should compare *Clann Allan*, his Irish form of Clonallan, which historically derives from *Cluain Dalláin*. There is good reason to believe that a form such as *Clann Allan* may represent quite closely the pronunciation of *Cluain Dalláin* in the local Irish dialect of McStay's day. There are other occasions, however, as in his attempt at providing an Irish form for **Donaghaguy** for example, when one might suspect that McStay was unsure of the correct Gaelic form of the name. It is clear, therefore, that the Irish-language forms in the *OSNB* should only be accepted when they are seen to be compatible with the earlier evidence.

(1) MacCana claims that the head of the family informed him of a papal bull sanctioning the right of the family chieftain to present the abbot of the monastery of Newry, which had been "founded by a chieftain of the same very ancient family, and endowed with considerable estates". He did not know whether this bull remained in his informant's possession or whether it had been lost in recent wars (*MacCana's Itinerary* 46–7).

(2) There is some confusion as to the correct spelling of Doyne's surname. In the 1632 inquisition he is referred to simply as Michael Doinegan (*Inq. Ult.* §30 Car. I), but in a later inquisition he appears as *Mic' Doyne de Tullerouse* in Co. Antrim (*Inq. Ult.* §71 Car. I). That this is a more accurate rendering of the name is clear from the *Book of Survey and Distribution* where Mabel is recorded as *Mabell Dunn alias Sexton* (*BSD* 112).

(3) On one occasion in his manuscript Mooney cites the *Newry Reporter*, February 1912, as his source for this deed (*Mooney* 52) but I have been unable to verify this.

(4) O'Donovan also mentions one Paddy Murphy of Ballyvally in a note at the end of the name book. It is impossible to say whether he ever actually met this individual or whether he was of any assistance to him.

PARISH NAME

Clonallan   *Cluain Dalláin*
                                              "Dallán's meadow"

1. Cluain Dallain		
i fail Chuain Snama Ech	CSH 120	1125c
2. Cluain Dallain	CSH 662.212	1125c
3. Clúain Dalláin		
i bfail Snámha Ech	Mart. Gorm. Apr. 2 p68n	1170c
4. Cluain (.i. Cluain Dalláin),		
i bfail Snamha Ech	Mart. Don. Apr. 2 p92	1630c
5. Cluain Dallain	Mart. Don. 388	1630c
6. Cluain-Dallain	Acta SS Colgan 205 col. 2	1645
7. Cluain-Dallain	Trias. Thaum. 381 col. 1	1648
8. Clondalan, Ecclesia de	Eccles. Tax. 112	1306c
9. Clondallan, ecc. de	Reg. Dowdall §129 275	1422
10. Cluandallan, parr. ecclesie de	Annates Ulst. 289	1423
11. Clonallon, vicarage of	Reg. Swayne 172	1437
12. Claondalan, prebende de	Annates Ulst. 291	1500
13. Clondallan, prebend of	Reg. Cromer x 171, §190	1534
14. Clondallan, prebend of	Reg. Dowdall §113 80	1546
15. T. Clann Allen	Bartlett Map (BM)	1600
16. Tempell Clonallen[?]	Bartlett Map (TCD)	1601
17. T[:] Clan Allen	Bartlett Maps (Esch. Co. Map) 2	1603
18. Clandallan rect.	CPR Jas. I 63b	1604
19. Clondallen	CPR Jas. I 104b	1607
20. Clandallan	CPR Jas. I 396a	1609
21. Clanall	Speed's Antrim & Down	1610
22. Clanall	Speed's Ulster	1610
23. Clandallon	CPR Jas. I 191b	1611
24. Clondollan	Inq. Ult. (Down) §13 Car. I	1629
25. Clonallan [Parish]	Inq. Down (Reeves 1) 89	1657
26. Cloneallen parish	Hib. Reg. Up. Iveagh	1657c
27. Clonallan [par.]	Census 74	1659c
28. Clanallan parish	BSD 111, 112	1661
29. Glannallen[?], Rector de	Trien. Visit. (Bramhall) 15	1661
30. Clonollan	Trien. Visit. (Margetson) 24	1664
31. Clonall et Kilbrony	Trien. Visit. (Margetson) 25	1664
32. Cloneallen	Hib. Del. Down	1672c
33. Clonealen	Hib. Del. Ulster	1672c
34. Clonallen Rectoria	Trien. Visit. (Boyle) 46, 48, 49	1679
35. Kill-Dallan, in Irish	MacCana's Itinerary 47	1700c

36. Clonallan	Harris Hist. map	1743
37. Clonallan	Dubourdieu's Map (OSNB) E42/100	1802
38. Clonallan	Civ. & Ecc. Top. (OSNB) E42/100	1806
39. Clonallan	Wm. Map (OSNB) E42/100	1810
40. Clonallen	Newry Tel. (OSNB) E42/100	1829
41. Clonallan Parish	Bnd. Sur. (OSNB) E42/100	1830c
42. Cluain Dalláin		
"lawn or meadow of St. Dallan"	OSNB E42/100	1834c
43. Clann Allan	OSNB Inf. E42/100	1834c
44. Cluain Dhallan		
"St. Dallan's Meadow"	Mooney 45	1950c
45. klɔ'nɑln	Local pronunciation	1990

Although *Cluain Dalláin* is associated with *Conall mac Áeda* in the earliest documents (1–5), it derives its name from another saint: *Dallán*, supposedly *Dallán Forgaill*, otherwise known as *Eochaidh Éigeas*. The latter occupies an important place in literary history as author of the *Amra Choluimb Chille*, a eulogy on the sixth-century Saint Columba, which is one of the oldest pieces of literature in the Gaelic language. Dallán is commemorated on January 29 in the martyrologies where he is described as *Dallan mac Forgaill ó Magin* (*Mart. Tal.* 13). This would suggest that Forgall was his father's name, although in a preface to the *Amra* his father's name is said to have been *Colla* (*Mart. Gorm.* 351). As to the place with which he is associated, Edward O'Reilly has suggested that it is the *Magin* located in *Mag Slecht* in Co. Cavan (*Atkinson's Dromore* 97–8), but there are other similarly-named places throughout Ireland (*Onom. Goed.* 533). Nevertheless, it is interesting that there is a *Cell Dalláin*, now Kildallon, near Killeshandra in Cavan (*Onom. Goed.* 188). Dallán also features in other place-names: *Glenn Dalláin*, now Glencar on the borders of Sligo and Leitrim, and *Tulach Dalláin* in Co. Donegal, to name but two (*Onom. Goed.* 441, 656). It is said that while Dallán was on a visit to Inniskeel in west Donegal, the abbey was attacked by pirates, probably Norsemen, and Dallán was murdered. He was subsequently buried at Inniskeel in the year 598 (*Atkinson's Dromore* 97–8).

The first person to speak of Dallán Forgaill in association with Clonallan appears to have been John Colgan who published his *Acta Sanctorum Hiberniae* in 1645:

> *Est ecclesia parrochialis in regione orientali Vltoniae, quae Iuechia dicitur,* **Cluain-Dallain** *appellata: quam Doctor Ketinus in Hystoria Regum Hiberniae, loquens de Rege Aido... indicat ab hoc sancto* **Dallano** *nomen sumpsisse* (*Acta SS Colgan* 205 col. 2).

> (There is a parish church called *Cluain Dalláin* in the eastern part of Ulster, known as Iveagh. Doctor Céitinn (or Keating), speaking of King Áed in his *History of the Kings of Ireland*, states that it derives its name from this saint *Dallán*.)

That Dallán is indeed one and the same as Dallán Forgaill is clear from the fact that he is stated to have been a contemporary of a certain king *Áed*, undoubtedly the 6th century high-king *Áed mac Ainmirech*. Colgan cites Seathrún Céitinn's *Hystoria Regum Hiberniae* as the source of his information, but this work, better known as *Forus Feasa ar Éirinn*, while referring to Dallán on numerous occasions, never mentions him in conjunction with Clonallan (*Céitinn*). Nevertheless, Colgan's interpretation of the name, whatever its source, is corroborated by the slightly later account of Edmund MacCana, who ventures the opinion that "the church called in Irish Kill-Dallan... the burial-place of the Magenis family... was dedicated to the famous panegyrist of our great Columba" (*MacCana's Itinerary* 47).

By the time O'Donovan visited the parish in 1834 there appears to have been no recollection of Dallán Forgaill in the locality. Oyne McStay's Irish form of Clonallan, i.e. *Clann Allan* (43), is clearly a misinterpretation of the original name but, nevertheless, there is good reason to believe that this form approximates quite closely to the pronunciation of the name in Irish at that time. There are linguistic reasons for this: the anglicized forms from the beginning of the 17th century suggest that by then the initial *D-* of *Dalláin* had been assimilated to the final *-n* of the preceding *Cluain* yielding forms like *Clann Allen* (15) in English. This also happened in the case of neighbouring **Clonduff** for which there are anglicized forms such as *Clonnyfe* and the like. The form *Clonallon* in *Reg. Swayne* (11) shows early evidence of this assimilation but, as this contrasts with the evidence gleaned from other 15th/16th-century ecclesiastical sources (9-10, 12-14), it is possible that the editor of that document may simply have adopted the modern form of the name. On the other hand, forms such as *Clondallan* are found in early 17th-century patents and inquisitions (18–20, 23–4), but it should be borne in mind that these documents are sometimes quite conservative for the simple reason that they often copy and recopy each other. We have seen that the origin of the name was still understood in the 17th century but, as the *D-* of *Dalláin* had by now been assimilated to the preceding *-n*, the original meaning was eventually forgotten. Whether the name had been re-interpreted as *Clann Allan* by 1834, or whether this is merely O'Donovan's interpretation of McStay's pronunciation, is a difficult question, but it is possible that the initial element *cluain* "meadow", which is unstressed, had been re-interpreted as *clann* "tribe, family", particularly if the second element was understood to be the personal name *Allan*. One final point in relation to the name is the fact that it is preceded by the element *teampall* on Bartlett's maps (15–7). *Teampall* in Irish means "a church" as does the element *cill* which is used by MacCana (35). Although *cill* names continued to be coined in post-Norman Ireland, they are usually earlier than the 12th century (Flanagan D. 1979(a)) and one wonders why *cill* is used by MacCana. It seems much more likely that Bartlett, in using the word *teampall*, has preserved the normal term for a "church" in the Irish of south Down at that time.

TOWNLAND NAMES

Aghavilly
J 1522

Achadh Bhile
"field of the sacred tree"

1. Achevyll	Reg. Swayne 160	1435
2. Ballyaghaville	CPR Jas. I 395b	1609
3. Ballyaghavilly	CPR Jas. I 235a	1612
4. Ballyaghivilly	Inq. Ult. (Down) §13 Car. I	1629
5. Aghevilly	Inq. Ult. (Down) §85 Car. I	1639
6. Aghaville al. Agherubuy	Hib. Reg. Up. Iveagh	1657c
7. Agherillie	BSD 112	1661
8. Aghavilly	Sub. Roll Down 276	1663
9. Aghavilly al. Agherillie	ASE 91a §4	1667
10. Agherubuy	Hib. Del. Down	1672c
11. (?)Aghavilly	Rent Roll Down 14	1692
12. Agharilly al. Aghatally	Rent Roll Down 8	1692
13. Aghavilly	Wm. Map (OSNB) E42/100	1810
14. Aughavilly	Bnd. Sur. (OSNB) E42/100	1830c
15. Aughavilly	Bnd. Sur. (OSNB) E42/100	1830c
16. Aghavilly	J O'D (OSNB) E42/100	1834c

17. Achadh bhile		
"Field of the old tree"	OSNB Inf. E42/100	1834c
18. Achadh a' bhile	Mooney 39	1950c
19. ˌɔxəˈvïlə	Local pronunciation	1990
20. ˌɑkəˈvïlə	Local pronunciation	1990
21. ˌɔxnəˈvïlə	Local pronunciation	1990

Aghavilly is a reasonably transparent place-name despite the fact that there appears to be two clearly distinct local pronunciations (19, 21). One of these (21) seems to introduce the article *na*, but there is absolutely no support for this in the forms and it must simply be a corruption of the name.

Aghavilly almost certainly derives from Irish *Achadh Bhile* "field or plain of the sacred tree." That the first element is indeed *achadh*, and not *áth* "a ford", is strongly supported by our earliest form (1) which appears in a grant of lands in Clonallan and Newry to Peter McGwyryn, canon of Dromore, in 1435. A spelling *Ach-* in English would be very unlikely to represent Irish *áth* at such an early date. It should be borne in mind that Oyne McStay, O'Donovan's local informant in 1834, also understood the first element as *achadh* (17).

The second element *bile* is also common in place-names (see *Joyce* i 499–501). It is quite possibly the element in question in place-names such as Aghavilly in the parish of Lisnadill, Co. Armagh, Aghavilla in the parish of Donaghmoyne, Co. Monaghan and Aghavilla in Drumlane, Co. Cavan (*Census* 1871), although one would need to see the historical documentation for these names to confirm this. It was generally applied not to any ordinary tree but to a tree which had some sacred or other significance. Quite often this was the tree under which the local chieftain was inaugurated and there are numerous references in the annals to the *bile* of a particular tribe having been cut down by its enemies. The gravity of this insult can be seen in the reaction of *Niall úa Lochlainn* in AD 1111 to the cutting down of the sacred trees of Tullyhogue in Co. Tyrone, known to later history as the inaugural site of the O'Neills:

> *Slogadh la hUlltu co Tealach nóc co ro thescsat a biledha. Crech la Niall H. Lochlainn co tuc mile no tri mile do buaibh ina ndighail.*

> "An expedition [was made] by the *Ulaid* to Telach óc, and they cut down its [sacred] trees. A raid [was made] by Niall ua Lochlainn, and [he] carried off a thousand or three thousand cows in revenge for them" (*AU (Mac Airt)* 552–3).

As to whether Aghavilly was an old inaugural site it is now impossible to say. If it was, it is possible that it was associated not with the Magennises but with their predecessors the *Méig Dhuibh Eamhna* who had close connections with the parish (see p. 51). As to the actual *bile* itself there appears to be no longer any recollection of it in the parish.

Aghnamoira
J 1121

Achadh na Maolrátha (?)
"field of the dismantled earthen fort"

1. Agheynmulragh	CSP Ire. 435	1570
2. Agheymulragh	Fiants Eliz. §1609	1570
3. Aghnemvillragh	CPR Jas. I 394b	1609
4. Aghnemvilragh	CPR Jas. I 190a	1611
5. Aghenemullraghe	Inq. Ult. (Down) §32 Car. I	1632
6. Aghnemullragh	Inq. Ult. (Down) §32 Car. I	1632
7. Aghnemaragh	Civ. Surv. x §72	1655c
8. Aghnemulragh	Hib. Reg. Up. Iveagh	1657c

9. Aghnemibragll	Census 74	1659c
10. Aughnemulragh	BSD 112	1661
11. Aghnemulleragh	Sub. Roll Down 276	1663
12. Aghnemutragh	ASE 107b §9	1666
13. Aghnemullragh	Hib. Del. Down	1672c
14. Aghnematragh	Rent Roll Down 9	1692
15. Aghnemulragh	Deeds & Wills (Mooney) 39	1712
16. Aghnemira	Map Hall Estates fol. 10	1800
17. Aghnamoyra	Wm. Map (OSNB) E42/100	1810
18. Aughnamoira	County Warrant (OSNB) E42/100	1830
19. Aghnemira	Bnd. Sur. (OSNB) E42/100	1830c
20. Aghnamoira	J O'D (OSNB) E42/100	1834c
21. Ath na maorach "Ford of the stewards"	OSNB Inf. E42/100	1834c
22. Achadh na maol-rátha "Field of the dilapidated rath"	Mooney 39	1950c
23. ˌɔxnəˈmairə	Local pronunciation	1990
24. ˈɑxnəˈmɑrə	Local pronunciation	1990

This is undoubtedly one of the most difficult names in the parish of Clonallan. The local Irish form in 1834 appears to have been *Ath na maorach* "ford of the stewards" (21), but the earlier evidence indicates quite clearly that this interpretation is historically incorrect. There is only one 17th-century form of the name that is in any way similar to the modern spelling. This is *Aghnemaragh* (7), a form which reflects quite accurately one of two current local pronunciations (24). However, the great weight of evidence suggests that *Aghnemulragh* (8) is a more accurate anglicization of the original Gaelic name, the *-l-* being lost as a result of its assimilation by the following *r*.

The first element is almost certainly either *achadh* "a field" or *áth* "a ford", but the second element is extremely difficult to interpret. There is the possibility that *-mulragh* might represent something like *maolrach* in Irish, where *maol* is a noun meaning "bare hill" and *-rach* a collective suffix. Joyce cites other examples of the use of this suffix in Irish place-names as in Boggeragh, Irish *Bograch* "a soft or boggy place", and Cleaveragh, Irish *Cliabhrach* "a place abounding in osiers" (*Joyce* ii 7–8). But there is a problem with this suggestion for it is clear from the anglicized form, *Aghnemulragh*, that if *maolrach* is the element in question then it must be a plural form as it is preceded by the article *na*. Although names of the form noun plus collective suffix are common throughout Ireland one would, in view of the collective meaning of the name, be surprised to find an example declined in the plural. Mooney's suggestion of an Irish form *Achadh na maol-rátha* "field of the dilapidated rath" (22) perhaps comes closest to satisfying the available evidence. The adjective *maol*, the primary sense of which is "bald, bare", is compounded with various nouns, most notably in the present context *cnoc* "a hill" and *sliabh* "a mountain", and the formation *maolráth* is attested in Irish texts (see *DIL* sv. 1 *mael*).

Aughnagon
J 1425

Achadh na nGabhann
"field of the smiths"

1. Aghynygony	Fiants Eliz. §4327	1583c
2. Aghenegowan	CPR Jas. I 394b	1609
3. Aghnegowan	CPR Jas. I 190a	1611

4. Aghenegoawn	Deeds & Wills (Mooney) 39	1618
5. Aghnegowne	Inq. Ult. (Down) §51 Car. I	1635
6. Aghnegon	Civ. Surv. x §72	1655c
7. Aghnegone	Census 74	1659c
8. Aghnagon	Deeds & Wills (Mooney) 39	1717
9. Aughnaconn	Deeds & Wills (Mooney) 39	1720c
10. Aghnagon	Wm. Map (OSNB) E42/100	1810
11. Aughnagon	County Warrant (OSNB) E42/100	1830
12. Aughnagun	Bnd. Sur. (OSNB) E42/100	1830c
13. Aughnagon	J O'D (OSNB) E42/100	1834c
14. Ath na g-con "Ford of the hounds"	OSNB Inf. E42/100	1834c
15. Athan Ui Ghobhain	Mooney 39	1950c
16. Athan a´ ghabhna	Mooney 39	1950c
17. Athan a´ ghabhainn	Mooney 39	1950c
18. Athan Mhig Dhuibheamhna	Mooney 39	1950c
19. ˈɔxnəˈgọn	Local pronunciation	1992
20. ˌɑxnəˈkọn	Local pronunciation	1992

There are at least two distinct pronunciations of Aughnagon in the locality. One of these (19) reflects quite accurately the modern spelling and is supported by the historical forms as far back as the middle of the 17th century (6). The alternative pronunciation (20) is also reflected by the early 18th-century form *Aughnaconn* (9) and, like the modern spelling, suggests that Oyne McStay's Irish form, *Ath na g-con* "ford of the hounds" (14), may indeed be correct. However, early forms of the name such as *Aghenegowan* (2) can only be interpreted as representing Irish *Achadh na nGabhann* "field of the smiths"; they certainly could not represent *Áth na gCon*. Forms 1, 2 and 4 indicate that the first element is *achadh*, followed by the plural form of the article *na*, and Mooney's suggestions can, therefore, be dismissed (15–8). Oyne McStay's form (14), however, cannot be similarly dismissed in the light of the historical and other evidence which seems to support it. One can only suggest that with the passage of time the original name *Achadh na nGabhann* was misunderstood and re-interpreted locally as *Áth na gCon*.

Reeves states that this townland was part of the ancient patrimony of the *Uí Ghairbhíth* (O'Garvey) who, like the *Méig Dhuibh Eamhna*, are included in Ó Dubhagáin's 14th-century topographical poem *Triallam timcheall na Fódla* "Let us travel around Ireland" (*Topog. Poems* l. 386). He also claims that it continued in the family's possession up until the beginning of the 19th century (*EA* 367). In the records of the 17th century, however, Aughnagon is listed among those possessions of Hugh McCon Magennis which later came into the hands of Edward Trevor (see p. 52).

Ballydesland	*Baile an Deiseáláin*	
J 1421	"townland of the righthand turn"	
1. Ballidesselan	CSP Ire. 435	1570
2. Balledesselan	Fiants Eliz. §1609	1570
3. Ballindeshelan	CPR Jas. I 395b	1609
4. Ballindeshellane	CPR Jas. I 235a	1612
5. Ballindeshallan	Inq. Ult. (Down) §13 Car. I	1629

6. Ballindeselan	Inq. Ult. (Down) §85 Car. I	1639
7. Ballideslane	Hib. Reg. Up. Iveagh	1657c
8. Ballydeslan	Census 74	1659c
9. Ballydeslane	BSD 111	1661
10. Ballydeslane	ASE 107b §9	1666
11. Ballideslane	Hib. Del. Down	1672c
12. Ballydeslane	Rent Roll Down 9	1692
13. Ballydeslan	Deeds & Wills (Mooney) 39	1712
14. Ballydesland	Map Hall Estates fol. 25	1800
15. Ballydesselan	Wm. Map (OSNB) E42/100	1810
16. Ballydesland	Reg. Free. (OSNB) E42/100	1829
17. Ballydesland	Bnd. Sur. (OSNB) E42/100	1830c
18. Baile deisealann "south town"	OSNB Inf. E42/100	1834c
19. Baile an deisealáin	Mooney 39	1950c
20. ˌbaliˈdɛ.zlən	Local pronunciation	1990

The historical spellings of this name are fairly consistent and point to an original Irish form *Baile an Deisealáin*. This is also the local Irish form which O'Donovan obtained from Oyne McStay although the definite article *an* seems to have been omitted (18). That the article indeed formed part of the name is clear from an entry in *CPR* dating to 1609 (3) and related documents (4-6), and these forms are also of value in establishing that the *s* in the name was palatal in Irish (represented by *sh* in English). In time, not only did the article and the palatal *s* disappear from the anglicized forms, but a vowel was dropped internally by a process known as syncope and the final syllable misinterpreted as "land" in English. *Ballindeshelan* (3), therefore, became at first *Ballideslane* (7) and later *Ballydesland* (14), although it should be noted that the *-d* is not usually heard in the local pronunciation (20) (cf. **Rathfryland**).

The element *deisealán* is not particularly common in Irish place-names. It appears to be a diminutive of *deiseal* "a turning to the right, righthand direction" (*Dinneen*; *Ó Dónaill*), which is an element in *An tIompú Deiseal*, the Gaelic form of Tempo in Co. Fermanagh (*GÉ* 119), and *Magh Deisiol*, Modeshil in Co. Tipperary (*Joyce* ii 428). The western and northern boundaries of Ballydesland follow the course of a river, which is unnamed on any of the modern maps. Their point of contact is where this river forms a sharp right turn on the south-eastern fringes of the village of Burren and this, presumably, is how Ballydesland got its name.

Ballydulany
J 1727

Of uncertain origin

1. Ballydowlaine	CPR Jas. I 394b	1609
2. Ballydowland	CPR Jas. I 190a	1611
3. Ballyvolany	CPR Jas. I 194b	1611
4. Ballydullany	Inq. Ult. (Down) §30 Car. I	1632
5. Ballydullany	Inq. Ult. (Down) §71 Car. I	1636
6. Ballydulany ½ towne	BSD 111	1661
7. Ballydulawny	Deeds & Wills (Mooney) 41	1712
8. Ballydulany	Deeds & Wills (Mooney) 41	1720c
9. Ballydilany[?]	Deeds & Wills (Mooney) 41	1720c
10. Ballydalany	Wm. Map (OSNB) E42/100	1810
11. Ballydoolany	County Warrant (OSNB) E42/100	1827
12. Ballydoolany	Reg. Free. (OSNB) E42/100	1830

13. Ballydulany	Bnd. Sur. (OSNB) E42/100	1830c
14. Baile Uí Dolaine "O'Delany's town"	OSNB Inf. E42/100	1834c
15. Baile Ui Dubhshláine "O'Delany's town"	Joyce iii 83	1913
16. Baile dubh láinne	Mooney 41	1950c
17. ˌbalədəˈleːni	Local pronunciation	1990

The remarkable thing about this name is that it is strongly stressed on the penultimate syllable, sounding more like Ballydelany than Ballydulany (17). Indeed, the local interpretation of the name was that it derived from *Baile Uí Dolaine* "O'Delany's town" (14), a form emended by Joyce to *Baile U[í] D[h]ubhshláine* (15), the correct historical spelling of the name in Irish. In Gaelic the stress would have fallen on the *Dubh-* element, which is at odds with the pronunciation of the name in English (17), but a comparable shift in stress seems to have occurred in similar names such as *Ó Duibhlearga* "Delargy", and *Ó Duibheannaigh* "Devanny", possibly on the analogy of Norman names such as de Lacy and de Courcy. The surname *Ó Dubhshláine* is normally associated with Cos Laois and Kilkenny but it is interesting that an earlier anglicized spelling of the name was O'Dulany, as in Felix O'Dulany, bishop of Ossory from 1178 to 1202 (MacLysaght 1957, 113). An obvious objection to deriving our place-name from the surname Delany is the fact that it is not attested either in Co. Down or anywhere else in Ulster.

There is the possibility, of course, that Ballydulany was misinterpreted locally because of its similarity to the surname in terms of pronunciation. It could also be suggested that this pronunciation is not historically accurate, but we cannot dismiss it as a relatively recent corruption for there is some evidence that the stress on *-lany* is at least as old as the early 18th century. This evidence is centred on a number of forms (8–10) which disagree as to the spelling of the *-du-* element, suggesting that the pronunciation of the *-u-* vowel was weak, whereas *Ballydulawny* (7) might possibly indicate that the stress fell on the vowel in the following syllable. We must also take the earliest form, *Ballydowlaine* (1), into account bearing in mind that forms 2 and 3, which occur in related documents, are probably corruptions of this. The difficulty with this form is in interpreting what vowel sound *-ow-* is supposed to represent and what implications this might have in terms of stress. If it is, indeed, a [uː] sound then *-dow-* and *-du-* may represent the adjective *dubh* "black", and the remaining part of the name may derive from a noun, in which case we might well expect it to be stressed. Mooney had obviously been thinking along these lines when he suggested that the original name was *Baile dubh láinne* (recte *lainne*) "black townland of the church" (16) to distinguish it from neighbouring *Baile Dubh*, Ballydoo, in Drumgath. Mooney's is an interesting suggestion but there is a problem in that there is no evidence for a church in the area. It is difficult to think of any other possibilities in the light of the present evidence.

Ballymaconaghy
J 1520

Baile Mhic Dhonnchaidh
"MacConaghy's townland"

1. Ballymakhowhe	CSP Ire. 435	1570
2. Ballemakhowhe	Fiants Eliz. §1609	1570
3. BallymcConeghie	CPR Jas. I 395b	1609
4. BallymcConeghie	CPR Jas. I 235a	1612
5. Ballinemacconoghy	Inq. Ult. (Down) §13 Car. I	1629
6. Ballymaconchye	Inq. Ult. (Down) §85 Car. I	1639

7.	Ballimacoughy	Hib. Reg. Up. Iveagh	1657c
8.	Ballymachonshy	BSD 112	1661
9.	Ballym'Conghy	Sub. Roll Down 276	1663
10.	BallymcCouchy	ASE 107b §9	1666
11.	B:mc:coghy	Hib. Del. Down	1672c
12.	BallymcShonchy	Rent Roll Down 9	1692
13.	Ballymaconaghy	Map Hall Estates fol. 29	1800
14.	Ballymaconachy	Map Hall Estates fol. 30	1800
15.	Ballymaconaghy	Wm. Map (OSNB) E42/100	1810
16.	Ballymaconaughey	Reg. Free. (OSNB) E42/100	1830
17.	Ballymaconaghy	County Warrant (OSNB) E42/100	1830
18.	Ballymaconaghy	Bnd. Sur. (OSNB) E42/100	1830c
19.	Baile mc Connachaigh		
	"Mac Conaghey's town"	OSNB Inf. E42/100	1834c
20.	Baile-Mic-Dhonchadha		
	"Mac Donaghy's town"	Joyce iii 104	1913
21.	Baile Mac Dhonnchaidh	Mooney 41	1950c
22.	Baile Mac Dhonnachaigh	Mooney 41	1950c
23.	ˌbaləməˈkɔnəgi	Local pronunciation	1990
24.	ˌbaləməˈkɔnəki	Local pronunciation	1990

It seems certain that the original Irish form of this name is *Baile Mhic Dhonnchaidh* "MacConaghy's townland". *Baile mic Dhonnchaidh* or *Baile mhac Dhonnchaidh* ("townland of the son of *Donnchadh*") are also possibilities, but place-names containing the element *mac* are normally derived from surnames. The fact that there is another Ballymaconaghy in the parish of Knockbreda seems to suggest that the surname *Mac D(h)onnchaidh* may once have been common in Co. Down. But is it an indigenous name? *Mac Dhonnchaidh* is normally associated with Scotland where it is variously anglicized as MacConaghy, MacConnachie, MacConkey and even Duncan, which is equated in English with the Gaelic personal name *Donnchadh*. It is particularly common in Perthshire, where the MacConnachies are a sept of Clan Robertson, but MacConnachie is also found as the name of a sept of Clan Campbell and Clan Gregor (Bell 1988, 53–4). We have seen in the introduction that Ballymaconaghy formed part of the patrimony of the senior branch of the Magennises, Lords of Iveagh. The name is at least as old as 1570 (1–2) and it is tempting to suggest that it derives its name from a band of Scottish gallowglasses who had been hired by the Magennises and granted lands in the area in reward for their services. This is entirely speculative. There is no reason why there could not have been a Co. Down family called *Mac D(h)onnchaidh* for the personal name *Donnchadh* was also common in Ireland. Donaghy, a common surname in Tyrone and Derry (MacLysaght 1957, 123), derives from an unlenited form of *Donnchadh*, i.e. *Mac Donnchaidh* as opposed to *Mac Dhonnchaidh*. The Co. Sligo surname MacDonagh is of similar origin but differs in that it derives from the Gaelic *Mac Donnchadha*, where *Donnchadha* is a variant gen. form of *Donnchadh*.

Ballyrussell   *Baile Ruiséil*
J 1421   "Russell's townland"

1.	Ballerussell	Fiants Eliz. §1609	1570
2.	Ballerussell	CSP Ire. 435	1570
3.	Ballyussell	CPR Jas. I 395b	1609

4.	Bally-Russell	CPR Jas. I 235a	1612
5.	Ballinrussell	Inq. Ult. (Down) §13 Car. I	1629
6.	Ballerussell	Inq. Ult. (Down) §85 Car. I	1639
7.	Ballirussell	Hib. Reg. Up. Iveagh	1657c
8.	Ballyrosse	Census 74	1659c
9.	Bally Russell	BSD 111	1661
10.	Ballyrussell	ASE 107b §9	1666
11.	Ballrussell (part)	ASE 91a §4	1667
12.	Ballirussell	Hib. Del. Down	1672c
13.	Ballyrussell	Rent Roll Down 8, 9	1692
14.	Ballyrussel	Map Hall Estates fol. 28	1800
15.	Ballyrussell	Wm. Map (OSNB) E42/100	1810
16.	Ballyrussell	Reg. Free. (OSNB) E42/100	1829
17.	Ballyrussell	Bnd. Sur. (OSNB) E42/100	1830c
18.	Baile Ruiseal "Russell's town"	OSNB Inf. E42/100	1834c
19.	"Russell's town"	Joyce iii 118	1913
20.	Baile (an) Ruiseil "Russell's town"	Mooney 41	1950c
21.	ˌbaləˈrɒsl	Local pronunciation	1990

Ballyrussell is not the only townland so named in Ireland. There is another Ballyrussell in the parish of Comber, Co. Down and a Ballyrussell in Cloyne, Co. Cork. There is also a Ballyrussel in Templemichael, Co. Waterford (*Census* 1871). The surname is found throughout Ireland and may be of Norman, English, Scottish, or Huguenot origin. It is most numerous in Ulster where the majority of Russells are probably descended from post-Plantation families. The Russells of Downpatrick, however, are descended from the Norman Osberto Russell who came to Co. Down with de Courcy in 1177 and settled in the barony of Lecale (Bell 1988, 225). Our Ballyrussell seems to preserve the memory of some branch of this family as the name is definitely pre-Plantation (1–2). In Irish it would have been *Baile Ruiséil*, although Mooney seems to have been influenced by the anglicized form *Ballinrussell* (5) in suggesting an alternative form *Baile an Ruiseil* (20). However, if the *-n-* of *Ballinrussell* is intended to represent the article and is not just a scribal error, then we should expect an Irish form *Baile an Ruiséalaigh*. When the article is used with a particular surname then that surname has the suffix *-ach* attached, e.g. *Puirséil/An Puirséalach* "Purcell", *Mac Domhnaill/An Domhnallach* "MacDonald". This is clearly not the case in this instance, so the *-n-* in form 5 is probably an error.

Ballyvally
J 1723

Baile an Bhealaigh
"townland of the path/pass"

1.	Ballymonycuggely	CPR Jas. I 394b	1609
2.	Ballaghmonynnecuggaly	CPR Jas. I 190a	1611
3.	Ballemoneyquigally	Inq. Ult. (Down) §32 Car. I	1632
4.	Ballaghnacugbille	Hib. Reg. Up. Iveagh	1657c
5.	Ballaghnecoglly	Census 74	1659c
6.	Ballaghmonicageale	BSD 112	1661
7.	Ballingingall al. Ballaghmonicageale	ASE 91a §4	1667
8.	Ballaghnecugalle	Hib. Del. Down	1672c

9. Ballynigillgall al. Ballaghmeeingageelle	Rent Roll Down 8	1692
10. Ballyvally	Wm. Map (OSNB) E42/100	1810
11. Ballyvalley	County Warrant (OSNB) E42/100	1827
12. Ballyvally	Reg. Free. (OSNB) E42/100	1829
13. Ballyvally	Bnd. Sur. (OSNB) E42/100	1830c
14. Baile an bhealaigh "Town of the way or pass"	OSNB Inf. E42/100	1834c
15. Baile bhealaigh "Town of the pass"	J O'D (OSNB) E42/100	1834c
16. Ba[i]le a(n) bhealaigh	Mooney 41	1950c
17. Bealach na coi-gcéilidhe	Mooney 41	1950c
18. Bealach na cómhdhala	Mooney 41	1950c
19. B. máighe na coi-gceilidhe	Mooney 41	1950c
20. ˌbalə'vali	Local pronunciation	1990

Ballyvally is clearly a shortened form of an older name *Ballaghmonynnecuggaly* (2) where the first element *ballagh* is derived from Irish *bealach* "a path or pass". The second element of the old name is possibly the Irish word *muine* "brake or thicket" or *mónadh*, gen. sing. of *móin*, "moor or bog". There is another word *monadh* "mountain, heath" which should be considered, but it is an element which is usually found only in Scottish place-names. The third element is preceded by the article *na* in form 2 and is quite likely a fem. word in the gen. sing. The word *coigeal*, gen. *coigile*, is strongly suggested by form 3 in particular and appears to be attested as an element both in Ballykeel, which is partly in Holywood and partly in Dundonald, and in Clooncogaile in the parish of Seskinan, Co. Waterford (Power 1907, 264). *Coigeal* basically means "a distaff" but *Ó Dónaill* records it as also meaning "a narrow channel". It is also found in Gaelic names of flowers. *Coigeal na mban sí*, for example, refers in both Ireland and Scotland to the flower known as "the great cat's tail or reed mace" (*Dinneen, Ó Dónaill* and *Dwelly*). This does not exhaust all the possibilities. *Dinneen* records *coigeal* as also meaning "a scarecrow", *Ó Dónaill* refers to *cluiche na coigile* "stick-play or cudgelling", and *Dwelly* states that *cuigeal* is attested in Scotland in reference to a "hand-rock". From this derives the adjective *cuigealach* "having rocks" (*Dwelly*).

There is the possibility that the final element of the old name is derived from something other than *coigeal* and Mooney makes a number of suggestions (17–19), none of which seem to be compatible with the anglicized forms. However, the modern name, which is our main concern, is definitely derived from the Gaelic *Baile an Bhealaigh* "townland of the path or pass", where *bealach* "a pass" is the first element of an older name *Ballaghmonynnecuggaly* (2). It appears that this older name was shortened at first to *Ballaghnecoglly* (5), but that by the early 19th century (10) the element *baile* "townland" had been introduced and most of the old name dispensed with. It is interesting that when John O'Donovan visited the area during the course of the Ordnance Survey in 1834 the pass or path could still be traced in many places (*OSNB* E42/100). Unfortunately, it does not appear to be marked on any of the modern maps.

Bavan
J 1528

An Bábhún
"the bawn/bailey"

1. Ballynbawen al. Ivane	CPR Jas. I 394b	1609
2. Ballynbawen al. Lavawne	CPR Jas. I 190a	1611

3. Bawne	CPR Jas. I 194b	1611
4. Ballybawne al. Lavawne	Inq. Ult. (Down) §30 Car. I	1632
5. Ballinebawne al. Levawne	Inq. Ult. (Down) §51 Car. I	1635
6. Bawne	Inq. Ult. (Down) §71 Car. I	1636
7. Bawne	Census 74	1659c
8. Bawne & Cullynn	BSD 112	1661
9. Bawne, Upper & Lower	Deeds & Wills (Mooney) 44	1712
10. Bawane	Deeds & Wills (Mooney) 43	1736
11. Bavan	Wm. Map (OSNB) E42/100	1810
12. Bavan	County Warrant (OSNB) E42/100	1827
13. Bavan	Reg. Free. (OSNB) E42/100	1829
14. Bavin	Reg. Free. (OSNB) E42/100	1830
15. Bavan	Bnd. Sur. (OSNB) E42/100	1830c
16. Badhbhun "A yard or enclosure"	OSNB Inf. E42/100	1834c
17. Badhbhdhun "a yard or castle enclosure"	OSNB E42/100	1834c
18. An Badhbhdhún "the bawn; enclosure"	Mooney 43	1950c
19. ba:vn	Local pronunciation	1990

The word *bábhún* (earlier *badhbhdhún*) is attested in both Ireland and Scotland as meaning "enclosure, bulwark, etc." (*Dinneen*; *Dwelly*). It is anglicized *bawn(e)* in post-plantation documents where it refers specifically to a "fortified enclosure around a castle" (see Mallory & MacNeill 1991, 303). There appears to be no evidence of any such castle in this area, although there is certainly an enclosure (*NISMR* sheet 47 §40). It may be that "an enclosure for cattle" is a more accurate translation of this particular *bábhún*.

It is interesting that Bavan is always spelt *Ballynbawen* (1) or *Bawne* (3) in the earliest documentation and that the modern spelling first makes its appearance at the beginning of the 19th century (11). *Bábhún* is normally anglicized Bawn in Irish townland names. It occurs independently as the name of fourteen townlands, whereas it appears to be an initial element in approximately one hundred townland names, the majority of which are in the extreme south of Ireland. Only two other townlands are anglicized Bavan, one in the parish of Carlingford, Co. Louth, and the other in Kilcar, Co. Donegal (*Census* 1871). These seem to be similar in origin to the Co. Down Bavan and one wonders whether all three may be indicative of some dialectal feature of Ulster Irish. Quiggin (1906, §196) notes that Irish *bábhún* is pronounced [bɑ:wən] in Donegal and it may be that the anglicized spelling Bavan is intended to distinguish this disyllabic sound from monosyllabic Bawn.

The historical documentation suggests that Bavan had been subdivided by the beginning of the 17th century. *Lavawne* (1–2, 4–5) seems to represent Irish *Leathbhábhún* "half of Bavan" and this may explain why Bavan is said to be in the possession of both George Sexton and Edward Trevor in the early documents (see p. 52). The reference in 1712 to *Bawne Upper and Lower* (9) clearly reflects this division and Bavan Upper and Lower is still marked on the 1:10,000 map (sheet 267).

Burren
J 1321

An Bhoirinn
"the rocky district"

1. (?)Boirne, la bachlachaibh	AFM i 204	565
2. (?)Bairne, la bachlachu	A. Tigern. 148	569

3. Ballibowrne al. Bowryn	CSP Ire. 435	1570
4. Ballebowrne al. Bowryn	Fiants Eliz. §1609	1570
5. Ballyburrin	CPR Jas. I 395b	1609
6. Balleburryne	CPR Jas. I 235a	1612
7. Ballybarrin	Inq. Ult. (Down) §13 Car. I	1629
8. Ballyburrin	Inq. Ult. (Down) §85 Car. I	1639
9. Buren	Civ. Surv. x §72	1655c
10. Burrine	Hib. Reg. Up. Iveagh	1657c
11. Burrin	BSD 111	1661
12. Burrin	ASE 107b §9	1666
13. Burrin	Hib. Del. Down	1672c
14. Burrin	Rent Roll Down 9	1692
15. Burren	Map Hall Estates fol. 1	1800
16. Burran	Wm. Map (OSNB) E42/100	1810
17. Burren[?]	County Warrant (OSNB) E42/100	1827
18. Burren	Reg. Free. (OSNB) E42/100	1829
19. Burren	Bnd. Sur. (OSNB) E42/100	1830c
20. An Buirrinn	OSNB Inf. E42/100	1834c
21. An Boirinn "the rocky district"	OSNB E42/100	1834c
22. Boireann	Post-Sheanchas 40	1905
23. An Bhoireann	Mooney 43	1950c
24. Boirinn	AGBP 114	1969
25. Boirinn	Éire Thuaidh	1988
26. Boirinn	GÉ 37	1989
27. bo.rn	Local pronunciation	1990
28. bọrn	Local pronunciation	1990

This name clearly derives from the word *boireann* in Irish which means "a rocky district" or "a large stone". It was declined as a feminine *ā* stem in Old Irish which means that in the acc. and dat. cases it would have been *bairinn* or *boirinn* and in the gen. *bairne* or *boirne* (*DIL* sv. *bairenn*). Oyne McStay's Irish form (21) preserves the old acc./dat. inflexion and Burren in Co. Clare is also derived from *Boirinn* in Irish (*GÉ* 195).

There is an element of doubt concerning the early Irish forms (1–2). These are taken from the annals and are concerned with the death of *Deman maic Cairill*, king of the *Ulaid*, at the hands of the shepherds of *Bairenn*. The annals disagree as to the date of this incident: *AFM* dates it to 565 and *A. Tigern.* to 569 although, linguistically, *A. Tigern.* is the earliest. It is clear from its association with Deman that *Bairenn* is located in east Ulster. Deman was a cousin of *Domangart* from whom **Slieve Donard** takes its name and this, presumably, is the reason why O'Donovan, in his edition of *AFM*, locates it in Co. Down. He suggests that Burren in Clonallan is the place intended (*AFM* i 204), but there is also a Burren in Magherahamlet (formerly Dromara), and there are the two townlands of Burrenbane and Burrenreagh in Kilcoo just a few miles north of Slieve Donard. It is impossible to decide to which, if any, of these places the annals may refer.

Cabragh *An Chabrach*
J 1430 "rough/bad land (?)"

1. Ballencabragh	CPR Jas. I 394b	1609
2. Ballencabbragh	CPR Jas. I 190a	1611

3. Ballynecabragh	Inq. Ult. (Down) §32 Car. I	1632
4. Ballinecabragh	Inq. Ult. (Down) §32 Car. I	1632
5. Cabragh	Civ. Surv. x §72	1655c
6. Cabragh	Hib. Reg. Up. Iveagh	1657c
7. Cabbragh	BSD 112	1661
8. Cabragh	Hib. Del. Down	1672c
9. Cabra	Hib. Del. Ulster	1672c
10. Cabbragh	ASE 273b §29	1681
11. Cabragh	Rent Roll Down 10	1692
12. Cabrah	Tombstone (OSNB) E42/100	1713
13. Cabra	Wm. Map (OSNB) E42/100	1810
14. Cabra	Porter's Map (OSNB) E42/100	1821
15. Cabragh	Reg. Free. (OSNB) E42/100	1829
16. Cabra	Bnd. Sur. (OSNB) E42/100	1830c
17. Cabrach "Rubbish"	OSNB Inf. E42/100	1834c
18. Cabrach "rough, bad land"	Mooney 43	1950c
19. ˈkʲabrə	Local pronunciation	1990

The townland names Cabra and Cabragh are most numerous in the northern half of Ireland and are found in all nine counties of Ulster (*Census* 1871). Elsewhere in Co. Down there is a **Cabragh** in Clonduff and also in Hillsborough. Joyce derives both Cabra and Cabragh from *Cabrach* in Irish which, he states, is "everywhere understood to mean bad, rough, unprofitable land" (*Joyce* iii 155). This is also the explanation given in O'Donovan's supplement to O'Reilly's Dictionary (*O'Reilly*) and it seems likely that O'Donovan was drawing on such local information as he received when working for the Ordnance Survey. In the *OSNB* for Clonduff, for example, *Cabrach* is translated "rough land" and it seems that our Cabragh was similarly understood (17). It should be stated that the land in this area does not appear to be any worse than in the neighbouring townlands, although it could be argued that this may not necessarily have been the case in the past.

The early historical forms of Cabragh (1–4) are preceded by the element *baile* "townland" plus the gen. form of the definite article. Two of these seem to suggest that the article is masc. sing. *an* (1-2) as opposed to fem. sing. *na* (3–4). However, the early forms of Cabragh in Clonduff suggest that the article is indeed fem. in which case Cabragh may derive from the word *cabrach* "a copse" (*Ó Dónaill*). Nevertheless, the evidence of both Joyce and O'Donovan cannot be dismissed lightly and it may be well to accept the local interpretation of the element even if it is otherwise unattested.

Carmeen
J 1826

Ceathrú Mhín
"smooth quarter"

1. Ballycharmen	CPR Jas. I 394b	1609
2. Ballycharmen	CPR Jas. I 190a	1611
3. Ballycarneny	Inq. Ult. §32 Car. I	1632
4. Caruemeene	Hib. Reg. Up. Iveagh	1657c
5. Caruemeen	Hib. Del. Down	1672c
6. Canoneene	Rent Roll Down 10	1692
7. Carrewmeene	Headfort Map (Mooney) 43	(?)
8. Carmeen	Wm. Map (OSNB) E42/100	1810

9. Carmeen	Reg. Free. (OSNB) E42/100	1829
10. Carmeen	Bnd. Sur. (OSNB) E42/100	1830c
11. Ceathramh mhín "smooth quarter"	OSNB Inf. E42/100	1834c
12. Carr-mín "smooth rock"	Joyce iii 167	1913
13. An Cheathramha Mhín "The smooth quarter"	Mooney 43	1950c
14. 'kʲarn'miːn	Local pronunciation	1990

Forms 4, 5 and 7 all suggest that the initial element in this place-name is Irish *ceathrú* "a quarter". *Ceathrú*, however, is usually anglicized *carrow-* in place-names, whereas both the earliest (1–3) and the more recent forms (8–10) of Carmeen agree in anglicizing the first element as *car-*. This led *Joyce* (iii 167) to suggest that the initial element is derived from *carr*, a word attested in *Ó Dónaill* with the meaning of "rough surface or rocky patch". Carmeen could certainly be considered a rocky district but, if *carr* is the first element, then it is unlikely to be qualified by an adjective such as *mín* "smooth". It is much more plausible to argue that the first element is possibly *carn* "a cairn or pile", particularly as the local pronunciation of Carmeen (14) clearly supports this. Furthermore, there are a couple of historical forms which might suggest an original *Carn Mín*, reading *n* for *u* in forms 4–5. On the other hand, form 7 can only be interpreted as representing *Ceathrú Mhín* in Irish, and the fact that this was the local understanding of the name in 1834 (11) is also difficult to argue against. This being the case the local pronunciation ['kʲarn'miːn] could have arisen by analogy with the townland of **Carnmeen** in the neighbouring parish of Newry.

Ballycarneny (3) must refer to Carmeen as it is recorded in the same position in this document as in earlier related documents (1–2). This unlikely spelling probably arose through confusion with **Carnany**, in neighbouring Drumgath, at some stage in the process of transcription.

Carrickcrossan *Carraig Uí Chrosáin (?)*
J 1428 "O'Crossan's rock"

1. Ballycarriccressan	CPR Jas. I 394b	1609
2. Ballycarrickrossan	CPR Jas. I 190a	1611
3. Carrick-Crossane	Deeds & Wills (Mooney) 46	1618
4. Ballicarrickorossan	Inq. Ult. (Down) §51 Car. I	1635
5. Carrickcrossan	Civ. Surv. x §72	1655c
6. Carrychnossan	Census 74	1659c
7. Crossan al. Carricrossan	Deeds & Wills (Mooney) 46	1717
8. Carrycrossan; Crossan	Deeds & Wills (Mooney) 45	1720c
9. Carricnecrossan	Maps (Mooney) 45	1767
10. Carrickcrossen	Wm. Map (OSNB) E42/100	1810
11. Carrickcrossan	County Warrant (OSNB) E42/100	1827
12. Crossan	Reg. Free. (OSNB) E42/100	1829
13. Crossen	Bnd. Sur. (OSNB) E42/100	1830c
14. Carrickcrossan	J O'D (OSNB) E42/100	1834c
15. Carraic Ui Chrosáin "O'Crossan's Rock"	OSNB Inf. E42/100	1834c
16. "rock of Crossan or Crosbie"	Joyce iii 174	1913

17. Carraig a' chrosain	Mooney 45	1950c
18. Carrach a' chrosain	Mooney 45	1950c
19. Ceathramha a' chrosain	Mooney 45	1950c
20. ˌkʲarïˈkrɔ.sn	Local pronunciation	1990

Mooney is clearly overcautious in his interpretation of the first element of this name; all the forms suggest *carraig* "a rock" and we can dismiss Mooney's other suggestions *carrach* (18) and *ceathramha* (19). It is the second element which is the problem for there is nothing in the historical documentation which would necessarily support Oyne McStay's local Irish form *Carraic Uí Chrosáin* "O'Crossan's rock" (15). The surname *Ó Crosáin* appears to be unattested although there is a surname *Mac an Chrosáin*, ultimately of Co. Donegal origin, but now more common in Cos Derry and Tyrone. It is normally anglicized MacCrossan and Crosbie (MacLysaght 1982, 69–70). Although it may be difficult to reconcile the historical forms with McStay's *Carraic Uí Chrosáin*, it must be stated that a postulated form *Carraig Mhic an Chrosáin* "MacCrossan's townland" is even less likely.

It is possible that the second element is not a surname, particularly as *Crossan* is attested independently in a number of historical documents (7–8, 12–13). If this is the case then the common noun *crosán* "cross-bearer; satirist; buffoon; villain; razorbill" (*Dinneen*) also has to be discounted for one might not expect such a word to be used alone in forming a place-name. On the other hand, historical forms such as *Crossan* may be misleading in that the element may have been unintentionally divorced from *Carrick* in the sources. If the spelling *Carricnecrossan* (9) is accurate then the original name may have been something like *Carraig na gCrosán* "rock of the razorbills". However, the plural form of the article *na* is not found in the other forms and may also be a scribal error. Furthermore, if Carrickcrossan derives from *Carraig na gCrosán* one might not expect it to be re-interpreted locally as *Carraig Uí Chrosáin*. In fact one might expect the reverse: the rare surname *Ó Crosáin* to be re-interpreted as the common noun *crosán*. It is difficult, therefore, to argue against McStay's Irish form on the basis of the present evidence.

Form 3 is taken from Mooney's manuscript where the source is described as a deed of purchase dating to June 23, 1618 (*Mooney* 46). Edward Trevor and Hugh McCon Magennis were the characters involved and we know that Trevor acquired much of the Magen
nis lands sometime between 1611 and 1625, the year of the death of James I (see p. 52). Mooney's evidence is important for it dates the transfer of Carrickcrossan to 1618.

Carrickmacstay
J 1422

Carraig Uí Mhaoilsté
"MacStay's rock"

1. Karricke, Emysteyoke	CSP Ire. 435	1570
2. Karricke Emysteyoke	Fiants Eliz. §1609	1570
3. Ballicarrickminstie	CPR Jas. I 395b	1609
4. Ballecarrigge Imuskey	CPR Jas. I 235a	1612
5. Ballycarrigg Inisteye	Inq. Ult. (Down) §13 Car. I	1629
6. Ballycarrickonnistey	Inq. Ult. (Down) §85 Car. I	1639
7. Carrigmusty	Hib. Reg. Up. Iveagh	1657c
8. Carricke Mastie	BSD 111	1661
9. Decarrickomustra	Sub. Roll Down 276	1663
10. Carrigmasby al. Carrickmastie	ASE 91a §4	1667
11. Carrickmastie	ASE 192b §45	1669

12. Carrigmusty	Hib. Del. Down	1672c
13. Carrickimusmusky	ASE 273b §29	1681
14. Carriginassy al. Carriginasty	Rent Roll Down 8	1692
15. Carrickmastead	Rent Roll Down 8	1692
16. Carrigunus Mully	Rent Roll Down 10	1692
17. Carrickmastay	Map Hall Estates fol. 1	1800
18. Carrickmackstay	Map Hall Estates fol. 27	1800
19. Carrickmacstay	Wm. Map (OSNB) E42/100	1810
20. Carrickmastay	County Warrant (OSNB) E42/100	1827
21. Carrickmastay	County Warrant (OSNB) E42/100	1830
22. Carrickmastay	Bnd. Sur. (OSNB) E42/100	1830c
23. Carrickmacstay	J O'D (OSNB) E42/100	1834c
24. Carraic mc Stéadhag "Mac Stay's rock"	OSNB Inf. E42/100	1834c
25. "MacStay's rock"	Joyce iii 175	1913
26. Carraig Uí Maoilstéighe "MacStay's Rock"	Mooney 45	1950c
27. ˈkʲarïgmǝkˈsteː	Local pronunciation	1990
28. ˈkʲarïk	Local pronunciation	1990

This townland appears to be derived from *Carraig Uí Mhaoilsté* (earlier *Mhaoilstéighe*) in Irish, "MacStay's rock". It is immediately obvious that the Gaelic surname *Ó Maoilstéighe* is quite different from the modern anglicized form MacStay. This is because the element *maol* was corrupted over the centuries due to the loss of palatal *-l-* in what must have been a difficult consonant cluster *-lst-*. After the loss of *-l-* the *Ó* prefix in the surname was retained for a time but, eventually, it also dropped out and historic *maol* was re-interpreted as *Mac*. Woulfe records earlier spellings of the surname which illustrate quite clearly the development from Gaelic *Ó Maoilstéighe* to the modern anglicized form: *O Molstaygh, O Mulstey, O Mustey, Mustay* and *Mac Stay* (Woulfe 1923, 602). The earliest spelling is particularly significant for it occurs in an entry in *Reg. Prene* concerned with the installation in 1461 of one Maurit[i]us O Hagan as vicar of Clonduff by John O Molstaygh (*EA* 115). The *-l-* in the surname had clearly disappeared by 1570 for there is no trace of it in our earliest anglicized form *Karricke Emysteyoke* (1–2). The name is similarly spelt in the first half of the 17th century although we now find that it is prefixed by the element *baile* "townland" (3–6). *Ballecarrigge Imuskey* (4) is probably the most accurate spelling although the *-k-* in the final element is a mistranscription of *-t-*. The *I-* in *Imuskey*, just like the *E-* in the earlier forms, probably represents *Uí* in Irish, gen. sing. of the surname prefix *Ó*. This *Uí/Ó* can still be traced in forms dating to 1663 (9) and 1681 (13) but, nevertheless, spellings such as *Carrigmusty* (7) suggest that it was in the process of being discarded. The forms in the *Rent Roll*, which dates to 1692, (14–16) are all corrupt forms of this *Carrigmusty*, which by the beginning of the 19th century had been re-interpreted as *Carrickmackstay* (18). The surname MacStay has long been established in Co. Down and frequently occurs in medieval lists of clergy relating to the diocese of Dromore (*Swanzy's Dromore* 67, 76 *et pass.*). It has obviously strong connections with Clonallan in particular, bearing in mind that O'Donovan's informant in 1834 was one Oyne McStay. His Irish form of the townland, *Carraic mc Stéadhag* (24), is particularly interesting in view of our earliest anglicized form *Karricke Emysteyoke* (1–2). It is unclear what the *-ag* and *-oke* may represent in Irish unless it is the diminutive suffix *-óg*.

Carrogs   *Corróga*
J 1223   "little round hills/peaks (?)"

1. Kerrokes, Little	CSP Ire. 435	1570
2. Karrokes, Great	CSP Ire. 435	1570
3. Korrokes, little	Fiants Eliz. §1609	1570
4. Korrokes, great	Fiants Eliz. §1609	1570
5. Coroge, little	Fiants Eliz. §4327	1583c
6. Corrorck	CPR Jas. I 394b	1609
7. Corrock, the	CPR Jas. I 195b	1610
8. Corrocks, the	CPR Jas. I 190a	1611
9. Corraggs	Inq. Ult. (Down) §32 Car. I	1632
10. Corrogs	Civ. Surv. x §72	1655c
11. Corroge	Hib. Reg. Up. Iveagh	1657c
12. Corroggs	Census 74	1659c
13. Corroge	BSD 112	1661
14. Coorroge	Hib. Del. Down	1672c
15. Carrocke	ASE 273b §29	1681
16. Carrock	Rent Roll Down 10	1692
17. Corrogs	Map Hall Estates fol. 1	1800
18. Corrogs	Wm. Map (OSNB) E42/100	1810
19. Carucks	Bnd. Sur. (OSNB) E42/100	1830c
20. Carrogs	J O'D (OSNB) E42/100	1834c
21. Carroga "Rocks"	OSNB Inf. E42/100	1834c
22. "little rocks"	Joyce i 419	1869
23. Cairrge "Rocks"	Mooney 47	1950c
24. Carracha	Mooney 47	1950c
25. 'kɔrïgz	Local pronunciation	1990

The original Irish form of this name is apparently *Corróga*, a plural form of the word *corróg*. In many of the anglicized forms the Irish plural *-a* has been replaced with the English plural *-s* and this is equally true of the modern form. In the earliest documents the townland is divided into two units (1–5), but forms such as *Little Kerrokes* (1) suggest that the English plural does not reflect this division but derives from the Irish plural form. *Corróg* is a diminutive of *corr* which has a wide variety of meanings in Irish. In the earlier language three different words are attested (*DIL*). Two of these are relevant here. The first is the noun *corr* "projecting part, peak, corner etc." which may be used adjectively: "tapering, peaked, pointed". It can also mean "rounded or curved" and *Dinneen* records *corr* "a conical hill" as in *An Chorr* (now the Sugar Loaf), *An Chorr Dhubh* "the black round hill", and *An Chorr Chuileannach* "the holly-clad round hill", all in Co. Kerry. The compound *corr-chnoc/corra-chnoc* "a round hill or a large hill" should also be mentioned here (*Dinneen*).

The second *corr* is usually translated "well, pool, depression containing water" and *corróg*, a diminutive of this, is attested as meaning "pit, hole, etc." (*DIL* sv. *corróc*). *Corróg*, and a variant *carróg*, are also found in *Dinneen*, but here they are translated "a corner, an angle; a little pit" which suggests that *corróg* could be a diminutive of either of the two *corr*s. To what, then, does it refer in our context: a little round or conical hill, a little peak, a little pool or depression? The local Irish form in 1834 was *Carroga* (21), where the initial *o* sound is lowered to [a] as might be expected in Ulster Irish. However, the element *corróg* appears to have been confused with *carraig* for McStay's form is translated "rocks" in the *OSNB* (21). Since the local interpretation is clearly unreliable one can only suggest that the *corróga* may refer to a couple of peaks on Carrogs Mountain (J 1224).

This is not the only instance of the element *corróg* in Co. Down. There is a **Corrog** in the parish of Ballytrustan and a **Carrigs** in Maghera, both of which have similar historical spellings. There is a place called *Corróca Cnámchoille* in the 12th-century Irish text *Acallam na Senórach*, and this appears to refer to the modern townlands of Corrogebeg and Corrogemore in Co. Tipperary (see *Onom. Goed.* 298; *Census* 1871). Corriga in the parish of Bourney in Co. Tipperary and Corriga in Cloone, Co. Leitrim may also be derived from Irish *Corróga*.

Finally, one should mention the name *Lyttell Corcaghe* which, in a document dating to 1552, is said to be one of "the two townships of Hytowelan". *Hytowelan* appears to refer to the modern townland of Ballyholland which is contiguous with Carrogs. Some of the 17th-century forms of this name, *Little Corragh* et var., are quite similar to *Little Coroge* above (5), but the historical evidence as a whole suggests that it is a different name (see **Ballyholland** in Newry parish).

Clonallan Glebe	*Baile na gCléireach*	
J 1419	"townland of the clerics"	

1. Ballynacleragh	Reg. Swayne 161	1435
2. Ballynegleragh al. Tonnycreman	CPR Jas. I 396a	1609
3. Ballynecleragh al. Tommemicknemarro, town of	CPR Jas. I 191b	1611
4. Clonallan, the town of, al. Ballinegleragh	Inq. Down (Reeves 1) 89	1657
5. Clonalle [td.]	Hib. Reg. Up. Iveagh	1657c
6. Conallan [td.]	Census 74	1659c
7. Glannallan belonging to ye Church of Clannallen	BSD 112	1661
8. Clonalle [td.]	Hib. Del. Down	1672c
9. Clonallon, Glebe of	Map Hall Estates fol. 32	1800
10. Clonallan Glebe	Civ. & Ecc. Top. (OSNB) E42/100	1806
11. Clonallan Glebe	Wm. Map (OSNB) E42/100	1810
12. Clonallen Glebe	Newry Tel. (OSNB) E42/100	1829
13. Clonallan Glebe	Bnd. Sur. (OSNB) E42/100	1830c
14. klɔ'naln 'glǝib	Local pronunciation	1990

References to Clonallan in the sources are normally either to the parish or to the church itself (see pp. 54–5). The lands which surrounded that church, the basis of the modern townland Clonallan Glebe, were known in earlier times as *Ballynegleragh* (1–4), Irish *Baile na gCléireach* "townland of the clerics". In two of the sources *Ballynegleragh* is recorded as having an alias *Tonnycreman* (2) or *Tommemicknemarro* (3). These may ultimately be two corrupt forms of the one name, but it is impossible to suggest on such little evidence what the original name may have been.

Clonta Fleece	*Cluainte Flís (?)*	
J 1623	"meadows of chickweed"	

1. Bally-clonteflish	CPR Jas. I 395b	1609
2. Ballyclonteflyish	CPR Jas. I 235a	1612

3. Ballyclontiffigges	Inq. Ult. (Down) §13 Car. I	1629
4. Clonte	Inq. Ult. (Down) §85 Car. I	1639
5. Clountiflus	Hib. Reg. Up. Iveagh	1657c
6. Clotefleyes	Census 74	1659c
7. Clontiflush	BSD 112	1661
8. Clontiflinch al. Clontiflush	ASE 91a §4	1667
9. Clontyflinch al. Clontyflush	Rent Roll Down 8	1692
10. Clunteflewich	Maps (Mooney) 45	1767
11. Clontifleece	Wm. Map (OSNB) E42/100	1810
12. Clontafleece	County Warrant (OSNB) E42/100	1827
13. Clontifleece	Reg. Free. (OSNB) E42/100	1829
14. Clontifleece	Bnd. Sur. (OSNB) E42/100	1830c
15. Clontafleece	J O'D (OSNB) E42/100	1834c
16. Cluainte Flís	OSNB Inf. E42/100	1834c
17. Cluainte Flidhise "Fleese's lawns or meadows"	OSNB E42/100	1834c
18. Cluainte Fliuchais\Flichis "Wet meadows"	Mooney 45	1950c
19. Cluainte Flaithgheasa\Flaithghis	Mooney 45	1950c
20. ˌklɔntəˈfliːs	Local pronunciation	1990

The first element of this place-name is probably *cluainte* in Irish, which is a plural form of *cluain* "a meadow". It is also possible that it derives from the sing. form *cluain*, plus *tí*, gen. of *teach*, "a house", but this seems less likely. The second part of the name is much more difficult to interpret. Oyne McStay's Irish form, *Cluainte Flís* (16), was emended by O'Donovan to *Cluainte Flidhise* (17), taking *Flís* to be a shortened form of the personal name *Fliodhais*, earlier *Flidais* or *Flidis*. There is no evidence for the final *-e* of *Cluainte Flidhise* in our historical forms but the loss of a vowel such as this is not unusual in Ulster Irish (Ó Dochartaigh 1987, 168–72). A much more serious reservation is the fact that *Fliodhais* is not a particularly common personal name. *Flidais*, a Connacht princess, is one of the principal characters in the early tale *Táin Bó Flidaise* "the Cattle-raid of Flidais", but there is a second *Flidais* in the genealogies who belonged to the *Eoganacht* dynasty of Munster (*CGH* 320b1 p. 362). It is also interesting that *Flidais* is believed to be an older name for the river Nore in Kilkenny (*Onom. Goed.* 426), as Clontafleece is bounded to a large extent by rivers. The Moygannon River forms part of its eastern boundary with Ballyagholy, a tributary of the Moygannon River forms the boundary with Lurgancanty, and another tributary forms the boundary with Aghavilly. One could argue that the second element of Clontafleece may possibly refer to one or other of these rivers but this is highly speculative to say the least.

Is it possible that the second element is derived from a common noun rather than a proper noun? Mooney obviously had thought along these lines and he offered two suggestions. One of these, *Cluainte Flaithgheasa* (19), seems to make little sense: *flaitheas* is attested in Irish only with meanings such as "kingdom, sovereignty, heaven" (*Dinneen*). His second suggestion centres on the word *fliuchas*, a variant of *fliuchras* "wetness, dampness, moisture" (*Ó Dónaill*), but this is incompatible with anglicized forms such as *Clotefleyes* (6) and *Clunteflewich* (10). There is, however, a word for the plant chickweed in Irish: normally *fliodh*, but with variants such as *flidh*, *flich* and *flíoch* (*Dinneen* & *Ó Dónaill*). The suffix *-as* is well attested in Irish place-names such as *Luachras* from *luachair* "rushes" (Ó Máille 1989–90, 136). If we postulate a similar formation *fliodhas*, then a gen. form *fliodhais* (after *cluainte*) might well be pronounced [fˈlˈiːʃ] or [fˈlˈöːʃ]. This does have the merit of being compatible with anglicized forms such as *Clonteflish* (1) and *Clontiflush* (7), and possibly even *Clotefleyes* (6) and *Clunteflewich* (10) depending on how we interpret them. Unfortunately, *fliodhas* does not seem to be attested in Irish place-names and so the original form of Clontafleece is a matter of some doubt. Our postulated form *Cluainte Fliodhais* has been emended to *Cluainte Flís* in accordance with the spelling conventions of standard Modern Irish.

Croan

J 1431

Cruán

"hard ground"

1.	Croan	CPR Jas. I 394b	1609
2.	Croan	CPR Jas. I 190a	1611
3.	Cluoyn	Civ. Surv. x §72	1655c
4.	Croune	Census 74	1659c
5.	Croan	Deeds & Wills (Mooney) 47	1710c
6.	Croon	Deeds & Wills (Mooney) 47	1710c
7.	Crowoan	Deeds & Wills (Mooney) 47	1710c
8.	Cruoan	Deeds & Wills (Mooney) 47	1710c
9.	Cran al. Crowoon	Deeds & Wills (Mooney) 47	1717
10.	Croan	Wm. Map (OSNB) E42/100	1810
11.	Crone	Bnd. Sur. (OSNB) E42/100	1830c
12.	Croan	Clergyman (OSNB) E42/100	1834c
13.	Croan	J O'D (OSNB) E42/100	1834c
14.	Cróan "Hard ground"	OSNB Inf. E42/100	1834c
15.	Cruan	J O'D (OSNB) E42/100	1834c
16.	Cruán/Cruadhán "hard ground"	Joyce iii 275	1913
17.	Cruadhan	Mooney 47	1950c
18.	kroən	Local pronunciation	1990

The historical forms of this place-name suggest that it derives from some disyllabic word in Irish such as *cruadhán/cruán*. *Cruadhán* is attested in Dinneen with the meaning "hard or concreted matter of any kind" and an example is cited in which the word clearly refers to hard ground (*Dinneen*). There are eight other examples of the anglicized element *croan* in Irish place-names, mostly in the south of Ireland but with one example in Killymard, Co. Donegal: Croankeeran. In most of these instances *croan* is unqualified but there are two other examples besides Croankeeran in which it is accompanied by another element: Croanrea in Cork and Croanruss in Carlow (*Census* 1871). We cannot be sure that *croan* derives from *cruadhán* in all these instances, but the anglicized form is clearly distinguishable from the element *crone*, Irish *crón*, which is also common in the south. There are over ten examples in Wicklow and a couple in Wexford (*Census* 1871) where it appears to refer to "a hollow" (*Joyce* iii 277). The origin of our place-name is clearly different and we can accept the local explanation of the name as *Cróan*, more correctly *Cruán*, "hard ground" (14).

Cullion

J 1530

Cuilleann

"a steep, unbroken slope (?)"

1.	Quillin	CPR Jas. I 394b	1609
2.	Quillin	CPR Jas. I 190a	1611

3. Quillin	Inq. Ult. (Down) §32 Car. I	1632
4. Cullin	Civ. Surv. x §72	1655c
5. Cullyn	Census 74	1659c
6. Cullynn & Bawne	BSD 112	1661
7. (?)Quilen	Sub. Roll Down 277	1663
8. Cullen	Wm. Map (OSNB) E42/100	1810
9. Cullen	Marriage Downshire (OSNB) E42/100	1811
10. Cullen	Reg. Free. (OSNB) E42/100	1829
11. Cullen[?]	Bnd. Sur. (OSNB) E42/100	1830c
12. Cullion	J O'D (OSNB) E42/100	1834c
13. Cuilleann "holly"	OSNB Inf. E42/100	1834c
14. An Cuileann "The holly tree"	Mooney 47	1950c
15. ˈkɔ̣ljən	Local pronunciation	1990

Cullion seems to be derived from *Cuilleann* in Irish, an obsolete word which usually describes "a steep, unbroken slope" in place-names (Ó Máille 1960). There is certainly a hill in this townland although it does not appear to be particularly steep. It may be that the term is generally applied to "an area of high ground" but there is no firm evidence for this. *Cuilleann* has been confused with *cuileann* "holly" in the *OSNB* (13) but the latter, when not in composition with some other element, is normally used in a collective sense in Irish place-names, e.g. *Cuileannach* "place of holly", anglicized Cullenagh in Co. Limerick (Ó Maolfabhail 1990, 147).

Donaghaguy Of uncertain origin
J 1320

1. Agheeghy	CSP Ire. 435	1570
2. Agheeghy	Fiants Eliz. §1609	1570
3. Ballyaghaeigh	CPR Jas. I 395b	1609
4. Ballyaghaeigh	CPR Jas. I 235a	1612
5. Balleaghaeigh	Inq. Ult. (Down) §13 Car. I	1629
6. Balleagheigh	Inq. Ult. (Down) §85 Car. I	1639
7. Aghegey	Hib. Reg. Up. Iveagh	1657c
8. Downagee	Census 74	1659c
9. Ballyaghegey	BSD 111	1661
10. Aghegeight al. Ballyaghegeigh	ASE 107b §9	1666
11. Aghegey	Hib. Del. Down	1672c
12. Aghegeigh al. Balleageigh	Rent Roll Down 9	1692
13. Aghegeight al. Ballyaghegeith	Deeds & Wills (Mooney) 48	1703
14. Donoghagyen	Maps (Mooney) 48	1767
15. Donaghaguy	Map Hall Estates fol. 21	1800
16. Donaghaguy	Wm. Map (OSNB) E42/100	1810
17. Donaghaguy	County Warrant (OSNB) E42/100	1827
18. Donoughaguy	Reg. Free. (OSNB) E42/100	1830
19. Donaghaguy	Bnd. Sur. (OSNB) E42/100	1830c
20. Domhnach a déigh "Church of the Lord or God"	OSNB Inf. E42/100	1834c

21.	Dun Achaidh Mhic Ghaoithe "Fort of Magee's plain"	Mooney 47	1950c
22.	ˌdɔnəxəˈgʲai	Local pronunciation	1990

The difficulty with this townland is in reconciling the modern pronunciation of the name, the local interpretation of it in 1834, and the historical forms. The local pronunciation of the final element resembles that of the English slang-word *guy* (22), but is this pronunciation historically accurate? Some of the earlier forms ending in *-geigh* (10, 12–13), for example, may reflect a similar pronunciation; but taken alongside such terminations as *-ghy* (1–2), *-gey* (7, 11) and *-gee* (8) it is more likely to represent an [i] sound rather than a diphthong [ai]. Oyne McStay's Irish form, *Domhnach a déigh* (20), suggests that we are dealing with a long [e] sound, but whereas this may be reconcilable with transcriptions such as *-geigh* and *-gey* it conflicts with the evidence of *-ghy* and *-gee*. There is also a problem with the initial *d-* of *déigh*, which is irreconcilable with the historical forms, and with the initial element of the name which is transcribed in the *OSNB* as if it were the word *domhnach* "a church". The form *Downagee* in the *Census* of c. 1659 (8) suggests that the first element is more correctly Irish *dún* "a fort" which, combined in unstressed position with the element *áth* "a ford" or *achadh* "a field", might well be misunderstood as *domhnach*. It should be borne in mind that the earliest form of the name is *Agheeghy* (1–2); *down-* or *don-* is not introduced until the middle of the 17th century (8) and did not become established until the second half of the following century (14–19). *Domhnach* "a church" ceased to be employed as a place-name element as early as the 7th century (Flanagan D. 1981–2(c), 70) and we should not expect it to be introduced as a place-name element in the early modern period. On the other hand, a fort is marked in Donaghaguy townland on the modern maps (J 139199) and this may well be the *dún* intended.

Having discussed the latest forms of the name we can now turn to the earliest: *Agheeghy* (1–2) in 1570, *Ballyaghaeigh* (3–6) in four related documents dating to the period 1609–39, *(Bally)Aghegey* (7, 9, 11) in sources dating to the period c. 1657–72, and *Aghegeigh(t) al. Ballyaghegeigh* (10, 12–13) in slightly later documents. In *Agheeghy* there should probably be only one *-e-*; and it is clear from a comparison with the later forms that *-g-* is missing from forms 3–6. If we dismiss the *bally* as a later accretion we have basically three independent forms: *Agheeghy* (recte *Agheghy*), *Aghegey* and *Aghegeigh*. It is interesting that the latter form resembles the modern townland of **Aghagheigh** in the parish of Layd, Co. Antrim. There is a word *gaoth* in Irish which can mean "the sea, a stream, an estuary" (*DIL* sv. *gáeth*), but which O'Donovan translates in a much narrower sense: "a shallow stream into which the tide flows and which is fordable at low water" (*O'Reilly*). *Dinneen* explains it as referring to "an inlet of the sea; a strand-stream left at low water" and states that it is common in Ulster place-names such as *Gaoth Dobhair*, Gweedore in Co. Donegal. This word *gaoth* is particularly common in the place-name *Tóin re/le Gao(i)th* familiar to us as Tanderagee, Tonregee, Tonlegee etc. in various parts of Ireland (see *GÉ* 168). A glance at a list of early anglicizations of *Tóin re/le Gao(i)th* is revealing, for the name is variously spelt *Tonragee, Tonelegey, Tonrageigh* etc. in 17th-century documents (Ó Maolfabhail 1982, 376–8). But if *gaoth* is also the final element in Donaghaguy, to what does it refer? Unlike Aghagheigh in Co. Antrim, Donaghaguy is not situated on the coast, although it is quite close to it. There is a river which flows from a lake in the townland into Carlingford Lough, but it could hardly be described as a *gaoth* as far up stream as Donaghaguy.

There is, however, another possibility suggested by the development of the name Aghagower in Co. Mayo. This name is attested in 17th-century Irish documentation as

Achadh Gabhair but it appears in the earlier language as *Ached Fobuir*. Ó Muraíle explains the *g* in the modern form as deriving from the pronunciation of *-dh* at the end of *achadh*, the following *F-* having disappeared through lenition (Ó Muraíle 1985, 32–33). This being the case, one could argue that *Aghegey* might derive from something like *Achadh Aoidh* in Irish, where *Aoidh* is the gen. form of the personal name *Aodh*. Similar names are *Achadh Conaire*, now Achonry in Co. Sligo, and *Achadh Dubhthaigh*, Aghadowey in Co. Derry; both *Conaire* and *Dubhthach* are also personal names. However, when *dún* is prefixed to *Achadh Aoidh* one might expect some such form as *Dún Achaidh Aoidh* in Irish where *achadh* appears in the gen. after *dún*. The problem here is that the final syllable in *achaidh* would not be realized as a [g] in the anglicized form. One might argue that the nom. form of *achadh* was used for the gen. as is the case in similar constructions in Modern Irish, but one would be surprised if this were the case in the 17th century. The original form of Donaghaguy, therefore, is clearly a matter of some doubt, although it certainly does not derive from either *Domhnach a déigh* (20) or *Dún Achaidh Mhic Ghaoithe* (22) in Irish.

Edentrumly
J 1726

Éadan Tromlaigh
"hill-face abounding in elder-trees"

1. Edentromley	CPR Jas. I 394b	1609
2. Edemtromlie	CPR Jas. I 190a	1611
3. Edem-Tromley	CPR Jas. I 373b	1618
4. Edem Dromley	Hib. Reg. Up. Iveagh	1657c
5. Edentrymby	Census 74	1659c
6. Edentromly	Sub. Roll Down 276	1663
7. Edendromly	Hib. Del. Down	1672c
8. Edentrumly	Wm. Map (OSNB) E42/100	1810
9. Edentrumly	Tombstone (OSNB) E42/100	1826
10. Edentrumley	Bnd. Sur. (OSNB) E42/100	1830c
11. Edentrumly	J O'D (OSNB) E42/100	1834c
12. Eadan a tromluídhe "Brow of the drying"	OSNB Inf. E42/100	1834c
13. Éadan (d)Tromlach "Hill-brow of the elder-trees"	Mooney 49	1950c
14. Eadan dromchlaidh	Mooney 49	1950c
15. 'e:dn'trọmli	Local pronunciation	1990
16. 'i:dn'trọmli	Local pronunciation	1990

The anglicized forms of this place-name are very consistent with the exception of *Edem Dromley* (4) and *Edendromly* (7) on Petty's maps. However, the majority of forms suggest that the second element begins with *t-*, not *d-*, in which case *Eadan dromchlaidh* (14) can be dismissed. One can also dismiss *Éadan (d)Tromlach* (13) where *Mooney* seems to suggest that *éadan* may be an old acc. form. causing eclipsis of the following noun. Nevertheless, the second element certainly seems to be *tromlach* in Irish, which is comprised of the noun *trom* "an elder tree" plus the collective suffix *-lach*. One would expect the gen. sing. form after *éadan* and a postulated form *Éadan Tromlaigh* is certainly in agreement with the historical forms. The *OSNB* form *Eadan a tromluídhe* (12) is possibly either a misinterpretation or a mistranscription of *Éadan Tromlaigh*, although the presence of *a* may be an indication that the definite article had been introduced.

77

Lurgancanty
J 1623

Lorgain Uí Cháinte
"ó *Cáinte*'s long low ridge"

1. Levallylurgancanty	CPR Jas. I 395b	1609
2. Levallylurganchantie	CPR Jas. I 235a	1612
3. Levallylurgancanty	Inq. Ult. (Down) §13 Car. I	1629
4. Largecanty	Hib. Reg. Up. Iveagh	1657c
5. Lorgancantie	BSD 112	1661
6. Lurganhanty al. Lorgacantie	ASE 91a §4	1667
7. Largecanty	Hib. Del. Down	1672c
8. Lurgahunty al. Lurgacanty	Rent Roll Down 8	1692
9. Lurgahunty	Deeds & Wills (Mooney) 49	(?)
10. Lurgancanty	Wm. Map (OSNB) E42/100	1810
11. Lurganecanthy	Atkinson's Tour (OSNB) E42/100	1823
12. Lurgancanty	Reg. Free. (OSNB) E42/100	1829
13. Lurgancanty	Bnd. Sur. (OSNB) E42/100	1830c
14. Lurgan Ui Chainte "O'Canty's long hill"	OSNB Inf. E42/100	1834c
15. Lurgan-Ui-Chainte "O'Canty's long hill"	Joyce iii 492	1913
16. Leargán Uí Cháinte "Canty's height; hill-slope"	Mooney 49	1950c
17. ˌlorgənˈkʲanti	Local pronunciation	1990

McStay's Irish form of this place-name has been recorded as *Lurgan Uí Chainte* "O'Canty's long hill" (14) in the *OSNB*. This interpretation of the second element has been accepted by both *Joyce* (15) and *Mooney* (16) but there is no conclusive evidence in the historical forms to support it. One could argue that spellings such as *Levallylurganchantie* (2) and *Lurganhanty* (6) indicate that the *c-* of the final element was lenited as in *Lurgan Uí Chainte*. However, the lenition could more easily be explained as indicating that the preceding word *lorgain* is dat. as in *Lorgain Cháinte* "long low ridge of the satirist". As against that, a transparent form such as *Lorgain Cháinte* is unlikely to have been misinterpreted by local Irish speakers as deriving from a surname which appears to be otherwise unattested.

The surname *Ó an Cháintigh(e)*, anglicized Canty, is attested in Cos Cork, Kerry and Limerick (MacLysaght 1982, 49; 1985, 36). However, there is no trace of the article *an* in McStay's form which is probably of different origin. MacLysaght (1982, 49) notes that a surname Canty is recorded in a survey of Armagh dating to 1618 and this may be the name which is preserved here. Oyne McStay's form has been transcribed as *Ó Cainte* in the *OSNB* but the *-a-* is probably long as in the noun *cáinte*. As regards the first element of the name, it is undoubtedly derived from *lorgain* in Irish, an oblique form of *lorga* "shin" which is applied to "a long low ridge, or to a long stripe of land" in place-names (*Joyce* i 527; Ó Maolfabhail 1987–8, 20).

Mayo
J 1526

Maigh Eo
"plain of the yew tree(s)"

1. Ballymoysh	CPR Jas. I 394b	1609
2. Ballymoyoh	CPR Jas. I 190a	1611
3. Ballymoyrogh	Deeds & Wills (Mooney) 49	1618

4. Ballymayogh	Inq. Ult. (Down) §51 Car. I	1635
5. Moyo	Census 74	1659c
6. Mayo	Wm. Map (OSNB) E42/100	1810
7. Mayo	Reg. Free. (OSNB) E42/100	1829
8. Mayo	Bnd. Sur. (OSNB) E42/100	1830c
9. Maigh Eo "plain of the yew"	OSNB Inf. E42/100	1834c
10. Maigh Eo	Mooney 49	1950c
11. mi'jo:	Local pronunciation	1990

Mayo is undoubtedly derived from *Maigh Eo* in Irish. Not only are the anglicized forms consistent with that view, but the village of **Mayobridge**, which takes its name from the townland, was known as *Droichead Mhaigh Eo* to Irish speakers in Omeath at the beginning of the century. The word *eo* "a yew tree" is now obsolete, but in the early language it was normally *i* in the gen. sing. and *eó* in the gen. pl. (*DIL*). In the modern language, however, it came to be declined as *eo* in both the gen. sing. and pl. and it is interpreted as sing. in the *OSNB* (9). Nevertheless, as place-names are often of great antiquity, *eo* is quite possibly pl. in this instance. This is almost certainly true of Co. Mayo which is also derived from *Maigh Eo* in Irish and is attested in Irish documentation as far back as the 8th century (Ó Muraíle 1985, 5–6, 72–5). Mayo is also a townland name in Cos Cavan, Leitrim and Laois (*Census* 1871) where it is quite likely to be of similar origin.

Milltown	*Baile an Mhuilinn*	
J 1324	"townland of the mill"	
1. Milton	CPR Jas. I 394b	1609
2. Miltown	CPR Jas. I 195b	1610
3. Milto(w)ne	CPR Jas. I 190a	1611
4. Miltowne	CPR Jas. I 194b	1611
5. Milltowne	Deeds & Wills (Mooney) 49	1618
6. Miltowne	Inq. Ult. (Down) §45 Car. I	1633
7. Milton	Inq. Ult. (Down) §51 Car. I	1635
8. Ballinvoline	Civ. Surv. x §72	1655c
9. Milbowne	Census 74	1659c
10. Ballywillin	Maps (Mooney) 49	1762
11. Milltown	Wm. Map (OSNB) E42/100	1810
12. Milltown	Educ. Rept. (OSNB) E42/100	1826
13. Milltown	County Warrant (OSNB) E42/100	1830
14. Milltown	J O'D (OSNB) E42/100	1834c
15. Baile mhuillinn "Town of the mill"	OSNB Inf. E42/100	1834c
16. 'mɪltəun	Local pronunciation	1990

Although it is clear that this townland was known as *Baile an Mhuilinn* in Irish (8, 10, 15) it is normally the English form that appears in the sources. It is possible that the name may have been originally coined in English but, as Clonallan does not appear to have been an area of significant Norman or early English influence, it may simply be a case of a transparent Irish name being recorded in translation in the early sources. Milltown is a common townland name throughout Ireland (*Census* 1871), but the anglicized form is also attested as in Ballymullen, Irish *Baile an Mhuilinn*, in Co. Kerry (*GÉ* 186).

| **Tamnaharry** | *Tamhnach an Choirthe (?)* | |
| J 1424 | "clearing/grassy upland of the (memorial) stone" | |

1. Tawnkaghharree	CPR Jas. I 394b	1609
2. Tawnagh-Harrie	CPR Jas. I 190a	1611
3. Tawnagh-harry	Deeds & Wills (Mooney) 52	1618
4. Tawnaghcharry, ½ vil´ & ter´ de	Inq. Ult. (Down) §45 Car. I	1633
5. Tawnagharee	Inq. Ult. (Down) §51 Car. I	1635
6. Tamnaharry	Wm. Map (OSNB) E42/100	1810
7. Tamnaharry	County Warrant (OSNB) E42/100	1831
8. Tamnaharry	J O'D (OSNB) E42/100	1834c
9. Tamhna-harry "Harry's Field"	OSNB Inf. E42/100	1834c
10. Tamhna harraidhe	OSNB E42/100	1834c
11. Tamhnach a´ chairthe	Mooney 51	1950c
12. ˌtɑmnəˈhɑri	Local pronunciation	1990
a. Tawnaghenrie	CSP Ire. 435	1570
b. Tawnaghenry	Fiants Eliz. §1609	1570
c. Tannaghhenrie	CPR Jas. I 395b	1609
d. Tawnaghenrie ½ townland	CPR Jas. I 235a	1612
e. Levallytawnaghhenry	Inq. Ult. (Down) §13 Car. I	1629
f. Tawnahenry	Hib. Reg. Up. Iveagh	1657c
g. Tawnahenry	BSD 112	1661
h. Townahenry	ASE 107b §9	1666
i. Taunahenery	Hib. Del. Down	1672c
j. Dromgehenry	Rent Roll Down 9	1692
k. Tavnahenry	Deeds & Wills (Mooney) 51	1712
l. Tunaherry	Deeds & Wills (Mooney) 52	(?)
m. Tamhnach Annraoi	Mooney 51	1950c

The history of Tamnaharry is quite complicated in that two similar names *Tawnkaghharree* (1) and *Tawnaghenrie* (a) are recorded in the early sources. When one considers that the personal name Harry is a pet form of the name Henry one can see why Mooney believed that both these names might possibly refer to one and the same place. However, *Tawnaghhenrie* is always located in the old district called the *Legan* in the early grants and inquisitions whereas *Tawnkaghharree* is said to be in *Clanawly* (see p. 51). Both places are sometimes termed half-townlands in 17th-century documents. *Tawnaghenrie* seems to refer to a small part of modern Donaghaguy and may for that reason have been considered a *leathbhaile* or "half-town". Tamnaharry, on the other hand, appears to have been divided in two just like **Bavan**. It had been acquired by Edward Trevor in 1618 but, in an inquisition dating to 1633, half of it appears to have been alienated by Hugh McCon Magennis to Dudley Garvey of Newry which suggests that Trevor had only purchased part of it in 1618.

The correct derivation of both Tamnaharry and *Tawnaghenrie* is still a problem. The latter looks as if it derives from the Irish *Tamhnach Énrí* "Henry's grassy upland or field". However, if this is correct, then the *OSNB* interpretation of Tamnaharry as "Harry's field" (9) can hardly be accurate as we should not expect two similarly named places within the one small parish. It is possible that *Tawnaghenry* does not derive from *Tamhnach Énrí* at all; Mooney refers to Donaghenry in Tyrone which appears to be *Domhnach Fhainre* in Irish (see *Onom. Goed.* 350). If this is the case then Tamnaharry may derive from *Tamhnach Énrí* in Irish but, nevertheless, Mooney's interpretation *Tamhnach a´ chairthe* "green field of the (memorial) stone" (11) may be preferable, particularly as there is a standing stone in the townland known as **Cloghadda**. Whereas the initial element of Tamnaharry is almost certainly *tamhnach* "grassy upland; arable place in a mountain" (*Ó Dónaill*) the second element can not be interpreted conclusively on the basis of the present evidence.

OTHER NAMES

Carlingford Lough
J 2013

Loch Cairlinn
"lake of the *kerling* (hag-shaped rock)"

1. do Shnamh Aighnech	AU (Mac Airt) 310	852
2. de Snam Aignech	AU (Mac Airt) 374	923
3. oc Snam Aignech	AU (Mac Airt) 376	926
4. ic Snam Ergda	Cogadh GG 18	1100c
5. co Snám Aignech	Cogadh GG 224	1100c
6. oc Snam Aignech	Cogadh GG 229	1100c
7. Chuain Snama Ech, Cluain Dallain i fail	CSH 120	1125c
8. Snámha Ech, ó Clúain Dalláin i bfail	Mart. Gorm. Apr. 2 p68n	1170c
9. Cuan Aidhneac[h]	Miscell. Ann. 68	1179
10. Carrlongphort, an	ALC i 250	1213
11. Cairlinne, ar	ALC ii 318	1539
12. Cuan Snamha Aighneach	C. Conghail Cláir. 182	1600c
13. o Cluain (.i. Cluain Dalláin), i bfail Snamha Ech	Mart. Don. Apr. 2 p92	1630c
14. imeall Chairlinn	Mac Cumhaigh (b) 16: 37 p. 109	1760c
15. imeall Cháirlinn na n-iasc	Mac Cumhaigh (b) 19: 34 p. 115	1760c
16. go Cairlinn	Mac Domhnaill 3: 13 p. 31	1835c
17. as Cairlinn	Mac Bionaid 7: 52 et pas.	1840c
18. Loch Cáirlinn	Omeath Infs. 157	1901
19. i gCáirlinn	Sgéalaidhe Óirghiall 85	1905c
20. Cáirlinn	Omeath Infs. 11	1925c
21. Carlingeford, aqua de	Cartae Dun. §8 421	1192c
22. Karlenfordiam, apud	Gir. Cambrensis 93	1200c
23. Kerlingford, aquam de	Pontif. Hib. i §59	1204
24. Kerlingefort, aquam de	Pontif. Hib. i §60	1204
25. Kerlingeford [castle]	CDI §1015	1221
26. Karlyngford	Great Rolls Pipe xxxv 41	1260c
27. Carlyngford	Reg. Sweteman §181	1366
28. Carlyngford	Reg. Sweteman §59	1369

29. Carlynforde	Reg. Sweteman §140	1375
30. Carlingford, castle or town of	CPR Hen. VII ii 443	1506
31. Carlyngford & Cowly, the manors & lordships of	CPR Hen. VII ii 443	1506
32. Carlingford, the castle of	Cal. Carew MSS §70 85	1535
33. Carlynford, the castle of	CPR (Tresham) ii 7	1536c
34. Carlyngford, the castle of	CPR (Tresham) ii 8, 9	1537c
35. Carlingford & Green Castle	CSP Ire. 45	1538
36. Carlingford Castle & Green Castle	CSP Ire. 104	1549
37. Carlingford	CSP Ire. 126	1552
38. Carlingford & Cowleye, the castle & manor of	CSP Ire. 192	1562
39. Carlingford, the Friar-house of	CSP Ire. 192	1562
40. Carlyngford	Mercator's Ire.	1564
41. Carlingford hauen	Goghe's Map	1567
42. Carlynford hauen	Lythe Map	1568c
43. Carlingford hauen	Ulster Map	1570c
44. Carlingforde	Nowel's Ire. (1)	1570c
45. Cralingford	Nowel's Ire. (2)	1570c
46. Carlinforde	Fiants Eliz. §1736	1570c
47. Carlyngford	Ortelius Map	1573
48. Carlingford	Fiants Eliz. §4312	1583c
49. C. Carlinford	Jobson's Ulster (TCD) 16	1590c
50. Carlingforde	Jobson's Ulster (TCD) 17	1590c
51. Carlinford hauen	Hondius' Map	1591
52. Carlyngford hauen	Mercator's Ulst.	1595
53. Carlingford hauen	Mercator's Ire.	1595
54. Hauen of Carlingford	Boazio's Map (BM)	1599
55. Hauen of Carlingforde	Bartlett Maps (Hayes McCoy) i	1602c
56. Carlingforde Hauen	Bartlett Maps (Esch. Co. Map) 1	1603
57. Carlingforde Hauen	Bartlett Maps (Esch. Co. Map) 2	1603
58. Carlingford haven	Speed's Ulster	1610
59. Carlingford haven	Speed's Ireland	1610
60. Carlingford hauen	Mercator's/Hole's Ire.	1610
61. Carlingforde hauen	Norden's Map	1610c
62. Curlingfoard, the sea of	Inq. Down (Reeves 1) 83	1657
63. Carlingfoard, Sea of	Inq. Down (Reeves 2) 89	1657
64. Lake Lir now Loch Carling	MacCana's Itinerary 45	1700c
65. Carlingford Bay	Harris Hist. map	1744
66. Cáirlinn	Post-Sheanchas 41	1905
67. Loch Cairlinn	Éire Thuaidh	1988
68. Loch Cairlinn	GÉ 127	1989
69. ˈkɑrlnfərd	Local pronunciation	1992

The old name for Carlingford Lough was *Snám Aignech* (5). The element *snámh* "sea-channel, ford, swimming-place" is treated in some detail under **Narrow Water**, whereas *aignech* is attested in Old Irish with the meaning "swift, spirited" (*DIL*). *Snám Aignech*, therefore, may be translated "swift sea-channel or ford" or "swift swimming-place". Elsewhere in early Irish documentation the lough is referred to as *(Cuan) Snámh(a) Ech* (7, 8, 13) which Flanagan translates "'bay of the horse-swimming", with reference to a crossing point which could be swum by horses, probably Narrow Water' (Flanagan D. 1978c, 26). In the Irish tale *Caithréim Conghail Cláiringhnigh*, however, this crossing place is referred to specifically as *Fertas Ruire* (*C. Conghail Clár.* 182). *Fertas* has been explained as "a raised bank or ridge of earth or sand, generally of a bar or shallow near the sea-shore or a ford in a river" (*DIL* sv. *fertas*). It is also an element in the Irish name of Belfast: *Béal Feirste* "mouth of the sand-bank". The element *ruire* is more difficult to explain. The word *ruiri* "a king or supreme ruler" can be dismissed here as it is only attested as *ruirech*, never *ruire*, in the gen. sing. There is another word *ruiriud* which is sometimes spelt *ruire*. The adjective *ruirthech* and the noun *ruirthecht* appear to be related to this. The former is explained as "swift, rapid" and the latter is attested as meaning "rapid course, flow" (*DIL*). If this is the word used in *Fertas Ruire* then it ties in quite nicely with the explanation of *Snám Aignech* above. As regards the form *Snam Ergda* (4) the second element appears to be the word *argda* "heroic, valiant" (*DIL*). It is interesting that in one early Irish text the word *aignech* is partially explained by the word *ágmhar*, and that *ághmhar* is similar in meaning to *argda*: "valorous, warlike; dangerous, terrible" (*DIL* sv. *ágmar*). Particularly interesting is the fact that according to MacCana, *Lake Lir* (64) was an old name for Carlingford Lough; and indeed the word *lear* (gen. *lir*) meaning "sea, ocean" (*Dinneen*) well befits it. This word is now obsolete, except in expressions such as *thar lear* "overseas, abroad", but it is familiar to students of early Irish literature and mythology in the name *Manannán mac Lir* "*Manannán* son of *Ler*" who was believed to have been a sea-god. Unfortunately, there appears to be no other record of this old name for Carlingford Lough.

Carlingford itself is a Scandinavian name which is thought to derive from Old Norse *kerling* "hag" and *fjörthr* (later *fjord*) "narrow inlet of the sea between cliffs or steep slopes" (*Longman Dict.* sv. *fiord*). Flanagan suggests that, by extension, *kerling* came to mean "rock shaped like a hag" and that it may have referred to "the three mountain tops, locally called The Three Nuns, frequently used as pilot points on entering the lough." It is interesting, as Flanagan points out, that the Irish word for "a nun" was *caillech* which also came to mean "a hag" (Flanagan D. 1978c, 26). Our earliest surviving form *Carlingeford* (21) is found in a Norman charter dating to c. 1192 and it is quite remarkable that a gaelicized form of this, *An Carrlongphort* (10), is found in the *Annals of Loch Cé* under the year 1213. In later documents, however, the name is gaelicized *Cairlinn/ Cáirlinn* and this is the form which was used by Irish speakers in Omeath at the beginning of this century (18–20).

Mayobridge   *Droichead Mhaigh Eo*
J 1527

1. Droichead Mhuigheó	Omeath Infs. 157	1901
2. Droichead Mhuigheó	Post-Sheanchas 95	1905
3. Droichead Mhaigh Eo	AGBP 118	1969
4. Droichead Mhaigh Eo	Éire Thuaidh	1988
5. Droichead Mhaigh Eo	GÉ 91	1989
6. miˈjoː ˈbrïdʒ	Local pronunciation	1992

See **Mayo**

For full discussion of the following names see *The Place-names of County Down, vol. iii: The Mournes*:

Cloghadda
J 1524

An Chloch Fhada
"the long stone"

Craignamona
J 1424

Creag na Móna
"crag/rock of the bog"

Slieveacarnane
J 1524

Sliabh an Charnáin
"mountain of the little cairn"

PARISH OF DONAGHMORE

The name Donaghmore is derived from the Irish *Domhnach Mór* "large, great church" (see below). The word *domhnach* is a borrowing from Latin *dominicum* and its presence in place-names is traditionally associated with the Patrician mission of the 5th century. The 8th-century *Liber Angeli* (Book of the Angel) states that "any place anywhere that is called *domnach* is ... in special union with bishop Patrick and the see of Armagh" (Flanagan 1981–2(c)) although the impression gained from the place-name evidence in its entirety is that some *domhnach*-names, particularly in the east and south of the country, may well have been independent of, but probably roughly contemporaneous with, the Patrician mission (*ibid.*). The founding of Donaghmore is attributed to both St Mac Erca and St Patrick (*Atkinson's Dromore* 230) and according to a number of medieval sources St Mac Erca was bishop of Donaghmore in the mid-5th century (*CSH* 159, 702.1.2, 722.92 and see *EA* 111–2, 189). No trace of his church remains, however, and the earliest archaeological evidence of an ecclesiastical site here is a stone cross of the 11th–12th century (*ASCD* 291) from which the townland of **Tullynacross** takes its name. In 17th-century documentation, many of the lands in Donaghmore were held of the See of Armagh and the parish seems to have maintained close links with the Primacy (*Cowan's Donaghmore* 55–6).

In early Irish sources, Donaghmore is frequently called *Domhnach Mór Maighe Cobha* "Donaghmore of *Má Cobha*" (1–5) to distinguish it from other ecclesiastical sites of the same name. According to the *Rennes Dindsenchus Má Cobha* "*Cobha*'s plain" was named after *Cobha*, the huntsman of the sons of Míl Espáine who was killed there after making the first trap in Ireland (*Rennes Dinds.* §93). In the *Annals of the Four Masters* we read that the plain of *Má Cobha* was cleared during the reign of Írial Fáidh mac Éireamhóin (*AFM* i 34–36; *Céitinn* ii 116 §xxv) although Cowan objects "with all due respect ... to such eminent authorities" that there were great forests in *Má Cobha* for many centuries after this date (*Cowan's Donaghmore* 5).

The name *Má Cobha* has long fallen out of use and the original extent of the district of that name is unclear but it would seem to have stretched as far north as Dromore for, according to an account of his Life, St Colmán of Dromore was instructed to build his monastery in *Má Cobha* (*in finibus campi Coba*) (*Acta Sanctorum* xxi June 7 p. 26 col.1; cited *EA* 105n). The modern townland of Ballyroney in the parish of Drumballyroney may also have been in *Má Cobha* if the identification of the castle at *Má Cobha* from which the English launched an attack into Tyrone in 1188 (*AFM*) as the site of Ballyroney motte and bailey castle is correct (*UJA* 4 (1941 supplement) 56-57; cited *ASCD*). It has further been suggested (*ASCD* 218–220) that this site was abandoned in the middle of the 13th century in favour of a stone fortress erected in Seafin townland, half a mile to the south-east, and both Irish and English sources inform us that a castle was erected in *Má Cobha* by Maurice Fitzgerald in 1252 (the castle of *Maicoue*, *CDI* §124 (1252); *caislén Mhuighi Cobha*, *AFM* iii 344).

The names of the townlands in the parish of Donaghmore are not recorded anywhere until the early part of the 17th century when they begin to appear in grants made by James I. As we have seen, however, the church of Donaghmore is of great antiquity and it makes its appearance correspondingly early in our ecclesiastical sources. In Irish sources, such as the *Martyrology of Tallaght* and the saints' genealogies, the church is invariably mentioned in connection with the bishop, Mac Erca (*Mart. Tal.* Sep. 17 72; *CGH passim*). In the Ecclesiastical Taxation of 1306 the church of *Donnachmore* is valued at 20 shillings (*EA* 110) and the name crops up time and again in the registers of the various archbishops of Armagh in the 14th and 15th centuries (*Reg. Fleming* §89, *Reg. Swayne* 68, 183, *Reg. Octavian (EA)* 112n, *Reg. Cromer* ii §192, *Reg. Dowdall* §113).

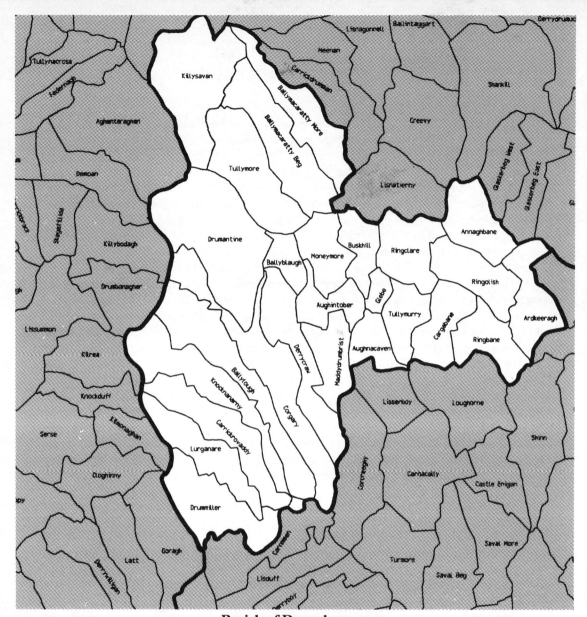

Parish of Donaghmore
Barony of Iveagh Upper, Upper Half

Townlands

Annaghbane	Buskhill	Knocknanarny
Ardkeeragh	Cargabane	Lurganare
Aughintober	Carrickrovaddy	Maddydrumbrist
Aughnacaven	Corgary	Moneymore
Ballyblaugh	Derrycraw	Ringbane
Ballylough	Drumantine	Ringclare
Ballymacaratty Beg	Drummiller	Ringolish
Ballymacaratty More	Glebe	Tullymore
	Killysavan	Tullymurry

Based upon Ordnance Survey 1:50,000 mapping, with permission of the Director of the Ordnance Survey of Northern Ireland, Crown copyright reserved.

In early 17th-century English documents, the townlands in the parish of Donaghmore do not appear together but are granted separately as the two manors of Donaghmore and Clanagan. The 10 townlands of Clanagan were granted to Murtagh McEnaspicke Magenis of *Corgirrie* (Corgary) at a rent of 10 Irish pounds in 1611 (*CPR Jas. I* 190a) and these names, with slight variations, appear again in *CPR Jas. I* 394b-395a. An inquisition taken at Downpatrick on March 30, 1630, (*Inq. Ult.* (Down) §14 Car. I) gives an account of this same grant which diverges from the original only in small details, such as *Corgerry* for earlier *Corgirrie*, and the superior reading *Balleknocknenarny* beside earlier *Balleknocknenarie* and *Balleknocknenary*. There is nothing in the two documents that can lead one to declare a direct relationship between them, although ultimately they are both derived from a single written source with no apparent oral intervention. Thus, for our purposes, they offer only limited assistance. The last document to be considered in this category is an inquisition taken at Newry c. 1650 (*Inq. Ult.* (Down) §106 Car. I). This is clearly independent of the others listed above and shows some later spellings such as *Dromenteane* (Drumantine) for earlier *Ballydromintighan*. In addition, it supplies further information, such as the extent of each of the townlands and the names of the heirs and tenants of each, which is not given in the other documents.

The manor of Donaghmore was created in 1611 when it was granted to Henry Ussher, Archbishop of Armagh, and his successors (*CPR Jas. I* 197a). These 12 townlands are excepted out of a grant made to Arthur Magenis the following year (*CPR Jas. I* 235a–b) and the two lists are clearly related. They give the names in the same order and are identical in all essentials so that the later list is almost certainly a copy of the grant of 1611. A further two documents (grants to Christopher, Archbishop of Armagh) list the townlands in the manor of Donaghmore and they form a distinct group on their own which shows very little correspondence with the earlier grants. The second of these (*CPR Jas. I* 479a) seems to have been compiled from at least two sources, probably including the earlier grant (*CPR Jas. I* 274b). Where the two lists contain the same names the spellings are practically identical but the second adds a number of variants not found in the first, presumably from another source. These additional forms are, of course, of independent value.

The great place-names scholar, John O'Donovan, travelled through Donaghmore in April of 1834 where he discovered a local man, 100 years old, to assist him in ascertaining the original Irish form of the local place-names (*OSL* 48–9). It was with great difficulty and much perseverance that O'Donovan found his informant and several people of whom he asked directions on the way to his house told him that he was dead "many and many a year" (*ibid.* 49). When he did find him he was blind and in a very feeble state and O'Donovan expresses astonishment at his intellectual powers:

> He is intimately acquainted with every field in the Parish of Donaghmore, where he was employed for half a century as a bailiff. He was able to give me the ancient name of every townland in the Parish in the most satisfactory manner... I certainly felt very shy in disturbing him, but as there was no substitute for him, I made bold to examine whether or not he had sufficient discernment to understand what he was about. He understood me immediately, and answered the questions I proposed him with great readiness. (*ibid.*)

He is often not far wrong in his attempts to understand the origins of the local names but, as can only be expected when one does not have access to the historical spellings of the names, he sometimes goes astray. Thus, he suggests an original *Doire Crádh* (standard *Doire Crá*) for **Derrycraw** where the early spellings clearly show an original final -*ch* and *Druim an tSian* (standard *Droim an tSiáin*, angl. **Drumantine**) where the early spellings have an internal *gh*.

Donaghmore *Domhnach Mór*
"large church"

1. o Domnuch Mór Maigi Coba	Mart. Tal. Sep. 17 p72	800c
2. i nDomnuch Mor Maige Coba	CSH 159	1125c
3. o Domnuch Mor in Maige	CSH 702.1.2	1125c
4. o Domnuch Mór Maige Coba	CSH 722.92	1125c
5. Domnaig Móir Maigi Coba, Secht noeb epscoip	Irish Litanies 68	1160c
6. Donnachmore, Ecclesia de	Eccles. Tax. 110	1306c
7. Domnachmore, rectory of St. Archanus of	Reg. Fleming §89	1408
8. Dompnaghmore	Reg. Swayne 68	1427
9. Donaghmore	Reg. Swayne 183	1440
10. Dompnachmor	Reg. Octavian (EA) 112n	1487
11. Donaghmore	Reg. Cromer ii §192	1534
12. Donaghmore, Rector of	Reg. Dowdall §113	1546
13. Donaghmore	CPR Jas. I 197a	1611
14. Donoghmore	CPR Jas. I 274b	1615
15. Donaghmore	CPR Jas. I 479a	1620
16. Donoghmore	Inq. Down (Reeves 1) 97	1657
17. Donnaghmore Parish	Hib. Reg. Up. Iveagh	1657c
18. Donoghmore	Hib. Del. Down	1672c
19. Donaghmore	Wm. Map (OSNB) 60	1810
20. Donaughmore	Bnd. Sur. (OSNB) 60	1830c
21. Don-agh-'more	OSNB 60	1834c
22. Donaghmore	J O'D (OSNB) 60	1834c
23. Domhnach Mór Muighe Cobha	Post-Sheanchas 60	1905
24. Domhnach Mór	AGBP 115	1969
25. ˌdͻnəx'moːr	Local pronunciation	1990

Irish sources clearly show that the name of the parish originates from *Domhnach Mór* "large, great church" (1–5). The loss of the internal *mh* in *domhnach* would be expected to produce a long vowel in the normal course of events and in modern Irish it is pronounced with a long closed *o* [doːnɑx] but as the stress in the name falls on the second element in our name (*mór*) the vowel in the first element has been shortened.

Annaghbane *Eanach Bán*
J 1136 "white bog"

1. Ballen, Ilandbane	CPR Jas. I 395b	1609
2. Balleen-Illanebane	CPR Jas. I 197a	1611
3. Ballen-Ilanbane	CPR Jas. I 235a	1612
4. Anaghbane orse Ilandbane	CPR Jas. I 274b	1615
5. Anaghbane al. Islandbane	CPR Jas. I 479a	1620

6. Anaghban	Hib. Reg. Up. Iveagh	1657c
7. Anaghban	Census 74	1659c
8. Anaghblane	BSD 104	1661
9. Annaghbann	Wm. Little (OSNB) 60	1810
10. Anaghban	Wm. Map (OSNB) 60	1810
11. Anaghbane	County Warrant (OSNB) 60	1827
12. Annaghbane	County Warrant (OSNB) 60	1827
13. Anoughbanne	Bnd. Sur. (OSNB) 60	1830c
14. An-nagh-'bann	OSNB 60	1834c
15. Annaghbane	J O'D (OSNB) 60	1834c
16. Eanach bán "white marsh"	OSNB Inf. 60	1834c
17. Eanach Ban "The white marsh"	Cowan's Donaghmore 41	1914
18. Eanach Bán	Mooney 69	1950c
19. ˌanəˈbɑːn	Local pronunciation	1990

According to the *Ordnance Survey Memoirs* (*OSM* iii 8), there were about 35½ acres of bog-land in Annaghbane in the 1830s and on *Hib. Reg.* Up. Iveagh a large portion of bog marked "Red Bog" appears on the northern boundary of the townland. The implicit opposition between the "Red Bog" and *Eanach Bán* or "white bog" is noteworthy and reveals something of the workings of the naming process.

The Irish element *eanach* "bog, marsh" was sometimes replaced by the English element "island", particularly in the place-names of east Ulster (Ó Mainnín 1989–90, 204–5). The *OSNB* for the parish of Loughgall, Co. Armagh, gives the form *Island McManus* for Annaghmacmanus and notes that "it is generally called 'the island'" (cited *ibid.* 204). In the same parish, the minor name Summer Island seems to derive from the townland in which it is situated, **Annasamry** (*Eanach an tSamhraidh* "summer marsh") and **Lambs Island** in the parish of Donaghcloney, Co. Down, may be similarly derived from the townland name of **Annaghanoon** (*Eanach an Uain* "lamb's marsh") (*ibid.* 204–5).

The majority of examples of *island* superseding earlier *annagh* seem to be no earlier than the beginning of the 19th century but Harris, in his *History of County Down* published in 1744, cites the variant *Islealong* for **Annalong** in Co. Down (*Harris Hist.* 140, 143) and our Annaghbane shows an even earlier alternation between the two elements (nos. 1–5). However, there is clear evidence in this latter instance that the element *island* is being used to translate Irish *oileán* "island" rather than *eanach*. Orthographically, there cannot be much difference between 17th-century English spellings of "island" and attempts to represent the Irish word *oileán* [iľ´an] but the former might be said to be characterized by the presence of either *d* as in *Iland* (1, 4) or *s* as in *Islan(d)* (5). However, scribes frequently tended to rationalize names which they could not understand to approximate to some more familiar English word(s) and the anglicized forms of Irish *oileán* must have been particularly prone to this tendency. This seems to have happened here for the earliest forms surely represent Irish *oileán*. Bilingual composition is extremely rare in Irish place-names so that we should not expect to find names composed of *island* plus an Irish adjective as would be the case here. The majority of names which appear to be bilingual are, in fact, late compounds formed by adding an English element to a pre-existent Irish name (e.g. **Bernish Rock** from Irish *Bearnas* "a gap" + English "rock"), or rationalizations of Irish names. **Ballycastle** in Co. Antrim, for example, goes back to Irish *Baile an Chaistil* (*GÉ* 182) and **Loughinisland** in Co. Down comes from *Loch an Oileáin* (*GÉ* 248). Moreover, the three earliest forms for Annaghbane are prefixed by an element *Balle(e)n-* which represents Irish *Baile an* "the townland of the..." and although *Bally et var.* is sometimes spuriously prefixed to Irish place-names in English documents the presence of the article *an* here clearly suggests that this particular instance is genuine. Thus, we may safely propose *Baile an Oileáin Bháin* "the townland of the white island" as an alternative, or possibly earlier, form of the name.

Ardkeeragh
J 1335

Ard Caorach
"hill of the sheep"

1.	Ballyardkeragh	CPR Jas. I 395b	1609
2.	Ballyardkeragh	CPR Jas. I 197a	1611
3.	Ballyardkeragh	CPR Jas. I 235a	1612
4.	Ardkyragh	CPR Jas. I 274b	1615
5.	Ardkyragh	CPR Jas. I 479a	1620
6.	Ardkiregh	Civ. Surv. x §72	1655c
7.	Ardkeragh	Hib. Reg. Up. Iveagh	1657c
8.	Ardkyragh	BSD 104	1661
9.	Ardkera	Hib. Del. Down	1672c
10.	Ardkeeragh	Wm. Map (OSNB) 60	1810
11.	Ardkeragh	Bnd. Sur. (OSNB) 60	1830c
12.	Ard-'ke-ragh	OSNB 60	1834c
13.	Ardkeeragh	J O'D (OSNB) 60	1834c
14.	Ard caorach "Sheep Hill"	OSNB Inf. 60	1834c
15.	Ard caorach "Sheep Hill"	J O'D (OSNB) 60	1834c
16.	Ard Caoragh "The hill of the sheep"	Cowan's Donaghmore 41	1914
17.	Ard Caorach	Mooney 69	1950c
18.	ˌarˈkiːrə	Local pronunciation	1990

There is no distinction in Irish, as in English, between the gen. sing. and pl. forms of *caora* "sheep" but we can probably assume that the pl. was originally intended.

Aughintober
J 0935

Achadh an Tobair
"field of the well"

1.	(?)Ballitullvar	CPR Jas. I 395b	1609
2.	(?)Ballytullyvar	CPR Jas. I 197a	1611
3.	(?)Ballytullyvar	CPR Jas. I 197b	1611
4.	(?)Ballytullyvar	CPR Jas. I 235b	1612
5.	(?)Tollyvare	CPR Jas. I 274b	1615
6.	(?)Tallysoare	CPR Jas. I 479a	1620
7.	(?)Tullymore	Hib. Reg. Up. Iveagh	1657c
8.	Aghantubber al. Aghantober	Deed (Cowan's Donaghmore) 62	1769
9.	Aughintuber	Wm. Little (OSNB) 60	1810
10.	Aughintuber	Bnd. Sur. (OSNB) 60	1830c
11.	Ahantobber	County Warrant (OSNB) 60	1831
12.	Augh-in-'tub-er	OSNB 60	1834c
13.	Aughintober	J O'D (OSNB) 60	1834c
14.	Ath an tobair	OSNB Inf. 60	1834c

15. Ath an tobair		
"ford of the well or spring"	J O'D (OSNB) 60	1834c
16. Achadh an Tobair	J O'D (OSNB) E42 no. 100	1834c
17. Achadh an Tobair		
"The field of the well"	Cowan's Donaghmore 41	1914
18. Achadh an Tobair	Mooney 69	1950c
19. ˌɑxənˈtoːbər	Local pronunciation	1990

Aughintober once had a celebrated spa well (*Cowan's Donaghmore* 41) and it is probably from this that the townland derives its current name *Achadh an Tobair* "the field of the well". The *OSNB* informant, followed by O'Donovan, suggests that the first element is *Áth* "ford" (14–15). The letters *gh* in anglicized spellings usually stand for Irish *ch*, originally pronounced [x], but in Ulster and north Meath, this was pronounced faintly in medial and final position and tends to be reduced to [h], so that it was easily confused with Irish *th* (O'Rahilly 1932, 210). Thus, **Aghanloo** in Co. Derry derives from Irish *Áth Lú* and **Aghory** in Co. Armagh goes back to *Áth Órai* (*GÉ* 173–4). Nevertheless, the close proximity of Aughintober to the townland of **Aughnacaven** would seem to indicate an original Irish *Achadh an Tobair*.

    The name Aughintober is of relatively late occurrence in our sources and it seems that the townland was formerly known as *Ballytullyvar* or *Tullyvar et var.* (1–7). The order of names in some early lists frequently follows the geographical layout of the land fairly closely, usually proceeding in an anti-clockwise direction. The name *Tullyvar* and its variants normally appear in our sources sandwiched between Moneymore, which lies to the north, and Aughnacaven, which adjoins it on the south, so that it is almost certainly the same place as the modern Aughintober. This is confirmed somewhat by the appearance of the (misspelt) form *Tullymore* on the map of Upper Iveagh in Petty's *Hib. Reg.* bounded on the north by *Moneymore* and on the south by *Monneydrombrest*. The forms (1–7) clearly suggest a first element *tulach* "hill, mound" (assuming, of course, that the *bally-* is not original) and we might tentatively suggest an original *Tulach Bhairr* "mound of the top" or, if we take the gen. as adjectival, "the upper mound", but this is by no means certain.

Aughnacaven

J 1034

Achadh Cabhán

"the field of the hollows"

1. Ballyaghacavan	CPR Jas. I 395b	1609
2. Ballyaghacavan	CPR Jas. I 235a	1612
3. (?)Aghathowen	CPR Jas. I 274b	1615
4. Aghacawen	CPR Jas. I 479a	1620
5. Aghecavan	Civ. Surv. x §72	1655c
6. Aghacavan	Hib. Reg. Up. Iveagh	1657c
7. Aghy Cauin ½ Towne	Census 74	1659c
8. Aghcaran	BSD 104	1661
9. Aghagevan	Hib. Del. Down	1672c
10. Aghacowen	Wm. Map (OSNB) 60	1810
11. Aughnacavan	Newry Tel. (OSNB) 60	1830
12. Augnacaven	Bnd. Sur. (OSNB) 60	1830c
13. 'Augh-na-'cav-an	OSNB 60	1834c
14. Aughnacaven	Wm. Little (OSNB) 60	1834c
15. Aughnacavan	J O'D (OSNB) 60	1834c

16. Achadh na ccabhán		
"field of the round dry hills"	J O'D (OSNB) 60	1834c
17. Achadh a Cabhain		
"The field of the hollow"	Cowan's Donaghmore 41	1914
18. Achadh a(n) Chabháin	Mooney 69	1950c
19. ˌaxnəˈkʲavən	Local pronunciation	1990

The element *cabhán* in this name is somewhat ambiguous and it could equally well be either singular or plural, although the plural is perhaps more likely given the later appearance of the plural article (*na*). It was probably this intrusion of the article, adding an extra syllable, which caused the final syllable in *achadh* to be elided.

Ballyblaugh	*Baile Bláthach* (?)	
J 0835	"townland abounding in flowers"	
1. Ballyblagh	CPR Jas. I 395a	1609
2. Ballyblagh	CPR Jas. I 190a	1611
3. Ballebleaghe	Inq. Ult. (Down) §14 Car. I	1630
4. Balleblagh	Inq. Ult. (Down) §106 Car. I	1650c
5. Ballebleagh	Inq. Ult. (Down) §106 Car. I	1650c
6. Ballyblegg	Census 74	1659c
7. Ballybleagh	ASE 112a §37	1667
8. Balybleagh	Rent Roll Down 12	1692
9. Ballyblaugh	Wm. Map (OSNB) 60	1810
10. Ballyblagh	County Warrant (OSNB) 60	1827
11. Ballyblough	Bnd. Sur. (OSNB) 60	1830c
12. Bal-ly-'blough	OSNB 60	1834c
13. Ballyblaugh	J O'D (OSNB) 60	1834c
14. Baile bládhach "noisy, talkative"	OSNB Inf. 60	1834c
15. Baile Blathach		
"The town of flowers"	Cowan's Donaghmore 41	1914
16. Baile bláchach	Mooney 71	1950c
17. ˌbaliˈblɔː	Local pronunciation	1990

According to the *OSNB*, the townland of **Ballyblagh** in Co. Tyrone derives its name from the Irish *Baile Blathach* meaning either "flowery town[land]" or "[townland] of the butter-milk" (*OSNB* Tyrone D23/39). The latter suggestion is perhaps not as fanciful as it might at first appear for this element occurs in a number of other place-names. Portnablagh (otherwise Portnablahy) in Co. Donegal comes from the Irish *Port na Bláiche* "port of the buttermilk" (*GÉ* 262) and *Caislén na Blathaighe* in Co. Wexford is now called Buttermilk Castle (*Onom. Goed.* sv. *Sliab Blathaige*), but the normal gen. sing. *bláiche* is somewhat at variance with the current pronunciation and with the written forms, although we may note the anglicization of the Donegal *Port na Bláiche* as Portnablagh.

Joyce suggests as a general rule that the second element in names such as Ballyblaugh comes from the Irish *bláthach* meaning "flowery" (ii 308–9) and there is nothing in the present evidence to contradict such an origin for our Ballyblaugh. Intervocalic *th*, having in-itially become [h], became much weakened in the Irish of east Ulster and eventually disappeared altogether, and this may explain its apparent absence from the forms listed above (cf. **Benagh**, Newry). However, its presence is still felt in a few names in Ulster where original -*atha* has come to be pronounced [ɔ:]. The name **Drumcaw**, Co. Down, for example, appears to derive from *Droim Catha*, and the name of the parish of **Ardstraw** in Co. Derry is attested in Irish documents as *Ard Sratha* (gen. sing. of *srath*). This also seems to be the case in the name Ballyblaugh, although we must add that the final *ch* has since also disappeared.

Ballylough	*Baile an Locha*	
J 0833	"townland of the lake"	
1. Balleenlalogh	CPR Jas. I 394b	1609
2. Ballenlogh	CPR Jas. I 190a	1611
3. (?)Ballylaghnan	CPR Jas. I 190b	1611
4. Ballenloghe	Inq. Ult. (Down) §14 Car. I	1630
5. Ballenlagh	Inq. Ult. (Down) §85 Car. I	1639
6. Ballinlogh	Wars Co. Down 79	1641
7. Ballenlagh	Inq. Ult. (Down) §106 Car. I	1650c
8. Ballylogh halfe towne	Census 74	1659c
9. Ballinlough	ASE 112a §37	1667
10. (?)Ballyloghaninis	Rent Roll Down 11	1692
11. Ballinlogh	Rent Roll Down 12	1692
12. Ballylough	Wm. Map (OSNB) 60	1810
13. Ballylough	Bnd. Sur. (OSNB) 60	1830c
14. Bal-ly-'lough	OSNB 60	1834c
15. Baile an locha "town of the lough"	OSNB Inf. 60	1834c
16. Baile an Lacha	J O'D (OSNB) 60	1834c
17. Baile an Locha "The town of the lake"	Cowan's Donaghmore 41	1914
18. Baile an Locha	Mooney 71	1950c
19. ˌbalˈlɔx	Local pronunciation	1990

The earliest forms with internal *n* clearly indicate the presence of the article *an* (1-2, 4-7, 9, 11). The variant spellings with *a* instead of *o* in the final element in some of the early sources (3, 5, 7), if they are not mere scribal errors, may reflect the variant form *lach* which was not uncommon in early Irish (see *DIL* sv. *1 loch*).

Ballymacaratty Beg	*Baile Mhic an Reachtaí Beag*
J 0837	"McRatty's townland, little"

Ballymacaratty More	*Baile Mhic an Reachtaí Mór*	
J 0937	"McRatty's townland, great"	
1. Ballyvickenrattie	CPR Jas. I 396a	1609
2. Ballyvickenratty	CPR Jas. I 235a	1612
3. Ballyvickenrattye	CPR Jas. I 235a	1612
4. BallymcEnratty	CPR Jas. I 305a	1616
5. Ballymacinratty	Inq. Ult. (Down) §85 Car. I	1639

6. Ballimackillrattybeg	Hib. Reg. Up. Iveagh	1657c
7. Ballimckillrattymore	Hib. Reg. Up. Iveagh	1657c
8. Ballyharnetty begg	Census 74	1659c
9. Ballyharnaty mor	Census 74	1659c
10. Ballynacraghtybegg	BSD 104	1661
11. B:mcKilrattibeg	Hib. Del. Down	1672c
12. Ballymcrattybegg	ASE 274a §29	1681
13. Ballymcrattimore	ASE 273a §29	1681
14. Bally McRattybegg	Rent Roll Down 11	1692
15. Bally McRattymore	Rent Roll Down 10	1692
16. Ballymacarettybeg	Wm. Map (OSNB) 60	1810
17. Ballymacarettymore	Wm. Map (OSNB) 60	1810
18. Ballymacaratteybeg	Bnd. Sur. (OSNB) 60	1830c
19. Ballymacaratteymore	Bnd. Sur. (OSNB) 60	1830c
20. Bal-ly-'mac-a-'rat-ty	OSNB 60	1834c
21. Bal-ly-'mac-a-'rat-ty-more	OSNB 60	1834c
22. Ballymacaratty-beg	J O'D (OSNB) 60	1834c
23. Ballymacaratty-more	J O'D (OSNB) 60	1834c
24. Baile mic Aireachtaigh		
"Macaratty town"	J O'D (OSNB) 60	1834c
25. Baile Mac Ionnreachtaigh Beag	Cowan's Donaghmore 41	1914
26. Baile Mac Ionnreachtaigh Mor	Cowan's Donaghmore 42	1914
27. Baile mhic an Reachtaidhe	Mooney 71	1950c
28. 'bɑlimɑkə'rɑti'moːr	Local pronunciation	1990

The townlands of Ballymacaratty Beg and Ballymacaratty More formed a single townland known as Ballymacaratty up until the mid 17th-century when the current division first appears (6–7). Cowan notes that, ironically, Ballymacaratty Beg is presently larger than Ballymacaratty More (*Cowan's Donaghmore* 42) and explains that the townland of Carrickdrummond in Aghaderg was formerly a portion of Ballymacaratty More (*ibid.* 42n). This is confirmed by the fact that the name **Carrickdrummond** does not occur in our records before 1747, approximately 100 years after the division of Ballymacaratty into two parts.

The name McEnrattie is attested in Co. Down in the early 17th century (*CPR Jas. I* 320b) and this would seem to represent the surname element in Ballymacaratty. Cowan suggests that this element derives from *Mac Ionnreachtaigh* (recte *Mac Ionrachtaigh*), anglicized Enright, the name of a family which lived in Co. Armagh (*Cowan's Donaghmore* 41–42). However, the stress in the townland-name falls on the penultimate syllable suggesting an Irish name something like *Mac an Reachtai*. This is supported by the name **Tullymacarath** in the parish of Dromore which clearly contains the same surname as we find in Ballymacaratty. In this name the stress falls on the final syllable giving the same stress pattern as we find in Ballymacaratty. It is further supported by the appearance of a certain James m'Ratty of Croreagh, Newry in *Sub. Roll Down* (p.280). This cannot be the name *Mac Ionrachtaigh*, as the initial *Ion-* would not be reduced under stress, but could very well represent something like *Mac an Reachtai* where the article, being in a position of weak stress, is liable to reduction.

The name *Mac an Reachtai* is unattested in any of the modern works on surnames but, as these are limited in their extent, this should hardly come as a surprise. There is ample evidence, both in the townland names of Ballymacaratty and **Tullymacarath** and in the spellings McEnrattie and M'Ratty cited above (although, it is true, the former may represent *Mac Ionrachtaigh*) to postulate a lost surname *Mac an Reachtaí*. A *reachtaidh* (O.Ir. *rechtaid*) was a member of the legal class, perhaps a judge (*DIL* sv. *rechtaid*) and names formed from the element *mac* + the article *an* + word signifying occupation, such as *Mac an Airchinnigh* (MacEnerney), *Mac an Bhaird* (MacAward) and *Mac an Bhreithiún* (McEvrehon), are relatively common in Irish nomenclature (see Woulfe 1923, 308-319).

Buskhill	*An Bhascoill* (?)	
J 1036	"round wood"	
1. Ballinebaskillye	CPR Jas. I 395b	1609
2. Ballinebaskilly	CPR Jas. I 197a	1611
3. Ballynebaskely	CPR Jas. I 235a	1612
4. Boskill otherwise Vaskill	CPR Jas. I 274b	1615
5. Boskyll al. Vaskyll	CPR Jas. I 479a	1620
6. Rosskill	BSD 104	1661
7. Boskill	Wm. Map (OSNB) 60	1810
8. Buskhill	Bnd. Sur. (OSNB) 60	1830c
9. 'Busk-ill	OSNB 60	1834c
10. Baile na Bascaille "The town of the hind or deer"	Cowan's Donaghmore 42	1914
11. 'bos'kɪl	Local pronunciation	1990

Cowan (10) suggests that this name goes back to *Baile na Bascaille* "the townland of the hind, deer" but this explanation is not without difficulties. As early as the 17th century we find forms without the *baile* element but it is extremely unlikely that a simple animal name could stand on its own as a place-name. In addition, the stress in *bascall* would fall on the first element whereas the current pronunciation shows even stress, suggesting that we may be dealing with a loose compound although it is quite possible that the stress shifted by analogy with names in English ending in "hill" (cf. **Forkhill** from Irish *oirceall*).

What appears to be the same name is found in the Co. Limerick townland of Boskill for which the Place-names Office in Dublin supplies a transliterated form *Boscail* (Ó Maolfabhail 1990, 72). The historical forms are similar to those for our townland of Buskhill save that they show no trace of the element *baile* (thus further weakening Cowan's suggestion). The same element seems to lie behind the name of the townland of Baskill in the parish of Culdaff, Co. Donegal, and may also be contained in the names of Ballyvoskillakeen in the parish of Kilcrumper and Ballyvouskill in the parish of Drishane, Co. Cork. We might tentatively suggest an original Irish form *Baschoill* from *bas* "hand" and *coill* "wood". While this etymology is consistent with the forms for the townlands in Limerick, Donegal and Down it does not provide very good sense. Dinneen gives the definition "anything flat" for *bas* but in his actual examples it is applied more specifically to small objects such as "the blade of an oar, a hurley" etc. In compounds its sense is invariably "hand, paw" etc. and this can hardly be the meaning in the place-name. Moreover, there is no evidence of the use of *bas* in place-names. The most likely derivation is, perhaps, from *basc*, which, although not widely attested, appears to have had the meaning "round, circular" (*DIL* sv. *2basc*), and *coill* "a wood". The compounding of the final *c* in *basc* with the initial *c* of *coill* would cause the latter to be delenited (*GOI* 86).

Cargabane
J 1134

An Charraigeach Bhán
"the white rocky place"

1.	Ballencarraghbane	CPR Jas. I 395b	1609
2.	Balleenecarraghebane	CPR Jas. I 197a	1611
3.	Ballencarraghbane	CPR Jas. I 235a	1612
4.	Cargeaghbane	CPR Jas. I 274b	1615
5.	Cargeabane al. Barrencarraghibane	CPR Jas. I 479a	1620
6.	Carraghbann	Hib. Reg. Up. Iveagh	1657c
7.	Cargaghban	Census 75	1659c
8.	Carraghbane	BSD 104	1661
9.	Cargaban	Wm. Map (OSNB) 60	1810
10.	Cargabawn	Newry Tel. (OSNB) 60	1830
11.	Carigbanne	Bnd. Sur. (OSNB) 60	1830c
12.	Car-rig-'bawn	OSNB 60	1834c
13.	Cargabane	J O'D (OSNB) 60	1834c
14.	Cairgeacha bana "white rocks"	OSNB Inf. 60	1834c
15.	An Cairgeach Bán	Post-Sheanchas 94	1905
16.	Cairgeach Ban "The white rocky place"	Cowan's Donaghmore 42	1914
17.	An Carraigeach, Carrach bán "The white rocky place = white rocks"	Mooney 73	1950c
18.	ˌkʲargəˈbaːn	Local pronunciation	1990

The first element in this name would seem to be *carraigeach*, an adjective derived from *carraig* and used substantively in the sense "a rocky place". The anglicized spellings seem to represent a syncopated form of the word (*cairr'geach < carraigeach*) (4–5, 7, 9–10, 13) and many of the forms show a loss of the internal *-g-* which is a relatively common development in names containing this element (1–3, 5b, 6, 8). For further discussion of this element see **Carrigenagh** in Kilkeel.

Carrickrovaddy
J 0632

Carraig Chró Mhadaidh (?)
"rock of the dog's shelter"

1.	Ballycarrickrovade	CPR Jas. I 395a	1609
2.	Ballycarrickrovade	CPR Jas. I 190a	1611
3.	Ballecarrickrovadde	Inq. Ult. (Down) §14 Car.I	1630
4.	Cargaghravaddy	Inq. Ult. (Down) §106 Car.I	1650c
5.	Corgaghravaddy	Inq. Ult. (Down) §106 Car.I	1650c
6.	Cargaghy, the halfe towne of	Census 74	1659c
7.	Carrickkerovadie	ASE 112a §37	1667
8.	Carrickrovaddy	Rent Roll Down 13	1692
9.	Carrickrovady	Wm. Map (OSNB) 60	1810
10.	Carrickrovady	Bnd. Sur. (OSNB) 60	1830c
11.	'Car-rick-ro-'vad-dy	OSNB 60	1834c
12.	Carrickrovaddy	J O'D (OSNB) 60	1834c
13.	Carraic a ro mhadaidh "the fox's rock"	OSNB Inf. 60	1834c

14. Carraig ruadh-mhadaidh	J O'D (OSNB) 60	1834c
15. Carraig an mhadaidh ruaidh	J O'D (OSNB) 60	1834c
16. Carraig an tsionaigh	J O'D (OSNB) 60	1834c
17. Carraic Ruadh Mhadaidh		
"The rock of the red dog"	Cowan's Donaghmore 42	1914
18. Carrach, Carraig ruadh-mhadaidh		
"The fox's rock"	Mooney 73	1950c
19. ˌkarəkroˈvɑdi	Local pronunciation	1990
20. ˌkargəˈvɑːdi	Local pronunciation	1990

The majority of the spellings listed above point to a first element *carraig* "rock" (1–3, 7–12). A small number of forms (4–6) may be adduced as evidence of an alternative initial element *cairrgeach* "rocky place" but as these are restricted to only two documents, of which at least one frequently throws up spurious spellings (*Census*), this possibility can be dismissed.

All previous attempts to unravel the meaning of this peculiar name have centred on the hitherto unattested compound *rua-mhadadh* (13–18). The word for fox in Irish is *madadh rua* (literally "red dog"), not *rua-mhadadh*, and in any case the postulated *rua-mhadadh* would produce a name with stress on the ante-penultimate rather than the penultimate syllable such as we find in the name Carrickrovaddy. Of course, this problem of stress could be circumvented if *rua* were taken as an attributive adjective qualifying *carraig* in which case the Irish may be rendered "the dog's red rock". However, the construction noun + adj. + noun in the gen. is rare and in such examples as do exist the noun in the gen. appears to be a noun or a proper name qualifying a name which may otherwise stand on its own, such as *Baile Nua na hArda* (**Newtownards**), *Baile Nua an Chaisil* (Newtown Cashel), *Cnoc Mór na nGaibhlte* (Galtymore Mountain), *Baile Nua Sheandroma* (Newtownshandrum), and *Domhnach Mór Maighe Cobha* (**Donaghmore**).

A number of other possibilities suggest themselves but no single etymology can be confidently proposed. The initial and final elements can be safely identified as *carraig* "rock" and *m(h)adaidh*, gen. sing. of *madadh* "dog, wolf" but the second element is problematic. We might take it as *cró* (O.Ir. *crú*) meaning "blood, gore", in which case the name might be translated "rock of the dog's blood", a reference, perhaps, to the colour of a rock in the area. There is another word *cró* meaning "byre, pen, fold" etc. which would be expected to produce the lenition we see in this name, with which we may compare *Curracha-cro-na-gcon* "the moors of the hut of the hounds", cited in *Joyce* (ii 220). We might also consider an original *Carraig Chroibh Mhadaidh* "rock of the dog's paw" where the "paw" may be some indentation in the rock. However, there is little to distinguish between all these suggestions and, indeed, it appears that we are dealing here with some type of allusive or fanciful name which will not easily reveal its composition.

Corgary	*Corrdhoire*	
J 0834	"round oak-wood"	
1. Corgirry	Fiants Eliz. §4218	1583
2. Corgirry, the island of	Fiants Eliz. §4327	1583c
3. Corrgirrie	CPR Jas. I 394b	1609
4. Corrgirrie	CPR Jas. I 195b	1610
5. Corgirrie	CPR Jas. I 190a	1611
6. Corgirrie	CPR Jas. I 190a	1611
7. Corgerry	Inq. Ult. (Down) §14 Car. I	1630

8. Corgerry	Inq. Ult. (Down) §106 Car. I	1650c
9. Corgerrie	Inq. Ult. (Down) §106 Car. I	1650c
10. Corgery	Census 74	1659c
11. Corgary	ASE 112a §37	1667
12. Corrgarry	Rent Roll Down 12	1692
13. Corgery	Wm. Map (OSNB) 60	1810
14. Corgary	County Warrant (OSNB) 60	1827
15. Corgerry	Newry Tel. (OSNB) 60	1830
16. Corgrey	Bnd. Sur. (OSNB) 60	1830c
17. 'Cor-gry	OSNB 60	1834c
18. Corgarry	J O'D (OSNB) 60	1834c
19. Corgrey	Ir. Wills Index iv 49	1838
20. Corrgarraidh "garison"	OSNB Inf. 60	1834c
21. Corgarbh "The rough round hill"	Cowan's Donaghmore 42	1914
22. Corr-dhoire "a round (or fairy) grove"	Mooney 73	1950c
23. ˈkɔːrgərɪ	Local pronunciation	1990
24. ˈkɔrgrɪ	Local pronunciation	1990

The interpretations of both O'Donovan's informant (20) and Cowan (21) hinge on the realization of the internal consonant usually represented in the spellings as *g* but this would have been lenited and thus indistinguishable from lenited *d*. Cowan's suggestion is wholly untenable because, although he writes it as a compound, the stress would fall on the adjective, *garbh*, providing a different stress pattern from the one indicated by the current pronunciation. Moreover, we should expect to see some trace in the early spellings of the final *bh* which in the Irish of Ulster is generally pronounced [w], earlier [v]. While, the *Corrgarraidh* proposed by the *OSNB* informant is somewhat more satisfactory there is no precedent for its use either in the lexicon or in the onomasticon and it may be safely dismissed as a possibility. *Corrdhoire*, on the other hand, as suggested by Mooney (22) is attested in both spheres. *Joyce* cites the example of Corgerry in Co. Galway which was understood locally as *Cordhoire* (sic) "odd oakwood" (iii 255) and we should also note the name of the townland of **Corderry** in the parish of Carnteel, Co. Tyrone, where we are dealing unmistakably with the element *doire*. Dinneen cites a word *corr-dhoire* "a round (or fairy) grove" where the first element is probably the adjectival prefix *corr-* "odd, occasional, pointed, round" which is also found in composition with *sceach* in the sense of "fairy thorn".

Derrycraw
J 0934

Doire Creathach (?)
meaning uncertain

1. Ballyderrycragh al. Ballecragh	CPR Jas. I 395a	1609
2. Ballyderricragh orse Ballechragh	CPR Jas. I 190a	1611
3. Ballederrycraghe	Inq. Ult. (Down) §14 Car. I	1630
4. Balledericraghe al. Ballecraghe	Inq. Ult. (Down) §14 Car. I	1630
5. Dirycragh	Civ. Surv. x §72	1655c
6. Dorrybragh	Hib. Reg. Up. Iveagh	1657c
7. Berecra	Census 74	1659c
8. Dyribragh	BSD 104	1661
9. Dorrybragh	Hib. Del. Down	1672c

---

10. Derrycra	Wm. Map (OSNB) 60	1810
11. Derrycraw	County Warrant (OSNB) 60	1827
12. Derrycraw	Bnd. Sur. (OSNB) 60	1830c
13. Der-ry-'craw	OSNB 60	1834c
14. Doire crádh "oak wood of oppression"	OSNB Inf. 60	1834c
15. Doire Creach "oak-wood of the herds or plunder"	Cowan's Donaghmore 42	1914
16. Doire Creamhach "garlic-grown oak-wood i.e. abounding in garlic"	Mooney 73	1950c
17. ˌdɛrɪ'krɔː	Local pronunciation	1990

The suggestion put forward by the *OSNB* informant (14) was based solely on the contemporary pronunciation (13) and it is not supported by the earlier spellings which almost invariably show a final -*gh*(*e*), most probably representing Irish *ch* (1–6, 8–9). Mooney's contribution (16) is rather more plausible as the element *creamh* "wild garlic" appears in a number of other place-names (*Joyce* ii 327–329) and we may note in particular Derrycraff in Co. Mayo and Derrycrave in Co. Westmeath, both of which derive from Irish *Doire Creamha* (*ibid*. 328). However, names containing this element almost always show some trace of the *mh*, either as a nasal element or as a [au], and we should certainly expect to find some evidence of this in the 17th-century forms. Joyce notes that *creamh* is generally anglicized *craff*, *crave*, *crew*, *cramph* etc. and cites numerous examples none of which produce any spellings like those for our Derrycraw (*Joyce* ii 327–9).

Cowan's identification (15) of the second element as *creach* "plunder", with which we may compare Craughwell, Co. Galway (from *Creach-mhaoil*, *Joyce* iii 271; *GÉ* 78), seems to better fit the available evidence but the modern pronunciation seems to call for a word containing the sound group *atha* (cf. **Ballyblaugh**). This suggests as the most likely origin of this element the adjective *creathach* which primarily means "shaking, trembling". In an article on the place-names of the Rosses in Co. Donegal, Dónall Mac Giolla Easpaig proposes that Craghy in the Rosses goes back to an original *Crathaigh* meaning "*talamh creathach* or "shaking ground", and that the name Crolly derives from Irish *Craithlí* (*craith* + *l(e)ach*) (1984, 52; see also *Joyce* ii 367–8). Its use in this particular instance, however, is not exactly parallel and we might argue instead for a connection with *crann creathach* "aspen tree" (*DIL* 508 sv. *crann*; *Dinneen* 265 sv. *criothach*; *Ó Dónaill* 309 sv. *crann*; *de Bhaldraithe* 36 sv. *aspen*), although the combination *doire* + *creathach* is unattested. Thus, some doubt remains as to the meaning of the Irish form.

Drumantine
J 0737

Droim an tSiáin
"ridge of the fairy-mound"

1. Ballydronintigham	CPR Jas. I 395a	1609
2. Ballydromintighan	CPR Jas. I 190a	1611
3. Balledromentighean	Inq. Ult. (Down) §14 Car. I	1630
4. Dromintanty	Wars Co. Down 79	1641
5. Dromenteane	Inq. Ult. (Down) §106 Car. I	1650c
6. Dromentean	Inq. Ult. (Down) §106 Car. I	1650c
7. Dromintreane	ASE 112a §37	1667
8. Dromisheane	Rent Roll Down 12	1692

9. Dromontain	PRONI T750/1	1732
10. Drumantine	Wm. Map (OSNB) 60	1810
11. Drumantine	Bnd. Sur. (OSNB) 60	1830c
12. 'Drom-an-'tine	OSNB 60	1834c
13. Druim an tSian "ridge of the fox-gloves"	OSNB Inf. 60	1834c
14. Druim an tSidheain "ridge of fairies, foxgloves"	Cowan's Donaghmore 42	1914
15. Drom an tSídheáin or tSíodháin "Hill ridge of the fairy-palace"	Mooney 75	1950c
16. ˌdrǫmən'tain	Local pronunciation	1990

The suggestion that the second element in this name is Irish *Sian* "foxglove" (13–14) cannot be easily dismissed as it would be indistinguishable in modern Irish from the proposed element *sián* "a fairy-mound". The early spellings with internal *-gh-* (1–3) might be adduced as evidence in favour of the latter suggestion as the word *sian* "foxglove" never contained this consonant whereas *sián* "a fairy-mound" goes back to a form *siodhán*. However, *siodhán* would have been reduced to *sián* by this period and it is more than likely that the *gh* in our earliest forms is silent. Nevertheless, Joyce notes that *sián* "a fairy-mound" is used throughout Ireland, usually applied to hills crowned by an old fort (*Joyce* i 186–7). In this particular instance, the rath to the east of Dromantine College (OS J 0835) may be the feature which gave rise to this name.

Drummiller
J 0746

Droim Iolair
"ridge of the eagle"

1. Ballydromiller	CPR Jas. I 395a	1609
2. Ballidromiller	CPR Jas. I 190a	1611
3. (?)Ballylisdromiller	CPR Jas. I 235a	1612
4. Balledromiller	Inq. Ult. (Down) §14 Car.I	1630
5. Dromiller (×3)	Inq. Ult. (Down) §21 Car. I	1631
6. Drommiller	Inq. Ult. (Down) §106 Car. I	1650c
7. Drumillere	ASE 112a §37	1667
8. Drumilree	Rent Roll Down 12	1692
9. Drumiller	Wm. Map (OSNB) 60	1810
10. Drumiller	Bnd. Sur. (OSNB) 60	1830c
11. 'Drum-mill-er	OSNB 60	1834c
12. Drummiller	J O'D (OSNB) 60	1834c
13. Drum Miller "Millers ridge"	OSNB Inf. 60	1834c
14. Druim Iolar "The eagle's ridge"	Cowan's Donaghmore 42	1914
15. Drom Mhuilleóra "Millar's Ridge"	Mooney 75	1950c
16. ˌdrǫ'Mɪlər	Local pronunciation	1990

The *OSNB* informant (13), followed by Mooney (15), suggested that the second element in Drummiller is a personal name, Millar (Miller), a name of English and Scottish origin (Bell 1988, 191). Millar or Miller was noted as a "principal name" in Co. Antrim in the mid-seventeenth century where the largest concentration of people of that name is now to be found (*ibid.*). However, as the name of the townland is recorded as early as the beginning of the 17th century at a time when there were still relatively few settlers in the area it seems unlikely that the final element represents the English or Scottish surname Millar. The most satisfactory solution is perhaps that given by Cowan (14) (recte *Droim Iolair*) although his suggestion that the name preserves the memory of an eagle from the Mourne Mountains which paid a visit to a sheep run here is purely conjectural (*Cowan's Donaghmore* 42). One might also postulate an original Irish *Droim Muilleora* "ridge of the miller" on the basis of the minor names found in the townland of Drummiller, namely, Mount Mill Bridge and Mount Mill House which might be supposed to be based on a translation of *Droim Muilleora*. It is true that the *ui* in *muilleoir* and similar words is usually fronted towards [i] under the influence of the following palatal consonant in Modern Irish, but in similar names, such as Drummullin in Co. Roscommon (*Droim an Mhuilinn*, *GÉ* 217), Mullingar in Co. Westmeath (*an Muileann gCearr*, *GÉ* 256) and Ballymullen in Co. Kerry (*Baile an Mhuilinn*, *GÉ* 186) the vowel is represented as *u* in the anglicized spellings. It seems probable, therefore, that the name Mount Mill was coined like so many other names of its type as a fancy name by the owner of the house which bears it and so little faith can be placed in its authenticity.

Glebe	*Tulach na Croise*	
J 1035	"mound of the cross"	
1. Tullynecrosse, hill or mountain of	CPR Jas. I 274b	1615
2. Collens or Mount Tolleneacrosse	CPR Jas. I 479a	1620
3. Tolleny Cross	Census 74	1659c
4. Glebe	Wm. Map (OSNB) 60	1834c
5. Tullagh or Tullynacross	Lewis' Top. Dict. 468	1837
6. Tulach na Cros "The hill of the cross"	Cowan's Donaghmore 42	1914
7. Tulach na Croise	Mooney 75	1950c
8. gli:b	Local pronunciation	1990

The Parliamentary Returns in PROI for the diocese of Dromore in the year 1768 report that Donaghmore had "a small Glebe, no house on it" and, according to an inscription on the west gable, the Glebe House was erected in that year (*Cowan's Donaghmore* 185, 189). The townland was previously known as *Tulach na Croise* "the hill of the cross" so called, according to Cowan (*ibid*. 43), from a Celtic Cross of the 10th or 11th century which stands in the churchyard (*ASCD* 291).

Killysavan	*Coillidh Sabháin* (?)	
J 0739	"wood of the savin"	
1. Tullimore al. Killasonn	Hib. Reg. Up. Iveagh	1657c
2. Killeshanan	Census 74	1659c
3. Tullymore al. Killasonne	BSD 104	1661
4. Tullymore al. Killsavan	ASE 274a §29	1681
5. Tullymore al. Killfarane	Rent Roll Down 11	1692
6. Killysaven	Wm. Map (OSNB) 60	1810
7. Killysavan	Reg. Free. (OSNB) 60	1829
8. Kil-ly-'sav-in	OSNB 60	1834c
9. Killysummon	OSNB Inf. 60	1834c

10. Killysavan	J O'D (OSNB) 60	1834c
11. Cill a saman "Savan's church"	J O'D (OSNB) 60	1834c
12. Coillidh Samhan "Hollantide bushes, wood"	Cowan's Donaghmore 43	1914
13. Coill Uí Sabháin "Savin's (or Savage's Wood)"	Mooney 75	1950c
14. ˌkɪliˈsavən	Local pronunciation	1990

The form suggested by O'Donovan (11) is peculiar in the extreme and can only be explained as an attempt to render in Irish words the pronunciation he heard from his informants (8–9). Judging by his translation, he took the final element to be a personal name, but in order to account for the second syllable he inserted what appears to be a form of the article (a' < an). Apart from the fact that the article would not be used with a personal name, this particular form (gen. sing. masc.) would prefix t to the s of Saman. Mooney postulates an original Irish Coill Uí Sabháin (13) but the name Ó Sabháin is largely confined to Cork, Kerry and Tipperary (Woulfe 1923, 637).

Cowan's suggestion (12) seems nearer the mark than the previous suggestions but we should expect a form Coillidh S(h)amhna which would produce a quite different anglicized form. We must also consider sabhán "a cub, whelp" or sabhán "a piece of V-shaped wood used for securing the bottom of a pannier" (here possibly used of a fork in the river), and, most notably sabhán, a variant of sabhan (gen. sing. sabhna), meaning "savin". Savin is a variety of juniper and both the English and Irish words derive from Latin sabina. According to Harris, the mountains of Mourne were "furnished with a considerable Variety of balsam-ick and pectoral Herbs", including Juniper and Savin, upon which the goats used to feed giving their milk the medicinal qualities of those herbs (Harris Hist. 179).

Two of the earliest forms (1b, 3b) are irreconcilable with the current form of the name and the other historical spellings. We might suggest that two forms of the name existed side by side, one derived from sabhán (angl. savan etc.) and the other from the more usual form of this word, sabhan (explaining the forms ending in -sonne). However, the variant spellings appear in closely related sources and they are quite conceivably based on a scribal error. A greater problem is raised by the form provided by O'Donovan's local informant, Killysummon (9), which, if reliable, suggests an internal -mh- which has since been delenited (cf. **Deehommed**).

It might be argued that the first element is to be identified as cill "church" following O'Donovan (11) but, in the absence of any evidence of the former existence of a church in this townland, this possibility may be dismissed. The first element may alternatively be explained, following Cowan (12), as Irish Coillidh, a by-form of coill "a wood" based on an oblique form (see Dinneen sv. coill), although the effect of the expected lenition is wholly absent from the forms. Coillidh is found in a number of other place-names such as Coillidh Léith (**Killylea**, Co. Armagh) and Coillidh Brón (Killybrone, Co. Monaghan) (GÉ 238), and it should be noted that lenition is not marked in the latter name.

Knocknanarny Cnoc na nAirní
J 0733 "hill of the sloes"

1. Balleknocknenarie	CPR Jas. I 394b	1609
2. Balleknocknenary	CPR Jas. I 190a	1611
3. Balleknocknenarny	Inq. Ult. (Down) §14 Car.I	1630

102

4. Knocknenarly	Inq. Ult. (Down) §106 Car.I	1650c
5. Knockenivary	Hib. Reg. Up. Iveagh	1657c
6. Knockenenarney	Census 74	1659c
7. Knocknarney	BSD 105	1661
8. Knockenwary	Hib. Del. Down	1672c
9. Knocknanerny or Knockneeverny	ASE 274a §29	1681
10. Knocknanerney	Rent Roll Down 11	1692
11. Knockanarney	Wm. Little (OSNB) 60	1810
12. Knocknenarny	Wm. Map (OSNB) 60	1810
13. Knockinarney	Bnd. Sur. (OSNB) 60	1830c
14. Knock-a-'nar-ney	OSNB 60	1834c
15. Knocknanarny	J O'D (OSNB) 60	1834c
16. Cnoc na náirneadh "the hill of sloes"	OSNB Inf. 60	1834c
17. Cnoc na n-Airne "The hill of the sloes"	Cowan's Donaghmore 43	1914
18. Cnoc na n-Áirneadh	Mooney 77	1950c
19. ˌnɔkənˈaːrnɪ	Local pronunciation	1990
20. ˌnɔknəˈnɑrni	Local pronunciation	1990

The final element seems to have been correctly identified as the gen. pl. of *airne* "sloe" (16–18). A small number of early forms do not show the internal *-n-* in the final element (1–2, 4–5, 8) but as these spellings occur sporadically in a small number of related documents (1 and 2, 5 and 8) they are probably due to scribal or editorial inaccuracies.

Lurganare   *Lorga an Áir*
J 0732   "the tract of the slaughter"

1. Ballylurrganmore	CPR Jas. I 395a	1609
2. Ballelurgannare	CPR Jas. I 190a	1611
3. Ballelurgoonar	Inq. Ult. (Down) §14 Car. I	1630
4. Ballelurganare	Inq. Ult. (Down) §14 Car. I	1630
5. Lurgonore	Inq. Ult. (Down) §21 Car. I	1631
6. Lurganore	Inq. Ult. (Down) §21 Car. I	1631
7. Luganore	Inq. Ult. (Down) §21 Car. I	1631
8. Largonery	Inq. Ult. (Down) §106 Car. I	1650c
9. Lurganary	Inq. Ult. (Down) §106 Car. I	1650c
10. Lurgmare	Census 74	1659c
11. Lorganare	ASE 112a §37	1667
12. Lorganare	Rent Roll Down 12	1692
13. Lurganar	Wm. Map (OSNB) 60	1810
14. Lurgan	Reg. Free. (OSNB) 60	1829
15. Lurganare	Bnd. Sur. (OSNB) 60	1830c
16. Lorg an áir "track of slaughter"	OSNB Inf. 60	1834c
17. Lurgan Air "The long low hill of slaughter"	Cowan's Donaghmore 43	1914
18. Lorga(n) mhor (O.I. mhár)	Mooney 77	1950c

19. Ár-mhagh "Battlefield or Slaughter"	Mooney 77	1950c
20. ˌlɒrganˈeːr	Local pronunciation	1990

The first element in this name is almost certainly a form of the word *lorga* which means primarily "shin" but has the extended meaning "a long thin tract of land" (see Ó Maolfabhail 1987–8, 20). However, some doubt hangs over the precise origins of the name for the spellings listed above may be satisfactorily explained as either *Lorga an Áir* "the tract of the slaughter" or *Lorgain Áir* "tract of slaughter". This latter contains an oblique form of the root word *lorga* which is more common in the north and west of the country where there are about thirty places called Lurgan and more than sixty others of whose name it forms a part (*Joyce* i 527; cf. Ó Maolfabhail, *art. cit.*).

Canon Mooney attempted to relate the final element in this name to Mod. Ir. *mór* through O.Ir. *már* (18) but this form became obsolete during the Mid. Ir. period and can hardly be the element in question. The most likely origin of the final element is that suggested by the *OSNB* informant (16) and Cowan (17), namely, *ár* "slaughter". In many places in Ireland names containing this element are still associated with some great battle. In Glenanair on the borders of Limerick and Cork the locals preserve a tradition of a dreadful battle fought at a ford over the river and at Coumanare in the parish of Ballyduff, a few miles from Dingle, there is a memory of a great battle in the valley (*Joyce* i 116–7).

Maddydrumbrist J 0933	*Mónaidh Droma Bhrisc* (?) "moor of the easily-broken ridge"	
1. Ballymanydrombrisk	CPR Jas. I 395b	1609
2. Ballymanydromvrish	CPR Jas. I 197a	1611
3. Ballymanydrombrish	CPR Jas. I 197b	1611
4. Ballymaindrombrishe	CPR Jas. I 235b	1612
5. Moneydrombristee	CPR Jas. I 274b	1615
6. Monidrombrestee	CPR Jas. I 479a	1620
7. Monneydrombrest	Hib. Reg. Up. Iveagh	1657c
8. Moneydrombrist	Census 74	1659c
9. Monidrombish	BSD 104	1661
10. Monydrombresk	Hib. Del. Down	1672c
11. Moneydrombriste al. Maddydrombriste	Deed (Cowan's Donaghmore) 62	1769
12. Maddydrumbrist	Bnd. Sur. (OSNB) 60	1830c
13. Maddydrumbrist	County Warrant (OSNB) 60	1831
14. Maide druim briste "stick of the broken ridge"	OSNB Inf. 60	1834c
15. Muine Droma Riasca "shrubbery of the moory ridge"	Cowan's Donaghmore 43	1914
16. Muine Droma Briste "the shrubbery of the hunch-backed ridge"	Mooney 79	1950c
17. ˌmadɪdrɒmˈbrɪsk	Local pronunciation	1990
18. ˌmadidrɒmˈbrɪst	Local pronunciation	1990

Cowan suggested that this name was derived from *Muine Droma Riasca* "shrubbery of the moory ridge" (15) but, as all the forms show an internal *b* or *v* (1–13), this possibility must be rejected. Even so the final element is problematic as the character of the original final consonant shows great and apparently erratic variation between *-st*, *-sk*, and *-sh*, even in the earliest sources. The local pronunciation with a final [k] deserves particular attention given the fact that the official spelling ends in *t* as local people sometimes preserve the older pronunciation of a name. However, only two of the early forms end in *k* (1, 10) and it might be suggested instead that the original ·[t] has gone to [k] in the current pronunciation. The alternation between [t´] and [k´] is attested in the Irish of east Ulster and, while most of the forms show a guttural instead of a dental, the replacement of [k´] by [t´] seems to become more common when it comes into contact with [ʃ] (Sommerfelt 1929, 168 §231). This would suggest that [k´] may have been the original final consonant in our name and we might propose an original final element *briosc* "brittle, friable", gen. sing. masc. *brisc*. The current pronunciation with final [k], therefore, may preserve the older form of the name, and the *h* in some early spellings (2–4) may have resulted from confusion with an original *k*.

The first element is just as problematic as the last. The earliest forms clearly indicate that it originally contained an internal *n* (1–10) which later became assimilated to the *d* in *droma* (11b–13). However, this still leaves a number of possibilities including *muine* "thicket, brake" (see 15–16), *mónaidh* (an oblique form of *móin* "turf, bog") and *monadh*, a Scottish Gaelic word meaning "hilly ground". This last word was used by the Place-Names Commission to explain the element "money" in a small number of Ulster place-names but there is no evidence of its use either in the lexicon or the onomasticon of Ireland (for further discussion see Toner 1991–92). *Muine*, on the other hand, is a well-attested element in Irish place-names and almost certainly forms the first element in the name of the nearby townland of **Moneymore**. However, the early spellings also accord well with a postulated origin in *mónaidh* for the long *o* would be shortened before the main stress in Ulster Irish. Moreover, unstressed long *o* sometimes becomes short *a* in Donegal Irish as, for example, in the name Cronaguiggy (original *Cró na gCúigeadh*) which is now pronounced as if it were *Crann na gCúigeadh* (Mac Giolla Easpaig 1986, 77–8), and this may explain the current pronunciation with short *a*. No similar development has been documented for *ui* and, although such a development is not inconceivable, this would seem to tip the balance of probability in favour of an origin in *mónaidh*.

Moneymore	*Muine Mór*	
J 0936	"large thicket"	
1. Ballymunnymore	CPR Jas. I 395b	1609
2. Ballymunnymoore	CPR Jas. I 197a	1611
3. Ballymunnymore	CPR Jas. I 197b	1611
4. Ballymunnymore	CPR Jas. I 235b	1612
5. Monymore	CPR Jas. I 274b	1615
6. Monamore	CPR Jas. I 479a	1620
7. Moneymore	Hib. Reg. Up. Iveagh	1657c
8. Mune More ½ towne	Census 74	1659c
9. Munimore	BSD 104	1661
10. Monymore	Hib. Del. Down	1672c
11. Moneymore al. Monimore al. Minimore	Deed (Cowan's Donaghmore) 62	1769
12. Mineymore	County Warrant (OSNB) 60	1827

13. Munnymore	Reg. Free. (OSNB) 60	1829
14. Minnymore	Bnd. Sur. (OSNB) 60	1830c
15. Moneymore	County Warrant (OSNB) 60	1831
16. Moneymore	J O'D (OSNB) 60	1834c
17. Muine mór "great brake, shrubbery"	J O'D (OSNB) 60	1834c
18. Muine Mor "The big shrubbery"	Cowan's Donaghmore 43	1914
19. Muine Mór	Mooney 77	1950c
20. ˌmɒnɪˈmoːr	Local pronuciation	1990

The spellings with internal -i- tend to confirm the postulated Irish original (11c, 12, 14; cf. **Maddydrumbrist**).

Ringbane   *An Rinn Bhán*
J 1234   "the white point"

1. Balleeneraghnabane	CPR Jas. I 197a	1611
2. Balleneraghnabane	CPR Jas. I 235a	1612
3. Ranbane	CPR Jas. I 274b	1615
4. Ranbane al. Ballineragherbane	CPR Jas. I 479a	1620
5. Rinbane	Civ. Surv. x §72	1655c
6. Ringban	Hib. Reg. Up. Iveagh	1657c
7. Ringban	Census 74	1659c
8. Ringbane	BSD Dn. 104	1661
9. Ringbane	Sub. Roll Down 276	1663
10. Ringban	Hib. Del. Down	1672c
11. Ringban	Wm. Map (OSNB) 60	1810
12. Ringbane	County Warrant (OSNB) 60	1827
13. Ringbanne	Bnd. Sur. (OSNB) 60	1830c
14. Ringbane	J O'D (OSNB) 60	1834c
15. Rin[n], or Roin[n] bán "white point or division"	OSNB Inf. 60	1834c
16. Rinn Ban "The white point"	Cowan's Donaghmore 43	1914
17. rɪŋˈbaːn	Local pronunciation	1990

While the second element in this name is undoubtedly *bán* "white" the first element might be either *roinn* "part, division" or *rinn* "point, promontory". However, several forms (1–2, 4) may point to a gen. sing. in -*ch*- and this is supported by a number of early spellings of the closely related name **Ringolish**. Whereas there is no evidence of such a declension for *roinn*, *rinn* has a variant gen. sing. *reannach* (pl. *reannacha*) (*Ó Dónaill* sv. *reannach*[3]) so that it would appear that we are dealing here with the latter of the two possibilities. *Rinn* is normally used in place-names in the sense of "promontory" and is generally restricted to coastal features but it can also be used of an inland promontory in a bog (*Dinneen* sv. *rinn*). Indeed, Harris takes the name of the Mournes to derive from Irish *Mor-rinn* which he translates "the great Ridge" (*Harris Hist*. 11) and, although his derivation is incorrect, it seems to indicate that *rinn* could designate "a ridge" in the Irish of this area.

The change of -*nn* to -*ng* is rather peculiar and, while it is normal in the Irish of Waterford, it is not found in Ulster Irish. Nevertheless, this same development is found in a great number of Ulster place-names, particularly in Co. Down where there are a total of 12 townland names with an initial element *Ring-* (*Top. Index 1961*). It might be suggested that the development first occurred in the name of the nearby townland of **Ringclare** as the combination [n] and [k] normally gives [ŋk] (see, for example, "bank, rink") and that it spread to this name by analogy, but the wide dispersal of this phenomenon suggests a different cause.

Ringclare *Rinn Chláir*
J 1036 "point of the plain"

1. Ringlare	Hib. Reg. Up. Iveagh	1657c
2. Ringcleare	BSD 104	1661
3. Ringcleare & Ringless	BSD 104	1661
4. Ringlare	Hib. Del. Down	1672c
5. Ringclare	Wm. Map (OSNB) 60	1810
6. Ringclare	Bnd. Sur. (OSNB) 60	1830c
7. 'Ring-clare	OSNB 60	1834c
8. Rin[n], or Roin[n] cláir "level division"	OSNB Inf. 60	1834c
9. Rinn Clair "The level point, point of the plain"	Cowan's Donaghmore 43	1914
10. An Rinn Chláir "The broad bogland Peninsula"	Mooney 79	1950c
11. riŋ'kle:r	Local pronunciation	1990

On the initial element, see **Ringbane**.

Ringolish *Rinn an Lis*
J 1135 "point of the fort"

1. Ballynnerannagh	CPR Jas. I 395b	1609
2. Ballynerannagh	CPR Jas. I 235a	1612
3. Rangilish orse Cashanahery	CPR Jas. I 274b	1615
4. Rangilish al. Cashanehery al. Ballynerany	CPR Jas. I 479a	1620
5. Ringilles	Hib. Reg. Up. Iveagh	1657c
6. Ringe Imulbeece	Census 74	1659c
7. Ringless	BSD 104	1661
8. Ringills	Hib. Del. Down	1672c
9. Ringolish	Wm. Map (OSNB) 60	1810
10. Ringalish	Bnd. Sur. (OSNB) 60	1830c
11. Ring-go-'lish	OSNB 60	1834c
12. Ringolish	J O'D (OSNB) 60	1834c
13. Roin[n] a lis "division of the fort"	OSNB Inf. 60	1834c
14. Rinn a' Lis "The point of the fort"	Cowan's Donaghmore 44	1914
15. Rinn mhaol-lis "Bogland peninsula of the defaced fort"	Mooney 79	1950c
16. ˌriŋgə'liʃ	Local pronunciation	1990

This name appears to contain the same initial element as **Ringclare** and **Ringbane** and the evidence of the early variant forms with guttural declension (1–2) clearly points to *rinn* as the origin of this part of the name (cf. **Ringbane**). The final element, *lis,* is gen. sing. of early *leas*, the dat. sing. of which produced the modern Irish word *lios* "enclosure, fort".

Tullymore　　　　　　　*Tulaigh Mhór*
J 0837　　　　　　　　　　"large mound"

1. Ballytullaghmore	CPR Jas. I 396a	1609
2. (?)Ballytolleymore	CPR Jas. I 181b	1610
3. Ballytullaghmore	CPR Jas. I 235a	1612
4. Ballytullaghmore juxta le Glynn	Inq. Ult. §13 Car. I	1629
5. Tullimore al. Ballimveigh	Hib. Reg. Up. Iveagh	1657c
6. Tollemor	Census 74	1659c
7. Tullymore al. Killasonne	BSD 104	1661
8. Tullymore al. Ballyveigh	BSD 104	1661
9. Ballimateige	Hib. Del. Down	1672c
10. Tullimor	Hib. Del. Down	1672c
11. Tullymore al. Ballyneveagh	ASE 274a §29	1681
12. Tullymore al. Killsavan	ASE 274a §29	1681
13. Tullymore al. Killfarane	Rent Roll Down 11	1692
14. Tullymore	Wm. Map (OSNB) 60	1810
15. Tullymore	Bnd. Sur. (OSNB) 60	1830c
16. Tulach mór "great hill"	OSNB Inf. 60	1834c
17. Tulach Mor "The big hill"	Cowan's Donaghmore 44	1914
18. An Tulach Mhór	Mooney 81	1950c
19. ˌto‌l‌t'mo:r	Local pronunciation	1990

The constant use of place-names in oblique cases after prepositions frequently leads to the oblique form being adopted as the nom. sing. as well and this seems to have occurred here. We might assume that some of the early forms represent the use of the nom. sing. (1, 3–4) but they could just as well represent the gen. sing. *tulcha* after *baile*.

Tullymurry　　　　　　*Tulaigh Uí Mhuirí*
J 1034　　　　　　　　　　"Murray's mound"

1. Ballytully-Inmerrie	CPR Jas. I 395b	1609
2. Ballytully-Inurie	CPR Jas. I 197a	1611
3. Ballyetullemurrie	CPR Jas. I 235a	1612
4. Ballitollywirie	CPR Jas. I 274b	1615
5. Ballytollywyry	CPR Jas. I 479a	1620
6. Tullyvory	Civ. Surv. x §72	1655c
7. Tullymery	Hib. Reg. Up. Iveagh	1657c
8. Tollenemary	Census 75	1659c
9. Tullymurry	BSD 104	1661
10. Tullamury	Hib. Del. Down	1672c
11. Tullymurry	Wm. Map (OSNB) 60	1810
12. Tullymurrey	Bnd. Sur. (OSNB) 60	1830c
13. Tul-ly-'mur-ry	OSNB 60	1834c

14. Tullymurry	J O'D (OSNB) 60	1834c
15. Tulach Muireadhaigh "Murray's hill"	OSNB Inf. 60	1834c
16. Tulach Mhuire "The hill of Mary"	Cowan's Donaghmore 44	1914
17. Tulach Mhuire	Mooney 81	1950c
18. ˌtɒlt'mörɪ	Local pronunciation	1990

In the absence of any evidence associating this townland with Marian devotion the suggestion by Cowan and Mooney (16–17) that the name originates in *Tulach Mhuire* may be safely rejected. Cowan (*Cowan's Donaghmore* 44) notes that the townland is close to the church and suggests that a chapel or place of devotion in the townland was dedicated to Mary but this is pure conjecture. The second element is almost certainly a name, probably the surname *Ó Muiri* (angl. Murray) but the suggestion made by the *OSNB* informant that it is the personal name *Muireadhach* (gen. sing. *Muireadhaigh*) should also be borne in mind (15).

OTHER NAMES

Cash, The	*An Cheis*	
J 1235	"the causeway"	
1. Cashanahery, Rangilish orse	CPR Jas. I 274b	1615
2. Rangilish al. Cashanehery al. Ballynerany	CPR Jas. I 479a	1620
3. ðə 'kʲaʃ	Local pronunciation	1990

This name comes from Irish *an Cheis*, an oblique form of *ceas* "causeway of hurdles", and may have originally referred to a causeway crossing the bogland which is characteristic of this area. Causeways built from hurdles were formerly very common in Ireland (*Joyce* i 362). The Four Masters record that Hugh Roe O'Donnell erected a wicker bridge (*ceasaigh-droichet*) across the Blackwater in Tyrone for his army and when they had crossed he let it float down the stream so that his enemies could not follow (*AFM* iv 1126–7). The element *ceis* is found in a number of other place-names such as **Kesh** in Co. Fermanagh and Kesh in Co. Sligo, as well as Keshcarrigan in Co. Limerick (*GÉ* 53).

Dane's Cast	*Gleann na Muice Duibhe*	
J 0639	"the valley of the black pig"	
1. 'diənz'kʲɑst	Local pronunciation	1990

The Dane's Cast is a linear earthwork, extending from a point one and a half miles east of Scarva village to ½ mile north of Jerretspass, Co. Armagh, where it disappears before resuming its course close to the south end of Camlough Reservoir and apparently terminating in Aghayalloge townland 3½ miles south-west of Newry (*ASCD* 144). In Co. Down the structure is discontinuous, consisting for the most part of short lengths of earthwork linking natural obstacles of bog which fringe the Newry Canal (*ibid.*). The Dane's Cast is one of a series of linear earthworks which are dotted along the southern borders of ancient Ulster, constructions such as the Dorsy and the Black Pig's Dyke. It differs somewhat from the other earthworks in that it follows a north-south path and it has been suggested that it represents a later defensive wall raised up by the Ulaid who occupied Co. Down after their expulsion from their ancient capital of *Emain Macha* (modern **Navan Fort**) c. 500 AD (Mallory and McNeill 1991, 152). An ancient tradition concerning the expulsion of the Ulaid from *Emain Macha* suggests the ditch may have been constructed by the *Uí Néill* or the *Airgialla* rather than by the Ulaid. This relates how the three Collas, who are to be identified with the three sons of Niall Noígiallach, the founders of the northern *Uí Néill* (O'Rahilly 1946, 222-234), drew a boundary between themselves and the defeated Ulaid along the Clanrye northwards from Newry (*CGH* 142b27; *LCABuidhe* 50).

A 19th-century native of the neighbourhood of Scarva is reported to have said that "the Kings of the Danes lived in Lisnagade, and had this 'Cast' made for a way through which to march their army out of sight of their Irish enemies to Warrenpoint, where they had their ships" (*UJA* 2 iii (1897) 27n; cf. *OSL* 28–9) and there was a tradition around Lisnabrague that the Cast was built by the Danes for defensive purposes, and that in old times there had been terrible fighting there (*UJA art. cit.* 28n).

The name "The Danes' Cast" is not attested anywhere before the 19th century and it seems to have originated in an account of the earthwork given by Dubourdieu in his *Statisical Survey of the county of Down* published in 1802. Dubourdieu gives no name to the earthwork but suggests that it may "have been intended as a line of communication between two distant posts, probably of the Danes, who are said to have penetrated as far to the west as the city of Armagh." (*Statist. Sur. Dn.* 276) The idea that certain earthworks in Ireland were the work of Scandinavians was first mooted by Giraldus Cambrensis in the 12th century (*ASCD* 146). Dr. James Stuart draws our attention to a remark made by Ranulf Higdon or Higden, a Benedictine monk who died c. 1363, in his *Polychron Ranulph Higdeni monachi Chestrensis* which he translates:

> After the coming of St. Patrick, till the reign of King Feidlim, thirty-three kings ruled in Ireland, during a period of four hundred years. In his reign came the Norwegians, under their commander Turgeseus, and occupied the land. This they intersected through various places with deep trenches, and they erected many castles, some singly, others doubly or triply, walled round... (*Stuart's Armagh* 585).

The inhabitants of Drummiller at the close of the last century knew the ditch as the Black Pig's Glen and apparently had never heard of the Dane's Cast (*UJA art. cit.* 68). It is also reported at the same time that the road running above the eastern shore of Lough Cam, which supposedly followed the line of the earthwork, was called by the inhabitants of the district "The Valley of the Black Pig" (*ibid.* 69n). Stuart notes that the ditch was called *Gleann na Muice Duibhe* "the glen of the black pig" by the native Irish and contrasts this with the practice of the settlers who used the name "The Danes' Cast" (*Stuart's Armagh* 585). Given all these circumstances, it is virtually certain that the Danes' Cast was originally known as *Gleann na Muice Duibhe* and that its present name, complete with the interpretation of the ditch's use, was adapted among settlers from Dubourdieu's work.

In a letter from Carrickmacross, dated 20th May 1835, John O'Donovan relates a story of how the Black Pig's Valley got its name. He writes:

> The tradition about *Gleann na muice Duibhe* is the wildest I ever heard. A schoolmaster lived in Drogheda a long time ago who used to work the magic art, and turn his scholars into pigs. One day that they were playing in the field adjoining the schoolhouse, in this shape, O'Neill, who was hunting in the neighbourhood with a fine pack of hounds, observed the playfulness and dexterity of the swine in the field. He set his dogs after them to their great sudden surprise. The swine ran in various directions through the country, and formed those ditches called *Gleannta (muce dubhe)*, which are

to be seen in various parts of the South of Ulster. One made its way towards Lough Neagh, another faced the west, and a third that was very closely pursued, swam across *Loch Mucshnámha* at Castleblayney, and gave it its name, and then proceeded in the direction of Meath. (*OSL* 35)

Sir Samuel Ferguson cites another tradition which relates that the Glen of the Black Pig was named after a mythical monster which was banished after the establishment of Christianity to the seas off the Hebrides "where his 'rootings' may be seen in stormy weather in the hollows of the waves, and his 'gruntings' heard from the caverned rocks of Mull and Isla." (cited *UJA art. cit.* 72). A story about a place called *Dubhchlais* (modern *Dúchlais*, literally "black ditch") near Moylen in Co. Offaly, which Lett and Berry erroneously identify with the Black Pig's Valley, (*UJA art. cit.* 71) is related in the 10th-century collection of place-name legends known as the *Dindshenchus*. It recounts how Léna, the swineherd, was delivering the famous Mac Da Thó's pig to the feast of Mac Da Thó when he fell asleep at *Dubhchlaiss* and was buried alive by the pig while it was rooting up the trench (*mucclais* literally "pig-ditch") (*SMMD* 23–4).

Alexander Knox, in his *History of the County Down*, mistakenly calls the Dane's Cast by the name "Tyrone ditches" (*Knox Hist.* 354) but Lett and Berry rightly point out that this was the name of a separate site two miles due west of Gambles Bridge, supposedly named after Hugh Earl of Tyrone who, in the 17th century, carried out many military exploits in Co. Armagh (*UJA art. cit.* 66n). Knox also calls it "the Dowagh" (*Knox Hist.* 357), which probably derives from *an Dumhach* "the sandbank", and this name is also used by a contributor to the *Newry Magazine* for that part of the rampart near Newry (vol. i, no.3 p. 210; cited *OSL* 38).

Five Mile Hill   An English form
J 0935

Five Mile Hill, so called because it is five miles from Newry, is the highest hill in the parish (*OSM* iii 7).

Four Mile House   An English form
J 0934

1. 4 Mile House	Harris Hist. Map	1743
2. Four-mile House	Taylor & Skinner 4	1777

This house is approximately four miles from Newry.

Frankfort   An English form
J 0935

1. Frankfort	Cowan's Donaghmore 61	1764
2. Frankford	Cowan's Donaghmore 391	1832
3. Frankfort	OSM iii 7-9	1834
4. fraŋkˈfort	Local pronunciation	1990

This name is clearly of English origin but its exact meaning is unclear. An advertisement of "the Auction of goods and Furniture of Thomas Fortescue, Esq., late of Frankfort, Co. Down, deceased" appears in the *Belfast News-Letter* of March 16, 1764 (*Cowan's Donaghmore* 61) and one wonders whether his surname might have had some influence on the naming of this place. Indeed, a certain "Francis Fortescue, Esq. of Donaghmore" is mentioned in an obituary notice which appeared in the *Belfast News-Letter* on Sept. 13, 1765, following the death of his daughter, the wife of the Rev. Robert Martin (*Cowan's Donaghmore* 61) and it is not beyond the bounds of reason that the name Frankfort may have been coined after his name. However, Cowan reminds us that there was formerly a very large rath at Frankfort which is now destroyed and that such earthworks were called "forts" by the local settler population, places such as Churchyard Fort, Cooley's Fort, Cunningham's Fort, Smith's Fort, and Thompson's Fort (*ibid.* 57, 128–131).

A more important objection to this explanation is the attachment of the name Frankfort or Frankford to a number of places throughout Ireland (see *Census 1871*, 456–7) and, although they all do not necessarily have the same origin, this would seem to indicate that the name is of more than purely local significance. Frankfort in Co. Limerick would appear to have been called *Baile na Fraince*, or some variation thereof, from as early as 1586 (Ó Maolfabhail 1990, 40), clearly associating the name in this instance with the French. Thus, the origin of all the places in Ireland bearing this name must be considered together before a firm conclusion can be reached.

Glen	*an Gleann*	
J 0836	"the valley/glen"	
1. Clanagan	CPR Jas. I 190a	1611
2. Clanagan	CPR Jas. I 235a	1612
3. Clanaggan	CPR Jas. I 394b	1617
4. Clovegan, vill in peinct		
[de] vocat Corgany [Corgarry]	PRONI T 750/1	1622
5. Clanagan	Inq. Ult. (Down) §14 Car. I	1630
6. Clarenagan	Civ. Surv. x §72	1655c
7. Glynn Wood	Harris Hist. map	1743
8. Glyn	Harris Hist. 86	1744
9. Glenn	Newry Tel. (OSNB) 60	1830
10. Gleann "a valley"	OSNB Inf. 60	1834c
11. 'sa' Ghleann	GJ 12	1902c
12. fá'n Ghleann	GJ 12	1902c
13. i ngleann	CCU 98	1915c
14. sa ghleann	CCU 98	1915c
15. glεn	Local pronunciation	1990

The parish of Donaghmore contained two manors, one called Donaghmore and the other called Clanagan. The manor of Donaghmore comprised 12 townlands covering the modern townlands of Maddydrumbrist, Aughintober, and Moneymore, and that part of Donaghmore to the east of these including the townland of Lisserboy in the parish of Newry. The precinct of Clanagan included the 10 townlands of Drummiller, Lurganare, Carrickrovaddy, Knocknanarny, Ballylough, Corgary, Derrycraw, Ballyblaugh, and Drumantine in the parish of Donaghmore, and Lisnatierny in the parish of Aghaderg. Cowan records that the area comprising Ballymacarattybeg, Ballymacarattymore, Tullymore and Killysavan was known as the Fourtowns and suggests that these too originally formed part of Clanagan (*Cowan's Donaghmore* 336–7). Indeed, this may be inferred from a grant to Sir Arthur Magennis made in the year 1617 which refers to "… Ballyvikenratty, Ballytullaghmore in Clanagan" (*CPR Jas I* 396a).

The modern name of this district is Glen which comes from Irish *Gleann* "a valley, glen". Harris, writing in 1744, uses the form *Glyn* (*Harris Hist.* 86), an oblique form *Glinn* of this *Gleann*. Cowan (*Cowan's Donaghmore* 336) suggests that the name Clanagan comes from the Irish diminutive *Gleannagán* "the little glen" but his conclusion seems to rest on the fact that the area in question was later known as Glen or Glyn. However, it seems rather unlikely that a common toponym such as *gleann* would have been replaced by the comparatively rare element *clann* and even the earliest spellings invariably show initial *c* (1–6; cf. **Clanrye River**). It might be argued that Clanagan was formed by analogy with other district names such as Clandeboy (from Irish *Clann Aodha Buí*) but the lack of evidence for an initial *g* at any stage of the name's development renders this scenario improbable. Instead, it might be suggested that, as the name was clearly obsolete at the time he was writing, Cowan mistakenly assumed that the stress fell on the first syllable whereas there is, in fact, no evidence of the original stress. Thus, it is distinctly possible, given the near certain identification of the first element as Irish *clann*, that we are here dealing with an old sept name, perhaps *Clann Aogáin* (from earlier *Clann Aodhagáin*).

Ó hAogáin was the name of a family who were lords of *Dartraighe* in Co. Monaghan and of *Uí Niulláin* in Co. Armagh in the 10th and 11th centuries (Woulfe 1923, 557). The church of SS Peter and Paul in Armagh was built by a certain *Iomhar Ua hAedhacáin* who died while on pilgrimage to Rome in 1134 and was reputedly tutor to St Malachy (*AFM* ii 1022, 1046; MacLysaght 1957, 169). *Scolaighe Ua hAedhacáin*, who died in 945, is described as lord of Dartry in Co. Armagh (*tighearna Dartraighe*) (*AFM* ii 658) and *Dubhghall Ua hAedhacáin*, lord of *Uí Niulláin* (the barony of O'Neallan, Co. Armagh) was slain in 1054 (*AFM* ii 864). Information linking the O'Hagans directly with Clanagan has not been forthcoming but there is ample evidence that they held land in the early part of the 17th century just across the county border in Co. Armagh. The townland of Lisnagree in Co. Armagh was granted to Laughlin O'Hagan in 1611 and, in the same year, the townland of Ballygorman was granted to Donogh Reogh O'Hagan (*CPR Jas. I* 196b; *Inq. Ult.* (Armagh) §18 Car. I). These two townlands are a matter of only two or three miles from Clanagan so that the case for associating the O'Hagans with that district is reasonably secure. Thus, we may conclude with some degree of certainty, despite the lack of evidence regarding its pronunciation, that the name Clanagan derives from Irish *Clann Aogáin*.

McGaffin's Corner   An English form
J 1135

McGaffin's Corner is named after a family of that name who have long been associated with this area. In 1773 the local church vestry appointed a certain Alexander McGoffin, among others, to carry out repairs to the school house (*Cowan's Donaghmore* 218) and in the 19th century, McGaffins are recorded living in and around Donaghmore (*Ir. Wills Index* iv 92 (1852), 103 (1823), 92 (1826)).

Mount Mill Bridge   See **Drummiller**
J 0831

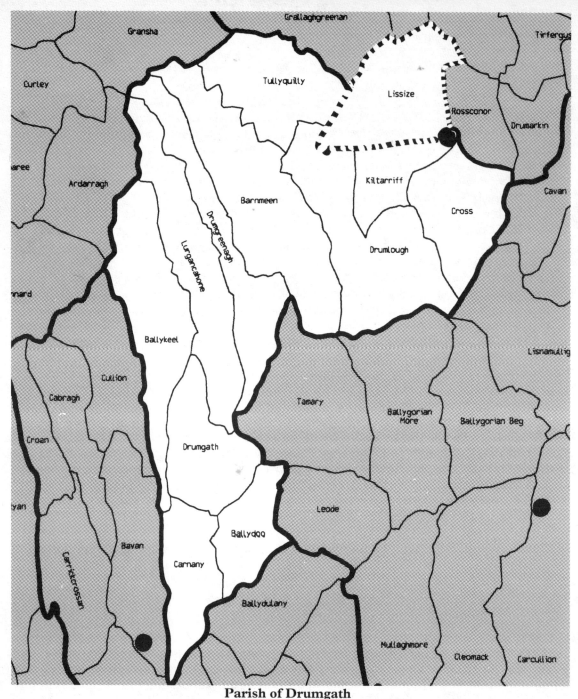

Parish of Drumgath

Barony of Iveagh Upper, Upper Half

Townlands
Ballydoo
Ballykeel
Barnmeen
Carnany
Cross
Drumgath

Drumgreenagh
Drumlough
Kiltarriff
Lissize
Lurgancahone
Tullyquilly

Town
Rathfriland

The townland of Lissize is divided between Drumgath and Drum-ballyroney parishes.

PARISH OF DRUMGATH

Drumgath parish, in south-west Co. Down, comprises approximately 5,330 acres (*Lewis' Top. Dict.* i 515), of which 81 acres were reported as "nearly exhausted turf bogs" in 1834 (*OSM* iii 19). It is a very hilly parish, the highest ground being Ballydoo Hill, 802 feet above sea level (*ibid.*).

The earliest reference to the church at Drumgath appears to be in a letter from Fleming, the archbishop of Armagh, dated 2 January 1407, appealing to Sir Milo "vicar of Drumgo" and other worthies of the diocese of Dromore to curtail the plunderous activities of Odo Magynassa (Hugh Magennis) who had "made hostile entry in the archbishop's lands and the city of Armagh" and "among other crimes" had taken a citizen of Armagh prisoner until he paid ransom for his release (*Reg. Fleming* §34). This same Milo, who was surnamed Omistega (modern McStay), died in 1431 and was succeeded as vicar of Drumgath by Michael O'Henean or O'Kaunan (*Swanzy's Dromore* 146). The vicarage fell vacant for a long time and was later held by a certain John Magyndehay "calling himself a priest, who has no title or sanction of law for his possession, which is but *de facto* and the outcome of his temerity and rashness." (*Annates Ulst.* 297) Pope Clement VII subsequently directed by papal bull that the Archdeacon of Dromore, Eugene Magnyssa (Magennis) and Cormac Osyegayl (O'Sheil), a canon of Dromore, should confer the vicarage on Nellanus Macyaydh "provided that ... no other had a special right therein" (*ibid.*)

Atkinson reported that the ruins of the ancient parish church still existed as late as 1925 about 3½ miles south-west of Rathfryland in the townland of Drumgath (*Atkinson's Dromore* 266). The *Archaeological Survey* (*ASCD*), however, has nothing to say about the church and the *Northern Ireland Sites and Monuments Record* merely notes the presence of a graveyard there.

The names of the townlands in the parish first make their appearance in early 17th-century grants. Documents such as these are often copied from one another and may not always afford independent evidence of the pronunciation of any name at this period. An examination of the grants and inquisitions used here, however, demonstrates that at least some are not directly related. On January 20, 1609, an order was made by the Lord Deputy and Council for "dividing and settling of the country of Iveagh, in the co. of Downe" according to which the five townlands of Ballyduff, Drumgreenagh, Barnmeen, Dromlough and Tullyquilly, along with "Rathfrillan, alias Rathrillan, with one castle and 4 towns", were to be held by Sir Arthur Magennis (*CPR Jas. I* 394b, 395b) and they were so granted in 1612 (*CPR Jas. I* 235a). These two documents are clearly closely related and they do not offer independent evidence as to the actual pronunciation of the names in them. A similar grant was also issued to the same Arthur Magennis in 1611 but a number of differences between this and the other two documents mentioned above seem to indicate that this grant is of independent value to the student of place-names (*CPR Jas. I* 188b–189a). Three of the four townlands of Rathfryland alluded to in these three documents may be identified with the modern townlands of Cross, Kiltarriff and Lissize, all of which neighbour on Rathfryland, as none of these places are to be found in any of our sources until 1657 when they appear, with the exception of Kiltarriff, on Sir William Petty's *Hibernia Regnum* (*Hib. Reg.* Up. Iveagh). As the name *Rathgriland* (Rathfryland) is located on the map precisely where we should expect to find Kiltarriff it would appear that at this stage the townland was known as Rathfryland and that it only came to be known as Kiltarriff when the older name became restricted to the town.

The lands held by Arthur Magennis were recorded at an inquisition held in Newry on June 5, 1629 (*Inq. Ult.* (Down) §13 Car. I). The contents of this document are similar to those of the grant of 1612 but a number of differences indicate that the relationship between them is not significantly close. Another inquisition, held 10 years later at Downpatrick, lists the lands held in his lifetime by Hugh Magennis, Arthur's son, and this differs considerably from the other documents discussed here (*Inq. Ult.* (Down) §85 Car. I). The order in which the townlands are listed is quite different and it contains additional information, particularly land measurements, not found in the earlier documents. The erratic ordering of the names in this list makes it difficult to identify the townlands that are mentioned in it with any degree of certainty and all names extracted from it are preceded by a question mark in the form-lists given below.

In the same order of 1609 mentioned above concerning the "dividing and settling of the country of Iveagh", John Magennis of Corrocks (Carrogs) was assigned a number of townlands in Clanawly including Lurgancahone and Ballykeel (*CPR Jas. I* 394b) and the grant was issued in 1611 (*CPR Jas. I* 190a; on Clanawly see pp. 51–2). There are a number of differences in spelling between the two documents but the large degree of similarity between them suggests that this variation is due to scribal or printing errors rather than to any intervention on the part of someone familiar with the names. At an inquisition taken at Newry in August of 1632 this same grant was recorded and a number of spelling differences, often reflecting the more modern forms of the names, allows us to adduce the forms in this document as independent evidence of the pronunciation of the names included in it (*Inq. Ult.* (Down) §32 Car. I).

The *OSNB* informant for Drumgath was John McLindon (*OSNB* 98). His suggested Irish forms are fairly reliable, although he does occasionally produce demonstrably inaccurate etymologies when faced with difficult names (see **Lurgancahone**). However, the interpretations provided by the *Ordnance Survey Memoirs* (*OSM*), evidently also of local provenance, are sometimes far superior. Of considerable note is the accurate analysis of the name **Drumgreenagh** as "thorny ridge", resisting the obvious interpretation as *Droim Grianach* "sunny ridge" made by McLindon.

PARISH NAME

Drumgath　　　　　　　　　　　　　*Droim gCath* (?)
J 1629　　　　　　　　　　　　　　　　"ridge of battles"

1. Drumgo	Reg. Flem. §34	1407
2. (?)Drumgan	Reg. Octavian (Swanzy) 146	1431
3. Drumgaa	Reg. Swayne 158	1435
4. Drumga, vic. of	Annates Ulst. 297	1530
5. Drumga, vicar of	Reg. Dowdall §113 80	1546
6. Drumgath	Jas. I to Dromore Cath. 314	1609
7. Dromgagh, vicarages of	CPR Jas. I 190b	1611
8. Dromgaghe vic.	CPR Jas. I 235a	1612
9. Dromgagh, vicar´ de ...	Inq. Ult. (Down) §13 Car. I	1629
10. Dromgath parish	Inq. Down (Reeves 1) 93	1657
11. Dromgah Parish	Hib. Reg. Up. Iveagh	1657c
12. Drumgagh (townland)	Hib. Reg. Up. Iveagh	1657c
13. Dromgagh halfe towne	Census 73	1659c
14. Dromgagh Parish	BSD 110	1661
15. Dromlagh al. Dromgagh	BSD 110	1661
16. D:gagh	Hib. Del. Down	1672c

17. Dromgah als Dromlagh	Hib. Del. Down	1672c
18. Drumlagh alias Drumgagh	ASE 273b §29	1681
19. Drumlagh alias Drumgigh	Rent Roll Down 10	1692
20. Drumgarth	Reg. Deeds abstracts ii §701	1784
21. Drumgath	Wm. Map (OSNB) 98	1810
22. Drumgath	Bnd. Sur. (OSNB) 98	1830c
23. Drumgath	EA 311	1833
24. Druim "a back" and Gah "a sting"	OSM iii 19	1834c
25. Druim a Ghath "Ridge of the dart"	OSNB Inf. 98	1834c
26. Druim gCat	Post-Sheanchas 62	1905
27. Druim gatha "ridge of the spear"	Mooney 135, 139	1950c
28. Droim Ga	AGBP 116	1969
29. Droim Ga	GÉ 93	1989
30. drom'gaθ	Local pronunciation	1990

Most modern scholars have agreed in deriving this name from an Irish form meaning "ridge of the spear" (24–25, 27–29) and the Rev. Bernard Treanor cites a legend of uncertain date which relates that St Patrick cast a spear from a spot in the townland of Tamary in the parish of Clonduff, declaring that where it should land would be the site of his church, and in this way, we are told, the location of the church of Drumgath was chosen (Treanor 1960, 5). There were originally two very similar words in Irish for "spear, dart", *gae* and *goth* or *gath*, which later fell together to give modern Irish *ga* (*DIL* svv. *gae*, 3 *goth*; Ó Dónaill svv. *gath(a)*, *ga*1). The earlier forms which end in a vowel (1–5) seem to support a derivation from *gae* but the appearance of a final spirant element in the later forms, represented either by *gh* or *th*, points to an origin in the synonymous *gath*. Irish *th* became [h] as early as the 13th century (O'Rahilly 1932, 207) so that the *th* of some early spellings must represent [h]: the re-emergence of [θ] in the current pronunciation is probably due to the influence of the written forms of the name. It is possible that this final element was re-analysed as *gath*, or that it represents the kind of *h* commonly found in modern Donegal Irish after a short stressed final vowel (see Quiggin 1906, 19), but it seems rather more probable that the spirant element was always there and that it was simply omitted by the earlier ecclesiastical scribes because it was relatively faint. We may compare Drumgath with Cloncagh in Co. Limerick which is thought to derive from *Cluain Cath* (Ó Maolfabhail 1990, 116). This name shows a similar pattern of spellings to those listed above with the earliest forms, dating from 1200 and 1306, ending in a vowel, and the later forms alternating in *gh*, *th*, and *h*.

This now forces us to consider the possibility that the name goes back to an original *Droim gCath*. As *droim* was neuter in O.Ir. it would have nasalized the following word and, although the neuter became obsolete c. 1000 AD, its effects were preserved in a few names such as **Slieve Gallion** in Co. Down (*Sliabh gCallann*) and **Slieve Gullion** in Co. Armagh (*Sliabh gCuillinn*) (*GÉ* 272). As we have seen, *cath* is attested as a place-name element elsewhere. As far as can reasonably be established at the present time, *ga* occurs in no other place-name in this country and these two facts tend to weigh in favour of *cath* as the origin of the second element of this name. Art Ó Maolfabhail (1990, 116) tentatively suggests a meaning "meadow of (the) battles" for Cloncagh in Co. Limerick but adds that *cath* might have another meaning besides "battle" in this name. In an article on the place-names of the Rosses in Co. Donegal, Dónall Mac Giolla Easpaig notes that a number of the places whose names contain this element are somewhat isolated and are thus unlikely locations for battles and proposes instead that it may refer to some natural feature (1984, 53–4).

There is another word *cáith*, gen. sing. *cátha*, meaning "chaff" and this must be considered as a strong possibility in all these names. Unfortunately, there is no way to distinguish between either of these words in the anglicized spellings with which we have to deal so that no firm conclusion as to the origin of the name Drumgath can yet be reached.

Hogan identifies a certain *Druim Gat*, which appears in a poem on the deaths of some Irish nobles attributed to Cináed úa hArtacáin (d. AU 975), with our Drumgath, but the rhyme *Gat: Abrat* clearly indicates a final [d] so that Drumgath cannot be intended (*Onom. Goed.* sv. *Druim Gat*; *Aid. Uais. Érenn* 312 §37).

TOWNLAND NAMES

Ballydoo　　　　　　　　　　*Baile Dubh*
J 1728　　　　　　　　　　　　"black townland"

1. Ballyduffe	CPR Jas. I 395b	1609
2. Balliduffe	CPR Jas. I 189a	1611
3. Ballyduffe	CPR Jas. I 235a	1612
4. Balleduffe	Inq. Ult. (Down) §13 Car. I	1629
5. Ballyduffe	BSD 110	1661
6. Ballyduffe	Rent Roll Down 8	1692
7. Ballydoo	Wm. Map (OSNB) 98	1810
8. Ballydoo	Bnd. Sur. (OSNB) 98	1830c
9. Baile-Dubh "the black townland"	OSM iii 21	1834
10. Baile Dubh	OSNB Inf. 98	1834c
11. Baile Dubh	Mooney 135	1950c
12. ˌbalˈdu	Local pronunciation	1990

Towards the summit of Ballydoo Hill in Ballydoo, black rock can be seen above the surface in many places and it is probably from this that the townland derives its name, *Baile Dubh* "black townland" (*OSM* iii 21). Historically, *bh* in Irish was pronounced as bilabial [v] (O'Rahilly 1932, 211) and this is frequently represented in anglicized spellings by *ff*. Thus, Lisduff in Co. Cavan comes from Irish *Lios Dubh* (*GÉ* 245) and Drumcliff in Co. Sligo derives from Irish *Droim Chliabh* (*GÉ* 216). In modern Ulster Irish, however, non-palatal *bh* has been vocalized so that *dubh*, which was formerly pronounced [duv], is now pronounced [duh], giving us the modern anglicized spellings that we see here ending in -*doo* (7–8).

Ballykeel　　　　　　　　　　*Baile Caol*
J 2531　　　　　　　　　　　　"narrow townland"

1. Ballykeehill (in Clawnawly)	CPR Jas. I 394b	1609
2. Ballikeehill (of Clanawlie)	CPR Jas. I 190a	1610
3. Ballykeele in Clanawlye	CPR Jas. I 191a	1611
4. Ballikeile in Clanawly	CPR Jas. I 266a	1614
5. Ballykeele in Clanawlie	CPR Jas. I 309a	1616
6. Ballykiele in Clanawley	Inq. Ult. (Down) §4 Jac. I	1617
7. Ballikeel	Inq. Ult. (Down) §32 Car. I	1632
8. Ballykeell	Census 73	1659c
9. Ballykeele	BSD 111	1661

10. Ballykeel	Sub. Roll Down 277	1663
11. Ballykeel	Wm. Map (OSNB) 98	1810
12. Ballykeel	Bnd. Sur. (OSNB) 98	1830c
13. Baile-Caol "the narrow townland"	OSM iii 21	1834
14. Baile Caol "narrow town"	OSNB Inf. 98	1834c
15. ˌbalʊˈkiːl	Local pronunciation	1990

The name Ballykeel was interpreted in the 19th century by O'Donovan's informant as *Baile Caol* "narrow townland" but some earlier forms (1–2) indicate that this may not have been the original form of the name. According to Reeves, writing c. 1847, the townland of **Kinghill** in Clonduff, which probably originates in Irish *Caomhchoill* "fair wood", was pronounced *Keehill* (*EA* 115) and this might be the same element as in our Ballykeel (*Baile Caomhchoille*). However, it might be argued that there is no evidence of the nasal element *mh* such as we find in the 17th-century forms for **Kinghill** and the separate development of the names should certainly be taken into consideration. A number of other tentative suggestions may be made including *Baile Caoithiúil* "pleasant townland" and *Baile Caochthoill* "townland of the bog-hole". However, *caoithiúil* is more commonly used in the sense "gentle, kindly" (*Dinneen* sv. *caoitheamhail*) and its application to a place here must be suspect. There is, indeed, a word *caochpholl* "boghole" but a variant *caochtholl* as required by our forms is unattested. Strangely enough, although the earliest forms seem to indicate a different origin, the name *Baile Caol* "narrow townland" is eminently suitable to the shape of Ballykeel which consists of a narrow strip of land running from north to south. It might also be noted that the forms with internal *h* are not unlike a spelling from 1527 *KilKahyll* for Kilkeel (*Reg. Cromer* ii §116), the second element of which is undoubtedly derived from some form of *caol*. Bearing these facts in mind, we may, therefore, tentatively suggest an original form, *Baile Caol* "narrow townland".

Ballykeel appears rather more frequently in our early 17th-century sources than most of the other townlands in the parish of Drumgath and the reason for this is that it was divided into two halves, one of which was granted by James I to John Magennis of Carrogs (*CPR Jas. I* 190a) in 1610, while the other was reckoned as church land. In 1611, a number of townlands in the barony of Iveagh, including "the moeity of Ballykeile in Clanawlye", was granted to William Worselely of Hallam in Nottingham county at a rent of 40 Irish shillings payable to the bishop of Dromore (*CPR Jas. I* 191a) but Worseley failed to fulfil the conditions attached to the grant and his holdings in the barony of Iveagh reverted to the bishop of Dromore in 1616 (*CPR Jas. I* 309a). In 1614, "Ballykeile in Clanawly, ½ plowland" was among a number of lands granted to Anthony Andrewes of Greenwich park in Kent to hold forever of the bishop of Dromore "in common soccage, as of the manor of Dromore in Iveagh, by fealty and suit of court" (*CPR Jas. I* 266a).

Barnmeen	*Bearn Mhín*	
J 1732	"smooth or level gap"	
1. Ballybannemine	CPR Jas. I 395b	1609
2. Bearmuyne	CPR Jas. I 189a	1611
3. Ballybarnemyne	CPR Jas. I 235a	1612
4. Barrmyne	Inq. Ult. (Down) §13 Car. I	1629
5. Ballybarnymyne	Inq. Ult. (Down) §13 Car. I	1629
6. (?)Barmeene	Inq. Ult. (Down) §85 Car. I	1639

7. (?)Bernameene	Inq. Ult. (Down) §85 Car. I	1639
8. Barninyn	Civ. Surv. x §72	1655c
9. Barnemyne	Census 73	1659c
10. Barninyn	BSD 111	1661
11. Barmyne	Sub. Roll Down 277	1663
12. Banemedne als Barnaneene	Rent Roll Down 9	1692
13. Barnmeen	Wm. Map (OSNB) 98	1810
14. Barnmean	Bnd. Sur. (OSNB) 98	1830c
15. Barnmeen	J O'D (OSNB) 98	1834c
16. Beirn Mhín, "smooth gap"	OSNB Inf. 98	1834c
17. Beárna Mín "smooth gap"	Mooney 137	1950c
18. Bearn Mhín	Éire Thuaidh	1988
19. bɑrn'miːn	Local pronunciation	1990

The townland of Barnmeen, situated on low ground with hills to the north and south, clearly derives its name, as indicated, from *Bearn Mhín* "level, arable gap" (cf. Treanor 1960, 5).

Carnany	*Carn Éanaigh*	
J 1628	"cairn of (the) birds"	
1. grange church land	Hib. Reg. Up. Iveagh	1657c
2. Carwey ½ towne	Census 73	1659c
3. (?)Grange	BSD 110	1661
4. Carnany ½ towne land	BSD 111	1661
5. Carnany	Wm. Map (OSNB) 98	1810
6. Carnany	Bnd. Sur. (OSNB) 98	1830c
7. Carrick-na-nean "birds' rock"	OSM iii 21	1834c
8. Carn Ean[n]aidh,		
"Enny's Carn or sepulchral heap"	J O'D (OSNB) 98	1834c
9. Carrach an éanaigh (coll)		
"Birds' Rock"	Mooney 137	1950c
10. Carn Aonaigh		
"Rock of the gathering"	Mooney 137	1950c
11. ˌkər'nɛnɪ	Local pronunciation	1990

There is no record of this name prior to its appearance on *Hib. Reg.* c. 1657 but, according to the *Book of Survey and Distribution*, in 1640 one half belonged to Rowland Savage (*BSD* 111) while the other, which was grange church land, was owned by a Mrs. Bagenal (*BSD* 110).

Despite various claims to the contrary (7, 9) there seems to be little doubt that the first element in the name is derived from Irish *carn* "mound, cairn" (8, 10). The second element is somewhat more problematic but it may derive from the gen. sing. of *éanach* (coll.) "birds" or *aonach* "fair, market". Tomás Ó Concheanainn notes that *aonach* in Scottish Gaelic has the meaning "a solitary place, a mountain top" etc. and he proposes that it had the same meaning in Irish (1966, 15–16) but the evidence is rather inconclusive. Although *carn* is qualified in many instances by a noun or adjective, it seems to be more usually qualified by a personal name (see *Onom. Goed.* 158–164, *Joyce* i 332–4) and, if this is indeed the case, we must consider the possibility that the second element here is a personal name such as that suggested by O'Donovan (8). Nevertheless, local authority had it that the name was associated with birds (form 7). As this same source has proved trustworthy and perceptive in relation to other names (see p. 116), the form *Carn Éanaigh* has been adopted here.

Cross *An Chros*
J 1932 "the cross"

1. Crosse	Hib. Reg. Up. Iveagh	1657c
2. Crosse	BSD 110	1661
3. Crosse	Hib. Del. Down	1672c
4. Crosse	ASE 273b §29	1681
5. Cross	Rent Roll Down 10	1692
6. Cross part	Rent Roll Down 13	1692
7. Crossquarter	Wm. Map (OSNB) 98	1810
8. Cross	Bnd. Sur. (OSNB) 98	1830c
9. Crois, "a cross"	J O'D (OSNB) 98	1834c
10. krɔs	Local pronunciation	1990
11. ðə ˈkrɔs	Local pronunciation	1990

The Irish word *cros* is frequently used in place-names, either with another element, as in the name of **Crossgar** in Co. Down, or independently, as here, in the sense of a "crossroads". The name **Crossmaglen** in Co. Armagh often appears in 17th-century sources as simply *Cross* but there is no indication that our Cross was ever qualified by another Irish element (but see 6–7).

Drumgath See parish name
J 1629

Drumgreenagh *Droim Draighneach*
J 1731 "thorny ridge"

1. Ballydrumduragh	CPR Jas. I 395b	1609
2. Dromdrinagh	CPR Jas. I 189a	1611
3. Ballydrumdrinagh	CPR Jas. I 235a	1612
4. Ballydromdrinagh	Inq. Ult. (Down) §13 Car. I	1629
5. (?)Balledromdrynagh	Inq. Ult. (Down) §85 Car. I	1639
6. Drumgrinagh	Hib. Reg. Up. Iveagh	1657c
7. Drumgungagh	Census 73	1659c
8. Dromgemagh	BSD 111	1661
9. Dromgrina	Hib. Del. Down	1672c
10. Drumgrenagh or Dromyghrenagh	ASE 273b §29	1681
11. Drumgronagh	Rent Roll Down 10	1692
12. Drumgreenan	Wm. Map (OSNB) 98	1810
13. Drumgreenagh	OSNB 98	1830
14. Drumgreena	Bnd. Sur. (OSNB) 98	1830c
15. Drumgreenagh	J O'D (OSNB) 98	1834c
16. Drumnadreen "blackthorn hill"	OSM iii 21	1834c
17. Drum gríanach "sunny ridge"	OSNB Inf. 98	1834c

18. ˌdrɔ̥m'griːnə	Local pronunciation	1990
19. ˌdrɔ̥m'griːnəx	Local pronunciation	1990

The element *bally* is frequently prefixed to townland names in official documents where it may not be original and this would appear to be the case in a number of early forms (1, 3–5). Nos. 7 and 8 may be discounted as scribal errors and no. 11 is not supported by the other forms. The remainder of the evidence points to a first element *droim* "a ridge" (1–14) and a second element *draighneach* "pertaining to blackthorn bushes" (1–5).

The peculiar development whereby the original -*d*- of this second element gives the current form with -*g*- (6–15) may be explained as dissimilation or, more probably, by the lenition of the second element following the gen. or dat. sing. of *droim*. In the 12th century, dental *dh* fell together with velar *gh* in Irish and the two sounds became indistinguishable. As English does not possess such a sound, it may be represented, as is probably the case here, by *g* (cf. Ballygorman *Baile Uí Ghormáin*, Ballygawley *Baile Uí Dhálaigh*, Kilgobnet *Cill Ghobnait*, Mogeely *Maigh Dhíle*, *GÉ passim*).

Drumlough
J 1832

Droim Locha
"ridge of the lake"

1.	Ballydrumlagh	CPR Jas. I 395b	1609
2.	Dromlagh	CPR Jas. I 189a	1611
3.	Ballydromlagh	CPR Jas. I 235a	1612
4.	Ballydromlagh	Inq. Ult. (Down) §13 Car. I	1629
5.	(?)Dromlagh	Inq. Ult. (Down) §85 Car. I	1639
6.	(?)Dromlagh	Inq. Ult. (Down) §85 Car. I	1639
7.	Dromlaugh	Hib. Reg. Up. Iveagh	1657c
8.	Dromlogh	Census 73	1659c
9.	Dromlagh al. Dromgagh	BSD 110	1661
10.	Dromgah al. Dromlagh	Hib. Del. Down	1672c
11.	Drumlagh alias Drumgagh	ASE 273b §29	1681
12.	Drumlagh alias Drumgigh	Rent Roll Down 10	1692
13.	Dromlogh part	Rent Roll Down 13	1692
14.	Drumlough	Wm. Map (OSNB) 98	1810
15.	Drumlough	Bnd. Sur. (OSNB) 98	1830c
16.	Druim a lacha, "Ridge of the Lough"	OSNB Inf. 98	1834c
17.	Drom Locha	Mooney 139	1950c
18.	drɔ̥m'lɔx	Local pronunciation	1990

This name goes back to Irish *Droim Locha* "ridge of the lake" although a number of spellings may indicate that this was once pronounced *Droim Lacha* (1–6, 9–12) where *lach* represents an early variant of *loch* "lake" (*DIL* sv. *1. loch*). The townland probably takes its name from the lake within its confines where the Newry River rises, now known as Drum Lough (see *OSM* iii 19).

Kiltarriff
J 1933

Coill Tarbh
"wood of bulls"

1.	Kiltariff part	Rent Roll Down 13	1692
2.	Kiltarriff	County Warrant (OSNB) 98	1827

3. Kiltariff	County Warrant (OSNB) 98	1830
4. Kiltarrif	Bnd. Sur. (OSNB) 98	1830c
5. Kiltarf	OSM iii 21	1834
6. Coill Tarbh, "Wood of the Bulls"	OSNB Inf. 98	1834c
7. ˌkɪl'tarəf	Local pronunciation	1990

There is a possibility that the second element in this name is gen. sing. *tairbh* "of the bull" but a comparison with other similar names in Ulster seems to support the suggested form in the gen. pl., *Coill Tarbh* "wood of bulls". **Cluntirriff** in Co. Antrim, Lochaterriff in the parish of Aghalurcher, Co. Fermanagh, and Edenterriff in the parish of Annagh, Co. Cavan, with internal *i* or *e*, all stem from forms with original gen. sing. *tairbh* (*Onom. Goed.* svv. *Cluain Tairbh, Loch an Tairbh, Etan Tairb*) whereas **Stranadarriff** in Co. Fermanagh, with its internal *a*, appears to derive from the gen. pl. *tarbh* (*Onom. Goed.* sv. *Srath na Tarbh*). This is much as we would expect and we can state with some confidence that Kiltarriff, with its forms invariably showing internal *a*, comes from *Coill Tarbh* "wood of bulls".

Lissize   *Lios Seaghsa*
J 1833   "enclosure of the wood/wooded height"

1. Lissyse	Hib. Reg. Up. Iveagh	1657c
2. Lyseyse	Hib. Reg. Up. Iveagh	1657c
3. Lisseise	BSD 110	1661
4. Lisseis	BSD 113	1661
5. Lisyse	Hib. Del. Down	1672c
6. Lisise	ASE 273b §29	1681
7. Lysise	Rent Roll Down 10	1692
8. Lissize	Rent Roll Down 13	1692
9. Lissize	Wm. Map (OSNB) 98	1810
10. Lissize	Bnd. Sur. (OSNB) 98	1830c
11. Lios sadhas "Size's lis fort"	OSNB Inf. 98	1834c
12. Lios Shaghas "Goat's Bog"	Mooney 31	1950c
13. lə'saiz	Local pronunciation	1990

The suggestions made by McLindon (11) and Mooney (12) as to the origin of this difficult name are both rather peculiar. McLindon was clearly puzzled by the name and either he or O'Donovan suggested as a second element a personal name of which there is no record anywhere else. Mooney's interpretation of this element as *saghas* is even stranger as no such word meaning "goat" is attested in any Irish dictionary. The most probable origin of this element is Irish *seaghais* (otherwise *seaghas*). It appears in the Irish names for the river Boyle (*Seaghais*) and for part of the Boyne (*Sruth Seaghsa*) (*Dinneen* sv. *seaghais*) and its close association with water features perhaps indicates that the meaning "wood, wooded height" attributed to it by Dinneen is secondary (see *DIL* sv. *segais*). The loss of a final syllable ending in a vowel is not unusual in Irish place-names and we may compare the name of the nearby townlands of **Drumlough** (*Droim Locha*) and **Ballylough** (*Baile an Locha*) which show no trace of the original final *-a*, even in the earliest sources. The final [s] in this name appears to have become voiced from quite an early date (8–10) and this is probably due to analogy with English words such as "size".

Lurgancahone
J 1631

Lorgain Chú Chonnacht
"Cú Chonnacht's long low ridge"

1.	Lurganconnaght	CPR Jas. I 394b	1609
2.	Lurgancoconaght	CPR Jas. I 190a	1611
3.	Lorgancooquoone	Inq. Ult. (Down) §32 Car. I	1632
4.	Lorgicoghoone	Civ. Surv. x §72	1655c
5.	Lurgancughan	Census 73	1659c
6.	Lurgankockhune	BSD 111	1661
7.	Lurgancahone	Wm. Map (OSNB) 98	1810
8.	Lurgancahone	Bnd. Sur. (OSNB) 98	1830c
9.	Lurgancahone	Ir. Wills Index iv 104	1841
10.	Lurgan Cháthon, "Cahan's Long Hill"	OSNB Inf. 98	1834c
11.	Lurgan Cuchonnacht "Cuconnaght's long hill"	Mooney 141	1950c
12.	ˈlọrgənˌkəˈhoːn	Local pronunciation	1990

This place seems to have been known in Irish as *Lorgain Chú Chonnacht* "Cú Chonnacht's long low ridge" (1–2). Cú Chonnacht, meaning "hound of Connacht", was a popular name in the 17th century (O'Rahilly 1922, 109) especially among the Maguires of Fermanagh who anglicized it Constantine (Ó Corráin & Maguire 1981, 63–64), but it is also found in Co. Down as, for example, in the person of "Coconaght O'Ronowe or O'Rony of Dycomed" who received a grant of land in 1611 from James I (*CPR Jas. I* 190b). Whereas the original form of the name is relatively transparent, its subsequent development is rather peculiar. Under normal circumstances, final *-cht* in East Ulster Irish becomes *t* as, for example, in Drumsnat, Co. Monaghan (*Droim Sneachta*) and **Ballybot** in Newry (*Baile Bocht*). However, some place-names have highly irregular, even haphazard, histories and sense cannot always be made of their present form.

Tullyquilly
J 1734

Tulaigh Uí Chaollaí (?)
"Kealy's mound"

1.	Ballytullchooly	CPR Jas. I 395b	1609
2.	Tullyquoile	CPR Jas. I 189a	1611
3.	Ballytullychooly	CPR Jas. I 235a	1612
4.	Balletullycooly	Inq. Ult. (Down) §13 Car. I	1629
5.	(?)Tullyncholy	Inq. Ult. (Down) §85 Car. I	1639
6.	(?)Tullyquily	Inq. Ult. (Down) §85 Car. I	1639
7.	Tullycoolie	Civ. Surv. x §72	1655c
8.	Tollyquillin	Census 73	1659c
9.	Tollighnally	BSD 111	1661
10.	Tullygnilly	Sub. Roll Down 277	1663
11.	Tullycoyle	Rent Roll Down 9	1692
12.	Tullyquilly	Wm. Map (OSNB) 98	1810
13.	Tullyquilly	Bnd. Sur. (OSNB) 98	1830c
14.	Tulaigh Chuaille, "hill of the pole, the tall branchless tree"	J O'D (OSNB) E42 no. 100	1834c

15. Tulach a chuaille, "Hill of the notable tall branchless tree"	Mooney 141	1950c
16. ˌt̥ɒlɪˈkʷĩlt	Local pronunciation	1990

The early spellings of this name are unusually inconsistent and this factor makes the process of discerning the original Irish rather difficult. The first element undoubtedly represents a form of Irish *tulach* "mound, hill" and we might follow O'Donovan in deriving the second element from *cuaille* "stake, pole, post". This derivation accords well with the majority of early forms (1, 3–5, 7) and *cuaille* is attested in several other names (*Onom. Goed.* 312), although caution should be exercised here as O'Donovan, unfamiliar with the pronunciation of the East Ulster *ao*, frequently mistakenly wrote *ua* (Flanagan 1978(c) 46). Indeed, a number of forms suggest an original internal vowel *ao* (2, 11) which is frequently anglicized *-oy-* (cf. **Islandmoyle**, Co. Down; **Dunmoyle** and **Knockmoyle** Co. Tyrone) and we might infer an original *Tulaigh Chaoille* "mound of the *caoille* (a division of land)", or *Tulaigh Uí Chaollaí* where the second element represents the surname *Ó Caollaí* which is attested in Ulster (Woulfe 1923, 452). The reduction of the vowel *ao* to the present [ɪ] is paralleled by the anglicization of the surname *Ó Caoindealbháin* as Quinlan, and the modern pronunciation of the place-names *Dún Chaoin* in Kerry and *Droim Caoin* in Tyrone as Dunquin and **Drumquin** respectively. Unfortunately, evidence of the use of the surname in the immediate area has not been forthcoming but, as Woulfe notes, it is now almost everywhere disguised under the anglicized form of Kelly (*ibid.* 452)

OTHER NAMES

Lisnashrean	*Lios na Srian*	
J 1733	"fort of the bridles"	
1. Lisnarean or the Bridle Fort hill	OSM iii 19	1834
2. Lisnabrean Rath	OS 1:10,000 Sh. 253	1983

Lisnashrean Hill in Barnmeen townland stands 323 feet above sea-level. In the *Ordnance Survey Memoirs*, it is called Bridle Fort hill (*OSM* iii 19) and, although it is not made clear in the text, this may reflect the local understanding of the name (cf. **Lisnastrean** in the parish of Drumbo). The name has been corrupted on the *OS 1:10,000* to *Lisnabrean*, apparently mistaking the original *sh* for *b*.

McGinn's Cross	An English form	
J 1734		
1. məˈgʲɪnz ˈkɔrnər (sic)	Local pronunciation	1990

The name McGinn or Maginn is common in Ulster and is found in most of the nine counties (Bell R. 1988, 160). It was borne by many members of the clergy of the diocese of Dromore from very early times, men such as Patrick McGynd, who was appointed rector of Clonduff and prebendary of Magheralin in 1407 (*Swanzy's Dromore* 106, 201), and John Magynd, who became a canon of Dromore in 1422 (*ibid.* 112). The name also crops up in later documents relating to Drumgath and most importantly a certain James Magin of Tullyquilly appears in the *Index to Irish Wills* for the year 1851 (*Ir. Wills Index*, 104). Apart from giving their name to McGinn's Cross, this family also gave its name to the townland of **Ballymaginn** in Magheralin.

Rathfriland   *Ráth Fraoileann* (?)
J 2133   "fort of *Fraoile*"

1. (?)Ráith Braoilein	Onom. Goed. 568	1646
2. an Mhullaigh, air chúrsa	Neilson's Intro. 104	1808
3. Ráith Fraoileann	SCtSiadhail 74	1852
4. Mullach Ráth' Fraoileáin	Omeath Infs. 157	1901
5. Raferilan	Fiants Eliz. §1583	1570
6. Raphrylan	Fiants Eliz. §4218	1583
7. Raphrilan	Fiants Eliz. §4218	1583
8. Rathphrilan	Fiants Eliz. §4327	1583c
9. Reagher insul:	Bartlett Map (BM)	1600
10. (?)Reagher Ile	Bartlett Map (TCD)	1601
11. (?)Rafer-Ile	Bartlett Map (Esch. Co. Map)2	1603
12. Rathfrillan	CPR Jas. I 395b	1609
13. Rathfrillan alias Rathrillan	CPR Jas. I 395b	1609
14. (?)Ragh Iland	Speed's Antrim & Down	1610
15. (?)Rafer	Norden's Map	1610c
16. Rathfrillane (×3)	CPR Jas. I 188b	1611
17. Rathfrillan	CPR Jas. I 189a	1611
18. Rathfrillan (×3)	CPR Jas. I 190b	1611
19. Rathfrillan	CPR Jas. I 235a	1612
20. Rathfrilland al. Rathkillan castle	CPR Jas. I 235a	1612
21. Rathfrilland	CPR Jas. I 235a	1612
22. Rathbrillane in Iveagh	PRONI T 750/1	1622
23. Rathfrylan (×2)	Inq. Ult. (Down) §13 Car. I	1629
24. Rathfrilan	Inq. Ult. (Down) §30 Car. I	1632
25. Rathfreelan	Inq. Ult. (Down) §85 Car. I	1639
26. Rafrylan	Civ. Surv. x §72	1655c
27. (?)Corintenvally	Hib. Reg. Up. Iveagh	1657c
28. Rathgriland	Hib. Reg. Up. Iveagh	1657c
29. Rathryland	Census 73	1659c
30. Rafriland ½ Towneland	BSD 110	1661
31. Corintanvally al. Rathfrilan	BSD 113	1661
32. Rathgriland	Hib. Del. Down	1672c
33. Rathfryland	ASE 273b §29	1681
34. Rathfryland	Rent Roll Down 10	1692
35. Rathfriland	Wm. Map (OSNB) 98	1810
36. Ráá-freelion	OSL 70	1834
37. Rathfryland	J O'D (OSNB) 98	1834c
38. Rathfraoileann	OSL 70	1834
39. Mullach Ráith Fraoileann "the summit of the fort of Fraoileann	OSL 69–70	1834
40. Ráth Fraoilean[n]	OSNB Inf. E42 no. 100	1834c
41. Mullach Ráith Fraoilean[n] "Summit of Rathfryland"	OSNB Inf. 98	1834c
42. Ráth Foircheálláin	Post-Sheanchas 107	1905
43. Rath Fearghaláin/Frighileán	Mooney 141	1950c
44. Ráth Fraoileann	AGBP 119	1969

126

| 45. Ráth Fraoileann | GÉ 149 | 1989 |
| 46. ˌrɑθˈfrailən | Local pronunciation | 1990 |

The castle of Rathfriland was probably built by the Magennis family in the late 16th or early 17th century (*ASCD* 248). Hugh Magennis resided at Rathfriland in the later 16th century (*Fiants Eliz.* §§ 1583, 4218) and Marshall Bagenal describes him living "very cyvillie and English-like in his house" in 1586 (*Bagenal's Descr. Ulst.* 152). Hugh's son, Arthur, also lived at Rathfriland and was in residence at the castle in 1611 (*CPR Jas. I* 190b). The castle was battered down in the rebellion of 1641 (*Atkinson's Dromore* 265) and much of the remainder was carried off by William Hawkins, the first Protestant proprietor after the Rebellion, to build the inn and a number of other houses in the town (*Harris Hist.* 87).

Josiah Bodley, writing c. 1603, describes a visit he made to a certain *Insula Magnesii* "Magennis' island", ten miles from Newry. The 19th-century editor of the text identifies this *Insula Magnesii* as Castlewellan, one of the strongholds of the Magennises (*Bodley's Lecale* 76) but it would appear, rather, to be the castle at Rathfriland for this was the home of Arthur Magennis (*CPR Jas. I* 190b) and his wife Lady Sara, daughter of the Earl of Tyrone, who played host to Bodley's companions while they awaited his arrival from Newry (*Bodley's Lecale* 77; see *UJA* 12 (1906) 74 n.2). The term "island" is frequently applied to raised pieces of land surrounded by bog and Rathfriland, at the time in question, aptly suited such a description (see Ó Mainnín 1989–90; *UJA* 12 (1906) 74 n.2).

B. S. Mac Aodha identifies *Ragh Is.* on Speed's map of Antrim and Down as our Rathfriland (*Maps Down (Mac Aodha)* 70–1) and, indeed, similar names are applied to a site in Upper Iveagh on a number of early 17th century maps (10–11, 14–15). The location varies considerably on these maps and it can hardly be doubted that the *Ragh Is.* et var. was to some extent confused with **Lough Island Reavy** in Kilcoo. The spellings also differ in important details from the majority of other early forms, most notably substituting *gh* for *f* (10, 14) and the addition of an extra syllable (10–11, 15), although in this latter respect they have something in common with our earliest extant anglicized spelling (5). There can be no doubt that these forms belong to a separate and distinct cartographic tradition and within this tradition the name seems to have been re-analysed as an Irish element followed by the English word "island". While this identification is of some interest, the forms with which it provides us are so confused that they can provide only the most limited assistance in attempting to ascertain the origin of the name. The most certain thing about the etymology of Rathfryland is that it has got nothing to do with "islands".

Some slight variation in the spelling of the name is found even in modern times. The name of the town is officially spelt with an *i* (Rathfriland) whereas the District Electoral Division has a *y* (Rathfryland) (see *Top. Index 1961* 32; *OS 1:50,000* 29 J 2033). This variation is, of course, wholly artificial and does not represent any difference in origin.

The first element of the name would appear to be *ráth* "fort" but the fort has long since disappeared (*ASCD* 149). O'Donovan thought he "could trace the ring of a very large fort on the eastern side of the town" but even in his day none of the inhabitants remembered it or recognized the ring as a fort (*OSL* 69–70).

The second element is now impossible to determine, although it is, in all likelihood, a personal name. The spellings found in most 19th- and 20th-century surveys are not very enlightening as to the origin of the name and they are probably mere transcriptions of the name. *Fraoileann* is not attested in the lexicon, nor is it found in any of the works on personal names, although it is supported by the spellings provided from Irish speakers. The forms suggested by Laoide and by Mooney (42–3) are hardly convincing and may fairly be regarded as speculative. Two spellings, one of which appears to be in Irish, suggest that the initial letter of the final element may have been *b* rather than *f* (1, 22: I have been unable to confirm the authenticity of the former spelling cited in Hogan's *Onom. Goed.* as his reference is inaccurate. Caution should therefore be exercised in accepting it as an Irish form as he elsewhere presents his own etymologies as original material). This same development is found also in the name Raphoe (*Ráth Bhotha*) in Co. Donegal and in the strikingly similar name Rathfreedy (*Ráth Bhroíle*) in Co. Limerick (Ó Maolfabhail 1990, 237).

It would appear from *Hib. Reg.* Up. Iveagh (27) and *BSD* (31) that another name for Rathfriland was *Corr an tSeanbhaile* "hill of the old homestead" or *Corr an tSeanbhealaigh* "hill of the old road". In a letter written in 1834, O'Donovan states that John McLindon had told him that, in the prophecies of St Columbkille, Rathfriland was called *Mullach Curraigh*, that is, "the hill over the bog" (*OSL* 69–70) but I have been unable to confirm this. Nevertheless, the evidence from Irish sources clearly shows that Rathfryland was also known as *an Mullach* "the summit" or *Mullach Rátha Fraoileann* "the summit of Rathfryland" among Irish speakers of the 19th and early 20th centuries (2, 4).

PARISH OF KILBRONEY

Kilbroney is situated in the barony of Upper Iveagh and bounded by the parishes of Kilkeel, Clonallan and Clonduff. It consists of 13,208¼ acres, more than half of which is mountainous (*Lewis' Top. Dict.* ii 58). It forms part of the diocese of Dromore and was historically considered a "bishop's mensal" i.e. "a parish whose revenues were in part devoted to supplying the bishop's table" (*Atkinson's Dromore* 249). The parish, or more particularly the eastern part of it, is often called **Killowen** in 17th-century documents, and as both names contain the element *cill* "a church" they undoubtedly have old ecclesiastical associations. Nevertheless, neither Killowen nor Kilbroney is recorded as such in early Irish documentation. What are preserved are references to Saint *Brónach* of *Glenn Sechis*, from whom Kilbroney takes its name. *Glenn Sechis* has been identified with the Kilbroney valley running inland between the mountains from Rosstrevor to Hilltown (*Atkinson's Dromore* 100).

The oldest occurrence of the name Kilbroney seems to be that in the *Register of Archbishop Sweteman* under the year 1366 (*Reg. Sweteman* §221); in the *Ecclesiastical Taxation* of 1302–6 the local church is simply called *ecclesia de Glentegys* or "the church of *Glenn Sechis*" (*Eccles. Tax.* 114). The old church ruins just outside Rosstrevor date to the 15th or 16th century (*ASCD* 303), but there is a pre-Norman cross in the graveyard nearby which provides evidence for ecclesiastical settlement in the area as much as 500 years earlier (*ASCD* 129, 303). There are many references to the parish in the registers of the medieval Archbishops of Armagh. In 1428, for example, we read of the grant to Gyllabrony McKewyn of the custody of the staff of Saint Brónach with all the privileges which that entailed (*Reg. Swayne* 101) and this, to quote Atkinson, appears to have been "the title by which the incumbent held the benefice from the Bishop" (*Atkinson's Dromore* 250). Reeves thinks it likely that Brónach's baculus or staff was a relic preserved in the local church (*EA* 309), but if so it has disappeared without trace. What does survive is another relic, the Kilbroney bell or *clog bán* ("white bell") as it was anciently called (*OSM* iii 37), and it can be seen in the Roman Catholic chapel of Rosstrevor up to this day (*ASCD* 140). The old church of Kilbroney was used by the Church of Ireland after the Reformation but was described in 1641 as "out of repaire". For a history of the various church buildings in the parish in more recent times see *Atkinson's Dromore* 249–55 and the *Ordnance Survey Memoirs* (*OSM*) iii 26–40.

The earliest surviving documentation of Kilbroney townlands dates to 1570. Under that year the *Fiants of Elizabeth I* record the leasing of a castle and a large number of townlands "in the barony of Legan in the country called M'Gennys, in the queen's hands by act of parliament" to one John Sanky, an Englishman, for a period of 21 years. The *Legan* (Irish *Lagán* "low-lying country") is an old district name which embraced eight of the modern townlands in western Kilbroney, the southern part of neighbouring Clonallan and all of Warrenpoint.[1] Six Kilbroney townlands are listed in the 1570 grant: Knockbarragh, Levallyreagh, Ballymoney, Drumreagh (including modern Drumreagh Upper), Drumsesk and Moygannon (*Fiants Eliz.* §1609).[2] As to the grantee, John Sanky, he disappears from the records. In 1583 we read of a "grant to Sir Hugh Magnisse, knight, of the entire country or territory of Iveaghe, alias the country of Magnisse..." the bounds of which extend "to the sea towards Dromseske in the Legan..." (*Fiants Eliz.* §4327) and it seems certain that these lands had historically formed part of the old Magennis patrimony. In 1609 the six aforementioned townlands, plus another contiguous townland Levallyclanone, are recorded in the possession of Arthur Magennis of Rathfriland (*CPR Jas. I* 395b), who had succeeded Hugh, his father, as lord of Iveagh in 1596 (Walsh 1930, 38). In 1612 the same townlands were granted by James I to Magennis (*CPR Jas. I* 235a) and are again recorded in his possession in an inquisition dating to 1629 the year of his death (*Inq. Ult.* §13 Car. I). They then

129

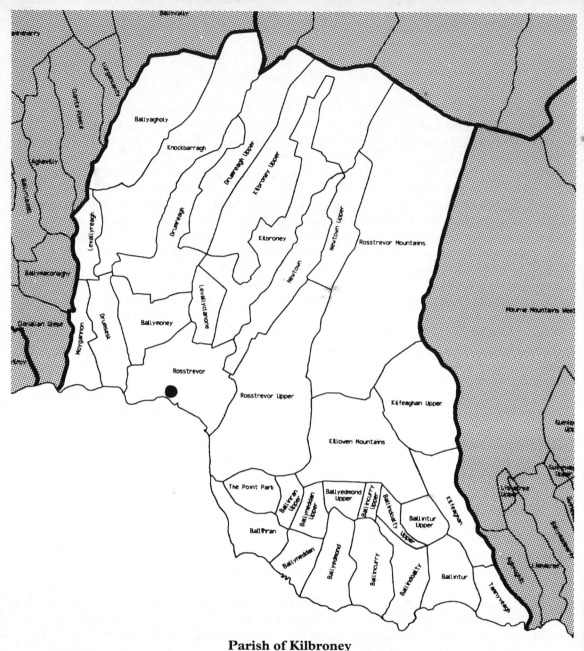

Parish of Kilbroney
Barony of Iveagh Upper, Upper Half

Townlands
Ballincurry	Ballyagholy	Kilbroney	Newtown
Ballincurry Upper	Ballyedmond	Kilbroney Upper	Newtown Upper
Ballindoalty	Ballyedmond Upper	Kilfeaghan	Point Park, The
Ballindoalty Upper	Ballymoney	Kilfeaghan Upper	Rosstrevor
Ballinran	Ballyneddan	Killowen Mountains	Rosstrevor Upper
Ballinran Upper	Ballyneddan Upper	Knockbarragh	Rosstrevor Mountains
Ballintur	Drumreagh	Levallyclanone	Tamnyveagh
Ballintur Upper	Drumreagh Upper	Levallyreagh	
	Drumsesk	Moygannon	*Town*: Rosstrevor

passed to his son Hugh whose lands are subject of another inquisition dating to 1639 (*Inq. Ult.* §85 Car. I). It is important to note that all of these early 17th-century documents list the Magennis lands in similar order. The spelling of names varies occasionally but, in so far as they relate to Kilbroney, all four lists appear to derive from a common original, the 1639 inquisition being the poorest copy.

The second half of the 17th century heralds a major decline in the fortunes of the Magennises. The *Book of Survey and Distribution* notes that the Kilbroney townlands had been held by Lady Sarah Evagh, i.e. Arthur's wife Sorcha, daughter of Hugh O'Neill, in 1640, but by 1661 five of them had been transferred to William Hawkins, while Levallyreagh was divided between Hawkins and Grace Swift and Moygannon between Hawkins and Joseph Deane (*BSD* 108). On the *Hibernia Regnum* map of c. 1657 all seven townlands are marked[3] whereas the rest of the parish, with the exception of Ballyagholy,[4] is simply designated "Protestant Lands." It would appear, therefore, that the Magennis lands were confiscated some time between 1657 and 1661. Unfortunately the *Census* of c. 1659 is of little help, since of these seven townlands only Levallyreagh, Knockbarragh and Drumreagh are listed (*Census* 72), nor is the *Subsidy Roll* of 1663, where Hawkins is named among those whose lands were taxed but the lands themselves are not specified (*Sub. Roll* 277). In the *Acts of Settlement and Explanation* the five townlands granted to William Hawkins are said to be in possession of his son John in 1681, as is that part of Moygannon which was also included in the original grant. All Hawkins' possessions, which included much of the old Magennis patrimony, are stated to have been created into the manor of Rathfryland later that same year (*ASE* 273b–274a §29). There appears to be no mention whatsoever of Levallyreagh, whereas the south part of Moygannon, granted to Joseph Deane, is mentioned no later than 1666, at which date it was still in his possession (*ASE* 107b §9). The *Rent Roll* of 1692 seems to follow the townland lists as they occur in *ASE* (*Rent Roll Down* 9–10). The spellings of the names, however, can be very inaccurate, and the rent roll is clearly a poor transcription.

Having discussed the records which deal with the Magennises we can turn to the seven Killowen townlands – Ballinran, Ballyneddan, Ballyedmond, Ballincurry, Ballindoalty, Ballintur and Tamnyveagh – which Donald and James McYawne are said to have alienated to Nicholas Bagenal in 1568 (*Ex. Inq. 34 Eliz. I*). Strangely enough, these townlands are not included in the *Bagenal Rental* of 1575 although we know from an independent source that Nicholas had indeed purchased these lands "from the Irish" (*Inq. Ult.* §15 Jac. I). In 1606 Arthur Bagenal was granted a licence to alienate his possessions in Killowen to Sir John Floyde and Edward Trevor (*CPR Jas. I* 86a). A year later both Bagenal and Trevor were licensed to alienate the same lands plus some in Mourne to Sir Arthur Chichester, Patrick Barnewall, Richard Trevor, Thomas Savadge and John Trevor (*CPR Jas. I* 102b-103a). Another copy of this latter document appears elsewhere in the patent rolls (*CPR* Jas. I 494b-495a). When in 1609 a record was made of the major freeholders in Iveagh, Bagenal still held these seven townlands (*CPR* Jas. I 395b) and in 1611 James I officially granted them to him (*CPR* Jas. I 190b). They are again included in a grant dating to 1613, when all the Bagenal possessions in Cos Down, Armagh and Louth were confirmed (*CPR Jas. I* 246b-247), in an inquisition dating to c. 1625 (*Inq. Ult.* §15 Jac. I), and finally in an inquisition dating to 1638 (*Inq. Ult.* §84 Car. I), Bagenal having died in 1637. Arthur was succeeded by his son Nicholas who is recorded as proprietor in the 1661 *Book of Survey and Distribution* (*BSD* 132). Here the seven Killowen townlands are said to be "parte and parcel of ye manor of Greene Castle" and are included in Kilkeel. The 1688 *Rent Roll of Mourne* also includes the Killowen townlands and notes that they were "given by Nich: Bagenall Esqr to Captn Trevor Loyd & afterwards to Mr. Price" (*Rent Roll Morne* 6).

It is important in analysing these names to be aware of the relationship which the various documents bear to one another. Although the spellings may differ slightly, the townland lists in the 1606 and 1607 grants and in the 1638 inquisition follow each other very closely. That all three lists are ultimately derived from the same source is almost certain, although the 1638 inquisition seems to be a poor copy. The 1613 patent and 1625 inquisition are also related and sometimes resemble the 1606 and 1607 lists in the ordering of townlands. They differ, however, in that they record aliases for some of the names, Ballintur and Ballinran for example, and should, therefore, be seen to provide independent evidence for the development of these names. The 1609 and 1611 grants are also similar but diverge sharply from the other groups. They complement the 1613 and 1625 documents in that they record an important stage in the process of name substitution which in the Killowen area was quite dramatic. In the past Ballyedmond was known as *Lurganleigh* and *Ballypoell*, Ballincurry as *Lurgenmore* and *Ballynelorgin*, Ballindoalty as *Rone-harragh*, Ballintur as *Eden-curren* and Ballinran as *Ballyrannaghmore*. We have seen that the 17th-century documentation sometimes ties the various names together in the form of aliases. For some of the townlands, however, the only way of identifying the older names correctly is by comparing the various sources and operating a process of elimination. As to how these places came to change their names one can only suggest that in the case of Ballintur, for example, we have a denomination of land which meared *Eden-curren* and which in the process of time amalgamated with and absorbed it. Developments of this nature are not unusual but it is nevertheless remarkable that four out of seven townlands in a given area should have changed so drastically, particularly in view of the fact that all four are contiguous! On the other hand, there are names in the parish which even now are in the process of being discarded. The late Bernard Mooney, who did some very important work on the locality, recorded over fifty previously undocumented minor names, many of which are in danger of being forgotten. For those who are interested in these names see *Mooney's Rostrevor* 35-40.

(1) The *Legan* is also mentioned in *Fiants Eliz.* §4327 and *Inq. Ult.* §13 Car. I. See further **Clonallan** parish.
(2) There is also a copy of this grant in the *Calendar of State Papers*, where the wording is slightly different but the spelling of names almost exactly the same (*CSP Ire.* 1570, 435).
(3) They are also found in *Hiberniae Delineatio*, the later atlas based on the same survey (*Hib. Del. Down*). The spellings here differ slightly.
(4) Ballyagholy, in the western extremity of the parish, formed a part of the ancient territory of *Clanawly* and as such is often included in townland lists concerned largely with Clonallan.

PARISH NAME

Kilbroney	*Cill Bhrónaí*	
	"*Brónach*'s church"	
1. Bronach uirgo o Glinn Sechis	Fél. Óeng. Apr. 2 p110n	1450c
2. Bronach ógh ó Chill Sechis	Mart. Don. Apr. 2 p92	1630c
3. Bronach ogh ó Ghlinn seichis	Mart. Don. 368	1630c
4. Chill' Brónaighe, reilic	Sgéalaidhe Óirghiall 87	1905c
5. i gCill Bhrónaighe	Sgéalaidhe Óirghiall 87	1905c
6. Glentegys al. de Nister, Ecclesia de	Eccles. Tax. 114	1306c

7.	Kyllwronaygh	Reg. Sweteman §221	1366
8.	Clonseys, ecclesia de	Reg. Dowdall §129 275	1422
9.	St. Bromana's parish church	Reg. Swayne 101	1428
10.	Parish churches of St. Bromana the virgin & Disertmoy	Reg. Swayne 85	1428
11.	Kilbrony, church of	Reg. Prene (EA) 116n	1433
12.	Cillbronaid, vicar of	Reg. Prene (EA) 116n	1442
13.	Kyllbronca and Dissertdubunnugi, rectories of	Reg. Prene (EA) 116n	1442
14.	Kilbroney	Reg. Cromer viii 343, §51	1526
15.	Kilbrony	Reg. Cromer x 174, §195	1534
16.	Killbronagh, vicar of	Reg. Dowdall §113 81	1546
17.	Kylbrayne	Lythe Map	1568c
18.	Kilbrayne	Mercator's Ulst.	1595
19.	Kylbraine	Mercator's Ire.	1595
20.	Kilbron	Bartlett Map (BM)	1600
21.	Kilbron	Bartlett Map (TCD)	1601
22.	Te: Kilbronie	Bartlett Maps (Hayes McCoy) i	1602c
23.	Kilbronie Mountaine[?]	Bartlett Maps (Hayes McCoy) i	1602c
24.	T: Kilbronie	Bartlett Maps (Esch. Co. Map) 2	1603
25.	Kilbronie	Bartlett Maps (Esch. Co. Map) 2	1603
26.	Kilbreny in Mackeyany's country	CPR Jas. I 86a	1606
27.	Kilbrony al. Killowen al. Mc Jawmes' country	CPR Jas. I 103a	1607
28.	Kilbroney parish al. Kilowen or Mc Jawme's country	CPR Jas. I 495a	1607
29.	Killbroney, parson of	CPR Jas. I 396a	1609
30.	(?)Polly	Speed's Antrim & Down	1610
31.	(?)Polly	Speed's Ulster	1610
32.	(?)Polly	Speed's Ireland	1610
33.	Kilbronagh al. Kilbroney, rectory/vicarage of	CPR Jas. I 190b	1611
34a.	Kilbrony, rectory of	Buckworth (EA) 310	1622
b.	Kilbroney, rectory of	Buckworth (Atkinson) 129	1622
35.	Kilbrony, church of	CPR Jas. I 305a	1623c
36.	Kilbroney [parish]	Inq. Down (Reeves1) 83	1657
37.	Kilbrony, parish of	Hib. Reg. Up. Iveagh	1657c
38.	Kilbrony [parish]	Census 72	1659c
39.	Kilbrony quarter	Census 72	1659c
40.	Kilbrony, Rector de	Trien. Visit. (Bramhall) 17	1661
41.	Kilbrony Parish	BSD 107	1661
42.	Kilbrony et Clonall	Trien. Visit. (Margetson) 25	1664
43.	Kilbron	Hib. Del. Ulster	1672c
44.	Kilbroney vicaria	Trien. Visit. (Boyle) 47;49	1679
45.	Cell of St. Broncha	MacCana's Itinerary 48	1700c
46.	Kilbroney	Harris Hist. map	1743
47.	Kilbrony	Wm. Map (OSNB) E164	1810
48.	Kilbrony	Bnd. Sur. (OSNB) E164	1830c
49.	Kilbroney Upper	Bnd. Sur. (OSNB) E164	1830c

50.	Cill Bronaighe		
	"Bronach's Church"	J O'D (OSNB) E164	1834c
51.	Cill Broinshe(a)cha		
	"St. Brony's church"	J O'D (OSNB) E164 & E175	1834c
52.	Cill Broncha	OSNB Inf. E164 & E175	1834c
53.	Teampoll Chill Broncha	OSNB E175	1834c
54.	Cill Bronaighe/Broncha		
	"Bronach's Church"	Mooney's Rostrevor 6	1950
55.	kɪl 'broːni	Local pronunciation	1990

The old name for Kilbroney parish was *Glenn Sechis*, a form attested not only in Irish (1–3), but also in Latin documents of the late medieval period where it appears in anglicized dress (6, 8). That it is to be identified with Kilbroney is clear from the papal taxation, where it is stated to be in the diocese of Dromore (*Eccles. Tax.* 114), and from the Irish sources where it is associated with Saint *Brónach*. Although the word *sechis* is of dubious origin Mooney believes that it may "be based on the Old-Irish word *sech*... sometimes used as a prefix meaning 'secluded'", and that *Glenn Seichis*, therefore, might mean "glen of seclusion". Furthermore, he suggests that *sechis* may be a native Irish synonym for the loan-word *díseart* (borrowed from Latin *desertum*) and that the alias *Nister* given in the *Eccles. Tax.* may be derived from *díseart* preceded by the article *an* where the *d-* is assimilated to the *-n* and *-eart* metathesised to *-ter* (*Mooney* 143–4; *Mooney's Rostrevor* 6–7). This theory does not seem so far-fetched when one considers that Kilbroney church is associated with two *díseart*s in the sources, *Disertmoy* (10) and *Dissertdubunnugi* (13), and that *díseart* is variously anglicized *isert, ister, ester* etc. throughout Ireland (*Joyce* i 325–6).

Whereas the old name *Glenn Sechis* lingered on in the records until the 17th century (2–3) Kilbroney first makes its appearance in 1366 (7). Although the name undoubtedly commemorates Saint *Brónach*, the form of its gen. case in Irish is a little uncertain. There are two possibilities: *Bróncha* and *Brónaí* (earlier *Brónaighe*); and our earliest example of the name, the gen. form *Brónchi uirginis* "*Brónach* the virgin" in the 9th-century text *Mart. Tal.* (p. 29), clearly indicates the former. *Cill Bhróncha* is not only supported by forms 13 and 45 but was also recorded by John O'Donovan from his local informant John Morgan as late as 1834 (52–3). However, the bulk of the historical documentation seems to point to an original *Cill Bhrónaí*, and this was the form used by Irish speakers in Omeath, Co. Louth, at the turn of the century (4–5). A third Irish form, *Cill Broinsheacha* (51), is also recorded in the *OSNB*, but for this curious form there appears to be no basis. It is interesting that the form of the personal name *Brónach* seems to have changed in Irish by the beginning of the century and that the nom./voc. form *Brónach* had been displaced by the acc./dat. form *Brónaigh*. The latter is recorded in the voc. in a piece of folklore of South Armagh provenance c. 1905 (*Sgéalaidhe Óirghiall* 116), whereas an anglicized form Broney survives in the name Broney's Well in the townland of Ballinran (*NISMR* sheet 54 §17). The Latin form Saint *Bromana* (9–10) is particularly odd as it is difficult to explain the internal *-m-* as anything other than a scribal mistranscription. As to the meaning of the name Atkinson notes that in *Mart. Gorm. Brónach* is described as *Bronach beoda*: "*Bronach* means in Gaelic 'mournful', while *beoda* means 'lively', so that we may at least infer that *Bronach* (the Mournful One) was of a much more cheerful temperament than her name would suggest!" (*Atkinson's Dromore* 100).

References to Kilbroney in the 17th- and pre-17th-century records are normally to the local church in particular or to the parish as a whole. On Bartlett's maps (22, 24) the name is preceded by *T:* for *teampall* which, as the Irish word for "church", appears to have been still in use in the locality over 200 years later (53). It is the middle of the century before

Kilbroney turns up in the townland lists; in the *Census* of c. 1659 it is termed a "quarter" (39). Presumably it absorbed "the half townland or parcel of Levallystrade otherwise Levallisrade" which in 1611 was held by the rector or parson of Kilbroney (*CPR Jas. I* 191b, 396a). In the perambulation of the bounds of Iveagh c. 1623 there is also a reference to "the ½ town of the glebe-land, belonging to the church of Kilbrony, called Covernuestrade" which clearly refers to the same place (*CPR Jas. I* 305a). Kilbroney townland seems to have been subdivided into Kilbroney and Kilbroney Upper some time in the late 18th or early 19th century.

For *Mackeyany's* or *Mc Jawmes' country* (26-8) see **Killowen** below.

Ballincurry	*Baile an Chorraigh*	
Ballincurry Upper	"townland of the bog/marsh"	
J 2115, 2116		

1. Lurgenmore	CPR Jas. I 86a	1606
2. Lurganmore	CPR Jas. I 103a	1607
3. Lurganmore	CPR Jas. I 495a	1607
4. Ballyluganmore	CPR Jas. I 395b	1609
5. Ballilurganmore	CPR Jas. I 190b	1611
6. Lurganmore	CPR Jas. I 247a	1613
7. Lurganmore	Inq. Ult. §15 Jac. I	1625
8. Lurgenmore	Inq. Ult. §84 Car. I	1638
9. Ballylurgan	Census 72	1659c
10. Ballynelorgin	BSD 132	1661
11. Ballycurrie	Sub. Roll Down 276	1663
12. Ballencorry	Rent Roll Morne 6	1688
13. Ballyncurry	Deeds & Wills (Mooney) 145	1731
14. Ballincurry	Wm. Map (OSNB) E164	1810
15. Ballincurry	Bnd. Sur. (OSNB) E164	1830c
16. Ballincurry Upper	Bnd. Sur. (OSNB) E164	1830c
17. Baile an churraigh "Town of the bog or moor"	OSNB Inf. E164	1834c

18. Baile an choire:
    "Townland of the caldron
    i.e. hollow"
	Mooney's Rostrevor 24	1950

19. ˌbalən ˈkọri	Local pronunciation	1990

Central to the correct identification of both Ballincurry (earlier *Lurgenmore* and *Ballylurgan*) and neighbouring Ballyedmond (earlier *Lurgenleigh*) in 17th-century records are the *Census* (9) and *BSD* (10). Here we get forms *Ballylurgan* and *Ballynelorgin* alongside *Ballyedmond* and *Ballyemun* which means the former must be identified with Ballincurry whereas Ballyedmond must be synonymous with *Lurganleigh* et var. in older documents. The oldest form of the name, *Lurgenmore*, is derived from *Lorgain Mhór* in Irish, where *lorgain* is an oblique (i.e. dative) case of the word *lorga*, which in place-names refers to "a long low ridge" or "a long stripe of land" (Ó Maolfabhail 1987-8, 20). The name was occasionally preceded by the element *baile*, already familiar to us from other parishes, with the result that *lorga* sometimes appears in the gen. sing. as in *Baile na Lorgan* (10). Ballincurry first enters the records in 1663 (11) but the second element is not immediately transparent in this instance. John Morgan understood it as *corrach* (17), variously spelt *cuirreach* and *currach* in Irish, which primarily means "marsh, moor, or bog" but can also indicate "a level, low-lying plain"

(*Dinneen* sv. *corrach*). These interpretations might well suit Ballincurry but there is a second possibility. This is the word *coire* which *Dinneen* explains "caldron; gulf, whirlpool, maelstrom; a mountain tarn." The word has been borrowed into English as "corrie" and adopted by physical geographers to indicate "a bowl-shaped depression on a mountain" (*Longman Dict.*). The Reverend Mooney, who had some knowledge of the locality, prefers this interpretation. He suggests that *lorga* in the old name referred to the ridge on which Ballincurry Heights (a name on neither the OS 1:10,000 nor OS 1:50,000 maps) is now sited and that "behind it lies the *coire*, between it and the mountain mass." In support of this he cites a pronunciation "Ballahurra", which he claims to have received locally (*Mooney's Rostrevor* 24), but no such pronunciation seems to be known any longer in the area (19). It may be that his is an older pronunciation of the name which in recent times has been superseded by a pronunciation more in keeping with the modern orthography. If this is the case then it is crucial, for "Ballahurra" is more likely to represent *Baile an Choire* than *Baile an Chorraigh* in Irish. On the other hand, if the original name was *Baile an Choire* it is hard to see how a local Irish speaker could have misinterpreted it as *Baile an Chorraigh* as both names would be easily distinguished, particularly in Ulster Irish. It is safer, therefore, to accept John Morgan's form *Baile an Chorraigh* "townland of the bog or marsh".

Ballindoalty
Ballindoalty Upper
J 2115, 2116

Baile an Dubhaltaigh
"*An Dubhaltach*'s townland"

1. (?)Reinmore	Bartlett Maps (Hayes McCoy) i	1602c
2. Rone-harragh	CPR Jas. I 86a	1606
3. Rono, Harragh	CPR Jas. I 103a	1607
4. Renoharragh	CPR Jas. I 495a	1607
5. Ballyrinnechary	CPR Jas. I 395b	1609
6. Ballyrinnecharry	CPR Jas. I 190b	1611
7. Rynnacharreh	CPR Jas. I 247a	1613
8. Rynnacharreh	Inq. Ult. §15 Jac. I	1625
9. Rawcharragh	Inq. Ult. §84 Car. I	1638
10. Ruinecharre	BSD 132	1661
11. Rinecarry	Rent Roll Morne 6	1688
12. Reancurry	Deeds & Wills (Mooney) 148	1730c
13. Raincurry	Deeds & Wills (Mooney) 145	1731
14. Ballyndooalty	Deeds & Wills (Mooney) 147	1731
15. Ballindooalty al. Beaucurry	Deeds & Wills (Mooney) 147	1732
16. Pt. Barry	Harris Hist. map	1743
17. Ballindo[oa]ty	Wm. Map (OSNB) E164	1810
18. Ballindoalty	Bnd. Sur. (OSNB) E164; E175	1830c
19. Ballindoalty Upper	Bnd. Sur. (OSNB) E164	1830c
20. Baile an Dubháltaigh "Dudley's town"	OSNB Inf. E164; E175	1834c
21. Baile an Dubhaltaigh "Dualtagh's or Dudley's homestead"	Mooney's Rostrevor 25	1950
22. ˌbalən ˈdoːlti	Local pronunciation	1990

The modern name for this townland, Ballindoalty, unquestionably derives from the Irish *Baile an Dubhaltaigh/Dubháltaigh*, there being some doubt as to the position of the stress and length of the *a* vowel in *An Dubhaltach/Dubháltach*. This is because the origin and meaning of this relatively rare Irish personal name is uncertain (for similarly constructed surnames see Woulfe 1923, 21–2). Ó Muraíle (1987(a), 1–26), who has done some excellent work on the name, outlines a number of possibilities, two of which seem to be particularly plausible. The most commonly suggested basis for the name is that first put forward by Woulfe (1923, 181) but more recently echoed by Ó Corráin and Maguire (1981, 77–8). This derives *dubhaltach* from the adjectives *dubh* and *altach* meaning "black-jointed" or "dark-limbed". The second suggestion is *dubháltach* where *áltach* is derived from the Old-Irish noun *álaig* meaning "habit, behaviour, practice" (*DIL*). Ó Muraíle notes the word *subhaltach/subháltach* "virtuous, cheerful, pleasant" and suggests that *dubháltach* may be an antonym meaning "unvirtuous, gloomy, morose". The other possibilities are (i) that *dubhaltach* is derived from an unattested place-name *Dubhalt*; (ii) that the name is more correctly *Dubhfholtach* "black-haired". It seems more likely, however, that his solitary example of *Dubhfholtach* is a misinterpretation of the more common *An Dubhaltach/Dubháltach*.

Whatever about the correct spelling and interpretation of the name Ó Muraíle has discovered that *An Dubhaltach/Dubháltach* is associated largely with the provinces of Ulster and Connacht, particularly in the 16th–17th centuries, with a nucleus centred on the Cos of Roscommon, Sligo and Donegal. In the case of Co. Down he has unearthed three instances of the name in *Fiants Eliz.* and six in *CPR Jas. I*. Two of the entries in the former concern a certain Dwalltagh or Dowaltagh O Doran, presumably the same person, who is listed among those followers of Magennis who obtained a pardon from Elizabeth I in 1590 (§5523) and 1602 (§6616). O'Doran is one of the most common indigenous surnames in southern Co. Down and the references to Dwalltagh are important in that they establish that this personal name was known in the area. However, one cannot agree with Mooney's suggestion (*Mooney's Rostrevor* 26) that the townland Ballindoalty may take its name from this particular individual as the townland name first appears in the records as late as 1731 (14). Prior to this the area was known variously as *Rone-harragh*, *Rynnacharreh*, *Ballyrinnechary* etc. The first element is undoubtedly *rinn* "a point" and refers to the headland marked *Pt. Barry* by Harris (16). Bartlett seems to call it *Reinmore* (1), Irish *Rinn M(h)ór*, although there is a slight possibility that it refers rather to Killowen Point. Mooney suggests that *Rone-harragh* derives from the Irish *Rinn Charrach* "rocky point" which might well befit the topography (see **Dickey's Rocks**), but with which there are a number of difficulties. One is the internal vowel in the anglicized forms which intrudes between the *rynn-* and *-charreh* as in *Rynnacharreh* (7–8). Mooney believes this is an epenthetic vowel (*Mooney's Rostrevor* 26) as in Killonahan, originally *Cill Onchon*, in Co. Limerick (Ó Maolfabhail 1990, 106). Another problem is the variation in endings between *-agh* and *-y*. It may be that in the case of the second element we are dealing with a masc. noun which in the nom. case ended in *-ach* and in the gen. *-aigh*, the latter normally realized as an [i] sound in Ulster Irish. This might explain the variation *-agh/-y* in the anglicized forms. If this is plausible then the internal vowel could be seen to reflect the definite article *an* which would probably have preceded the noun in Irish. However, there does not seem to be any noun which might suit in the present circumstances.

Ballinran
Ballinran Upper
J 1915, 1916

Baile an Reanna
"townland of the point"

1. Ballyrane	CPR Jas. I 86a	1606
2. Ballirane	CPR Jas. I 103a	1607

3. Ballyranie	CPR Jas. I 495a	1607
4. Ballyrannaghmore	CPR Jas. I 395b	1609
5. Ballyrannaghmore	CPR Jas. I 190b	1611
6. Ballinrane al. Ballirannaghmore	CPR Jas. I 247a	1613
7. Ballinran al. Ballyrannaghmore	Inq. Ult. (Down) §15 Jac. I	1625c
8. Ballyran al. Ballyrame	Inq. Ult. (Down) §84 Car. I	1638
9. Ballyran	Census 73	1659c
10. Ballinrane	BSD 132	1661
11. Balleran	Rent Roll Morne 6	1688
12. Ballyran	Deeds & Wills (Mooney) 145	1731
13. Ballynran	Deeds & Wills (Mooney) 145	1736
14. Ballinran	Wm. Map (OSNB) E164	1810
15. Ballinran	Bnd. Sur. (OSNB) E164	1830c
16. Ballinran Upper	Bnd. Sur. (OSNB) E164	1830c
17. Baile an rann		
"Town of the division"	OSNB Inf. E164	1834c
18. Baile an ranna "division"	OSNB E175	1834c
19. Baile na reanna		
"Townland of the point"	Mooney's Rostrevor 23	1950
20. ˌbɑlən ˈrɑːn	Local pronunciation	1990

Although O'Donovan interpreted John Morgan's form as *Baile an Rann[a]* "townland of the division" (17), there are several preferable suggestions. One is *Baile an Raithin* "townland of the ferns or bracken" which seems to be the original form of **Ballinran** in the parish of Kilkeel. If this is correct then Ballyrannaghmore (4–7) must derive from *Baile Raithneach Mór*, *raithneach* and *raithean* simply being variant forms of *raith*, the Old-Irish word for "ferns" or "bracken" (*DIL*). As *raithneach* is a collective noun it is usually declined in the singular while referring to "ferns" in the plural. In *Baile Raithneach Mór*, however, *raithneach* can only be in the gen. pl. which is both unnecessary and unlikely.

A more acceptable explanation of the name is that Ballinran is derived from Irish *Baile an Reanna* "townland of the point". The spellings in forms 4–7 may point to a variant form *Baile Reannach* "pointed townland", although the *gh* may be silent. Mooney takes *rinn* "a point" to be feminine as is the case in Modern Irish (19). The forms, however, may suggest that in this instance *rinn* is masculine as it was in Old Irish and sometimes even in Classical Irish (*DIL*). If this derivation is correct then the *rinn* must refer to what is now known as Killowen Point. As to the significance of the additional element *mór* in *Ballyrannaghmore* it is difficult to say, but Mooney believes that it referred to the larger of the two modern townlands, Ballinran and Ballinran Upper (*Mooney's Rostrevor 23*).

Ballintur   *Baile an Toir*
Ballintur Upper   "townland of the bush (?)"
J 2214, 2216

1. Eden-Curren	CPR Jas. I 86a	1606
2. Edencurrane	CPR Jas. I 103a	1607
3. Edencurran	CPR Jas. I 495a	1607
4. Bally-Intuyr	CPR Jas. I 395b	1609
5. Ballyadenkuyrin al. Bally-Inknir	CPR Jas. I 190b	1611

6. Ballintor al. Edengwiran		
al. Ballyadenkinrin	CPR Jas. I 247a	1613
7. Ballyinter al. Edenguyran		
al. Ballyedenkmrin	Inq. Ult. (Down) §15 Jac. I	1625c
8. Lingenlegh(eden, Corran)	Inq. Ult. (Down) §84 Car. I	1638
9. Ballytue	Census 72	1659c
10. Ballintuir	BSD 132	1661
11. Ballintur	Rent Roll Morne 6	1688
12. Ballyntur	Deeds & Wills (Mooney) 147	1731
13. Ballinturr	Deeds & Wills (Mooney) 147	1732
14. Ballinturr	Wm. Map (OSNB) E164	1810
15. Ballinturr	Bnd. Sur. (OSNB) E164	1830c
16. Ballinturr Upper	Bnd. Sur. (OSNB) E164	1830c
17. Baile an tuir		
"Bushtown; Town of the Bush"	OSNB Inf. E164	1834c
18. Baile an tuir		
"Townland of the bush"	Mooney's Rostrevor 26	1950
19. ˌbɛlən 'tɔ.r	Local pronunciation	1990
20. ˌbɑln 'tǫr	Local pronunciation	1990

The forms suggest that Ballintur is derived from *Baile an Toir* in Irish but the correct interpretation of the second element *tor* is a little more problematic. John Morgan's form is translated "bushtown, town of the bush" in the *OSNB* (17) but it is impossible to say whether this is Morgan's own interpretation or whether the translation was supplied by John O'Donovan. As well as *tor* "a bush" there is also another word *tor*, which basically means "tower, steeple or mansion" (*Dinneen*), but which *Joyce* (i 399) notes is often "applied to a tall rock resembling a tower" in place-names. In the case of Ballintur it is difficult to see to what feature, if any, this particular *tor* might apply. There is a third possibility: that the element in question is *tur* not *tor*, which although normally an adjective meaning "dry" etc. can also be used substantivally to refer to "a dry place" (*Dinneen*). As it is virtually impossible to decide between any of these interpretations it is best to accept the translation provided in the *OSNB* as it may possibly be based on some local evidence.

Ballintur first appears in the records in 1609 (4). There was an older name, however, variously spelt *Eden-Curren* (1–3, 8) or *Edengwiran al. Ballyadenkinrin* (6–7). Mooney derives this from *Éadan Mhig/Mhic Uidhrín* "Maguirin's or Magivern's hill-face" and notes that MacGivern is still a common name in the area (*Mooney's Rostrevor* 26–7). A major objection to this is the fact that there is no trace of *Mac* in any of the forms. Mooney believes that this is because the aspirated *m* in *Mhig/Mhic* fell silent so that the name developed in Irish from *Éadan Mhic/Mhig Uidhrín* to *Éadan 'ic/'ig Uidhrín*. Furthermore, he notes that some of the early anglicized spellings of MacGivern were McGwyryn and Maguryn which are reminiscent of some of the spellings of *Eden-Curren*. However, it is much easier to interpret *Eden-Curren* as deriving from something like *Éadan Corráin* in Irish. Both elements are well attested in the onomasticon: *éadan* as "a brow of a hill" (*Joyce* i 523) and *corrán* as a crescent-shaped topographical feature, usually a ridge or hill, or a pronounced bay or bend on a lakeshore or seashore (Ó Máille 1962(a)). There are two points on Ballintur's coastline which could be considered crescent-shaped, but as the element *corrán* is preceded by *éadan* it may be that the name refers to some point of the mountain mass. If, however, forms such as *Ballyadenkuyrin* (5–7) are accurate then an Irish original such as *Éadan Coireáin* "hillface of the campion" also needs to be considered although earlier forms such as *Eden-Curren* are probably more accurate. The variation *c/g* in spellings such as *Eden-Curren* and *Edengwiran* may best be explained as arising from a mistranscription of *c/q* as *g* in a couple of related sources (6–7).

Ballyagholy	*Baile Eachmhílidh*	
J 1723	"*Eachmhílidh's*/Agholy's townland"	
1. Balleagholee	CPR Jas. I 394b	1609
2. Ballyagholye	CPR Jas. I 190a	1611
3. Bally-Agholly	CPR Jas. I 373b	1618
4. Ballaghcully	Hib. Reg. Up. Iveagh	1657c
5. Ballyagholly	Census 72	1659c
6. Ballyaholie	BSD 107	1661
7. Balligcully	Hib. Del. Down	1672c
8. B cully	Hib. Del. Ulster	1672c
9. Ballyahhally	Wm. Map (OSNB) E164	1810
10. Ballaghally	Bnd. Sur. (OSNB) E164	1830c
11. Baile eachmhilíd[h] "Agholy's Town"	OSNB Inf. E164	1834c
12. Baile Eachmhilidh "Agholy's homestead"	Mooney's Rostrevor 8	1950
13. bəˈlɔxli	Local pronunciation	1990
14. bəˈlɔkli	Local pronunciation	1990

Agholy, Irish *Eachmhílidh* "horse-soldier", is a name with strong Co. Down associations. It was very popular among the Magennises and MacCartans from the 15th to the 17th centuries (Ó Corráin & Maguire 1981, 83) but it was also in use among the O'Hanlons (*Wars Co. Down* 88). An Agholy Mc Dermydan is recorded as custodian of the staff of Saint Brónach c. 1427 (*Reg. Swayne* 101; *EA* 115) and it may be from an individual such as this that the townland takes its name. Mc Dermydan is probably a patronymic, as no such surname is attested, and it is quite possible that he was a Magennis.

Ballyedmond	*Baile Éamainn*	
Ballyedmond Upper	"*Éamann's*/Edmond's townland"	
J 2015, 2016		
1. Lurganleigh	CPR Jas. I 86a	1606
2. Lurganleigh	CPR Jas. I 103a	1607
3. Lurganbeagh	CPR Jas. I 495a	1607
4. Ballypoell	CPR Jas. I 395b	1609
5. Ballypoell	CPR Jas. I 190b	1611
6. Lurganclogh al. Ballipoell	CPR Jas. I 247a	1613
7. Lurganclogh al. Ballypoell	Inq. Ult. §15 Jac. I	1625
8. Linganlegh(eden) al. Lingenlegh(eden, Corran)	Inq. Ult. §84 Car. I	1638
9. Ballyedmond	Census 72	1659c
10. Ballemun	BSD 132	1661
11. Ballyedmond	Sub. Roll Down 276	1663

12. Balle Edmond	Rent Roll Morne 6	1688
13. Ballyedmund	Deeds & Wills (Mooney) 143	1731
14. Ballyedmond	Wm. Map (OSNB) E164	1810
15. Ballyedmond	Bnd. Sur. (OSNB) E164	1830c
16. Ballyedmond Upper	Bnd. Sur. (OSNB) E164	1830c
17. Baile Emoinn "Edmond's Town"	OSNB Inf. E164	1834c
18. Lurga(n) Chloiche "long-hill of the stone"	Mooney's Rostrevor 24	1950
19. Baile Puill "townland of the hollow"	Mooney's Rostrevor 24	1950
20. Baile Eamoinn "Eamon's or Edmond's homestead"	Mooney's Rostrevor 24	1950
21. ˌbɑli ˈɛdmənd	Local pronunciation	1990

The modern name for this townland clearly derives from *Baile Éamainn* in Irish, "*Éamann's* or Edmond's townland". Edmond is in origin an English name introduced into Ireland by the Normans "where it became popular in the later middle ages" (Ó Corráin & Maguire 1981, 86). As Ballyedmond first appears in the records c. 1659 (9) our Éamann must have lived in the 17th century, if not earlier. Unfortunately there is no evidence to suggest to what particular family he may have belonged.

There seem to have been two older names for the area: *Ballypoell*, and *Lurganleigh* or *Lurganclogh* (see p. 132). Mooney suggests that the latter derives from Irish *Lurga(n) Chloiche* "long-hill of the stone" (18), and believes that the *lurga/lorga* in question is the spur in the north of the parish upon which the great stone known as **Cloghgarran** is situated. However, the anglicized forms indicate that we are dealing with an oblique form of *lorga* which should be spelt *lorgain*, not *lurgan* as suggested by Mooney. Furthermore, *Lurganleigh* may be a more accurate transcription than *Lurganclogh* in which case *Lorgain Léith* "grey spur" may be the original form. The other obsolete name has also been discussed by Mooney. This, he suggests, is *Baile Puill* (modern *Poill*) "townland of the hollow" in Irish, and he locates this hollow, through which runs a stream, between the *lorga* or "spur" and the mountain mass (*Mooney's Rostrevor 24–5*).

Ballymoney
J 1820

Baile na Muine
"townland of the brake/thicket"

1. Ballenemoney	CSP Ire. 435	1570
2. Ballenemoney	Fiants Eliz. §1609	1570
3. Ballynemony	CPR Jas. I 395b	1609
4. Ballynemony	CPR Jas. I 235a	1612
5. Ballynymony	CPR Jas. I 305a	1623c
6. Ballynemony	Inq. Ult. (Down) §13 Car. I	1629
7. Ballimony	Hib. Reg. Up. Iveagh	1657c
8. Ballynamony	BSD 107	1661
9. Ballimony	Hib. Del. Down	1672c
10. Ballynamony	ASE 273b §29	1681
11. Ballynamoney	Rent Roll Down 10	1692
12. Ballymoney	Wm. Map (OSNB) E164	1810
13. Ballymony	Bnd. Sur. (OSNB) E164	1830c

14. Baile na muine
    "Town of the brake or shrubbery" OSNB Inf. E164   1834c
15. Baile na muine "Townland of the
    brake or thicket"   Mooney's Rostrevor 8   1950

16. ˌbalə ˈmǫni   Local pronunciation   1990

Although Ballymoney as a townland name is found in Cos Wicklow, Wexford and Galway, it is particularly common in Ulster where it is most numerous in Cos Down, Derry and Antrim. There is a solitary example in Donegal (*Census* 1871). The element *money* may represent two different words in Irish place-names: *muine* "brake or thicket" and *mónaidh*, an oblique form of *móin*, "moor or bog". There is also another word *monadh* "mountain, heath, etc." which is normally found in Scotland. The latter, a masc. word, can be dismissed here, as the second element in the historical forms of Ballymoney is preceded by the fem. form of the article *na*. Furthermore, this historical evidence together with the modern pronunciation indicates that John Morgan's form *Baile na Muine* (14) is indeed correct.

Ballyneddan   *Baile an Fheadáin*
Ballyneddan Upper   "townland of the stream"
J 1915, J 2016

1. Ballenden	CPR Jas. I 86a	1606
2. Ballenden	CPR Jas. I 103a	1607
3. Ballenden	CPR Jas. I 495a	1607
4. Ballyneaden	CPR Jas. I 395b	1609
5. Ballyneaden	CPR Jas. I 190b	1611
6. Ballynedan	CPR Jas. I 247a	1613
7. Ballynedan	Inq. Ult. (Down) §15 Jac. I	1625c
8. Ballenden	Inq. Ult. (Down) §84 Car. I	1638
9. Ballynedan	Census 73	1659c
10. Ballynedane	BSD 132	1661
11. Balleneddan	Rent Roll Morne 6	1688
12. Ballyneddan	Deeds & Wills (Mooney) 149	1731
13. Ballyneddan	Deeds & Wills (Mooney) 149	1736
14. Ballyneddan	Wm. Map (OSNB) E164	1810
15. Ballyneddin	Bnd. Sur. (OSNB) E164	1830c
16. Ballyneddin Upper	Bnd. Sur. (OSNB) E164	1830c

17. Baile an fheadáin
    "Town of the brook or runnell"   OSNB Inf. E164   1834c
18. Baile an fheadain
    "Townland of the brook"   Mooney's Rostrevor 23   1950

19. ˌbɑli ˈnɛdn   Local pronunciation   1990

Considered in isolation the historical forms of this townland are ambiguous. The second element could be derived from *éadan* "brow of a hill", or *feadán* "stream or brook". However, the local interpretation of the name in 1834 (17) points to its derivation from *feadán*, the stream in question rising in Slieveban (J 2016) in the townland of Ballyneddan Upper and entering the sea in the townland of Ballyedmond (J 2014). This stream is not named either on the OS 1:50,000 or OS 1:10,000 maps.

Drumreagh
Drumreagh Upper
J 1719, 1822

Droim Réidh
"smooth ridge"

1.	Dromrey	CSP Ire. 435	1570
2.	Dromrey	Fiants Eliz. §1609	1570
3.	Ballydrumrey	CPR Jas. I 395b	1609
4.	Ballydrumrey	CPR Jas. I 235a	1612
5.	Ballydromry	Inq. Ult. (Down) §13 Car. I	1629
6.	Dromreagh	Hib. Reg. Up. Iveagh	1657c
7.	Dromreagh ½ town	Census 72	1659c
8.	Dromreage	BSD 107; 108	1661
9.	Dromreagh	Hib. Del. Down	1672c
10.	Dromreagh	ASE 274a §29	1681
11.	Dromreage	Rent Roll Down 11	1692
12.	Drumreagh	Wm. Map (OSNB) E164	1810
13.	Drumreagh	Bnd. Sur. (OSNB) E164	1830c
14.	Drumreagh Upper	Bnd. Sur. (OSNB) E164	1830c
15.	Drum réidhe "smooth ridge" (rectius aimhreidh)	OSNB Inf. E164; E175	1834c
16.	Drom Riabhach "Grey ridge"	Mooney 149	1950c
17.	Druim reidhe "Hill-ridge of the upland moor" or "Mountain flat"	Mooney's Rostrevor 8	1950
18.	drọm 're:	Local pronunciation	1990

As is the case with **Ballyneddan** the second element of Drumreagh could be derived from a number of different words in Irish: (i) *riabhach* "grey, brindled etc."; (ii) *réidh* "smooth"; (iii) *ré* (earlier *réidh*) "a clearing, a level plain, moorland" as in *réidh sléibhe* "a level tract of moorland or smooth hillside" (*Dinneen*).When Mooney first turned his attention to this name he suggested that *riabhach* was the element in question (16). This is highly unlikely, however, when one considers the earliest anglicized forms (1–5) as a spelling *-rey* in English could not represent Irish *riabhach*. Furthermore, *Drum réidhe* was the form obtained locally by John O'Donovan over 150 years ago (15). This caused Mooney to reconsider his earlier decision and to suggest that the second element was *réidh* "an upland moor or mountain flat" (17). He rejected the translation "smooth ridge" in the *OSNB* (15) for two reasons: firstly *réidhe* is not an adjective but rather the gen. form of the noun *réidh*; and secondly Drumreagh is not smooth, which is why he believes O'Donovan suggested emending the *OSNB* form to *Drum aimhreidh*, *aimhréidh* meaning "rough, uneven etc." in Irish (*Mooney's Rostrevor* 8–9). There are a number of points to be considered here. If *Droim Réidh* is the correct Irish form, then it is not impossible to reconcile this with the local topography, for we need only look for a single flat spur or ridge in the area like the one in Ballymoney Wood (J 1820). Furthermore, *réidhe* need not be a substantive but may be merely an orthographic variant of the adjective *réidh*. This being the case *Droim Réidh* "smooth ridge" is probably the correct interpretation.

There is another Drumreagh in the parish of Killinchy, Co. Down and a few more examples throughout Ireland (*Census* 1871), but it is impossible to say whether these names are of similar origin without consulting the historical evidence.

| **Drumsesk** | *Droim Seasc* | |
| J 1619 | "barren ridge" | |

1. Dromseske	Fiants Eliz. §1609	1570
2. Dromseske	CSP Ire. 435	1570
3. Dromseske	Fiants Eliz. §4327	1583c
4. Ballydromsheske	CPR Jas. I 395b	1609
5. Ballydrumsheske	CPR Jas. I 235a	1612
6. Dromseske	CPR Jas. I 305a	1623c
7. Ballydromsheaske	Inq. Ult. (Down) §13 Car. I	1629
8. Ballydromseske	Inq. Ult. (Down) §85 Car. I	1639
9. Dromsaske	Hib. Reg. Up. Iveagh	1657c
10. Dromsealke	BSD 107	1661
11. Drumsack	Hib. Del. Down	1672c
12. Drumseske	ASE 273b §29	1681
13. Drumseske	Rent Roll Down 10	1692
14. Drumsesk	Wm. Map (OSNB) E164	1810
15. Drumsesk	Bnd. Sur. (OSNB) E164	1830c
16. Drum Seasc "Barren ridge; sedge-barren"	OSNB Inf. E164	1834c
17. Druim Seasc "Barren ridge"	OSNB E122; E175	1834c
18. Drom seasc "Barren hill-ridge"	Mooney's Rostrevor 9	1950
19. ˌdrọm ˈsɛsk	Local pronunciation	1990

This townland probably derives from Irish *Droim Seasc* "barren ridge", although *Droim Seisce* "ridge of the sedge" may also be a possibility. Mooney notes that part of the "barren ridge", which he locates in the centre of the townland, is "still uncultivated and over-run by furze" (*Mooney's Rostrevor* 9). The ridge he has in mind is presumably that located near St. Brigid's Cottages (J 1619).

Kilbroney	*Cill Bhrónaí*
Kilbroney Upper	"*Brónach*'s church"
J 1920, 1922	

See **Kilbroney** Parish.

Kilfeaghan	*Cill Fiacháin (?)*	
Kilfeaghan Upper	"*Fiachán*'s church"	
J 2216, 2118		

1. Killfeagan	CPR Jas. I 395b	1609
2. Kilpheighan	CPR Jas. I 195b	1610
3. Kilfeaghan	CPR Jas. I 191a	1611
4. Kilfeighan	CPR Jas. I 191a	1611
5. Kilphekan or Kilpheighan al. Ballymcknevan	CPR Jas. I 191a	1611
6. Killuegary	Hib. Reg. Up. Iveagh	1657c
7. Killfeighan	Inq. Ult. (Down) Temp. Interreg.	1658
8. Killneghane	BSD 108	1661

9. Killuegen	Hib. Del. Down	1672c
10. Kilvegan	Hib. Del. Ireland	1672c
11. Kilfeghan	Wm. Map (OSNB) E164	1810
12. Killfeaghan	Bnd. Sur. (OSNB) E164	1830c
13. Kilfeaghan Upper	Bnd. Sur. (OSNB) E164	1830c
14. Cill Fiacháin "Fiachan's church"	OSNB Inf. E164	1834c
15. Cill Fheichin "St. Fechin's church"	Mooney's Rostrevor 27	1950
16. Baile Mhic Chnaimhin "Mac Nevin's homestead"	Mooney's Rostrevor 27	1950
17. kïl ˈfɛ.hən	Local pronunciation	1990
18. kïl ˈfe:xən	Local pronunciation	1990
19. kïl ˈfi:hən	Local pronunciation	1990

There are a number of reasons why the first element of Kilfeaghan must derive from Gaelic *cill* "a church" as opposed to *coill* "a wood." Not only is the townland marked as an ecclesiastical site on the mid-17th-century map *Hibernia Regnum* (6), but it is consistently referred to as see land pertaining to the bishop of Dromore in various patents dating to the beginning of that century (1–5). Furthermore, there is a field in Kilfeaghan which up to very recently was still known by the name of Shankill, Irish *Seanchill* "old church" (*Mooney's Rostrevor* 27).

The second element in Kilfeaghan is not as easy to interpret. It was John Morgan, the local informant in the *OSNB*, who provided John O'Donovan with the Irish form *Cill Fiacháin* "Fiachan's church" (14). There does not appear to be any definite instance of the personal name *Fiachán* in the early genealogies (*CGH*; *CSH*), although the evidence of the surname *Ó Fiacháin*, anglicized Feighan, Feghan, Feehan etc. (Woulfe 1923, 524; MacLysaght 1982, 97), certainly confirms its existence. The fact that the townland of **Cross** in Kilcoo may be derived from an earlier *Cros Tí Fhiacháin* also strengthens the case for *Cill Fiacháin*, as does one of three pronunciations of the townland in the area itself (19).

On the other hand, the alternative pronunciations (17–18) may support Mooney's suggestion that Kilfeaghan derives from the personal name *Féichín* rather than *Fiachán*. *Féichín* is certainly well-attested as a saint's name. There are five bearers of the name in all, the most famous of whom, *Féichín* of Fore, is thought to be commemorated in the name Termonfeckin in Co. Louth (*Mooney's Rostrevor* 27).

There is nothing to connect any of these saints with the diocese of Dromore, but it is noteworthy that Archbishop Swayne's register does contain a direction for the veneration of St. Feghin in the neighbouring diocese of Armagh (*Reg. Swayne* 13, 191). Nevertheless, despite the considerable evidence to suggest that the personal name *Féichín* could possibly be the second element in Kilfeaghan, there is nothing in the historical documentation to suggest that *Cill Féichín* is more likely to be the original Irish name than *Cill Fiacháin*, the form recorded by John O'Donovan from a local Irish speaker in 1834. It is also worth noting that both *Fiachán* and *Féichín* are diminutives of *fiach* "a raven", but that the diminutive suffix *-ín* is rare in East Ulster Irish.

There are a number of other points to be considered. First and foremost is the initial *f-* of *Fiachán* which does not appear to be lenited (orthographic *fh*) as might be expected when qualifying a fem. noun such as *cill*. This absence of lenition is evident in other Irish placenames such as Kilfrush, Irish *Cill Frois*, in Co. Limerick (Ó Maolfabhail 1990, 100), and it may even be that Irish speakers felt that the [f] sound represented a lenited *p* (orthographic *ph*). It is also possible that the lenition of *f-*, which would have rendered it silent, may have been avoided in order not to obscure the origin of the name. The second point to be considered is the anglicized form *Kiluegen* which occurs, with minor variations in spelling, in a number of related sources (6, 8–10). It is hard to see how the *-u-* or *-v-* in these forms can be anything other than a mistranscription of the bilabial [f] sound in Irish. Finally, there is the alias *Ballymcknevan* (5) which Mooney derives from *Baile Mhic Chnaimhin* "Mac Nevin's homestead" (16). It is rash, however, to base such a firm conclusion on just one form, especially since no such surname is attested in the area.

Killowen Mountains	*Cill Eoghain (?)*	
J 2017	"*Eoghan*'s church"	
1. Cill Eoin	Sgéalaidhe Óirghiall 87	1905c
2. Kelcone	Mercator's Ulst.	1595
3. Killowen al. Kilbrony al. Mc Jawmes' country	CPR Jas. I 103a	1607
4. Kilowen al. Kilbroney parish or Mc Jawme's country	CPR Jas. I 495a	1607
5. Killownie, Patrick Grome & Donnogh McJawnie of	CPR Jas. I 175a	1610
6. Killowen, precinct of/lands of	CPR Jas. I 247a	1613
7. Kilowen, territory... called	Inq. Ult. (Down) §15 Jac. I	1625c
8. Kelcone	Hondius Map (Mooney) 156	1630c
9. Killowen, lez 7 vil' de	Inq. Ult. (Down) §68 Car. I	1636
10. Killowen	Rent Roll Morne 6	1688
11. Killowen, the point of	Rent Roll Morne 6	1688
12. Killone Bay	Collins C'ford Lough	1693
13. Killone	Deeds & Wills (Mooney) 155	1731
14. Killowen Point	Harris Hist. 141	1744
15. Killowen Mountains	Bnd. Sur. (OSNB) E164	1830c
16. Cill Eóghain "Owen's church"	OSNB E164	1834c
17. Cill Eoghain	Post-Sheanchas 83	1905
18. Cill Abhann "The church of the river"	Mooney 155	1950c
19. Cill Eoghain "Owen's church"	Mooney's Rostrevor 18	1950
20. Cill Eoin	AGBP 117	1969
21. Cill Eoin	GÉ 56	1989
22. kïˈloən	Local pronunciation	1990
23. kïˈləuən	Local pronunciation	1990

Killowen itself is not a townland name; it is an old territorial name historically comprising the seven townlands of Ballinran, Ballyneddan, Ballyedmond, Ballincurry, Ballindoalty, Ballintur and Tamnyveagh. The modern townland Killowen Mountains first appears in the records of the early 19th century and may never have been known as such in Irish.

All authorities agree that Killowen derives its name from some old ecclesiastical site (16–21). There are, however, no references to a church in any of the historical documents which refer to the district, and the only evidence for Killowen church is the name itself and the testimony of Samuel Lewis. The latter, writing in 1836, notes that some remains of the old church of Killowen were still visible in his time (*Lewis' Top. Dict.* ii 540), but he does not specify where and nothing appears to have been discovered in the area in the course of the archaeological survey (*ASCD*; *NISMR*). Mooney suggests that Killowen and Kilfeaghan "both refer to the same church, or at least the same site" (*Mooney's Rostrevor* 19) but this is unlikely to be the case.

In the 17th-century documentation Killowen is sometimes referred to as *Killowen al. Kilbrony al. Mc Jawmes' country*; the area in question is presumably the same as *Kilbreny in Mackeyany's country* referred to elsewhere (see **Kilbroney**). Mooney suggests that the surname is more correctly McJawnie/McYawny *et var.*, a family who held Killowen before alienating it to Nicholas Bagenal in 1568 (see p. 131). He also suggests that McJawnie derives from *Mac Eoghain* in Gaelic and that the *Eoghan* from whom the clan takes its name may be one and the same as the *Eoghan* he believes is commemorated in the place-name Killowen: Irish *Cill Eoghain* "*Eoghan*'s church" (*Mooney's Rostrevor* 18–23). It is difficult to see how *Mac Eoghain* in Irish could ever yield McJawnie in English. There was, however, a family in south Down known as the *Méig Dhuibh Eamhna*, chiefs of *Ceinél nAmholghaidh* (*Topog. Poems* ll. 399–400), anglicized *Clanawly*, an old district which included Ballyagholy in this parish and much of the neighbouring parish of **Clonallan**. It would be surprising if a surname which was once so prominent in the area could become totally obsolete and it may well be that it is now barely recognizable in some other form. One might argue that *Mac Dhuibh Eamhna* > McJawnie is a radical phonological change, but note *MacDuibhne*, which appears to be an intermediate form of the name in Irish, in *MacCana's Itinerary* (46–7). If MacCana's form is accurate then the third element of the name has been reduced. Alternatively, one could argue for the loss of the second element *dubh*, and compare the similar name *Mac Dhubhdara* which is sometimes shortened to MacDara (Woulfe 1923, 353).

Having discussed the McJawnies and rejected any connection with the district name we must consider whether John O'Donovan is correct in transcribing the Irish form of Killowen as *Cill Eoghain* (16). This form should probably be ascribed to John Morgan who provided O'Donovan with Irish forms for most of the names in Kilbroney. On the other hand, Morgan's form of **Levallyclanone** has been transcribed as *Leathbhaile Clann Eoin* in the *OSNB*. The problem here is that while the native name *Eoghan* and the borrowed name *Eoin* (from Latin *Johannes*) are distinct in the nom. case in Modern Irish, there can be no phonetic distinction when *Eoghan* is modified to *Eoghain* in the gen. (the *-gha-* is silent). It is for this reason that Seosamh Laoide, who heard the Irish form of the name in Omeath, transcribed it variously as *Cill Eoghain* and *Cill Eoin* in two different publications dating to c. 1905 (1, 17). Similarly, we have no way of knowing whether John Morgan had made clear that Killowen contained the personal name *Eoghan* and Levallyclanone contained *Eoin*, or whether the distinction has really no basis and should be ascribed solely to O'Donovan? The only way John Morgan himself could have distinguished between *Cill Eoghain* and *Cill Eoin* is if there had been some tradition of a saint named *Eoghan* or *Eoin* in the area. If there ever had been any such tradition then, unfortunately, there is no longer any recollection of it in the locality.

There have been other suggestions. *Cill Abhann* "church of the river" (18) has been suggested by Mooney on the basis of what is believed to be an older pronunciation of Killowen (23). However, it is difficult to reconcile this pronunciation with the other evidence. Saint *Lóichéin* of *Uibh Eathach* (Iveagh), who has been included by Reeves in his calendar of local saints (*EA* 376–81), must also be considered. Atkinson notes that "it has been suggested by Monsignor O'Reilly... of Kilbroney that he may have been the Founder and Patron of Killowen (*Cill loicen*) in that parish" (*Atkinson's Dromore* 97). There are a number of problems with this for there is nothing in the martyrologies to suggest that *Lóichéin* was associated with Iveagh. There is a *Lochan i nUíb Echach* in the saints' genealogies (*CSH* 298.2, 662.238, 730) and this may be the individual Reeves had in mind. However, *Uibh Eachach* in this instance could well be *Uíbh Eachach Mumhan*, *Uíbh Eachach* of Munster, now Evaugh in the barony of West Carbery in Co. Cork. There is no tradition of any such *Lóichéin* or *Lóchán* in the Kilbroney area and, more importantly, it is unlikely that a postulated Irish form *Cill Lóichéin* could become Killowen in English for, although *ch* might be reduced to zero in East Ulster Irish, the resultant anglicized form would have been something like *Killone*.

It seems, therefore, that Killowen must derive from either *Cill Eoghain* or *Cill Eoin* in Irish. The element *cill* is the most common ecclesiastical settlement term in Irish parish, townland and minor names and may have been used in the formation of place-names as early as the 5th-century mission of St Patrick (Flanagan D. 1979(a), 1–3). There is some evidence to show that it continued to be used in the coining of place-names after the 12th-century reforms and it seems to be largely during this period that names of Latin origin came to form the qualifying element (*ibid.* 4–6). Thus, St Mary's Abbey, Dublin, is called *Cell Muire Átha Cliath* in 1238; Christ Church, Dublin, is called *Cell Críst* in 1283; Kilpeddar in Co. Wicklow, which was probably an Anglo-Norman foundation, comes from Irish *Cill Pheadair* "Peter's church"; and, most notably in the present context, Killone in Co. Clare derives from *Cill Eoin*, an abbey of St John the Baptist built for Augustinian nuns c. 1189. As there is no evidence of any great Anglo-Norman influence in this area, let alone of an Anglo-Norman church, it is more probably from St *Eoghan* rather than St John that the church derived its name.

| **Knockbarragh** | *Cnoc Bearach* | |
| J 1722 | "hill of heifers" | |

1. Knockberaghe	CSP Ire. 435	1570
2. Knockberagh	Fiants Eliz. §1609	1570
3. Ballyknockbyragh	CPR Jas. I 395b	1609
4. Ballyknockviragh	CPR Jas. I 235a	1612
5. Ballyknockeecragh	Inq. Ult. (Down) §13 Car. I	1629
6. Knockbiragh	Hib. Reg. Up. Iveagh	1657c
7. Knockebearagh	Census 72	1659c
8. Knockbereagh	BSD 108	1661
9. Knockbragh	Hib. Del. Down	1672c
10. Knockboragh	ASE 273b §29	1681
11. Knockeragh al. Knockberagh	ASE 274a §29	1681
12. Knockberagh	Rent Roll Down 10	1692
13. Knockeragh al. Knockberagh	Rent Roll Down 12	1692
14. Knockbereagh	Rent Roll Down 12	1692
15. Knockbarragh	Wm. Map (OSNB) E164	1810
16. Knockbarragh	Bnd. Sur. (OSNB) E164	1830c
17. Cnoc bearrach "hill of the heifers"	OSNB Inf. E164	1834c
18. Cnoc bearach "Hill of heifers"	Mooney's Rostrevor 9	1950
19. nɔk'barə	Local pronunciation	1990
20. nɔk'bɔrə	Local pronunciation	1990

The historical spellings of this place-name are, with one important exception, fairly consistent. The exception is *Ballyknockviragh* (4) with a *-v-*, whereas in a related source we get a *-b-* (3). Mooney suggests that this *-v-* represents *-bh-* (i.e. a lenited *b*) caused by the prefixing of *baile* to the place-name: *Baile Chnoic Bhearrach* in Irish. Whether this is correct or not has no bearing on the meaning of the name; it seems to derive from Irish *Cnoc Bearach* "hill of heifers", which was the local understanding of the name in 1834 (17). A couple of forms, such as *Knockbiragh* (6) with an *i* vowel, could be taken to suggest that the original name was *Cnoc Biorach/Bearach* "pointed hill" but it is more likely that the local interpretation is correct and that the *i* is a mistranscription.

Levallyclanone	*Leathbhaile Chlann Eoghain*	
J 1918	"half-townland of *Eoghan*'s descendants"	
1. Clanawen	CPR Jas. I 395b	1609
2. Clynowen ½ townland	CPR Jas. I 235a	1612
3. Levallycloneowin	Inq. Ult. (Down) §13 Car. I	1629
4. Clynowen, ½ vil' de	Inq. Ult. (Down) §85 Car. I	1639
5. Clonowen	Hib. Reg. Up. Iveagh	1657c
6. Clonowen	BSD 108	1661
7. Clanowen	Sub. Roll Down 276	1663
8. Cloneowen	Hib. Del. Down	1672c
9. Clanowen	ASE 273b §29	1681
10. Canoneene	Rent Roll Down 10	1692
11a. Levallyclanine	Bnd. Sur. (OSNB) E175	1830c
b. Levallyclanone	Bnd. Sur. (OSNB) E164	1830c
12a. Leth baile Eoin		
"John's half town"	OSNB Inf. E164	1834c
b. Leth bhaile clann Eoin		
"Half town of the Clann Keon"	OSNB Inf. E175	1834c
13. Leath-bhaile Chloinne Eoghain		
"Half-town of Owen's family"	Mooney's Rostrevor 10	1950
14. ˈlɛvli ˌklɑ ˈnoːn	Local pronunciation	1992

The older form of this name is simply *Clanowen* which appears to be comprised of the element *clann* "offspring, descendants, clan" (*DIL*) and one or other of the personal names *Eoghan* or *Eoin*. It is also possible that the first element is *cluain* "a meadow". However, the earliest anglicized form *Clanawen* (1) plus the evidence of the *OSNB* suggests, rather, that it is territorial in origin referring to the district held by the descendants of *Eoghan* or *Eoin*. We have already discussed the difficulty in distinguishing between *Eoghan* and *Eoin* when they occur in genitival position (see **Killowen**). While John Morgan's Irish form of Levallyclanone is recorded as *Leth bhaile clann Eoin* (12b), Killowen is said to derive from *Cill Eoghain*, and we have wondered whether there is any basis in reality for such a distinction. Mooney obviously does not think so and takes *Eoghan* as the element in both names. He is probably right for one might expect *clann* to be qualified by an old native name rather than by a name of comparatively recent origin. Unfortunately, there is no mention of an Eoghan in the *Uí Echach* or Iveagh genealogies (*CGH*) and so the original form of Clanowen is a matter of some doubt.

Note the two forms ascribed to John Morgan. Presumably *clann* has been omitted through oversight in the former (12a) and the name has been mistranslated "John's half town" as a result. The other form (12b) has also been mistranslated; *clann Eoin* could not possibly yield anything like "Clann Keon" in English. It seems likely that in this instance the translator was thinking of the surname *Mac Eoin* "MacKeon."

Levallyreagh   *Leathbhaile Riabhach*
J 1620   "dun/grey half-townland"

1.	Balleryogh	Fiants Eliz. §1609	1570
2.	Ballerioghe	CSP Ire. 435	1570
3.	Leallyreogh	CPR Jas. I 395b	1609
4.	Levallyreogh	CPR Jas. I 235a	1612
5.	Leavallyreagh	Inq. Ult. (Down) §13 Car. I	1629
6.	Leaualreagh	Hib. Reg. Up. Iveagh	1657c
7.	Levollyreagh ½ towne	Census 72	1659c
8.	Levallyreagh	BSD 108	1661
9.	Leaghuallrea	Hib. Del. Down	1672c
10.	Levallyreagh	Map Hall Estates fol. 31	1800
11.	Levalyreagh	Wm. Map (OSNB) E164	1810
12.	Levylareagh	Bnd. Sur. (OSNB) E164	1830c
13.	Leth b(h)aile riach "Grey half town"	OSNB Inf. E175; E164	1834c
14.	Leath-bhaile riach "Grey half-town"	Mooney's Rostrevor 11	1950
15.	ˌlavli 're:	Local pronunciation	1990
16.	'lɛvli 're:	Local pronunciation	1990

This townland, known as *Balleryogh* in the earliest sources (1–2), has been confused with Drumreagh by Mooney (*Mooney's Rostrevor* 8). *Balleryogh* clearly derives from *Baile Riabhach* in Irish, the adjective *riabhach* having a variety of applications such as "grey, dun, speckled, striped and furrowed" (*Dinneen*). By 1609 it had come to be considered a *leathbhaile* "half-townland", and so the modern form is derived from *Leathbhaile Riabhach* not *Baile Riabhach*.

Moygannon   *Maigh Ó gCanann*
J 1618   "plain of the O'Cannons"

1.	Moyoganan	CSP Ire. 435	1570
2.	Moyoganon	Fiants Eliz. §1609	1570
3.	Ballymoyagonan	CPR Jas. I 395b	1609
4.	Ballymoyagonan	CPR Jas. I 235a	1612
5.	Ballymoyagenan	Inq. Ult. (Down) §13 Car. I	1629
6.	Ballymoyganon	Inq. Ult. (Down) §85 Car. I	1639
7.	Balleyaunane	Hib. Reg. Up. Iveagh	1657c
8.	Moygannan	BSD 108	1661
9.	Moygannon (south part)	ASE 107b §9	1666
10.	Balliganon	Hib. Del. Down	1672c
11.	Moygannon	ASE 273b §29	1681
12.	Moygownan	Rent Roll Down 9	1692
13.	Moygannon	Rent Roll Down 10	1692
14.	Moygannon Upper	Map Hall Estates fol. 32	1800
15.	Moygannon	Wm. Map (OSNB) E164	1810
16.	Moygannon	Bnd. Sur. (OSNB) E164	1830c

17. Moighe Geanainn		
"Gannon's plain"	OSNB Inf. E164	1834c
18. Magh Ui Gheannáin/Ghionnáin	Mooney 153	1950c
19. Magh Mhig Fhionnain		
"MacGannon's/MacGennan's		
plain"	Mooney's Rostrevor 12	1950
20. Baile I Ghionnain/Gheannain		
"O'Gannon's homestead"	Mooney's Rostrevor 12	1950
21. mɔiˈgʲanən	Local pronunciation	1990

Although Moygannon may be reasonably transparent in appearence it is in fact quite difficult to interpret. The first element is undoubtedly *maigh*, an oblique form of *má* (earlier *magh*) "a plain", but the second element is a problem. The historical forms indicate that in origin the name is more correctly *Moyoganan* or *(Bally)moyagonan*, where *Moyoganan* has four syllables as opposed to its present three. If these forms are accurate then it seems likely that the name contains an *Ó* surname in the gen. pl.: *Maigh Ó gCanann*, *Maigh Ó gCanáin* or the like. Mooney suggests *Ó Gionnáin*, which is occasionally a corruption of an earlier *Mag Fhionnáin* (*Mooney's Rostrevor* 12), but the evidence provided by the historical forms of Moygannon clearly rejects this. *Ó Canann* is much more likely to be the surname in question. It is significant that some of the early anglicized forms of Glennagannon in Co. Donegal, Irish *Gleann Ó gCanann* "glen of the *Uí Chanann* [or O'Cannons]", resemble those of Moygannon: particularly *Clonagannan*, AD 1608, and *Glanoganan*, AD 1661 (Ó Canann 1989–90, 115–21). John Morgan's form *Moighe Geanainn* (17) appears to dismiss *Maigh Ó gCanann* as a possibility , but it may be that *Ó gCanann* has been misinterpreted as the personal name *Geanann*, attested in the more familiar place-name *Dún Geanainn* (**Dungannon**, Co. Tyrone). Whether this analysis of Morgan's form is correct or not, the historical forms suggest that Moygannon is more likely to be derived from *Maigh Ó gCanann* rather than *Moighe Geanainn* in Irish.

Newtown An English form
Newtown Upper
J 1919, 2021

1. Newtown	Wm. Map (OSNB) E164	1810
2. Newtown	Bnd. Sur. (OSNB) E164	1830c
3. Newtown Upper	Bnd. Sur. (OSNB) E164	1830c
4. ˈnjutəun	Local pronunciation	1990

As its name suggests Newtown is quite simply a new townland. It first appears in our records in 1810 (1) and Mooney suggests that it owes its creation to Catholic settlers from Co. Armagh who cleared the Kilbroney valley around the end of 18th century (*Mooney's Rostrevor* 12). By 1830 it had been redivided into Newtown and Newtown Upper.

It seems that the whole of northern and central Kilbroney, which is quite mountainous, was only carved up into administrative divisions relatively recently. Newtown, Newtown Upper and The Point Park are first recorded in the early 19th century, and although Kilbroney, Rosstrevor and Drumreagh appear in earlier documents, the townland names Kilbroney and Kilbroney Upper, Rosstrevor Upper, Rosstrevor Mountains and Drumreagh Upper are also of recent origin.

Point Park, The   An English form
J 1916

  1. The Point Park   Bnd. Sur. (OSNB) E164   1830c

This, like the townlands of Newtown and Newtown Upper, is a name of late origin and does not appear to be commonly used in the locality. The point in question may be Killowen Point but the latter falls within the modern boundaries of neighbouring Ballinran. It is difficult to see, however, what other point might be intended.

Ros(s)trevor   *Ros Treabhair (?)*
Rosstrevor Mountains   "Trevor's wood"
Rosstrevor Upper
J 1718, 2221, 1918

  1. C[aislén] Trever   Cín Lae Ó M. 42   1646
  2. Ros Treibheor   Sgéalaidhe Óirghiall 87   1905c
  3. Caisleán Ruaidhrí   Sgéalaidhe Óirghiall 152   1905c
  4. An Caisleán Ruadh   Sgéalaidhe Óirghiall 152   1905c

  5. Rose Trevor, Edward Trevor of   Parliamentary Records
                                     (Mooney's Rostrevor) 12 & 16   1613
  6. Rose Trevor, the landes of   Inq. Ult. (Down) xliii   1618
  7. Rosetrevor, Edw' Trevor de   Inq. Ult. (Down) §11 Jac. I   1621
  8. Rose-Trevor, the lands of   CPR Jas. I 305a   1623c
  9. Rossetrevor, Edw' Trevor de   Inq. Ult. (Down) §51 Car. I   1635
10. Rostrever   Civ. Surv. x §72   1655c
11. Rosse Trevor   Census 72   1659c
12. Rosse, Baron Trevor of   Mooney 156   1662
13. Rostrever   Hib. Del. Down   1672c
14. Rostrever   Maps Down (Mac Aodha) 71   1690
15. Rosstrevor   Rent Roll Down 14   1692
16. Rosetreuer   Collins C'ford Lough   1693
17. Rostrevor   Maps Down (Mac Aodha) 71   1712
18. Rostrepor   Maps Down (Mac Aodha) 71   1714
19. Carrickbrackian   Marriage Settlement
                                     (Mooney's Rostrevor) 12   1726
20. Rose Trevor   Harris Hist. map   1743
21. Rose-trevor   Harris Hist. 141   1744
22. Rostrevor Estate   Map Hall Estates fol. 32   1800
23. Rosstrever   Wm. Map (OSNB) E164   1810
24. Rosstrevor   Bnd. Sur. (OSNB) E164   1830c
25. Rosstrevor Mountains   Bnd. Sur. (OSNB) E164   1830c
26. Rosstrevor Upper   Bnd. Sur. (OSNB) E164   1830c

27. Carrickavraghad (ancient name)   OSM iii 32   1836
28. Castle Roe or Rory   Lewis' Top. Dict. ii 539   1837
29. Rostrevor or Rosetrevor   Lewis' Top. Dict. ii 539   1837

30. Cairge breaca "Spotted Rocks"   OSNB Inf. E164   1834c
31. Cairge breaca, anciently called   OSNB E175   1834c

32. Carrac an Bhraghad		
al. Caistel Ruad	Onom. Goed. 164	(?)
33. Caisleán Ruaidhrí	Post-Sheanchas 111	1905
34. An Caisleán Ruadh	Post-Sheanchas 111	1905
35. Caisleán Treibheor	Post-Sheanchas 111	1905
36. Rois Treibheor	Post-Sheanchas 111	1905
37. Rose Trevor	Mooney's Rostrevor 12	1950
38. Caislean Trever		
"Trever's castle"	Mooney's Rostrevor 12	1950
39. Caislean Ruaidh "Roe's castle"	Mooney's Rostrevor 12	1950
40. Ros Treabhair	AGBP 119	1969
41. Ros Treabhair	Éire Thuaidh	1988
42. Ros Treabhair	GÉ 153	1989
43. rə'strɛvər	Local pronunciation	1990

Of all the names in the parish of Kilbroney this is the one that has generated the most discussion. The first to comment on the derivation of the name was Walter Harris who in 1744 wrote that "this Place was so called from an Heiress, whose Name was Rose, that married into the Family of the Trevors..." (*Harris Hist.* 87). Almost 100 years later we have two similar accounts of the origin of the name, one contained in a memoir written in October 1836 by J. Hill Williams for the Ordnance Survey (*OSM* iii 32) and the other in Samuel Lewis's *Topographical Dictionary* published in 1837. Both Hill and Lewis derive the name from Rose, daughter of Sir Marmaduke Whitchurch, "after whose marriage with Trevor, Viscount Dungannon, the family seat... was invariably called Rosetrevor" (*Lewis' Top. Dict.* ii 539).

The association of Rosstrevor with the surname Trevor is undoubtedly correct. Edward Trevor, a Welshman, first appears in Co. Down as commander of the English garrison at Newry towards the end of the Nine Years War (*Mooney's Rostrevor* 14). By 1609 he held lands in Iveagh, not in Kilbroney itself but further north in the Aghaderg, Garvaghy and Shankill areas (*CPR Jas. I* 395). The following year he appears on record as "Edw. Trevor of Narrow-water" (*CPR Jas. I* 195b) and in 1611 not only was he confirmed in his possessions by the king but he was also granted "common of pasture on the mountain or waste of Cortlewe, and Beaniborphies [The Mournes]" (*CPR Jas. I* 190b). Trevor had now moved closer to home. That same year the plantation commissioners reported that "he had all the materials ready for the bylding of a castle at Kilbroney..." and by 1613 he had been returned to the Irish Parliament for the borough of Killileagh, as "Edward Trevor, Esq. K[nigh]t., of Rose-Trevor" (*Mooney's Rostrevor* 15–6).

Whereas there is little doubt as to the derivation of the second element in Rosstrevor, the initial element is more difficult to interpret. It should be noted that Harris, the first to discuss the name, was prone to fanciful etymologies; he derived **Mourne**, for example, from *Mor-Rinn* in Irish which he explained as "the great Partition, or great Hill" and **Binnian** from *Bin* or *Bein Gan*, "the Pinnacle of difficult Ascent" (*Harris Hist.* 120). Neither of these has any basis in reality. Nevertheless, one wonders were they simply Harris's concoctions, or might there have been some re-interpretation, or indeed misinterpretation, of the names locally? The same question needs to be posed in the case of Rosstrevor. Was Harris' explanation of the name purely his own or was there some local tradition behind it? One way or another the interpretation of the first element in Rosstrevor as the personal name Rose was later accepted by both Hill and Lewis, who disagreed merely on whether Rose was the only daughter or the youngest daughter of Marmaduke Whitchurch. In fact neither is correct.

The Rose who married Edward Trevor in 1612 was not a daughter of Marmaduke Whitchurch but rather of Henry Ussher, Archbishop of Armagh from 1595 to 1613 (Hamilton 1915, 313). It is remarkable that the first occurrence of Rosstrevor in the records dates to 1613 (5), less than a year after the marriage, and that both here and in the other early records the name is consistently spelt **Rose** Trevor *et var.* (6–8)! But are these spellings misleading? How would they have been pronounced? The modern pronunciation of the first element is nothing like the pronunciation of the name Rose and one wonders if this has always been the case? As early as 1875 Alexander Knox interpreted it as Irish *ros* (*Knox Hist.* 363), a word which, with such a wide range of meaning as "wood, copse; point, promontory; level tract of arable land" (*Dinneen*), could well have been applied to Rosstrevor. Hamilton suggests that *ros* in the meaning of "wood" is very appropriate to the locality, and that Trevor, who was familiar with the Welsh word *ros* "a moor or marshy place", simply added his own name to it. He also notes that *ros* in Irish place-names is often corrupted to *rose* as in Rosedermot in Co. Antrim. Furthermore, New Ross in Co. Wexford, Irish *Ros mhic Treoin* "the wood of the son of *Treon*", is locally interpreted as deriving from a mythical Rose Macrone (Hamilton 1915, 313–4). Hamilton probably goes too far when he suggests that Rosstrevor may originally have been Irish *Ros tsruthar* "wood of the stream" for there is absolutely no evidence for this. His explanation of the first element, however, and how it may have been corrupted is not at all far-fetched, especially if the form "Baron Trevor of Rosse" is accurate (12). The fact that the name is variously spelt *Rosetrevor*, *Rostrevor* and *Rosstrevor* in historical documents has caused some confusion, for Rosstrevor has been adopted as the correct spelling of the townland names whereas the village is more commonly spelt Rostrevor. The spelling in -*ss*- may have been popularised as a result of the disposal of a large part of the old Trevor estates to Robert Ross, Lord Mayor of Dublin in 1740 (see further *OSM* iii 32).

The complicated history of Rosstrevor does not end here for Lewis tells us that "this place was anciently called Castle Roe or Rory, from its original founder, Rory, one of the family of the Magennises, Lords of Iveagh, of whose baronial castle, subsequently occupied by the Trevor family, there are still some remains near the town..." (*Lewis' Top. Dict.* ii 539). Of this castle there is no longer any trace but as recently as 1846 it was described as being situated "near the centre of the town, between the main street and the shore..." (*ASCD* 263). Is Lewis correct in stating that this is the same castle as that occupied by the Trevors? It has been noted already that Edward Trevor had "all the material ready for the bylding of a castle at Kilbroney" in 1611 and this would seem to indicate that he was starting from scratch as opposed to rebuilding or renovating an older site. In Ó Mealláin's diary under the year 1646 *C[aislén] Trever* "Trevor's castle" (1) is treated as if it were a place-name in its own right and this form has been accepted by both Lloyd (35) and Mooney (38). As regards *Castle Roe* or *Castle Rory* both names were known to Irish speakers in Omeath at the beginning of the century as *An Caisleán Ruadh* (4) and *Caisleán Ruaidhri* (3). Mooney suggests that ultimately they are one and the same name, which he would derive from a Gaelic form *Caisleán Ruaidh* (39), *Ruadh* being a personal name meaning "red-haired". However, postulating a third form *Caisleán Ruaidh* does not necessarily contribute to solving the problem, especially when there seems to have been an historical personage called Rory Magennis. It is much more likely that *Caisleán Ruaidhrí* "Rory's castle" is the original form and that *Caisleán Ruadh* is the result of a process known as apocope whereby the end of a word is simply dropped or lost.

There are a couple of other names associated with Rosstrevor which need to be discussed. Firstly there is *Carraic an Bhraghad alias Caistel Ruad* (32) which Hogan cites in *Onom. Goed.* Although these may appear to be *bona fide* Irish forms there are a number of difficulties. The biggest problem is undoubtedly the fact that we cannot establish the source of this reference; Hogan merely remarks that it has been "omitted by a scribe" (*Onom. Goed.* xiv, 164). This is particularly worrying when one considers that Hogan's researchers sometimes transliterated anglicized forms of names when it seemed to them that the original Gaelic was fairly obvious. Killowen in Co. Derry is an example. Hogan cites an Irish form of this name, *Cell Eoghain*, supposedly taken from Archbishop Colton's *Visitation of the Diocese of Derry*. When one checks the visitation, however, one discovers that Killowen is merely included in an appendix to that document and there is no trace of an Irish-language form (*Colton Vis.* 131). There is, as Mooney suggests (*Mooney's Rostrevor* 13), the possibility that our "Irish" forms are equally artificial. Only once does *Carrac an Bhraghad* appear in the records proper; Hill in his memoir on Rostrevor states that "the ancient name of the place was Carrickavraghad" (*OSM* iii 32). Two years earlier John O'Donovan had noted that Rosstrevor was "anciently called *Cairrge Breaca*", a form which he received from John Morgan (30–1). To make matters even more complicated Mooney refers to a *Marriage Settlement* of 1726 in which the towns and lands of *Shread, Aughcarney, Ballitonwelly* and *Carrickbrackian* are said to be known by the general name of Rosstrevor (*Mooney's Rostrevor* 12). The similarity between *Carrac an Bhraghad, Cairrge Breaca* and *Carrickbrackian* is disturbing and one wonders might they ultimately derive from the one name? It is difficult, however, to come to any firm conclusion on the basis of the present evidence.

Tamnyveagh
J 2314

Tamhnaigh Bheithe
"clearing/grassy upland
of the birch"

1. Tawnebegg	CPR Jas. I 86a	1606
2. Tawnebeg	CPR Jas. I 103a	1607
3. Townebegg	CPR Jas. I 495a	1607
4. Tawnevehe	CPR Jas. I 395b	1609
5. Tawninevehe	CPR Jas. I 190b	1611
6. Toneveigh	CPR Jas. I 247a	1613
7. Toneveigh	Inq. Ult. (Down) §15 Jac. I	1625c
8. Tawnebegge	Inq. Ult. (Down) §84 Jac. I	1638
9. Tanyvea quarter	Census 72	1659c
10. Tawnyvea	BSD 132	1661
11. Taniveagh, ¼ of	Rent Roll Morne 6	1688
12. Taveneveagh	Deeds & Wills (Mooney) 155	1731
13. Tumnevea[?]	Wm. Map (OSNB) E164	1810
14. Tomniveagh	Bnd. Sur. (OSNB) E164	1830c
15. Tamnyveagh	J O'D (OSNB) E164	1834c
16. Tamhnaidh bhéith "Field of the Birch"	OSNB Inf. E164	1834c
17. Tamhnaidh bhféich	OSNB E175	1834c
18. Tamhnach a(n) bheithe "Field of the birch"	Mooney's Rostrevor 28	1950
19. ˈtɑmnə ˈveː	Local pronunciation	1990
20. ˌtɑmnə ˈviə	Local pronunciation	1990

The element *tamhnach*, which has been translated "a cultivated or arable spot in a waste; a green field" by *Dinneen* and "a grassy upland; arable place in mountain" by *Ó Dónaill*, is very common in the place-names of both Ulster and Connacht. It is variously anglicized *Tamna(gh)*, *Tamny*, *Tawna(gh)*, etc. but *Tamna(gh)* and *Tamny*, where the *-mh-* of the Gaelic form is delenited to *-m-* in English, are most common in East Ulster. Here we are dealing with an oblique case of the noun, *tamhnaigh*, which historically may be either dat. or acc. If dat. then *tamhnaigh* would lenite the following noun; a form *Tamhnaigh Bheithe* is quite plausible and this is undoubtedly the form which John Morgan had in mind (16). If *tamhnaigh* is acc., however, then according to the rules of early Irish the following noun should be eclipsed. This, presumably, is the reason why an alternative form *Tamhnaigh bhféich* (*féich*, gen. sing. of *fiach*, "a raven") has been suggested in the *OSNB* (17), although Morgan's suggestion makes the best sense. The early forms *Tawnebegg* et var. (1–3, 8) might be taken to suggest that the second element is historically the adjective *beag* "little", but it is important to remember that these sources are related and that a mistranscription of, or indeed in, the earliest source would simply have been repeated in the others. The majority of anglicized forms indicate quite clearly that *beith* is the original element.

OTHER NAMES

Arno's Vale   An English form
J 1618

1. Arnoes Vale	Taylor & Skinner 11		1777
2. Arno's Vale	Map Hall Estates fol. 39		1800
3. Arno's Vale	Wm. Map (OSNB) E122		1810
4. Arnoe's-Vale	Downshire Direct. 315		1823
5. Arno's Vale	Bnd. Sur. (OSNB) E122		1830c
6. 'arnoz 've:l	Local pronunciation		1992
7. 'ɑːrnəz 'viəl	Local pronunciation		1992

Arno's Vale originally appears to have referred to a cottage built on this site by the Rev. McArthur, curate of Rosstrevor, and so named by his daughter. As to whom or what Arno may refer is not clear; it may be an anagram of some sort or a fanciful association with the river Arno in Italy. A house was later built here by John Darley which by 1815 was in the possession of one James Moore (Ó Muirí 1989, 116). Subsequent owners were Dean Carter in 1834 (*OSNB* E122) and Robert M'Blain in 1875 (*Knox Hist.* 362).

Carpenham   An English form
J 1718

Carpenham was coined by one Henry Hamilton, brother-in-law of the Duke of Wellington, who, on building a house here, named it after his wife Caroline Penelope Hamilton using the first three letters of each part of her name (*Atkinson's Dromore* 255). Mr. Hamilton was still resident here in the time of O'Donovan, who notes that the grounds of this "beautiful villa... which are not very extensive, are laid out in the most tasteful manner" (*OSNB* E122). It subsequently came into the possession of a certain Major Ford (*Knox Hist.* 362).

Carrickbawn Wood   A hybrid form
J 1719

1. Carrickbawn [House]	OSNB E122		1834c
2. Carraig bhán "White Rock"	OSNB E122		1834c

The references to Carrickbawn in the *OSNB* do not refer to the wood but to a mansion which O'Donovan described as having an "excellent garden, with well laid out but not extensive pleasure grounds" (*OSNB* E122). At that time it belonged to a certain Honourable Justice Jebb, but Atkinson states that it was subsequently acquired by the Ross family and renamed Rosstrevor House (*Atkinson's Dromore* 253). It was still the seat of that particular family as Atkinson wrote, i.e. in the year 1925, but there is no longer any trace of it, at least under that name, on the modern maps. Carrickbawn itself is also absent from the maps; it may be that it was introduced into the area as a nice name for a house. O'Donovan is probably correct in his interpretation of Carrickbawn as *Carraig Bhán* "white rock" (2).

Dickey's Rocks An English form
J 2114

These rocks form an outcrop on a point of land which, despite its prominence, is not named on any of the modern maps. In the 17th century, however, it was known as *Rone-harragh*, *Rynnacharreh* etc. which, although difficult to decipher, seems to contain the element *rinn* "a point". The name was also applied to the townland in which the point is situated, but is now obsolete having been replaced in the 18th century by **Ballindoalty**. On either side of Dickey's Rocks we have two other rocks named **Carrigaroan** and **Carriganean**. For these we have no historical evidence but they appear to represent Irish *Carraig an Róin* "seal's rock", and *Carraig an Éin* "bird's rock", respectively. Dickey's Rocks seems to derive from the surname Dickey and a William Dickey of **Carcullion** in neighbouring Clonduff is on record in the year 1837 (*Ir. Wills Index* iv 33).

Dobbin's Point An English form
J 1518

   1. Dobbin's Point Mr. Dobbin (OSNB) E122 1834c

As O'Donovan's authority for the orthography of this name was one Mr. Dobbin, it seems likely that Dobbin's Point took its name from some member of his particular family. The surname Dobbyn is found in the south of the country since the 13th century, but the first bearer of the name in Ulster (spelt Dobbin) appears as Constable of Carrickfergus Castle in the year 1400. The two surnames are unrelated according to MacLysaght. Seventeen Dobbins were sheriffs and eight mayors of Carrickfergus between the years 1571 and 1666, and the name is more numerous today in Antrim and adjacent counties than in any other part of Ireland (MacLysaght 1982, 82; 1985, 83). As regards Co. Down a number of Dobbins are associated with the parish of Moira in early 18th-century wills (*Ir. Wills Index* iv 35), but the name does not appear to be particularly common in this part of the county.

Killowen
J 1815

For the village of Killowen see the townland called **Killowen Mountains**.

For full discussion of the following names see *PNI, County Down, vol. iii: The Mournes*:

Cloghgarran *Cloch Ghearráin*
J 2015 "stone of the horse"

157

Cloghmore J 1817	*An Chloch Mhór* "the big stone"
Crenville J 2018	Of uncertain origin
Crockbane J 2217	*Cnoc Bán* "white hill"
Cross River J 2023	*Crosabhainn* "transverse river"
Curraghknockadoo J 2217	*Corrach Chnoc Dubh* "marsh of *Cnoc Dubh* (black hill)"
Fallow, The J 2119	An English form
Ghann River, The J 1721	*An Abhainn Ghann* "the scanty river"
Knockshee J 2216	*Cnoc Sí* "hill of the fairy mound"
Leckan Beg	*Leacain Bheag* "little brow/hillside"
Leckan More J 1821	*Leacain Mhór* "great brow/hillside"
Rowans, The J 2118	*Na Ruáin* "the red patches"
Slieveanowen J 2218	Of uncertain origin
Slieveban J 2016	*Sliabh Bán* "white mountain"
Slievedermot J 1918	*Sliabh Diarmada* "Dermot's mountain"
Slievefadda J 2117	*Sliabh Fada* "long mountain"
Slievemartin J 2017	*Sliabh Mártain* "Martin's mountain"

Slievemeel
J 2120

Sliabh Míol
"mountain of the ants"

Slievemeen
J 2017

Sliabh Mín
"smooth mountain"

Slievemiskan
J 2219

Sliabh Meascán
"mountain of the cairns"

Slieve Roe
J 1823

Sliabh Rua
"red mountain"

Slieve Roosley
J 1922, 2024

Sliabh Mhic Rúslaing
"*Mac Rúslaing*'s mountain"

Thunder's Hill
J 1719

An English form

Yellow Water River
J 2122

An Abhainn Bhuí
"the yellow river"

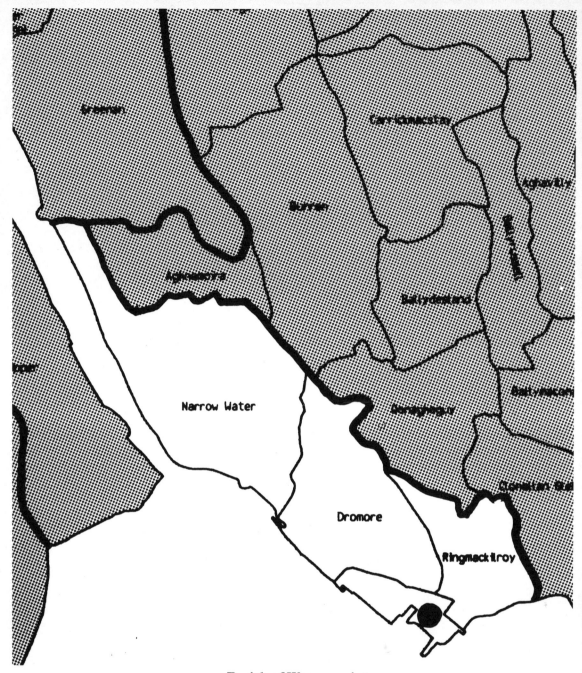

Parish of Warrenpoint
Barony of Iveagh Upper, Upper Half

Townlands   *Town*
Dromore   Warrenpoint
Narrow Water
Ringmackilroy

WARRENPOINT PARISH

For the introduction to this parish see **Clonallan**.

Warrenpoint
An Pointe
"the point"

1. A' Púinte	Omeath Infs. 157	1901
2. ins an Phuinte	Sgéalaidhe Óirghiall 94	1905c
3. An Poinnte	Omeath Infs. 11	1925c
4. Waring's Point	Harris Hist. 141	1744
5. Warren's-point	Post Chaise Comp. (OSNB) E42/100	1795
6. Warrenspoint	Civ. & Ecc. Top. (OSNB) E42/100	1806
7. Warren's-point	Downshire Direct. 315	1823
8. Warrenpoint	County Warrant (OSNB) E42/100	1830
9. Warrenpoint	Reg. Free. (OSNB) E42/100	1830
10. Warrenpoint	Bnd. Sur. (OSNB) E42/100	1830c
11. Warrenpoint	Maps Down (Mac Aodha) 72	1830c
12. Warrens Point	Maps Down (Mac Aodha) 72	1831
13. Warrenspoint	J O'D (OSNB) E42/100	1834c
14. Warren Point	Maps Down (Mac Aodha) 72	1851c
15. Warrenspoint	Maps Down (Mac Aodha) 72	1864
16. Pointe an Bháirínigh		
"Warren's Point"	OSNB Inf. E42/100	1834c
17. An Púinte	Post-Sheanchas 123	1905
18. An Pointe	AGBP 120	1969
19. An Pointe	Éire Thuaidh	1988
20. An Pointe	GÉ 145	1989
21. 'wɔrn 'pɔint	Local pronunciation	1990
22. 'wɛrn 'pɔint	Local pronunciation	1990

Warrenpoint is a comparatively modern name; the earliest reference to it in the sources dates to 1744 (4) and historically it formed a part of the district of the *Legan* and parish of Clonallan (see p. 49). As late as 1780 there were only two houses in the village, "with a few huts for the occasional residence of the fishermen during the oyster season..." In the succeeding 50 years, however, its scenic beauty and coastal location seem to have instigated its rapid development and in 1837 it contained 462 houses (*Lewis' Top. Dict.* ii 675).

It has been suggested by both *Mooney* (p. 53) and Laoide (*Sgéalaidhe Óirghiall* 152) that *Rinn Mhic Giolla Ruaidh*, anglicized Ringmackilroy, is the old Irish name for Warrenpoint. This is because the Irish element *rinn* "a point" clearly refers to the same topographical feature as *-point* in Warrenpoint. The modern urban district is virtually co-extensive with the townland of Ringmackilroy but Warrenpoint was never referred to as *Rinn Mhic Giolla Ruaidh* by the last generations of Irish speakers in the area. O'Donovan recorded the form *Pointe an Bháirínigh* "Warren's Point" (16) from Oyne McStay in 1834 whereas Irish speakers in Omeath at the beginning of the century simply referred to it as *An Púinte* or *An Pointe* (1–3). The origin of the first element in Warrenpoint is, nevertheless, a problem.

McStay clearly understood it to be a surname but Lewis, writing in 1837, states that "the site of the present town was originally a rabbit warren, whence it has received its name" (*Lewis' Top. Dict.* ii 675). These two interpretations are possibly reflected in varying spellings such as *Warren Point* (14) and *Warrenspoint* (15), which postdate the first Ordnance Survey when the spelling of most Irish place-names was finally settled. Lewis' explanation is possibly a folk etymology but, if this is the case, does Warrenpoint derive from the surname Warren or Waring? MacLysaght states that these two names are not related: Warren derives from the French *de la Varenne* whereas Waring derives from the Norman–French personal name *Guarin* (MacLysaght 1985, 296). They are sometimes confused, however, and Harris spells Warrenpoint *Waring's Point* in 1744 (4). **Waringstown** in the parish of Donagh-cloney, on the other hand, derives its name from a certain William Waring who purchased lands in the area in 1658. It is interesting that in a document lodged by Waring with the Court of Claims in 1662 he spells his surname *Warring* and *Warren* (*Atkinson's Donaghcloney* 24 & 144). While Waring is well attested in Co. Down, Warren is normally associated with the Pale (MacLysaght 1985, 296); but as neither surname is attested in this particular area the precise origin of the name Warrenpoint remains a matter of some doubt.

TOWNLAND NAMES

Dromore
J 1319

Droim Mór
"large/great ridge"

1. Dromore	Fiants Eliz. §1609	1570
2. Dromore	CSP Ire. 435	1570
3. Ballydromore	CPR Jas. I 395b	1609
4. Ballydromore	CPR Jas. I 235a	1612
5. Ballydromore	Inq. Ult. (Down) §13 Car. I	1629
6. Ballydromore	Inq. Ult. (Down) §85 Car. I	1639
7. Dromore	Hib. Reg. Up. Iveagh	1657c
8. Dromor	Census 74	1659c
9. Dromore	BSD 111	1661
10. Drumore	ASE 107b §9	1666
11. Dromore	Hib. Del. Down	1672c
12. Drumore	Rent Roll Down 9	1692
13. Dromore	Map Hall Estates fol. 17	1800
14. Dromore	Wm. Map (OSNB) E42/100	1810
15. Dromore	Reg. Free. (OSNB) E42/100	1829
16. Dromore	Bnd. Sur. (OSNB) E42/100	1830c
17. Druim Mór "Great Ridge"	OSNB E42/100	1834c
18. Druim mór "The Great Ridge"	Mooney 49	1950c
19. An drom mór	Mooney 49	1950c
20. drọ 'moːr	Local pronunciation	1990

Droim is an extremely common element in Irish townland names. *Joyce* (i 524) states that it occurs initially in approximately 2,400 townlands, towns and villages where it is variously anglicized as *drum/drom/drim*. There are over 50 Dromores in Ireland, the majority of which are located in the northern half of the country. There are examples in all the Ulster counties other than Armagh (*Census* 1871) and there are also a couple of examples from Scotland: Drummore in the parish of Kirkmaiden in Wigtown and Drumore in the parish of Campbeltown in Argyll (*Scot. Census* 1971).

Narrow Water	*Caol Uisce*	
J 1219	"narrow channel of water"	
1. (?)Chaoil uiscce, la Gallaibh	AFM i 462	841
2. Cáol, an Cúan laimh risan – i n-Uibh Eachach	Mart. Gorm. Apr. 2 p68n	1170c
3. (?)chaoiluiscce, Caisslen	AFM iii 344	1252
4. Caol, an cuan láimh risin – in Uibh Eachach Uladh	Mart. Don. Apr. 2 p92	1630c
5a. ó chaol an Éigse	Cathal Buí 150	1720c
b. ó chaol an uisg'	Cathal Buí 151	1720c
c. ó chaol an Eisge	Cathal Buí 151	1720c
d. ó chaol an Éisge	Cathal Buí 151	1720c
e. ó chaol an eisg	Cathal Buí 151	1720c
6. ag báda an Chaoil	Mac Bionaid 12: 40	1840c
7. Snámh a' Chaoil	Omeath Infs. 157	1901
8. Bád a' Chaoil	Omeath Infs. 157	1901
9. aige Bád an Chaoil	Sgéalaidhe Óirghiall 94	1905c
10. Narowwater[?], castell of	Lythe Map	1568c
11. Aghekhork, the castle in	Fiants Eliz. §1609	1570
12. Aghekhorke	CSP Ire. 435	1570
13. Narowater, John Sancky of	Fiants Eliz. §1736	1570c
14. Narro water	Ulster Map	1570c
15. Narrowe water castell	Ireland E. Coast	1580c
16. Narrow Water	Fiants Eliz. §4327	1583c
17. C: narrow water	Jobson's Ulster (TCD) 17	1590c
18. Narrow water	Mercator's Ulst.	1595
19. N.W.	Mercator's Ire.	1595
20. Ca: narrow water	Boazio's Map (BM)	1599
21. N. Water ca:	Bartlett Map (BM)	1600
22. Ca: Narowater	Bartlett Map (TCD)	1601
23. Ca: Narowater	Bartlett Maps (Hayes McCoy) i	1602c
24. Narawater Castle	Bartlett Maps (Esch. Co. Map) 1	1603
25. Ca Narowater	Bartlett Maps (Esch. Co. Map) 2	1603
26. Narrow-water, the	CPR Jas. I 56b	1604
27. Narrowater	CPR Jas. I 395b	1609
28. Narrowater	Speed's Antrim & Down	1610
29. Ca. Narrowater	Speed's Antrim & Down	1610
30. Narrowater	Speed's Ulster	1610
31. Ca. Narrowater	Speed's Ulster	1610
32. Ca Narrowater	Speed's Ireland	1610
33. C Narrowater	Norden's Map	1610c
34. Narrowe-Water	CPR Jas. I 190b	1611
35. Narrowater	CPR Jas. I 235a	1612
36. Narrow-Water	CPR Jas. I 235b	1612

37.	Narrow-Water, castle of	CPR Jas. I 337a	1614
38.	Narrowater	Inq. Ult. (Down) §13 Car. I	1629
39.	Narrow-water	Inq. Ult. (Down) §85 Car. I	1639
40.	Narrowater	Civ. Surv. x §72	1655c
41.	Castlekeele	Civ. Surv. x §77	1655c
42.	Narrow water	Hib. Reg. Up. Iveagh	1657c
43.	Narowe Water	Census 74	1659c
44.	Narrow Water	BSD 111	1661
45.	Narrow-Water	Sub. Roll Down 276	1663
46.	Narrow-Water	ASE 107b §9	1666
47.	Narrow water C:	Hib. Del. Down	1672c
48.	Narowater Castle	Hib. Del. Ireland	1672c
49.	Narrowwater	Rent Roll Down 9	1692
50.	Caol, the castle of	MacCana's Itinerary 46	1700c
51.	Narrow-water, the	Harris Hist. 141	1744
52.	Narrow-water	Map Hall Estates fol. 13	1800
53.	Narrow Water	Wm. Map (OSNB) E42/100	1810
54.	Narrow-water	Reg. Free. (OSNB) E42/100	1829
55.	Narrow-water	Bnd. Sur. (OSNB) E42/100	1830c
56.	Caol "a narrow or strait"	OSNB Inf. E42/100	1834c
57.	Caol Uisce	Mooney 53	1950c
58.	'narə 'watər	Local pronunciation	1990

Narrow Water is a translation of *Caol Uisce* in Irish, literally "a narrow channel of water". The first definite reference to our *Caol Uisce* in the historical documentation is in the form of a gloss added to the 12th-century text known as the *Martyrology of Gorman*:

> *Conall mor mac Aeda, o Clúain Dalláin i bfail Snámha Ech .i. an Cúan laimh risan Cáol i n-Uibh Eachach Uladh* (*Mart. Gorm.* 68).

> (Great Conall, son of Aed, from Clonallan near Carlingford, i.e. the haven beside Narrow Water in Iveagh of Ulster).

There are other references to *Caol Uisce* in Irish documents but it is sometimes difficult to say whether the Co. Down Narrow Water or *Caol Uisce* on the Erne is intended. The annals refer to the destruction of Tristeldermot in Meath by the Vikings of *Caol Uisce* in 841 (1), for example, and this has been taken to refer to the latter. However, the Vikings were equally prominent in this part of Co. Down and the name **Carlingford Lough** bears witness to that fact. The annals also refer to the castle of *Caol Uisce* in 1252 but there is some confusion as to which Narrow Water is intended. Reeves (*MacCana's Itinerary* 46), Hennessy (*ALC* i 399) and O'Donovan (*AFM* iii 344) equate it with our Narrow Water, but Freeman (*A. Conn.* 106) takes it to be Narrow Water in Fermanagh and refers to Orpen (1911–20, iii 268). Orpen states that the name in question refers to the castle built by Gilbert de Nangle on the Erne in 1212 but rebuilt by Maurice Fitzgerald in 1252, and says that Hennessy and others have confused it with *Caol Uisce* in Co. Down. However, there is a reference to *Magh Cobha*, which is also in southern Co. Down (see **Donaghmore**), in the same entry in the annals and one wonders if this has any bearing on the matter. Presumably Orpen had other information which put his identification beyond any doubt but unfortunately he does not cite such.

It is interesting that the first castle at Narrow Water in Co. Down is also said to have been built in 1212, not by Gilbert de Nangle but by Hugh de Lacy. Lewis states that it remained entire until 1641 and suggests that its ruins may possibly be located on Nun's Island not far from the present castle. The latter, he claims, was built by the Duke of Ormond in 1663 (*Lewis' Top. Dict.* i 348) but the Archaeological Survey would date its construction to shortly after 1560. It notes that John Sanky was paid £361 4s. 2d. for the construction and fortification of the castle and that he was warder of Narrow Water from October 1568 at the latest. By 1580 it appears to have changed hands for Hugh Magennis was then in possession of the castle (*ASCD* 241). This confirms what we know from other 16th-century records for we have seen that Sanky was granted the *Legan* in 1570 but that the area was held by Magennis c. 1583 (see p. 129). The 1570 document speaks of a lease to John Sanky "of a new castle, containing two chambers and a cellar, a hall covered with straw, nine cottages covered with earth within the precinct of the castle in Aghekhork, Co. Down..." (*Fiants Eliz.* §1609), but elsewhere the castle is referred to simply as *Castlekeele* (41) or *the castle of Caol* (50), Irish *Caisleán an Chaoil*. The number of historical forms of the name could undoubtedly be multiplied, especially for the early medieval period, and this is indicative of its importance commanding the entry to the Newry River.

The Irish word *caol* is found elsewhere in Co. Down as in **Quoile**, Irish *An Caol* "the narrow water", in the parish of Saul (Flanagan D. 1978(e)). It is also found in Scotland as in the Kyle of Lochalsh, for example, between the Isle of Skye and the mainland. *Caol Uisce* is mentioned in a poem by the 18th-century poet Cathal Buí Mac Giolla Ghunna, but as he was a Fermanagh poet one wonders might *Caol Uisce* on the Erne be intended? In the various manuscript copies of his poetry the name has been corrupted and all the variant spellings have been listed here (5a–e). The two Irish forms from Omeath at the beginning of the century are interesting. The first is *Snámh a' Chaoil* (7) where *snámh* refers to "part of a river passed or passable by swimming, a sea channel or ford, a swimming place" (*Dinneen*). Laoide informs us that there is an old churchyard in Omeath called *Cill an tSnáimh* in Irish (*Sgéalaidhe Óirghiall* 151) and it clearly derives its name from *Snámh a' Chaoil*. A similar name *Snámh Dá Éan* "ford or channel of the two birds" is located on the Shannon and in Hogan's edition of the *Lives of the Saints* this is translated *Vadum-duorum-avium* in Latin (*DIL* sv. *snám*). The word *vadum* is reminiscent of the element *bád* which is preserved in the second name from Omeath *Bád a' Chaoil* (8–9). *Bád* normally means "a boat" in Irish and this is the word which precedes *Caol* in Mac Bionaid's poem (6). However, *bád*, as in *Bád a' Chaoil*, is clearly of different origin and a meaning akin to Irish *snámh* and Latin *vadum* would seem to be more appropriate.

Ringmackilroy	*Rinn Mhic Giolla Ruaidh*	
J 1418	"McIlroy's point"	
1. Portyneile	CSP Ire. 435	1570
2. Portynele	Fiants Eliz. §1609	1570
3. Ballyportineale	CPR Jas. I 395b	1609
4. Ballyport-Ineale	CPR Jas. I 235a	1612
5. Ballyporteinele	Inq. Ult. §13 Car. I	1629
6. Ballyporteneale	Inq. Ult. §85 Car. I	1639
7. Roungelleroe	Hib. Reg. Up. Iveagh	1657c
8. Ring McIlroy	Census 74	1659c
9. Kingleroye	BSD 112	1661
10. Ringleroge	Sub. Roll Down 276	1663

11. Ringleroy	ASE 107b §9	1666
12. Rougelliroe	Hib. Del. Down	1672c
13. Ringleroy	DS (Mooney) 53	1677
14. Kingleroy	BSD 9	1692
15. Ringmackilroy	Map Hall Estates fol. 33	1800
16. Ringmacilroy	Wm. Map (OSNB) E42/100	1810
17. Ringmacelroy	Reg. Free. (OSNB) E42/100	1829
18. Ringmackilroy	Reg. Free. (OSNB) E42/100	1830
19. Ringmacleroy	Bnd. Sur. (OSNB) E42/100	1830c
20. Ringmackilroy	J O'D (OSNB) E42/100	1834c
21. Rinn mhic Giolla ruaidh "MacGilroy's point"	OSNB Inf. E42/100	1834c
22. Rinn mhic Ghilruaidhe	OSNB E42/100	1834c
23. Rinn Mhic Giolla Ruaidh	Post-Sheanchas 123	1905
24. Rinn Mhic Ghiolla Ruaidh "MacIlroy's point"	Mooney 53	1950c
25. ˌrɪŋmakəl ˈrɔi	Local pronunciation	1990

This name is clearly derived from *Rinn Mhic Giolla Ruaidh* in Irish: "MacIlroy's point". *Rinn* is a common element in the place-names of Co. Down. It occurs initially in ten townland names, three of which are in the parish of **Donaghmore**. The surname MacIlroy can be of local or Scottish origin (Bell 1988, 165–6). Woulfe states that it was common in Cos Down, Cavan, Roscommon and Offaly in the 16th century, although our Ringmackilroy first appears in the records in the middle of the 17th century. It is particularly associated with Co. Fermanagh where the name is preserved in the townland of **Ballymackilroy** in the parish of Aghalurcher (Woulfe 1923, 379). There is also a **Ballymackilroy** in Errigal Keerogue in Tyrone and a **Ballymacilroy** in Drummaul, Co. Antrim (*Census* 1871). It seems that *Portyneile* (1) was an earlier name for this townland. It appears to derive from the Irish *Port Uí Néill* "O'Neill's port", or possibly even *Port an Aoil* "port of the limestone".

APPENDIX A

ASPECTS OF IRISH GRAMMAR RELEVANT TO PLACE-NAMES

The following types of place-names can be identified:

1. Those which consist of a noun only:

> Sabhall "a barn" (Saul, Dn)
> Tuaim "a tumulus" (Toome, Ant.)

There is no indefinite article in Irish, that is, there is no word for *a*, e.g. *Sabhall* means "barn" or "a barn".

English nouns generally have only two forms, singular and plural, and the plural is normally formed by adding *s*, e.g. *wall, walls; road, roads*. Occasionally a different ending is added – *ox, oxen* – and occasionally the word is changed internally – *man, men*; sometimes there is both addition and internal change – *brother, brethren*. Irish nouns have not only distinctive forms for the plural but also for the genitive singular and sometimes for the dative and vocative as well. These distinctive forms are made by addition, by internal change and sometimes by both. Five principal types of noun change are identified in Irish and nouns are therefore divided into five major groups known as *declensions*. Examples of change will be seen later.

2. Singular article + masculine noun:

> An Clár "the plain" (Clare, Arm.)
> An Gleann "the valley" (Glen, Der.)

The only article in Irish is the definite article, that is, the word corresponding to *the* in English.

The singular article *an* "the" prefixes *t* to masculine nouns beginning with a vowel in certain cases. The nouns *éadan* "front, forehead" and *iúr* "yew tree", for example, appear in the place-names:

> An tÉadan "the face (of a hill)" (Eden, Ant.)
> An tIúr "the yew tree" (Newry, Dn)

3. Singular article + feminine noun:

> An Chloch "the stone" (Clough, Dn)
> An Bhreacach "the speckled place" (Brockagh, Der.)

The article *an* aspirates the first consonant of a following feminine noun.

Aspiration is indicated by putting *h* after the consonant (*cloch* "a stone"; *an chloch* "the stone") and the sound of that consonant is modified, just as in English the sound of *p*, as in the word *praise*, is changed when *h* is added, as in the word *phrase*. Only *b, c, d, f, g, m, p, s*, and *t* are aspirated. The other consonants, and vowels, are not aspirated.

The singular article *an* does not affect feminine nouns beginning with a vowel, e.g.

> An Eaglais "the church" (Eglish, Tyr.)

4. Masculine noun + adjective:

> Domhnach Mór "great church" (Donaghmore, Tyr.)
> Lios Liath "grey ring fort" (Lislea, Arm.)

In Irish the adjective normally follows the noun (but see §8).

167

5. Feminine noun + adjective:

> Bearn Mhín "smooth gap" (Barnmeen, Dn)
> Doire Fhada "long oak-wood" (Derryadd, Arm.)

The first consonant of the adjective is aspirated after a feminine noun.

6. Singular article + masculine noun + adjective:

> An Caisleán Riabhach "the brindled castle" (Castlereagh, Dn)
> An Baile Meánach "the middle town" (Ballymena, Ant.)

7. Singular article + feminine noun + adjective:

> An Charraig Mhór "the large rock" (Carrickmore, Tyr.)
> An Chloch Fhionn "the white stone" (Cloghfin, Tyr.)

Note that the first consonant of the feminine noun is aspirated after the definite article as in §3 above and that the adjective is aspirated after the feminine noun as in §5 above.

8 Adjective + noun:

> Fionnshliabh "white mountain" (Finlieve, Dn)
> Seanchill "old church" (Shankill, Ant.)

Sometimes an adjective precedes a noun. In such cases the two words are generally written as one and the second noun is usually aspirated. In compounds aspiration sometimes does not occur when *d, t* or *s* is preceded by *d, n, t, l* or *s.*

9. Article + adjective + noun:

> An Seanmhullach "the old summit" (Castledawson, Der.)
> An Ghlasdromainn "the green ridge" (Glasdrumman, Dn)

Dromainn is a feminine noun and the initial consonant of the compound is aspirated in accordance with §3 above.

10. Masculine noun + genitive singular of noun:

> Srath Gabhláin "(the) river valley of (the) fork" (Stragolan, Fer.)
> Port Rois "(the) harbour of (the) headland" (Portrush, Ant.)

These two examples contain the genitive singular forms of the nouns *gabhlán* and *ros.* Many nouns form the genitive singular by inserting *i* before the final consonant.

11. Feminine noun + genitive singular of noun:

> Maigh Bhile "(the) plain of (the) sacred tree" (Movilla, Dn)
> Cill Shléibhe "(the) church of (the) mountain" (Killevy, Arm.)

Note that in these examples the qualifying genitive is aspirated after the feminine noun. However the forms *maigh* and *cill* are also both old datives, and in the older language aspiration followed any dative singular noun.

Two other types of genitive are illustrated here: many nouns which end in a vowel, like *bile*, do not change at all, whereas others, like *sliabh*, form their genitive by adding *e* (and sometimes an internal change is necessary).

12. Noun + *an* + genitive singular:

> Léim an Mhadaidh "(the) leap of the dog" (Limavady, Der.)
> Baile an tSéipéil "(the) town of the chapel" (Chapeltown, Dn)

The noun *an madadh* "the dog" has a genitive *an mhadaidh* "of the dog". Note that, as well as the end of the noun changing as in §10 above, the genitive is aspirated after *an*.

Instead of aspirating *s* the article *an* prefixes *t* to it: *an sac* "the sack", *an tsaic* "of the sack"; *an séipéal* "the chapel", *an tséipéil* "of the chapel".

13. Noun + *na* + genitive singular:

> Muileann na Cloiche "(the) mill of the stone/the stone mill" (Clogh Mills, Ant.)
> Coill na Baice "(the) wood of the river bend" (Cullybacky, Ant.)

The genitive singular feminine article is *na*. It does not aspirate the following noun: *an chloch* "the stone", *na cloiche* "of the stone".

It prefixes *h*, however, to words beginning with a vowel e.g.

> Baile na hInse "(the) town of the water-meadow" (Ballynahinch, Dn)

The genitive in all these examples is formed by adding *e* to the nominative singular and making a slight internal adjustment.

14. Plural noun:

> Botha "huts" (Boho, Fer.)

The plural form of a substantial group of nouns in Irish is formed by adding -*a*. In the examples in §15 below an internal adjustment has also to be made.

15. *Na* + plural noun:

> Na Creaga "the rocks" (Craigs, Ant.)
> Na Cealla "the churches" (Kells, Ant.)

Na is also the plural article. *Creaga* and *cealla* are the plural forms of the nouns *creig* "rock" and *cill* "church".

16. Noun + genitive plural:

> Droim Bearach "(the) ridge of (the) heifers" (Dromara, Dn)
> Port Muc "(the) harbour of (the) pigs" (Portmuck, Ant.)

As in the case of *bearach* "a heifer" and *muc* "a pig" the genitive plural form is the same as the nominative singular.

17. Noun + *na* + genitive plural:

> Lios na gCearrbhach "(the) fort/enclosure of the gamblers" (Lisburn, Dn)
> Lios na nDaróg "(the) fort/enclosure of the little oaks" (Lisnarick, Fer.)

After *na* the first letter of the following genitive plural is eclipsed. Eclipsis involves adding to the beginning of a word a consonant which obliterates the sound of the original consonant, e.g.

bó "a cow", pronounced like English "bow" (and arrow)
(*na*) *mbó* "(of the) cows", pronounced like "mow"

The following are the changes which take place:

Written letter	Is eclipsed by
b	m
c	g
d	n
f	bh
g	ng
p	b
t	d
vowel	n

The other consonants are not eclipsed, e.g.

Áth na Long "(the) ford of the ships" (Annalong, Dn)

18. Noun + genitive of personal name:

Dún Muirígh *"Muiríoch*'s fort" (Dunmurry, Ant.)
Boith Mhéabha "Maeve's hut" (Bovevagh, Der.)

In the older language the genitive of a personal name was not aspirated after a masculine noun but it was after a feminine noun. In the above examples *dún* is masculine and *boith* is feminine. In current Irish aspiration of the personal name is also usual after a masculine noun and this is reflected in many place-names in areas where Irish survived until quite recently, e.g.

Ard Mhacha, interpreted as "the height of Macha" (Armagh, Arm.)

19. Noun + genitive singular of *Ó* surname:

Baile Uí Dhonnaíle "Donnelly's townland" (Castlecaulfield, Tyr.)
Coill Uí Chiaragáin "Kerrigan's wood" (Killykergan, Der.)

Surnames in *Ó*, e.g. Ó Dochartaigh "(O') Doherty", Ó Flannagáin "Flannagan", etc. form their genitive by changing *Ó* to *Uí* and aspirating the second element – Uí Dhochartaigh, Uí Fhlannagáin.

20. Noun + genitive singular of *Mac* surname:

Lios Mhic Dhuibhleacháin *"Mac Duibhleacháin*'s town"
(Lisnagelvin, Der.)
Baile Mhic Gabhann *"Mac Gabhann*'s town (angl. McGowan, Smith, etc.)
(Ballygowan, Dn)

Surnames in *Mac*, e.g. Mac Dónaill "McDonnell", Mac Muiris "Morrison, Fitzmaurice", etc. form their genitive by changing *Mac* to *Mhic* and aspirating the second element (except those beginning with *C* or *G*).

23. Noun + genitive plural of Ó surname:

> Doire Ó gConaíle "the oak-wood of the Ó *Conaíle* family (angl. Connelly)" (Derrygonnelly, Fer.)

In the genitive plural of Ó surnames the second element is eclipsed.

25. Neuter noun + genitive or adjective:

> Sliabh gCuillinn "mountain of (the) steep slope" (Slieve Gullion, Arm.)
> Loch gCaol "(the) narrow lake" (Loughguile, Ant.)

The neuter gender no longer exists in Irish but traces of it are found in place-names. The initials of nouns and adjectives were eclipsed after neuter nouns.

APPENDIX B

LAND UNITS

TERRITORIAL DIVISIONS IN IRELAND

The old administrative system, used in the arrangement of these books, consisted of land units in descending order of size: province, county, barony, parish and townland. Theoretically at least the units fit inside each other, townlands into parishes, parishes into baronies, baronies into counties. This system began piecemeal, with the names of the provinces dating back to prehistoric times, while the institution of counties and baronies dates from the 13th to the 17th century, though the names used are often the names of earlier tribal groups or settlements. Parishes originate not as a secular land-unit, but as part of the territorial organization of the Christian Church. There they form the smallest unit in the system which, in descending order of size, goes from provinces to dioceses to deaneries to parishes. Some Irish parishes derive from churches founded by St Patrick and early saints, and appear as parish units in Anglo-Norman church records: parish units are thus older than counties and baronies. Townlands make their first appearance as small land units listed in Anglo-Norman records. However the evidence suggests that land units of this type (which had various local names) are of pre-Norman native origin.

The 17th-century historian Geoffrey Keating outlined a native land-holding system based on the *tríocha céad* or "thirty hundreds", each divided in Ulster into about 28 *baile biadhtaigh* "lands of a food-provider" or "ballybetaghs", and about 463 *seisrigh* "six-horse plough-teams" or "seisreachs" (*Céitinn* iv 112f.). The term *tríocha céad*, which seems to relate to the size of the army an area could muster, is not prominent in English accounts, though there is a barony called Trough (*Tríocha*) in Co. Monaghan. The ballybetagh (land of a farmer legally obliged to feed his lord and retinue while travelling through the area) is mentioned in Plantation documents for west Ulster, and there is some evidence, from townlands grouped in multiples of three and four, that it existed in Armagh, Antrim and Down (McErlean 1983, 318).

Boundaries of large areas, such as provinces and dioceses, are often denoted in early Irish sources by means of two or four extreme points (Hogan 1910, 279–280; *Céitinn* iii 302). There was also a detailed native tradition of boundary description, listing landmarks such as streams, hills, trees and bogs. This can be demonstrated as early as the 8th century in Tírechán's record of a land grant to St Patrick (*Trip. Life (Stokes)* ii 338–9),[1] and as late as the 17th century, when native experts guided those surveying and mapping Ireland for the English administration. The boundary marks on the ground were carefully maintained, as illustrated in the *Perambulation of Iveagh* in 1618 (*Inq. Ult.* xliii), according to which the guide broke the plough of a man found ploughing up a boundary. However very often Irish texts, for example the "Book of Rights" (*Lebor na Cert*), the "topographical" poems by Seaán Mór Ó Dubhagáin and Giolla-na-naomh Ó hUidhrín (*Topog. Poems*), and "The Rights of O'Neill" (*Ceart Uí Néill*), refer to territories by the names of the peoples inhabiting them. This custom has been preserved to the present in some place-names, particularly those of provinces and baronies.

SECULAR ADMINISTRATIVE DIVISIONS

Townlands

Twelfth-century charters provide the earliest documentary evidence for the existence in Ireland of small land units, although we do not know what these units were called. Keating's smallest unit, the *seisreach*, a division of the ballybetagh, is given as 120 acres (the word *acra* is apparently borrowed from English). The size of the *seisreach* seems to have been approximately that of a modern townland, but the word does not occur much outside Keating's *schema*. Many other terms appear in the sources: *ceathrú* "quarter" (often a quarter of a ballybetagh), *baile bó* "land providing one cow as rent" (usually a twelfth of a ballybetagh), *seiseach* "sixth" and *trian* "third" (apparently divisions of a ballyboe). In most of Ulster the ballyboe and its subdivisions are the precursors of the modern townlands, and were referred to in Latin sources as *villa* or *carucata*, and in English as "town" or "ploughland" (the term used for similar units in 11th-century England in the Domesday Book). The Irish term *baile* (see below) seems to have been treated as equivalent to English "town", which had originally meant "settlement (and lands appertaining)"; and the compound term "townland" appears to have been adopted to make the intended meaning clear. It was used in 19th-century Ireland as a blanket term for various local words. In the area of Fermanagh and Monaghan the term for the local unit was "tate". In an English document of 1591 it is stated that the tate was 60 acres in size and that there were sixteen tates in the ballybetagh (*Fiants Eliz.* §5674). Tate appears in place-names in composition with Gaelic elements, but was regarded by Reeves (1861, 484) as a pre-1600 English borrowing into Irish.

There is no evidence for the use of the word *baile* in the formation of place-names before the middle of the 12th century. The earliest examples are found in a charter dating to c. 1150 in the Book of Kells which relates to lands belonging to the monastery of Kells. At this period *baile* seems to mean "a piece of land" and is not restricted to its present-day meaning "hamlet, group of houses", much less "town, village". After the coming of the Normans, *baile* appears more frequently in place-names, until it finally becomes the most prevalent type of townland name. By the 14th century, *baile* had acquired its present-day meaning of "town", probably in reference to small medieval towns, or settlements that had arisen in the vicinity of castles. Price suggests that the proliferation of the use of the word in place-names was a result of the arrival of settlers and their use of the word "town" (*tūn*) in giving names to their lands (Price 1963, 124). When the Irish revival took place in the 14th century many English-language names were translated into Irish and "town" was generally replaced by *baile*. The proportion of *baile* names is greatest in those parts of Ireland which had been overrun by the Anglo-Normans but subsequently gaelicized, and is lowest in the counties of mid-Ulster in which there was little or no English settlement (*ibid.* 125).

Despite attempts at schematization none of the units which predated the modern townlands was of uniform size, and it is clear from the native sources that evaluation was based on an area of good land together with a variable amount of uncultivated land. Thus townlands on bad land are usually larger than those on good land. The average size of a townland in Ireland as a whole is 325 acres, and 357 acres in the six counties of Northern Ireland, though these averages include huge townlands like Slievedoo (4551 acres, Co. Tyrone) and tiny townlands like Acre McCricket (4 acres, Co. Down). There is also considerable local variation: townlands in Co. Down average 457 acres (based on the ballyboe), compared to 184 acres (based on the tate) in Fermanagh (Reeves 1861, 490).

Parishes

Early accounts of the lives of saints such as Patrick and Columcille refer to many church foundations. It seems that land was often given for early churches beside routeways, or on the boundaries of tribal territories. Some of the same church names appear as the names of medieval parishes in the papal taxation of 1302-06 (*Eccles. Tax.*). Some parish names include ecclesiastical elements such as *ceall*, *domhnach*, *lann*, all meaning "church", *díseart* "hermitage" and *tearmann* "sanctuary", but others are secular in origin. Parish bounds are not given in the papal taxation, but parishes vary considerably in size, probably depending on the wealth or influence of the local church. The medieval ecclesiastical parishes seem to have come into existence after the reform of the native Irish church in the course of the 12th century; in Anglo-Norman areas such as Skreen in Co. Meath the parochial system had already been adopted by the early 13th century (Otway-Ruthven 1964, 111–22). After the Reformation the medieval parish boundaries were continued by the established Church of Ireland, and used by the government as the bounds of civil parishes, a secular land unit forming the major division of a barony. (The boundaries of modern Roman Catholic parishes have often been drawn afresh, to suit the population of worshippers).

As well as the area inhabited by local worshippers, lands belonging to a medieval church often became part of its parish. These were usually close by, but it is quite common, even in the early 19th century when some rationalization had occurred, for parishes to include detached lands at some distance from the main body (Power 1947, 222–3). Kilclief in the barony of Lecale, Co. Down, for example, has five separate detached townlands, while Ballytrustan in the Upper Ards and Trory in Co. Fermanagh are divided into several parts. While an average parish might contain 30 townlands, parishes varied in the number of townlands they contained; for example, Ballykinler in Co. Down contained only 3 townlands, while Aghalurcher contained 237 townlands (including several islands) in Co. Fermanagh plus 17 townlands in Co. Tyrone. Although most of its townlands are fairly small, Aghalurcher is still much larger than Ballykinler. There were usually several parishes within a barony (on average 5 or 6, but, for example, only 2 in the barony of Dufferin, Co. Down, and 18 in the barony of Loughinsholin, Co. Derry). Occasional parishes constituted an entire barony, as did Kilkeel, for example, which is coterminous with the barony of Mourne. However parish units also frequently extended across rivers, which were often used as obvious natural boundaries for counties and baronies: Newry across the Newry River, Clonfeacle over the Blackwater, Artrea over the Ballinderry River, Blaris over the Lagan. This means that civil parishes may be in more than one barony, and sometimes in more than one county.

Baronies

The process of bringing Irish tribal kingdoms into the feudal system as "baronies" under chieftains owing allegiance to the English crown began during the medieval period, although the system was not extended throughout Ulster until the early 17th century. Many of the baronies established in the later administrative system have population names: Oneilland, Irish *Uí Nialláin* "descendants of Niallán" (Arm.); Keenaght, Irish *Cianachta* "descendants of Cian" (Der.); Clankelly, Irish *Clann Cheallaigh* "Ceallach's children" (Fer.). Others have the names of historically important castles or towns: Dungannon (O'Neills, Tyr.), Dunluce (MacDonnells, Antr.), Castlereagh (Clandeboy O'Neills, Down). The barony of Loughinsholin (Der.) is named after an island fortification or crannog, *Loch Inse Uí Fhloinn* "the lake of O'Flynn's island", although by the 17th century the island was inhabited by the O'Hagans, and the O'Flynn area of influence had moved east of the Bann.

The barony system was revised and co-ordinated at the same time as the counties, so that later baronies always fit inside the county bounds. Both counties and baronies appear on maps from 1590 on. These later baronies may contain more than one older district, and other district or population names used in the 16th and 17th centuries, such as *Clancan* and *Clanbrasil* in Armagh, *Slutkellies* in Down, and *Munterbirn* and *Munterevlin* in Tyrone, gradually fell out of use. Baronies were not of uniform size, though in many cases large baronies have been subdivided to make the size more regular. The barony of Dungannon in Co. Tyrone has three sections (Lower, Middle and Upper) while Iveagh in Co. Down has been divided into four (Lower, Lower Half; Lower, Upper Half; Upper, Lower Half; Upper,

Upper Half). The number of baronies in a county in Ulster varies between five in Co. Monaghan and fifteen in Co. Antrim. Armagh, Fermanagh and Tyrone have eight.

Counties

Over the centuries following the Anglo-Norman invasion the English government created a new administrative system in Ireland, adapting the native divisions of provinces, tribal districts (as baronies), parishes and townlands, and dividing each province of Ireland into counties. The counties were equivalent to the shire in England, where a sheriff exercized jurisdiction on behalf of the King. To begin with the county system applied to only those areas where English rule was strong, but was eventually extended, through the reigns of Elizabeth and James I, to cover the whole of the country. Although a commission to shire Ulster was set up in 1585 (*Fiants Eliz.* §4763), the situation in 1604 was expressed, rather hopefully, in a document in the state papers:

> "each province, except Ulster and other uncivil parts of the realm, is subdued into counties, and each county into baronies and hundreds, and every barony into parishes, consisting of manors, towns and villages after the manner of England."
> (*CSP Ire.* 1603–6, 231).

Most of the counties created in the north were given the names of important towns: Antrim, Armagh, Coleraine (later Londonderry), Down, Donegal, Monaghan and Cavan. Fermanagh and Tyrone, however, have population names. *Fir Manach* "the men of the *Manaig*" (probably the *Menapii* of Ptolemy's *Geography*) had been important in the area before the Maguires. *Tír Eoghain* "Eoghan's land" derives its name from the *Cenél nEógain* branch of the *Uí Néill*, who had expanded southwards from *Inis Eógain* (Inishowen) during the centuries and whose dominant position continued right up until the Plantation. Counties were generally formed out of an amalgam of smaller territorial units, some of which were preserved as baronies within each county.[2] The bounds of these older units were often of long standing, and usually followed obvious physical features, like the lower Bann, the Blackwater, and the Newry River.

Down and Antrim, as part of the feudal Earldom of Ulster (see below), had been treated as counties since the 13th or 14th century (Falkiner 1903, 189; *Inq. Earldom Ulster* ii 141, iii 60). However other districts within the earldom could also be called counties, and up to the mid-16th century the whole area was sometimes called the "county of Ulster" (*Cal. Carew MSS* 1515–74, 223–4). The settling of Down and Antrim with their modern bounds began in 1570–1 (*Fiants Eliz.* §1530, §1736). Coleraine had also been the centre of an Anglo-Norman county (*Inq. Earldom Ulster* iv 127). Jobson's map of 1590 shows *Antrym, Armagh, Colrane, Downe, Manahan, Farmanaugh, Terconnel,* and *Upper and Nether Terone* as the names of counties. However, Ulster west of the Bann was still referred to as "four seigniories" (Armagh? plus *Terreconnell, Tyren, Formannoche*) in 1603 (*Cal. Carew MSS* 1601–3, 446–454), although Tyrone had been divided into baronies from 1591 (*Colton Vis.* 125–130). Armagh was settled into baronies in 1605 (*CSP Ire.* 1603–6, 318). The "nine counties of Ulster" were first listed in 1608: *Dunegal or Tirconnel, Tirone, Colraine, Antrim, Downe, Ardmagh, Cavan, Monoghan,* and *Fermanagh* (*CSP Ire.* 1606-8, 401), and these counties are shown on Hole's adaptation of Mercator's map of Ireland for Camden's atlas *Britannia* (1610). The county of Coleraine was renamed as a result of the plantation grant to the London companies. Under the terms of the formal grant of the area in 1613, the barony of Loughinsholin, which had hitherto been part of Tyrone, was amalgamated with the old county of Coleraine, and Londonderry was made the new county name (Moody 1939, 122–3).

Provinces

Gaelic Ireland, in prehistory and in early historic times, was made up of many small native kingdoms (called *tuatha*), but a sense of the underlying unity of the island is evident from the name of the earliest division in Ireland, that represented by the four modern provinces of Connaught, Leinster, Munster and Ulster. In Irish each is called *cúige* (older *cóiced*) "a fifth", followed by a district or population name. *Cúige Chonnacht* means "the fifth of the Connaughtmen" *Cúige Laighean* "the fifth of the Leinstermen", *Cúige Mumhan* "the fifth of Munster", *Cúige Uladh* "the fifth of the Ulstermen". The connection between population and place-names is evident at this very early stage. The ancient fifth "fifth" making up the whole was that of Meath, in Irish *Midhe* "middle". The division into these five provinces was taken over when Henry II of England invaded Ireland: Leinster, (North and South) Munster, Connaught, Ulster and Meath *quasi in medio regni positum* (as if placed in the middle of the kingdom), but the number was reduced by the 17th century to the modern four (*CSP Ire.* 1603–6 §402, 231), by incorporating Meath in Leinster.

The Province of Ulster

As mentioned above, the province of Ulster took its name from the tribal name *Ulaid* "Ulstermen" (Flanagan 1978(d)). The earliest record of the tribal name is the form quoted by the 2nd-century Greek geographer Ptolemy, as *Uoluntii* (O'Rahilly 1946, 7). The precise origin of the English form of the name is obscure, though it has been suggested that it derives from something like *Ulaðstir*, an unusual combination of the original Irish name plus the Norse possessive suffix *-s* and the Irish word *tír* "land" (Sommerfelt 1958, 223–227). Ptolemy mentions various other tribes in the north of Ireland, but it appears that the *Ulaid* were the dominant group.

The ancient province of the Ulstermen, according to the native boundary description, stretched south to a line running between the courses of the rivers *Drobáis* (Drowse, on the border between Donegal and Leitrim) and *Bóann* (Boyne, Co. Meath). The "fifth" of the legendary king of the Ulaid, Conchobar, (*Cóiced Conchobair*) thus included modern Co. Louth (Hogan 1910, 279b). It became contracted in historical times, as a result of the expansion of the *Uí Néill* "descendants of Niall", who drove the rulers of the Ulaid from the provincial capital at *Emain Macha* (Navan fort near Armagh) across the Bann into modern Antrim and Down.[3] From the 5th century the area stretching south from Derry and Tyrone to Monaghan and most of Louth belonged to a confederation of tribes called the *Airgialla*, who have been described "as a satellite state of the Uí Néill" (Byrne 1973, 73). Three groups of Uí Néill established themselves in the west, *Cenél Conaill* "Conall's kin" in south Donegal, *Cenél nÉndae* in the area around Raphoe, and *Cenél nEógain* in Inishowen (*Inis Eógain* "Eógan's island"). On the north coast, east of the river Foyle, the *Cianachta* maintained a separate identity, despite continuing pressure from *Cenél nEógain*.

East of the Bann the *Dál Fiatach* (the historic Ulaid) shared the kingship of the reduced Ulster with *Dál nAraide* and *Uí Echach Coba*, both originally *Cruthin* tribes.[4] In the 12th century the Anglo-Norman conquest of Antrim and Down resulted in the creation of a feudal lordship of the area under the English crown called the Earldom of Ulster. During the same period the kings of Cenél nEógain had extended their influence eastward, and after the extinction of the Dál Fiatach kingship in the 13th century they assumed the title of *rí Ulad* "king of the Ulaid" to forward their claim to be kings of the whole of the North. It is this greater Ulster which was the basis for the modern province, although there was some doubt at the beginning of the 17th century as to whether or not this included Co. Louth. By the time of the Plantation in 1609 Ulster had been stabilized as nine counties and Louth had been incorporated into the neighbouring province of Leinster.

ECCLESIASTICAL ADMINISTRATIVE DIVISIONS

Dioceses

Under the Roman Empire Christianity developed an administrative structure of dioceses led by bishops based in the local towns. In early Christian Ireland a bishop was provided for each *tuath*, but since the main centres of population were the monasteries established by the church, the bishop often became part of the monastic community, with less power than the abbot. The invasion of the Anglo-Normans in the 12th century encouraged the re-organization and reform of the native church along continental lines, and by the beginning of the 14th century the territories and boundaries for Irish bishops and dioceses had been settled. Most dioceses are named after important church or monastic foundations: Armagh, Clogher, Connor, Derry, Down, Dromore, Kilmore and Raphoe in the North. The ancient secular province of Ulster was included in the ecclesiastical province of Armagh, which became the chief church in Ireland. The bounds of individual dioceses within the province reflect older tribal areas, for example Derry reflects the development of *Cenél nEógain*, Dromore *Uí Echach Coba*. In the 8th century *Dál Fiatach*, who had settled in east Down, pushed northward into the land of *Dál nAraide*, and the bounds of the diocese of Down reflect their expansion as far north as the river *Ollarba* (the Larne Water). The diocesan bounds differ from those of similarly-named later counties because by the time the county boundaries were settled in the 17th century the leaders of many of the larger native territories had been overthrown. County boundaries were generally not based on large native kingdoms but were put together from an amalgam of smaller districts.

Deaneries

The medieval church divided dioceses into rural deaneries, the names of which often derive from old population names. *Blaethwyc* (modern Newtownards) in the diocese of Down, for example, derives from *Uí Blathmaic* "the descendants of Blathmac", whereas *Turtrye*, in the diocese of Connor, derives from *Uí Thuirtre* "the descendants of (Fiachra) Tort". The deaneries of Tullyhogue (Irish *Tulach Óc*) in the diocese of Armagh and *Maulyne* (Irish *Mag Line*) in Connor are named after royal sites. *Mag Line* was the seat of the *Dál nAraide* and *Tulach Óc* was probably the original seat of the Uí Thuirtre, whose area of influence had by this time moved east across the Bann, as the deanery name reveals. The deanery of Inishowen reflects the earlier homeland of the Cenél nEógain. Deanery names are often a useful source of information on important tribal groups of medieval times. Some of these same population names were used later as the names of baronies, while in other cases the earlier population group had lost its influence and the area had become known by another name.

TRIBAL AND FAMILY NAMES

Many personal or population names of various forms have been used as place-names or parts of place-names in Ireland, from provinces, counties, deaneries and baronies to townlands. As with different types of land divisions, different types of family names have come into being at various times.

The names of early Irish tribal groupings were sometimes simple plurals, for example *Ulaid, Cruthin*, and sometimes the personal name of an ancestor or some other element in composition with various suffixes: *Connachta, Dartraige, Latharna*. Other types prefixed *uí* "grandsons", *cenél* "kin", *clann* "children", *dál* "share", *moccu* "descendants", *síol* "seed", *sliocht* "line" to the name of the ancestor, for example *Dál nAraide* "share of (Fiacha)

Araide", and *Uí Néill* "grandsons of Niall", who are supposedly descended from the 5th-century *Niall Noígiallach* "Niall of the Nine Hostages".

In early Ireland individuals were often identified by patronymics formed by using *mac* "son" or *ó* (also written *ua*) "grandson" plus the name of the father or grandfather, rather than by giving the name of the larger group to which the individual belonged. Thus the most straightforward interpretation of *Eoghan mac Néill* is "Eoghan son of Niall", *Eoghan ó Néill* "Eoghan grandson of Niall". Sometimes the same formation can occur with female names. However, in the course of the 10th and 11th centuries patronymics began to be used as surnames. In Modern Irish orthography surnames are distinguished from simple patronymics by using capital *M* or *Ó*: *Eoghan Ó Néill* "Eoghan O'Neill", *Eoghan Mac Néill* "Eoghan MacNeill". However, in early documents, in either Irish or English, it is often difficult to distinguish between surnames and patronymics. This is particularly true of sources such as the *Fiants* where a name such as Donagh M'Donagh may represent the patronymic Donagh, son of Donagh, or the surname Donagh MacDonagh.

As families expanded it was common for different branches to develop their own particular surnames. Some of these have survived to the present, while others, which may have been important enough in their time to be incorporated in place-names, have either died out or been assimilated by similar, more vigorous surnames. In cases such as this the place-name itself may be the only evidence for the former existence of a particular surname in the locality.

Kay Muhr

(1) See also *Geinealach Chorca Laidhe* (O'Donovan 1849, 48–56); *Críchad an Caoilli* (Power 1932, 43–47).
(2) See *Fiants Eliz.* §1736 (1570) for Co. Down; *Colton Vis.* 125–30 (1591) for Cos Derry and Tyrone.
(3) North-east Derry and Louth were also held by the Ulaid, but their influence had been reduced to Down, Antrim and north Louth by the 7th century (Flanagan 1978d, 41).
(4) The *Cruthin* were a population group widespread in the north of Ireland. The name is of the same origin as "Briton".

ABBREVIATIONS

acc.	Accusative	Mid. Ir.	Middle Irish
adj.	Adjective	Mod. Eng.	Modern English
al.	Alias	Mod. Ir.	Modern Irish
angl.	Anglicized	MS.	Manuscript
Ant.	Co. Antrim	MSS	Manuscripts
Arm.	Co. Armagh	n.	(Foot)note
art. cit.	In the article cited	neut.	Neuter
BM	British Museum	NLI	National Library of
c.	About		Ireland, Dublin
cf.	Compare	no.	Number
Co(s).	County (-ies)	nom.	Nominative
col.	Column	O.Ir.	Old Irish
coll.	Collective	op. cit.	In the work cited
d.	Died	OSI	Ordnance Survey, Dublin
dat.	Dative	OSNI	Ordnance Survey, Belfast
Der.	Co. Derry	p(p).	Page(s)
Dn	Co. Down	par.	Parish
eag.	Eagarthóir/Curtha in	pass.	Here and there
	eagar ag (= ed.)	pl.	Plural
ed.	Edited by	PRO	Public Record Office,
edn	Edition		London
Eng.	English	PROI	Public Record Office,
et pass.	And elsewhere		Dublin
et var.	And variations (thereon)	PRONI	Public Record Office,
f.	Following page		Belfast
fem.	Feminine	pt.	Part
Fer.	Co. Fermanagh	RIA	Royal Irish Academy,
ff.	Folios/Following pages		Dublin
fol.	Folio	s.	Shilling
gen.	Genitive	sa.	Under the year
HMSO	Her Majesty's Stationery	sect.	Section
	Office	ser.	Series
ibid.	In the same place	sing.	Singular
IE	Indo-European	SS	Saints
iml.	Imleabhar (= vol.)	St	Saint
IPA	International Phonetic	sv(v).	Under the word(s)
	Alphabet	TCD	Trinity College, Dublin
l(l).	Line(s)	trans.	Translated by
lit.	Literally	Tyr.	Co. Tyrone
loc.	Locative	uimh.	Uimhir (= no.)
loc. cit.	In the place cited	Up.	Upper
Lr.	Lower	viz.	Namely
masc.	Masculine	voc.	Vocative
Mid. Eng.	Middle English	vol(s).	Volume(s)

PRIMARY BIBLIOGRAPHY

A. Conn. *Annála Connacht: the annals of Connacht (AD 1224–1544)*, ed. A. Martin Freeman (Dublin 1944).

Acta SS Colgan *Acta sanctorum veteris et majoris Scotiae seu Hiberniae*, John Colgan (Lovanii 1645).

Ad. Dána *Aithdioghluim dána*, ed. Lambert McKenna, 2 vols (Dublin 1939–40).

AFM *Annála Ríoghachta Éireann: annals of the kingdom of Ireland by the Four Masters from the earliest period to the year 1616*, ed. John O'Donovan, 7 vols (Dublin 1848–51; reprint 1990).

AGBP *Ainmneacha Gaeilge na mbailte poist*, Oifig an tSoláthair (Baile Átha Cliath 1969).

Aid. Uais. Érenn "Aideda forni do uaislib hÉrenn (On the deaths of some Irish heroes)", by Cináed húa hArtacáin, ed. Whitley Stokes, *Rev. Celt.* xxiii (1902), 303–348, 438; xxvii (1906), 202.

Ainm *Ainm: bulletin of the Ulster Place-name Society* (Belfast 1986–).

ALC *The annals of Loch Cé: a chronicle of Irish affairs from AD 1014 to AD 1590*, ed. William Hennessy, 2 vols (London 1871; reprint Dublin 1939).

Anal. Hib. *Analecta Hibernica* (Dublin 1930–69; Shannon 1970–).

Annates Ulst. *De annatis Hiberniae: a calendar of the first-fruits' fees levied on papal appointments to benefices in Ireland, AD 1400–1535*, vol. i (Ulster), ed. Michael A. Costello and Ambrose Coleman (Dundalk 1909; reprint Maynooth 1912).

Archiv. Hib. *Archivium Hibernicum; or, Irish historical records*, ser. 1, vols i–vii (Maynooth 1912–21); ser. 2, vol. viii– (1941–).

ASCD *An archaeological survey of County Down*, Archaeological Survey of Northern Ireland (Belfast 1966).

ASE "Abstracts of grants of lands and other hereditaments under the acts of settlement and explanation, AD 1666–84", compiled by John Lodge and published in the appendix to the *15th Annual report from the commissioners... respecting the public records of Ireland* (1825) 45–340.

A. Tigern. "The annals of Tigernach", ed. Whitley Stokes, *Rev. Celt.* xvi (1895), 374–419; xvii (1896), 6–33, 116–263, 337–420; xviii (1897), 9–59, 150–303, 374–91.

Atkinson's Donaghcloney *Donaghcloney, an Ulster parish*, Edward Dupre Atkinson (Dublin 1898).

Atkinson's Dromore | *Dromore: an Ulster diocese*, Edward Duprè Atkinson (Dundalk 1925).

Atkinson's Tour (OSNB) | Atkinson's Tour, cited in *OSNB, passim.*

AU | *Annála Uladh: annals of Ulster; otherwise Annála Senait, annals of Senait: a chronicle of Irish affairs, 431–1131, 1155–1541*, ed. William Hennessy and Bartholomew MacCarthy, 4 vols (Dublin 1887–1901).

AU (Mac Airt) | *The annals of Ulster* (vol. i to 1131 AD), ed. Seán Mac Airt and Gearóid Mac Niocaill (Dublin 1983).

Bagenal's Descr. Ulst. | "Marshal Bagenal's description of Ulster, anno 1586", ed. Herbert F. Hore, *UJA* ser. 1, vol. ii (1854), 137–60.

Bagenal Rental | *Rental of the Bagenal estate, AD 1575*, Bodleian Library, Oxford MS 103, ff. 116–134. This document has been published (O'Sullivan 1985) but some of the place-names have been mistranscribed.

B. Aodha Ruaidh | *Beatha Aodha Ruaidh: the life of Aodh Ruadh Ó Domhnaill, transcribed from the Book of Lughaidh Ó Cléirigh*, ed. Paul Walsh, 2 vols, Irish Texts Society xlii & xlv (Dublin 1948–57).

Bartlett Map (BM) | A map of south-east Ulster, AD 1600, by Richard Bartlett, British Museum, Cotton MS, Augustus i, vol. ii, no. 37.

Bartlett Map (TCD) | *The descriptione of a parte of Ulster containing the p[ar]ticuler places of the Righte Ho. the Lo. Montjoie now Lo. Deputie of Irelande his jorneies & services in the North part of that kingdome, from his entrie therinto until this present August 1601*, by Richard Barthelett (Bartlett), TCD MS 2379 (formerly 21 U 19). Reproduced in reduced form as frontspiece in *Dúiche Néill* vol. 1, no. 2 (1987).

Bartlett Maps (Esch. Co. Maps) | Three maps by Richard Bartlett published together with the *Esch. Co. Maps*: (i) *A Generalle Description of Ulster*; (ii) South-east Ulster; (iii) North-west Ulster (PRO MPF 35–37; copies in PRONI T1652/1–3). These maps have been dated to 1603 by G.A. Hayes-McCoy, *Ulster and Other Irish Maps, c. 1600*, p. 2, n. 13 (Dublin 1964).

Bartlett Maps (Hayes McCoy) | A set of twelve picture plans and maps of various forts, passes and other places of importance in Ulster by Richard Bartlett, c. 1600–1603. Reproduced in *Ulster and Other Irish Maps, c. 1600*, G.A. Hayes-McCoy, nos. i-xii (Dublin 1964).

Béaloid. | *Béaloideas: the journal of the Folklore of Ireland Society* (Dublin 1927–).

Beaufort's Mem. Map | *Memoir of a map of Ireland illustrating the topography of that kingdom, and containing a short account of its present state, civil and ecclesiastical; with a complete index to the map*, Daniel Augustus Beaufort (London 1792).

181

Bnd. Sur. (OSNB)	Boundary Survey sketch maps, c. 1830, cited in *OSNB*, *passim*.
Boazio's Map (BM)	*Gennerall discription or Chart of Irelande*, AD 1599, by Baptista Boazio. Three impressions are known, one in the British Museum, one in TCD, and a third in private hands.
Bodley's Lecale	"Bodley's visit to Lecale, County of Down, AD 1602–3", *UJA* ser. 1, vol. 2 (1854), 73–99.
BSD	*Book of survey & distribution, AD 1661: Armagh, Down & Antrim* (Quit Rent Office copy), PRONI T370/A.
Buckworth (Atkinson)	"Bishop Buckworth's report of the diocese [of Dromore], AD 1622", *Atkinson's Dromore* 127–32.
Buckworth (EA)	"Bishop Buckworth's return", *EA* 310–11.
BUPNS	*Bulletin of the Ulster Place-name Society*, ser. 1, vols i–v (Belfast 1952–7); ser. 2, vols 1–4 (1978–82).
C. Conghail Cláir.	*Caithréim Conghail Cláiringhnigh: Martial career of Conghal Cláiringhneach*, ed. Patrick M. MacSweeney, Irish Texts Society v (London 1904).
Cal. Canc. Hib. (EA)	*Calendarium Rot. Cancellar. Hib.*, cited in *EA, passim*. Probably the same as *CPR (Tresham)*.
Cal. Carew MSS	*Calendar of the Carew manuscripts preserved in the Archiepiscopal Library at Lambeth*, ed. J.S. Brewer and W. Bullen, 6 vols (London 1867–73).
Cal. Papal Letters	*Calendar of entries in the papal registers relating to Great Britain and Ireland: papal letters AD 1198–1498*, ed. W.H. Bliss, C. Johnson, J.A. Twelmow, Michael J. Haren, Anne P. Fuller, 16 vols (London 1893–1960, Dublin 1978, 1986). In progress.
Carlisle (OSNB)	Carlisle's Topographical Dictionary, cited in *OSNB, passim*.
Cartae Dun.	"Cartae Dunenses XII–XIII céad", eag. Gearóid Mac Niocaill, *S. Ard Mh.* vol. 5, no. 2 (1970), 418–28.
Cathal Buí	*Cathal Buí: amhráin*, eag. Breandán Ó Buachalla (An Charraig Dhubh 1975).
CCU	*Céad de cheolta Uladh*, Énrí Ó Muireasa a chruinnigh agus a chuir in eagar (Baile Átha Cliath 1915). An Br. T.F. Beausang a d'atheagraigh (Iúr Cinn Trá 1983).
CDI	*Calendar of documents relating to Ireland, 1171–1307*, ed. H.S. Sweetman and G.F. Handcock, 5 vols (London 1875-86).
Ceart Uí Néill	*Ceart Uí Néill*, ed. Myles Dillon, *Stud. Celt.* 1 (1966), 1–18. Trans. Éamonn Ó Doibhlin, "*Ceart Uí Néill*, a discussion and translation of the document", *S. Ard Mh.* vol. 5, no. 2 (1970), 324–58.

Céitinn	*Foras Feasa ar Éirinn: the history of Ireland by Seathrún Céitinn (Geoffrey Keating)*, ed. Rev. Patrick S. Dinneen, 4 vols, Irish Texts Society (London 1902–14).
Celtica	*Celtica*, Dublin Institute for Advanced Studies (Dublin 1946–).
Census	*A census of Ireland, circa 1659, with supplementary material from the poll money ordinances (1660-1)*, ed. Séamus Pender (Dublin 1939).
Census 1851	*Census of Ireland, 1851. General alphabetical index to the townlands and towns, parishes and baronies of Ireland...* (Dublin 1861).
Census 1871	*Census of Ireland, 1871. Alphabetical index to the townlands and towns of Ireland...* (Dublin 1877).
CGH	*Corpus genealogiarum Hiberniae*, vol. 1, ed. M.A. O'Brien (Dublin 1962).
Cín Lae Ó M.	*Cín lae Ó Mealláin*, ed. Tadhg Ó Donnchadha (alias Torna), *Anal. Hib.* 3 (1931), 1–61.
Civ. & Ecc. Top. (OSNB)	*Topographia Hibernica*, William Wenman Seward (Dublin 1795). Cited in *OSNB, passim*.
Civ. Surv.	*The civil survey, AD 1654–6*, ed. Robert C. Simington, 10 vols, Irish Manuscripts Commission (Dublin 1931–61).
Clergyman (OSNB)	Local clergyman, cited in *OSNB, passim*.
CMR	*The Banquet of Dun na nGedh and the Battle of Magh Rath, an ancient historical tale...*, ed. John O'Donovan, Irish Archaeological Society (Dublin 1842).
Cogadh GG	*Cogadh Gaedhal re Gallaibh: the war of the Gaedhil with the Gaill*, ed. J.H. Todd (London 1867).
Collect. Hib.	*Collectanea Hibernica: sources for Irish history* (Shannon 1958–).
Collins' C'ford Lough	Chart of Carlingford Lough by Captain Grenville Collins for Mr. Reeve Williams, AD 1693. Copy in the Ewart Collection, Queen's University, Belfast.
Colton Vis.	*Acts of Archbishop Colton in his metropolitical visitation of the diocese of Derry, AD 1397*, ed. William Reeves (Dublin 1850).
County Warrant (OSNB)	County warrant, cited in *OSNB, passim*.
Cowan's Donaghmore	*An ancient Irish parish past and present being the parish of Donaghmore, County Down*, J.D. Cowan (London 1914).
CPR Ed. VI	*Calendar of the patent rolls preserved in the Public Record Office: Edward VI, 1547–53*, 6 vols (London 1924–29).

CPR Hen. IV (EA)	*Calendar of patent rolls, Henry IV,* cited in *EA, passim.*
CPR Hen. VII	*Calendar of patent rolls of chancery, Henry VII, 1485–1509,* 2 vols (London 1914–16).
CPR Jas. I	*Irish patent rolls of James I: facsimile of the Irish record commissioners' calendar prepared prior to 1830,* with a foreword by M.C. Griffith (Dublin 1966).
CPR (Tresham)	*Rotulorum patentium et clausorum cancellariae Hiberniae calendarium,* 2 vols, ed. Edward Tresham (Dublin 1828–[1830]).
CSH	*Corpus genealogiarum sanctorum Hiberniae,* ed. Pádraig Ó Riain (Dublin 1985).
CSP Ire.	*Calendar of the state papers relating to Ireland, 1509–1670,* ed. H.C. Hamilton, E.G. Atkinson, R.P. Mahaffy, C.P. Russell and J.P. Prendergast, 24 vols (London 1860–1912).
Custom of County (OSNB)	Spelling or pronunciation current in the county c. 1834, cited in *OSNB, passim.*
de Bhaldraithe	*English–Irish dictionary,* ed. Tomás de Bhaldraithe (Baile Átha Cliath 1959).
Deed (Cowan's Donaghmore)	A deed of partition, dated September 11, 1769, *Cowan's Donaghmore* 61–2.
Deeds & Wills (Mooney)	A variety of unspecified deeds and wills, largely 18th century, cited in *Mooney, passim.*
de Lacy Char.	"Charter of Hugh de Lacy to the Cistercian abbey of Newry, confirming the grants of Muirchertach Mac Lochlainn and other Irish kings made prior to the coming of the Normans", ed. M.T. Flanagan, *Monastic charters from Irish kings of the 12th and 13th centuries,* M.A. thesis vol. ii, 247–9 (University College Dublin 1973).
Diary War Jas. II	"An Irish diary of the war against James II: 12 August–23 October 1689", ed. Anselm Faulkner, *Collect. Hib.* 20 (1978), 21–9.
DIL	*Dictionary of the Irish language: compact edition* (Dublin 1983).
Dinneen	*Foclóir Gaedhilge agus Béarla: an Irish–English dictionary,* Rev. Patrick S. Dinneen (Dublin 1904; reprint with additions 1927 and 1934).
Dinnsean.	*Dinnseanchas,* 6 vols (Baile Átha Cliath 1964–75).
Dongl. Ann.	*Donegal Annual: journal of the County Donegal Historical Society* (1947–).
Downshire Direct.	"Directory to the seats of Downshire, with their respective post towns alphabetically arranged", A. Atkinson, *Ireland exhibited to England, in a political and moral survey of her population* i, 315–30 (London 1823).

DS (Mooney)   Down Survey, cited in *Mooney passim.*

Dubourdieu's Map (OSNB)   Dubourdieu's map, cited in *OSNB passim.* See *Statist. Sur. Dn.*

Dúiche Néill   *Dúiche Néill: journal of the O'Neill Country Historical Society* (Benburb 1986–).

Dwelly   *The illustrated Gaelic–English dictionary*, Edward Dwelly (Glasgow 1901–11; reprint 1920 etc.).

EA   *Ecclesiastical antiquities of Down, Connor and Dromore, consisting of a taxation of those dioceses compiled in the year 1306*, ed. William Reeves (Dublin 1847).

Eccles. Tax.   "Ecclesiastical taxation of the dioceses of Down, Connor, and Dromore", ed. William Reeves, *EA* 2–119.

Educ. Rept. (OSNB)   Education report, cited in *OSNB, passim.*

Éire Thuaidh   *Éire Thuaidh/Ireland North: a cultural map and gazetteer of Irish place-names*, Ordnance Survey of Northern Ireland (Belfast 1988).

Enc. Brit.   *The new Encyclopaedia Britannica*, 15th edn (Chicago...).

Esch. Co. Map   *Barony maps of the escheated counties in Ireland, AD 1609*, 28 maps, PRO. Published as *The Irish Historical Atlas*, Sir Henry James, Ordnance Survey (Southampton 1861).

Exch. Accounts Ulst.   "Ancient exchequer accounts of Ulster", *UJA* ser. 1, vol. iii (1855), 155–62.

Ex. Inq. 3 Ed. VI   *Inquisition of the court of exchequer in Ireland taken at Greencastle, August 10, 3rd year of the reign of Edward VI, AD 1549.* All the original exchequer inquisitions have been lost, but there is a manuscript calendar in PROI and transcripts of some of the Ulster inquisitions in PRONI.

Ex. Inq. 34 Eliz. I   *Inquisition of the court of exchequer in Ireland taken at Newry, March 14, 34th year of the reign of Elizabeth I, AD 1591* (recte 1592). See *Ex. Inq. 3 Ed. VI.*

Ex. Inq. 2 Jac. I   *Inquisition of the court of exchequer in Ireland taken at Downpatrick, August 10, 2nd year of the reign of James I, AD 1604.* See *Ex. Inq. 3 Ed. VI.*

Ex. Inq. 8 Car. I (DF)   *Inquisition of the court of exchequer in Ireland taken at Downpatrick, March 25, 8th year of the reign of Charles I, AD 1633.* This particular copy was transcribed by Deirdre Flanagan from the calendar in PROI.

Féil. Torna   *Féilscríbhinn Torna .i. tráchtaisí léanta in onóir don Ollamh Tadhg Ua Donnchadha...*, eag. Séamus Pender (Corcaigh 1947).

Fél. Óeng.   *Félire Óengusso Céli Dé: the martyrology of Oengus the culdee*, ed. Whitley Stokes (London 1905; reprint 1984).

Fiacc's Hymn	"Fiacc's Hymn", ed. Whitley Stokes and John Strachan, *Thesaurus Palaeohibernicus: a collection of Old-Irish glosses, scholia, prose and verse*, ii, 307–21 (Cambridge 1903; reprint Dublin 1975).
Fiants Eliz.	"Calendar and index to the fiants of the reign of Elizabeth I", appendix to the *11–13th, 15–18th and 21–22nd Reports of the Deputy Keeper of public records in Ireland* (Dublin 1879–81, 1883–86, 1889–90).
Fiants Hen. VIII	"Calendar to the fiants of Henry VIII", appendix to the *7th Report of the Deputy Keeper of the public records of Ireland* (1875).
Forfeit. Estates	"Abstracts of the conveyances from the trustees of the forfeited estates and interests in Ireland in 1688", appendix to the *15th Annual report from the commissioners... respecting the public records of Ireland* (1825), 348–99.
GÉ	*Gasaitéar na hÉireann/Gazetteer of Ireland: ainmneacha ionad daonra agus gnéithe aiceanta*, Brainse Logainmneacha na Suirbhéireachta Ordanáis (Baile Átha Cliath 1989).
Gir. Cambrensis	*Giraldi Cambrensis opera*, vol. v: *Topographia Hibernica et expugnatio Hibernica*, ed. James F. Dimock (London 1867).
GJ	*Gaelic Journal: Irisleabhar na Gaedhilge*, 19 vols (Dublin 1882–1909).
Goghe's Map	*Hibernia: Insula non procul ab Anglia vulgare Hirlandia vocata, AD 1567*, by John Goghe, PRO MPF 68. Reproduced in *SP Hen. VIII* vol. ii, pt. 3.
GOI	*A grammar of Old Irish*, Rudolf Thurneysen, trans. D.A. Binchy and Osborn Bergin (Dublin 1946).
Great Rolls Pipe	"Accounts on the great rolls of the pipe of the Irish exchequer, 13 Henry III to 22 Edward III", ed. M.J. McEnery, *35th–54th Reports of the Deputy Keeper of public records in Ireland* (Dublin 1903–27).
Gwynn Cat.	*Catalogue of the Irish manuscripts in the Library of Trinity College, Dublin*, T.K. Abbott and E.J. Gwynn (Dublin & London 1921).
Harris Hist.	*The antient and present state of the county of Down*, Walter Harris (Dublin 1744).
Headfort Map (Mooney)	*Headfort map*, cited in *Mooney, passim*. Possibly belongs to the collection referred to by Goblet 1932, vii.
Hermathena	*Hermathena: a Dublin University review* (Dublin 1873–).

Hib. Del.	*Hiberniae Delineatio*: an atlas of Ireland by Sir William Petty comprised of one map of Ireland, 4 maps of provinces and 32 county maps. It was engraved c. 1671–72 and first published in London c. 1685 (Goblet 1932, viii). A facsimile reprint was published in Newcastle-Upon-Tyne in 1968 and a further reprint, with critical introduction by J.H. Andrews, in Shannon, 1970.
Hib. Reg.	*Hibernia Regnum:* a set of 214 barony maps of Ireland dating to the period AD 1655–59. These maps were drawn at the same time as the official parish maps which illustrated the Down Survey of Sir William Petty. The original parish maps have been lost but the *Hibernia Regnum* maps are preserved in the Bibliothèque Nationale, Paris (Goblet 1932, v–x). Photographic facsimiles of these maps were published by the Ordnance Survey, Southampton in 1908.
HMR Murray (1940)	"Hearth money rolls – barony of Fewes, AD 1664", *Murray's Creggan* 36-40.
HMR Murray (1941)	*The Co. Armagh hearth money rolls, AD 1664*, ed. L.P. Murray, *Archiv. Hib.* viii (1941), 121-202.
Hondius Map	*Hyberniae Novissima Descriptio, AD 1591*, drawn by Jodocus Hondius and engraved by Pieter van den Keere, Linen Hall Library, Belfast.
Hondius Map (Mooney)	A map by Jodocus Hondius, c. 1630, now in the National Library, Dublin. Cited by *Mooney, passim*.
IB	*The Voyage of Bran son of Febal to the Land of the Living...*, ed. Kuno Meyer, 2 vols (London 1895–7).
Inq. Arm. 1657	"Cromwellian inquisition as to parishes in County Armagh in 1657", ed. T.G.F. Patterson, *UJA* ser. 3, vol. ii (1939), 212–49.
Inq. Down (Reeves 1)	*An inquisition of Down, AD 1657*, transcribed by William Reeves, PRONI DIO/1/24/8/2.
Inq. Down (Reeves 2)	*An inquisition of Down, AD 1657*, transcribed by William Reeves, PRONI DIO/1/24/24/2.
Inq. Earldom Ulster	"The earldom of Ulster", Goddard H. Orpen, *JRSAI* xliii (1913), 30-46, 133–43; xliv (1914), 51–66; xlv (1915), 123–42.
Inq. (Mon. Hib.)	"An inquisition taken on August 10, 3rd year of the reign of Edward VI, AD 1549", ed. M. Archdall, *Mon. Hib.*, 286–8.
Inq. Ult.	*Inquisitionum in officio rotulorum cancellariae Hiberniae asservatarum repertorium*, vol. ii (Ulster), ed. James Hardiman (Dublin 1829).

Ireland E. Coast	A map of the east coast of Ireland from Dublin to Carrickfergus, c. 1580, PRO MPF 86. There is also a copy in PRONI T1493/43.
Irish Litanies	*Irish litanies*, ed. Charles Plummer, Henry Bradshaw Society lxii (London 1925).
Ir. Wills Index	*Indexes to Irish wills*, ed. W.P. Phillimore and Gertrude Thrift, 5 vols (London 1909–20; reprint Baltimore, 1970).
Jas. I to Dromore Cath.	"Grant of James I to the cathedral of Dromore, AD 1609", ed. William Reeves, *EA* 262–4.
JDCHS	*Journal of the Down and Connor Historical Society*, 10 vols (Belfast 1928-39).
J Louth AS	*Journal of the County Louth Archaeological Society* (Dundalk 1904–).
Jobson's Ulster (TCD)	A set of three maps of Ulster by Francis Jobson, the first of which dates to AD 1590, TCD MS 1209, 15–17.
J O'D (OSNB)	Irish and anglicized forms of names attributed to John O'Donovan in the *OSNB*.
Joyce	*The origin and history of Irish names of places*, P.W. Joyce, 3 vols (Dublin 1869–1913).
JRSAI	*Journal of the Royal Society of Antiquaries of Ireland* (Dublin 1849–). Also called *Transactions of the Kilkenny Archaeological Society* (vols i–ii, 1849–53); *Proceedings and Transactions of the Kilkenny and South-east Ireland Archaeological Society* (vol. iii, 1854–55); *Journal of the Kilkenny and South-east Ireland Archaeological Society* (2nd ser. vols i–vi [consecutive ser. vols iv–ix] 1856–67); *Journal of the Historical and Archaeological Association of Ireland* 3rd ser. vol. i [consecutive ser. vol. x], 1868–89); *Journal of the Royal Historical and Archaeological Association of Ireland* (4th ser. vols i–ix [consecutive ser. vols xi–xix] 1870–89); *Journal of Proceedings of the Royal Society of Antiquaries of Ireland* (5th ser. vol. i [consecutive ser. vol. xxi] 1890–91); 5th ser. vols ii–xx [consecutive ser. vols xxii–xl] (1892–1910); 6th ser. vols i–xx [consecutive ser. vols xli–lx] (1911–30); 7th ser. vols i–xiv [consecutive ser. vols lxi–lxxiv] (1931–44); thereafter numbered only as consecutive series vol. lxxv– (1945–).
Knox Hist.	*A history of the county of Down from the most remote period to the present day*, Alexander Knox (Dublin 1875; reprint Ballynahinch 1982).
Lamb Maps	*A Geographical Description of ye Kingdom of Ireland Collected from ye actual Survey made by Sir William Petty...Containing one General Mapp of ye whole Kingdom, with four Provincial Mapps, & 32 County Mapps...Engraven & Published for ye benefit of ye Publique* by Francis Lamb (London [c. 1690]).

L. an tS.	*Ar lorg an tseanchaidhe*, Peadar Ó Dubhda (Dundalk 1905).
LASID	*Linguistic atlas and survey of Irish dialects*, Heinrich Wagner and Colm Ó Baoill, 4 vols (Dublin 1958–69).
LCABuidhe	*Leabhar Cloinne Aodha Buidhe*, ed. Tadhg Ó Donnchadha alias Torna (Dublin 1931).
Leabharlann	*An Leabharlann*: journal of *Cumann na Leabharlann* (later, the Library Association of Ireland), vols 1–29 (Dublin 1906–71); new ser., vols 1–11 (1972–82); 2nd new ser., vol. 1– (1984–).
Lebor na Cert	*Lebor na Cert: the Book of Rights*, ed. Myles Dillon, Irish Texts Society xlvi (Dublin 1962).
Lewis' Top. Dict.	*A topographical dictionary of Ireland, comprising the several counties, cities, boroughs, corporate, market and post towns, parishes and villages with statistical descriptions*, ed. Samuel Lewis, 2 vols and atlas (London 1837; 2nd edn 1842).
LGD Map	*Local government district series showing townlands and wards within the various districts and showing the layout of the OS 1:10,000 sheets*, Ordnance Survey of Northern Ireland (Belfast 1974).
L. Log. Lú	*Liostaí logainmneacha: Contae Lú/County Louth*, arna ullmhú ag Brainse Logainmneacha na Suirbhéireachta Ordanáis (Baile Átha Cliath 1991).
L. Log. Luimní	*Liostaí logainmneacha: Contae Luimní/County Limerick*, arna ullmhú ag Brainse Logainmneacha na Suirbhéireachta Ordanáis (Baile Átha Cliath 1991).
L. Log. P. Láirge	*Liostaí logainmneacha: Contae Phort Láirge/County Waterford*, arna ullmhú ag Brainse Logainmneacha na Suirbhéireachta Ordanáis (Baile Átha Cliath 1991).
Local Inf.	Local informant.
Lochlann	*Lochlann: a review of Celtic studies* (Oslo 1958–).
Longman Dict.	*Longman Dictionary of the English language* (Harlow 1984, 2nd edn 1991).
Lythe Map	A map of Cooley, Omeath, Newry, Mourne and Lecale c. 1568 AD, by Robert Lythe, PRO MPF 89.
Mac Bionaid	*Mac Bionaid: dánta*, ed. Tomás Ó Fiaich and Liam Ó Caithnia (Baile Átha Cliath 1979).
MacCana's Itinerary	"Irish itinerary of Father Edmund MacCana", trans. William Reeves, *UJA* ser. 1, vol. 2 (1854), 44–59. Reeves' dating of the document appears to be inaccurate; we have dated it on internal evidence to c. 1700.

Mac Cumhaigh (a)	*Abhráin Airt Mhic Chubhthaigh agus abhráin eile*, eag. Énrí Ó Muirgheasa (Dundalk 1916).
Mac Cumhaigh (b)	*Art Mac Cumhaigh: dánta*, eag. Tomás Ó Fiaich (Baile Átha Cliath 1973).
Mac Domhnaill	*Aodh Mac Domhnaill: dánta*, eag. Colm Beckett (Dún Dealgan 1987).
Map Hall Estates	*Maps of the manor of Mullaglass in the county of Armagh and Narrow-Water in the county of Down, the estates of Savage Hall Esqr., from a survey taken by Pat O'Hare in 1800*, PRONI T2821/1A.
Map of Down (OSNB)	Unspecified map(s) of Co. Down, cited in *OSNB passim*.
Maps Down (Mac Aodha)	"Fianaise chartagrafach i dtaobh ainmneacha bhailte an Dúin, 1573–1864", Breandán S. Mac Aodha, *Ainm* ii (1987), 55–75.
Maps (Mooney)	Unidentified maps, cited in *Mooney, passim*.
Marriage Downshire (OSNB)	Marriage settlement of the Marquis of Downshire, AD 1811, cited in *OSNB, passim*.
Mart. Don.	*The martyrology of Donegal: a calendar of the saints of Ireland*, trans. John O'Donovan, ed. James H. Todd and William Reeves (Dublin 1864).
Mart. Gorm.	*Félire Húi Gormáin: the martyrology of Gorman*, ed. Whitley Stokes (London 1895).
Mart. Tal.	*The martyrology of Tallaght*, ed. R.I. Best and H.J. Lawlor (London 1931).
Mercator's/Hole's Ire.	A map of Ireland, AD 1610, drawn by Gerard Mercator and engraved by William Hole, and published in William Camden's atlas *Britannia, sive florentissimorum regnorum Angliae, Scotiae, Hiberniae, et insularum adiacentium....*
Mercator's Ire.	*Irlandiae Regnum*, by Gerard Mercator, first published in his atlas entitled *Atlas sive Cosmographicae Meditationes de Fabrica Mundi et Fabricati Figura*, AD 1595.
Mercator's Ulst.	*Ultoniae Orientalis Pars* by Gerard Mercator, first published in his *Atlas sive Cosmographicae Meditationis de Fabrica Mundi et Fabricati Figura*, AD 1595.
Met. Dinds.	*The metrical Dindshenchas*, ed. Edward J. Gwynn, 5 vols (Dublin 1903–35).
Miscell. Ann.	*Miscellaneous Irish annals (AD 1114–1437)*, ed. Séamus Ó hInnse (Dublin 1947).
Mon. Ang.	*Monasticon Anglicanum: a history of the abbies and other monasteries, hospitals and frieries...in England and Wales*, William Dugdale (London 1661). New edn John Caley, Sir Henry Ellis and Bulkeley Bandinel, 6 vols (London 1846).

Mon. Hib.
Monasticon Hibernicum: or a history of the abbeys, priories and other religious houses in Ireland, Mervyn Archdall, 3 vols (Dublin 1786). New edn Patrick F. Moran (Dublin 1873–6).

Mooney
An unpublished study of the townlands of the diocese of Dromore and the barony of Iveagh by Bernard J. Mooney (Ballynahinch Library, Co. Down).

Mooney's Rostrevor
The Place-names of Rostrevor, Rev. Bernard J. Mooney (Newry 1950).

Murray's Creggan
The history of the parish of Creggan in the 17th and 18th centuries, L.P. Murray (Dundalk 1940).

Neilson's Intro.
An introduction to the Irish language, William Neilson, 3 parts in 1 vol. (Dublin 1808; reprint Belfast 1990).

Newry Char. (EA)
Extract from the Charter of Newry, *EA* 117.

Newry Char. (Flanagan)
"Confirmation charter and grant of protection of Muirchertach Mac Lochlainn, king of Cenél nEógain and high-king of Ireland, to the Cistercian abbey of Newry, Co. Down", ed. M.T. Flanagan, *Monastic charters from Irish kings of the 12th and 13th centuries,* M.A. thesis, vol. ii, 245–6 (University College Dublin 1973).

Newry Char. (Mon. Ang.)
"Charter of Newry", ed. W. Dugdale, *Mon. Ang.* vi, 1133–4.

Newry Exam. (OSNB)
Newry Examiner, cited in *OSNB, passim.*

Newry Tel. (OSNB)
Newry Telegraph, cited in *OSNB, passim.*

NISMR
Northern Ireland sites and monuments record: stage 1 (1979), published privately by the Department of the Environment (NI) and the Archaeological Survey (Belfast 1979).

Norden's Map
"The plott of Irelande with the confines", formerly included in *A discription of Ireland,* c. 1610, by John Norden. This map had been preserved in the State Paper Office but is now in PRO MPF 67. It is reproduced in *SP Hen. VIII* vol. ii, pt. 3.

Norsk. Tids.
Norsk tidsskrift for sprogvidenskap, under medvirkning av Olaf Broch..., utgitt av Carl J.S. Marstrander (Oslo 1928–).

Nowel's Ire. (1)
A map of Ireland, c. 1570, attributed to Laurence Nowel, dean of Lichfield (d. 1576). British Museum Cotton MS, Domitian A18, ff. 101–103. Reproduced by the Ordnance Survey, Southampton.

Nowel's Ire. (2)
A map of Ireland c. 1570 attributed to Laurence Nowel, dean of Lichfield (d. 1576). British Museum Cotton MS, Domitian A18, f. 97. Reproduced by the Ordnance Survey, Southampton.

Ó Doirnín	*Peadar Ó Doirnín: a bheatha agus a shaothar*, eag. Seán de Rís (Baile Átha Cliath 1969).
Ó Dónaill	*Foclóir Gaeilge-Béarla*, eag. Niall Ó Dónaill (Baile Átha Cliath 1977).
O'Laverty	*An historical account of the diocese of Down and Connor ancient and modern*, Rev. James O'Laverty, 5 vols. (Dublin 1878–95).
Omeath Infs. (1901)	"Dinnseanchas: [Irish forms of place-names supplied by two natives of Omeath]", *GJ* xi (1901), 156–7.
Omeath Infs. (1925c)	"Canúintí an Tuaiscirt, vii: Gaeilge Óméith", Donn S. Piatt, *Ultach* iml. 44, uimh. 8 (Lúnasa 1967), 10–11.
Onoma	*Onoma: bibliographical and information bulletin*, International Centre of Onomastics (Louvain 1950–).
Onom. Goed.	*Onomasticon Goedelicum locorum et tribuum Hiberniae et Scotiae*, Edmund Hogan (Dublin 1910).
O'Reilly	*An Irish–English dictionary*, Edward O'Reilly. Revised and corrected, with a supplement by John O'Donovan (Dublin 1864).
Ortelius Map	*Eryn. Hiberniae, Britannicae Insulae, Nova Descriptio. Irlandt* by Abraham Ortelius. Published in the second edition of his *Theatrum Orbis Terrarum* (Antwerp 1573).
OS 1:10,000	*The Ordnance Survey 1:10,000 series maps*, Ordnance Survey of Northern Ireland (Belfast 1968–).
OS 1:50,000	*The Ordnance Survey 1:50,000 series maps*, also known as *The Discoverer Series*, Ordnance Survey of Northern Ireland (Belfast 1978–88).
OS 6-inch	*The Ordnance Survey six-inch series maps*, first published in the 1830s and 1840s with numerous subsequent editions. It has now been replaced by the OS 1:10,000.
OSL	"Letters [written by John O'Donovan] containing information relative to the [history and] antiquities of the County of Down collected during the progress of the Ordnance Survey in 1834", published as a supplement to *Leabharlann* iii (Dublin 1909).
OSM	*Ordnance Survey memoirs of Ireland*, ed. Angélique Day and Patrick McWilliams (Belfast 1990–).
OSNB	Name-books compiled during the progress of the Ordnance Survey in 1834–5 and preserved in the Ordnance Survey, Phoenix Park, Dublin.
OSNB Inf.	Informants for the Irish forms of place-names in the *OSNB*.

PBNHPS	*Proceedings and reports of the Belfast Natural History and Philosophical Society*, 74 vols (Belfast 1873–1955).
Pipe Roll John	"The Irish pipe roll of 14 John, 1211–2", ed. Oliver Davies and David B. Quinn, supplement to *UJA* ser. 3, vol. iv (1941).
Pontif. Hib.	*Pontificia Hibernica: medieval papal chancery documents concerning Ireland, 640–1261*, ed. Maurice P. Sheehy, 2 vols (Dublin 1962–5).
Porter's Map (OSNB)	Porter's map, cited in *OSNB, passim*.
Post Chaise Comp. (OSNB)	*Post Chaise Companion*, cited in *OSNB, passim*.
Post-Sheanchas	*Post-Sheanchas i n-a bhfuil cúigí, dúithchí, conntaethe, & bailte puist na hÉireann*, Seosamh Laoide (Baile Átha Cliath 1905).
Prerog. Wills Index	*Index to the prerogative wills of Ireland, 1536–1810*, ed. Arthur Edward Vicars (Dublin 1897).
PRIA	*Proceedings of the Royal Irish Academy* (Dublin 1836–). Published in three sections since 1902 (section C: archaeology, linguistics and literature).
PRONI T750/1	Magennis extracts from Sir Thomas Philips' *Revencionum Provinciae Conatiae et Ultoniae*, PRONI T750/1.
Reg. Cromer	"Archbishop Cromer's register", ed. L.P. Murray, *J Louth AS* vii (1929–32), 516–24; viii (1933–6), 38–49, 169–88, 257–74, 322–51; ix (1937–40), 36–41, 124–30; x (1941–44), 116–27; completed by Aubrey Gwynn, 165–79.
Reg. Deeds abstracts	*Registry of Deeds, Dublin. Abstracts of wills, 1708–1832*, ed. P. Beryl Eustace and Eilish Ellis, 3 vols (Dublin 1954–84).
Reg. Dowdall	"A calendar of the register of Primate George Dowdall, commonly called the *Liber Niger* or 'Black Book'", ed. L.P. Murray, *J Louth AS* vi (1925–8), 90–101, 147–58, 211–28; vii (1929–32), 78–95, 258–75.
Reg. Dowdall (EA)	*Register of Primate George Dowdall*, cited in *EA, passim*.
Reg. Fleming	"A calendar of the register of Archbishop Fleming", ed. Rev. H.J. Lawlor, *PRIA* vol. xxx, sect. C (1912), 94–190.
Reg. Free. (OSNB)	*Register of Freeholders*, cited in *OSNB, passim*.
Reg. Mey	*Registrum Johannis Mey: the register of John Mey, Archbishop of Armagh 1443–56*, ed. W.G.H. Quigley and E.F.D. Roberts (Belfast 1972).
Reg. Octavian (EA)	*Register of Octavian de Palatio, Primate 1478–1513*, cited in *EA, passim*.

Reg. Octavian (Swanzy)	*Register of Octavian de Palatio, Primate 1478–1513*, cited in *Swanzy's Dromore, passim.*
Reg. Prene (EA)	*Register of John Prene, Primate 1439–43*, cited in *EA, passim.*
Reg. Swayne	*The register of John Swayne, Archbishop of Armagh and Primate of Ireland 1418–39*, ed. D.A. Chart (Belfast 1935).
Reg. Sweteman	"A calendar of the Register of Archbishop Sweetman", ed. Rev. H.J. Lawlor, *PRIA* vol. xxix, sect. C (1911), 213–310.
Regal Visit. (Reeves)	*Regal visitation of Down, Connor & Dromore, AD 1633–34*, transcribed by William Reeves, and collated and corrected from originals in the Prerogative Office [now the Record Office] Dublin, PRONI DIO/1/24/2/4.
Rennes Dinds.	"The prose tales in the Rennes Dindsenchas", ed. Whitley Stokes, *Rev. Celt.* xv (1894), 272–336, 418–84; xvi (1895), 31–83, 135–67, 269–312.
Rent Roll Down	*Strangford and Lisburn rent roll no. 21, AD 1692*, PRONI T372/E.
Rent Roll Morne	*The rent roll of the Lordship of Morne, AD 1688*, PRONI D619/7/1/1.
Rev. Celt.	*Révue Celtique*, 51 vols (Paris 1870–1934).
Rocque's Map (Coote)	*John Rocque's map of Co. Armagh*, AD 1760, PRONI D602. Reproduced in part in Charles Coote's *Statistical survey of the county of Armagh* (Dublin 1804).
San. Corm. (LB)	"Cormac's Glossary from *Lebor Brecc*", ed. Whitley Stokes, *Three Irish Glossaries* (London 1862).
S. Ard Mh.	*Seanchas Ard Mhacha: journal of the Armagh Diocesan Historical Society* (Armagh 1954–).
Scáthlán	*Scáthlán: iris Chumann Staire agus Seanchais Ghaoth Dobhair* (Béal Átha Seanaigh 1984–).
Scot. Census 1971	*Index of Scottish place names from the 1971 census, with location and population (over 100 persons)*, General Register Office, Scotland (Edinburgh HMSO, 1975).
Scot. Stud.	*Scottish Studies*, School of Scottish Studies (Edinburgh 1957–).
SCtSiadhail	*Seachrán Chairn tSiadhail: amhrán ilcheardaidheachta agus seanchas síor-chuartaidheachta...*, eag. Seosamh Laoide (Baile Átha Cliath 1904).
S-E Ulster Map	A map of south-east Ulster (from Olderfleet in the north to Dundrum in the south), c. 1580, PRO MPF 87.
Sgéalaidhe Óirghiall	*Sgéalaidhe Óirghiall .i. Sgéalaidhe Fearnmhuighe agus tuilleadh leis*, eag. Seosamh Laoide (Baile Átha Cliath 1905).

Shaw Mason's Par. Sur.   *A statistical account, or parochial survey of Ireland, drawn up from the communications of the clergy*, William Shaw Mason, vol. i (Dublin 1814).

SMMD   *Scéla Mucce Meic Dathó*, ed. Rudolph Thurneysen, Medieval and Modern Irish Series iv (Dublin 1935).

S. Patrick Homily   "The Lebar Brecc Homily on S. Patrick", *Trip. Life (Stokes)* ii, 428–489.

Speed's Antrim & Down   A map entitled *Antrym and Downe*, AD 1610, by John Speed. Reproduced in *UJA* ser. 1, vol. i (1853) between pp. 123 and 124.

Speed's Ireland   *The Kingdome of Irland devided into severall Provinces and then againe devided into Counties. Newly described*, AD 1610, by John Speed. Also published in his atlas *The Theatre of the Empire of Great Britain* (Sudbury & Humble 1612).

Speed's Ulster   *The Province Ulster described*, AD 1610, by John Speed. Also published in his atlas *The Theatre of the Empire of Great Britain* (Sudbury & Humble 1612).

SP Hen. VIII   *State papers published under the authority of His Majesty's Commission: King Henry VIII*, 11 vols (London 1830–52).

Statist. Sur. Dn.   *Statistical survey of the county of Down, with observations on the means of improvement...*, John Dubourdieu (Dublin 1802).

Stuart's Armagh   *Historical memoirs of the city of Armagh*, James Stuart (Newry 1819).

Stud. Celt.   *Studia Celtica*, published on behalf of the Board of Celtic Studies of the University of Wales (Cardiff 1966–).

Sub. Roll Down   *Subsidy roll for the county of Down, AD 1663*, PRONI T/307.

Sur. Ulst.   "MS Rawlinson A. 237, The Bodleian Library, Oxford: [A survey of Ulster, AD 1608]", ed. James Hogan, *Anal. Hib.* iii (1931), 151–218.

Swanzy's Dromore   *Succession lists of the diocese of Dromore*, Henry B. Swanzy, ed. J.B. Leslie (Belfast 1933).

Taylor & Skinner   *Maps of the roads of Ireland, surveyed 1777*, by George Taylor and Andrew Skinner (Dublin 1778).

TBC (LL)   *Táin Bó Cúailnge from the Book of Leinster*, ed. Cecile O'Rahilly (Dublin 1967).

TBC (Rec. I)   *Táin Bó Cúailnge Recension I*, ed. Cecile O'Rahilly (Dublin 1976).

Tempest's Louth   *Gossiping guide to County Louth*, H. Tempest (Dundalk 1952).

Terrier (O'Laverty)   "Terrier or ledger book of Down and Connor, c. 1615", *O'Laverty* v, 318–334.

Terrier (Reeves)   *Terrier or ledger book of Down and Connor, c. 1615*, transcribed by William Reeves, PRONI DIO/1/24/2/3.

TNCT   *Townland names of County Tyrone with their meanings*, P. M'Aleer (c. 1920; reprint Portadown & Draperstown 1988).

Tombstone (OSNB)   Tombstone inscription cited in *OSNB, passim.*

Top. Index 1961   *Census of population 1961: topographical index*, Government of Northern Ireland, General Register Office (Belfast 1962).

Topog. Poems   *Topographical poems: by Seaán Mór Ó Dubhagáin and Giolla-na-Naomh Ó hUidhrín*, ed. James Carney (Dublin 1943).

Townland Index Map   *Index maps showing townlands and other administrative units and the disposition of six-inch sheets and 1:2,500 plans*, Ordnance Survey of Northern Ireland (Belfast 1970).

Trias. Thaum.   *Trias Thaumaturga*, tom. ii, John Colgan (Lovanii 1647).

Trien. Visit. (Boyle)   Boyle's *Triennial visitation of Down, Connor and Dromore, AD 1679*, transcribed by William Reeves, PRONI DIO/1/24/16/1, pp. 34–49.

Trien. Visit. (Bramhall)   Bramhall's *Triennial visitation of Down, Connor and Dromore, AD 1661*, transcribed by William Reeves, PRONI DIO/1/24/16/1, pp. 1–16.

Trien. Visit. (Margetson)   Margetson's *Triennial visitation of Down, Connor and Dromore, AD 1664*, transcribed by William Reeves, PRONI DIO/1/24/16/1, pp. 19–33.

Trip. Life (Stokes)   *The tripartite life of Saint Patrick, with other documents relating to that Saint*, ed. Whitley Stokes, 2 vols (London 1887).

UJA   *Ulster Journal of Archaeology*, 1st ser., 9 vols (Belfast 1853–62); 2nd ser., 17 vols (1894–1911); 3rd ser. (1938–).

Ulster Map 1570c   *A plat of Ulster*, c. 1570, annotated by Lord Burghley, AD 1590, PRO MPF 90. There is a copy in PRONI T1493/6.

Ulster Map 1587   *Ulster. The lands to be divided between the Earl of Tyrone and Turlough Lynagh*, AD 1587, PRO MPF 307. There is a copy in PRONI T1493/51.

Ulst. Plant. Paps.   "Ulster Plantation papers 1608–13", ed. T.W. Moody, *Anal. Hib.* viii (1938), 179–297.

Ulster Visit. (Reeves)   *The state of the diocese of Down and Connor, 1622, as returned by Bishop Robert Echlin to the royal commissioners*, copied from TCD E.3.6. by William Reeves, PRONI DIO/1/24/1.

Ultach	*An tUltach: iris oifigiúil Chomhaltas Uladh* (1923–).
Wars Co. Down	"The wars of 1641 in County Down: the deposition of High Sheriff Peter Hill (1645)", transcribed and annotated by Thomas Fitzpatrick with additional notes by Rev. Monsignor O'Laverty and Edward Parkinson, *UJA* ser. 2, vol. x (1904), 73–90.
Wm. Little (OSNB)	William Little, cited in *OSNB, passim*.
Wm. Map (OSNB)	James Williamson's map of Co. Down, AD 1810, cited in *OSNB, passim*.

SECONDARY BIBLIOGRAPHY

Andrews, J.H. 1974 "The maps of the escheated counties of Ulster, 1609–10", *PRIA* vol. lxxiv, sect. C, 133–70.

1975 *A paper landscape; the Ordnance Survey in nineteenth-century Ireland* (Oxford).

1978 *Irish maps: the Irish heritage series, no. 18* (Dublin).

1985 *Plantation acres: an historical study of the Irish land surveyor and his maps* (Belfast).

Arthurs, J.B. 1952–3(d) "Clanrye: the Newry River", *BUPNS* ser. 1, vol. i, 38–40.

1955–6 "The Ulster Place-name Society", *Onoma* vi, 80–2.

Barber, Charles 1976 *Early Modern English* (London).

Bell, Robert 1988 *The book of Ulster surnames* (Belfast).

Byrne, F.J. 1973 *Irish kings and high-kings* (London).

Canavan, Tony 1989 *Frontier town: an illustrated history of Newry* (Belfast).

de hÓir, Éamonn 1964(a) "An t-athru *onga > ú* i roinnt logainmneacha", *Dinnsean.* iml. i, uimh. 1, 8–11.

Falkiner, C.L. 1903 "The counties of Ireland: an historical sketch of their origin, constitution, and gradual delimitation", *PRIA* vol. xxiv, sect. C, 169–94.

1904 *Illustrations of Irish history and topography, mainly of the seventeenth century* (London).

Flanagan, Deirdre 1971 "The names of Downpatrick", *Dinnsean.* iml. iv, uimh. 4, 89–112.

1978(c) "Seventeenth-century salmon fishing in County Down (river-name documentation)", *BUPNS* ser. 2, vol. 1, 22–6.

1978(d) "Transferred population or sept-names: *Ulaidh* (a quo Ulster)", *BUPNS* ser. 2, vol. 1, 40–3.

1978(e) "Places and their names: Quoile and British", *BUPNS* ser. 2, vol. 1, 44–7; 51–2.

1979(a) "Common elements in Irish place-names: *ceall, cill*", *BUPNS* ser. 2, vol. 2, 1–8.

1979(f) "Review of *The meaning of Irish place names* by James O'Connell (Belfast 1978)", *BUPNS* ser. 2, vol. 2, 58–60.

1981–2(b) "Some guidelines to the use of Joyce's *Irish names of places*, vol. i", *BUPNS* ser. 2, vol. 4, 61–9.

1981–2(c) "A summary guide to the more commonly attested ecclesiastical elements in place-names", *BUPNS* ser. 2, vol. 4, 69–75.

Goblet, Y.M.   1932   *A topographical index of the parishes and townlands of Ire-*
                                   land in Sir William Petty's Mss. barony maps (c. 1655–9)…
                                   and Hiberniae Delineatio (c. 1672) (Dublin).

Hamilton, G.E.   1915   "Rostrevor, County Down: its name", *JRSAI* xlv, 313–4.

Kenney, J.F.   1929   *The sources for the early history of Ireland: an introduction*
                                   and guide, vol. i: ecclesiastical (New York).

Mac Airt, Seán   1958   "The churches founded by Saint Patrick" in *Saint*
                                   Patrick, ed. John Ryan, 67–80 (Dublin).

McCracken, Eileen   1971   *The Irish woods since Tudor times; distribution and exploita-*
                                   tion (Belfast).

McErlean, Thomas   1983   "The Irish townland system of landscape organisation"
                                   in *Landscape archaeology in Ireland*, ed. Terence Reeves-
                                   Smyth and Fred Hamond, 315–39 (Oxford).

Mac Giolla Easpaig, D. 1984   "Logainmneacha na Rosann", *Dongl. Ann.* vol. 36, 48–60.
                       1986   "Logainmneacha Ghaoth Dobhair", *Scáthlán* vol. 3,
                                   64–88.

MacLysaght, Edward   1957   *Irish families: their names, arms and origins* (Dublin).
                       1964   *A guide to Irish surnames* (Dublin).
                       1982   *More Irish families: a new revised and enlarged edition of*
                                   "More Irish families" (1960), incorporating "Supplement
                                   to Irish families" (1964), with an essay on Irish chieftain-
                                   ries (Dublin).
                       1985   *The surnames of Ireland* (Dublin, 4th edn; 1st edn 1957).

Mallory, J.P.   1991   *The archaeology of Ulster from colonization to plantation*
& McNeill, T.E.   (Belfast).

Moody, T.W.   1939   *The Londonderry plantation, 1609–41: the city of London*
                                   and the plantation in Ulster (Belfast).

Mooney, B.J.   1952–3(c)   "Kilcorway and Clanrye", *BUPNS* ser. 1, vol. i, 38.

Morton, Deirdre   1956–7   "Tuath-divisions in the baronies of Belfast and
                                   Masserene", *BUPNS* ser. 1, vol. iv, 38–44; v, 6–12.

Munn, A.M.   1925   *Notes on the place names of the parishes and townlands of*
                                   the County of Londonderry (1925; reprint Ballinascreen
                                   1985).

Nicolaisen, W.F.H.   1958   "Notes on Scottish place-names: 5. Shin", *Scot. Stud.*
                                   vol. 2, 189–92.

Ó Canann, Tomás   1989–90   "Notes on some Donegal place-names", *Ainm* iv, 107–24.

Ó Concheanainn, T.   1966   "*Ainmneacha éideimhne*", *Dinnsean.* iml. ii, uimh. 2, 15–19.

Ó Corráin, D. & Maguire, F.	1981	*Gaelic personal names* (Dublin).

O'Curry, Eugene | 1861 | *Lectures on the manuscript materials of ancient Irish history* (Dublin).

Ó Dochartaigh, C. | 1987 | *Dialects of Ulster Irish* (Belfast).

O'Donovan, John | 1849 | *Miscellany of the Celtic Society...* (Dublin).

Ó Foghludha, R. | 1935 | *Log-ainmneacha .i. dictionary of Irish place-names...* (Dublin).

Ó Máille, T.S.
1955(b) "*Muiceanach* mar áitainm", *JRSAI* lxxxv, 88–93.
1960 "*Cuilleann* in áitainmneacha", *Béaloid.* xxviii, 50–64.
1962(a) "*Corrán, Curraun, Corrane, Craan*", *Béaloid.* xxx, 76–88.
1987 "Place-name elements in -*ar*", *Ainm* ii, 27–36.
1989–90 "Irish place-names in -*as*, -*es*, -*is*, -*os*, -*us*", *Ainm* iv, 125–43.

Ó Mainnín, M.B.
1989–90 "The element *island* in Ulster place-names", *Ainm* iv, 200–210.

Ó Maolfabhail, Art
1974 "*Grianán* i logainmneacha", *Dinnsean.* iml. vi, uimh. 2, 60–75.
1982 "An logainm *Tóin re Gaoith*", *S. Ard Mh.* vol. 10, no. 2, 366–79.
1987–8 "Baill choirp mar logainmneacha", *Ainm* ii, 76–82; iii, 18–26.
1990 *Logainmneacha na hÉireann, iml. I: Contae Luimnigh* (Baile Átha Cliath).

Ó Muirí, Réamonn
1989 "Newry and the French revolution, 1792", *S. Ard Mh.* vol. 13, no. 2, 102–20.

Ó Muraíle, Nollaig
1985 *Mayo places: their names and origins* (Dublin).
1987(a) "The Gaelic personal name *(An) Dubhaltach*", *Ainm* ii, 1–26.

O'Rahilly, T.F.
1922 "Irish poets, historians, and judges in English documents, 1538–1615", *PRIA* vol. xxxvi, sect. C, 86–120.
1932 *Irish dialects past and present* (Dublin; reprint 1976).
1933 "Notes on Irish place-names", *Hermathena* xxiii, 196–220.
1946 *Early Irish history and mythology* (Dublin; reprint 1976).

Orpen, G.H.
1911–20 *Ireland under the Normans, 1169–1333*, 4 vols (Oxford; reprint 1968).

O'Sullivan, Harold	1985	"A 1575 rent-roll, with contemporaneous maps, of the Bagenal estate in the Carlingford Lough district", *J Louth AS* vol. xxi, no. 1, 31–47.
Otway-Ruthven, A.J.	1964	"Parochial development in the rural deanery of Skreen", *JRSAI* xciv, 111–22.
Petty, William	1672	*The political anatomy of Ireland* (1672), reprinted in *Tracts and treatises illustrative of Ireland* ii, 72–3 (Dublin 1860–1).
Power, Patrick	1907	*The place-names of Decies* (London).
	1932	*Crichad an chaoilli: being the topography of ancient Fermoy* (Cork).
	1947	"The bounds and extent of Irish parishes", *Féil. Torna* 218–23.
Price, Liam	1945–67	*The place-names of County Wicklow*, 7 vols. (Dublin).
	1963	"A note on the use of the word *baile* in place-names", *Celtica* vi, 119–26.
Quiggin, E.C.	1906	*A dialect of Donegal, being the speech of Meenawannia in the parish of Glenties* (Cambridge).
Reeves, William	1861	"On the townland distribution of Ireland", *PRIA* vii, 473–90.
Reid, Professor	1957	"A note on *cinament*", *BUPNS* ser. 1, vol. v, 12.
Sommerfelt, Alf	1929	"South Armagh Irish", *Norsk Tids.* ii, 107–91.
	1958	"The English forms of the names of the main provinces of Ireland", *Lochlann* i, 223–7.
Stockman, Gearóid	1991	"Focail: Loisc", *Ultach iml.* 68, *uimh.* 3 (Márta), 26.
Taylor, Isaac	1896	*Names and their histories* (1896), reprinted in the Everyman edition of his *Words and places* (1911).
Toner, Gregory	1991–2	"*Money* in the place-names of east Ulster", forthcoming in *Ainm* v.
Treanor, Bernard	1960	*The story of Drumgath* (Newry).
Walsh, Paul	1930	*The will and family of Hugh O'Neill, Earl of Tyrone [with an appendix of genealogies]* (Dublin).
Watson, William	1926	*The history of the Celtic place-names of Scotland* (Edinburgh; reprint Shannon 1973).
Woulfe, Patrick	1923	*Sloinnte Gaedheal is Gall: Irish names and surnames; collected and edited with explanatory and historical notes* (Dublin).

GLOSSARY OF TECHNICAL TERMS

advowson   The right of presenting a clergyman to a vacant benefice.

affricate   A plosive pronounced in conjunction with a fricative; e.g. the sounds spelt with *(t)ch* or *-dge* in English.

alveolar   Pronounced with the tip of the tongue touching the ridge of hard flesh behind the upper teeth; e.g. *t* in the English word *tea*.

analogy   The replacement of a form by another in imitation of words of a similar class; e.g. in imitation of *bake – baked, fake – faked, rake – raked* a child or foreigner might create a form *shaked*.

anglicize   Make English in form; e.g. in place-names the Irish word *baile* "homestead, townland" is anglicized *bally*.

annal   A record of events in chronological order, according to the date of the year.

annates   Later known as First Fruits; a tax paid, initially to the Pope, by a clergyman on appointment to a benefice.

apocope   The loss of the end of a word.

aspiration   (i) The forcing of air through a narrow passage thereby creating a frictional sound; e.g. *gh* in the word *lough* as pronounced in Ireland and Scotland is an aspirated consonant, (ii) the modification of a consonant sound in this way, indicated in Irish writing by putting *h* after the consonant; e.g. *p* aspirated resembles the *ph* sound at the beginning of *phantom*; also called **lenition**.

assimilation   The replacing of a sound in one syllable by another to make it similar to a sound in another syllable; e.g. in some dialects of Irish the *r* in the first syllable of the Latin *sermon-* was changed to *n* in imitation of the *n* in the second syllable, giving a form *seanmóin*.

ballybetagh   Irish *baile biataigh* "land of a food-provider", native land unit, the holder of which had a duty to maintain his lord and retinue when travelling in the area (*Colton Vis.* p.130).

ballyboe   Irish *baile bó* "land of a cow", a land unit equivalent to a modern townland, possibly so-named as supplying the yearly rent of one cow (*Colton Vis.* p. 130).

barony   In Ireland an administrative unit midway in size between a county and a civil parish, originally the landholding of a feudal baron (*EA* p. 62).

benefice   An ecclesiastical office to which income is attached.

bilabial   Articulated by bringing the two lips together; e.g. the *p* in the English word *pea*.

Brittonic   Relating to the branch of Celtic languages which includes Welsh, Cornish and Breton.

202

calendar A précis of an historical document or documents with its contents arranged according to date.

carrow Irish *ceathrú* "a quarter". See **quarter**.

cartography The science of map-making.

cartouche An ornamental frame round the title etc. of a map.

carucate Latin *carucata* "ploughland", a territorial unit, the equivalent of a townland.

Celtic Relating to the (language of the) Irish, Scots, Manx, Welsh, Cornish, Bretons, and Gauls.

centralized Pronounced with the centre of the tongue raised; e.g. the vowel sound at the beginning of *again* or at the end of *the*.

cess Tax.

cinament A territorial unit of lesser size than a **tuogh** (which see). Three derivations have been suggested: (i) from Irish *cine* "a family", (*cineamhain?*) (*EA* 388); (ii) from French *scindement* "cutting up, division" (Morton 1956–7, 39); (iii) from French *(a)ceignement* "enclosure(?)" (Reid 1957, 12).

civil parish An administrative unit based on the medieval parish.

cluster See **consonant cluster.**

coarb Irish *comharba*, originally the heir of an ecclesiastical office, later a high-ranking hereditary tenant of church land under the bishop. The coarb may be in charge of other ecclesiastical tenants called **erenaghs**, which see.

compound A word consisting of two or more verbal elements; e.g. *aircraft, housework*.

consonant (i) An element of the alphabet which is not a vowel, e.g. *c, j, x*, etc., (ii) a speech sound in which the passage of air through the mouth or nose is impeded, e.g. at the lips *(b, p, or m)*, at the teeth *(s, z)*, etc.

consonant cluster A group of two or more consonants; e.g. *bl* in *blood, ndl* in *handle, lfths* in *twelfths*.

contraction (i) The shortening of a word or words normally by the omission of one or more sounds, (ii) a contracted word; e.g. *good-bye* is a contraction of *God be with you; can not* is contracted to *can't*.

county Feudal land division, equivalent to an English shire, created by the English administration in Ireland as the major subdivision of an Irish province.

deanery Properly called a rural deanery, an ecclesiastical division of people or land administered by a rural dean.

declension   A group of nouns whose case-endings vary according to a fixed pattern. (There are five declensions in modern Irish).

delenition   Sounding or writing a consonant as if it were not aspirated; see **aspiration**.

dental   A sound pronounced with the tip of the tongue touching the upper teeth; e.g. *th* in the English *thumb*.

devoicing   Removing the sound caused by the resonance of vocal cords; see **voiced**.

dialect   A variety of a language in a given area with distinctive vocabulary, pronunciation or grammatical forms.

digraph   A group of two letters expressing a single sound; e.g. *ea* in English *team* or *ph* in English *photograph*.

diocese   The area or population over which a bishop has ecclesiastical authority.

diphthong   A union of two vowel sounds pronounced in one syllable; e.g. *oi* in English *boil*. (Note that a diphthong cannot be sung on a single sustained note without changing the position of the mouth).

dissimilation   The replacing of a sound in one syllable by another to make it different from a sound in another syllable e.g. Loughbrickland comes from an original Irish form, *Loch Bricrenn*.

eclipsis   The replacement in Irish of one sound by another in initial position as the result of the influence of the previous word; e.g. the *c* of Irish *cór* "choir" (pronounced like English *core*) is eclipsed by *g* in the phrase *i gcór* "in a choir" due to the influence of the preposition *i*, and *gcór* is pronounced like English *gore*; also called **nasalization**.

elision   The omission of a sound in pronunciation; e.g. the *d* is elided in the word *handkerchief*.

emphasis   See **stress**.

epenthetic vowel   A vowel sound inserted within a word; e.g. in Ireland an extra vowel is generally inserted between the *l* and *m* of the word *film*.

erenagh   Irish *airchinnech* "steward", hereditary officer in charge of church lands, later a tenant to the bishop (*Colton Vis.* pp. 4–5).

escheat   Revert to the feudal overlord, in Ireland usually forfeit to the English crown.

etymology   The facts relating to the formation and meaning of a word.

fiant   A warrant for the making out of a grant under the royal seal, or (letters) patent.

fricative   A speech sound formed by narrowing the passage of air from the mouth so that audible friction is produced; e.g. *gh* in Irish and Scottish *lough*.

Gaelic   Relating to the branch of Celtic languages which includes Irish, Scottish Gaelic and Manx.

glebe   The house and land (and its revenue) provided for the clergyman of a parish.

glide   A sound produced when the organs of speech are moving from the position for one speech sound to the position for another; e.g. in pronouncing the word *deluge* there is a *y*-like glide between the *l* and the *u*.

gloss   A word or phrase inserted in a manuscript to explain a part of the text.

Goedelic = **Gaelic**   which see.

grange   Anglo-Norman term for farm land providing food or revenue for a feudal lord, frequently a monastery.

haplology   The omission of a syllable beside another with a similar sound; e.g. *lib(ra)ry, deteri(or)ated*.

hearth money   A tax on the number of hearths used by a household.

impropriator   The person to whom rectorial tithes of a monastery etc. were granted after the Dissolution.

inflect   To vary the form of a word to indicate a different grammatical relationship; e.g. *man* singular, *men* plural.

inquisition   A judicial inquiry, here usually into the possessions of an individual at death.

International Phonetic Alphabet   The system of phonetic transcription advocated by the International Phonetic Association.

labial = **bilabial** which see.

lenition   See **aspiration**.

lexicon   The complete word content of a language.

lowering   Changing a vowel sound by dropping the tongue slightly in the mouth; e.g. pronouncing *doctor* as *dactor*.

manor   Feudal estate (Anglo–Norman and Plantation), smaller than a barony, entitling the landowner to jurisdiction over his tenants at a manor court.

martyrology   Irish *féilire*, also translated "calendar", a list of names of saints giving the days on which their feasts are to be celebrated.

mearing   A boundary.

metathesis   The transposition of sounds in a word; e.g. saying *elascit* instead of *elastic*.

moiety   French *moitié*, "the half of", also a part or portion of any size.

morphology   The study of the grammatical structure of words.

nasalization   See **eclipsis**.

oblique   Having a grammatical form other than nominative singular.

onomasticon   A list of proper names, usually places.

orthography   Normal spelling.

palatal   A sound produced with the tongue raised towards the hard palate.

parish   A subdivision of a diocese served by a single main church or clergyman.

patent   (or letters patent), an official document conferring a right or privilege, frequently here a grant of land.

patronymic   A name derived from that of the father.

phonemic   Relating to the system of phonetic oppositions in the speech sounds of a language, which make, in English for example, *soap* a different word from *soup*, and *pin* a different word from *bin*.

phonetic   Relating to vocal sound.

phonology   The study of the sound features of a language.

plosive   A sound formed by closing the air passage and then releasing the air flow suddenly, causing an explosive sound; e.g. *p* in English *pipe*.

ploughland   Medieval English land unit of about 120 acres, equivalent to a townland.

prebend   An endowment, often in land, for the maintenance of a canon or prebendary, a senior churchman who assisted the bishop or had duties in the cathedral.

precinct   *Ad hoc* land division (usually a number of townlands) used in Plantation grants.

prefix   A verbal element placed at the beginning of a word which modifies the meaning of the word; e.g. *un-* in *unlikely*.

proportion   *Ad hoc* land division (usually a number of townlands) used in Plantation grants.

province   Irish *cúige* "a fifth": the largest administrative division in Ireland, of which there are now four (Ulster, Leinster, Connaught, Munster) but were once five.

quarter   Land unit often a quarter of the ballybetagh, and thus containing three or four townlands, but sometimes referring to a subdivision of a townland. See also **carrow**.

206

GLOSSARY OF TECHNICAL TERMS

raising Changing a vowel sound by lifting the tongue higher in the mouth; e.g. pronouncing *bag* as *beg*.

realize Pronounce; e.g. *-adh* at the end of verbal nouns in Ulster Irish is realized as English *-oo*.

rectory A parish under the care of a rector supported by its tithes; if the rector cannot reside in the parish he appoints and supports a resident vicar.

reduction (i) Shortening of a vowel sound; e.g. the vowel sound in *board* is reduced in the word *cupboard*, (ii) = **contraction** which see.

register A document providing a chronological record of the transactions of an individual or organization.

rounded Pronounced with pouting lips; e.g. the vowel sounds in *oar* and *ooze*.

seize To put in legal possession of property, especially land.

semantic Relating to the meaning of words.

semivowel A sound such as *y* or *w* at the beginning of words like *yet*, *wet*, etc.

sept Subgroup of people, for instance of a tribe or ruling family.

sessiagh Irish *seiseach* "a sixth", usually referring to a subdivision of a townland or similar unit. Apparently three sessiaghs were equivalent to a ballyboe (*Colton Vis.* 130).

shift of stress The transfer of emphasis from one syllable to another; e.g. *Belfast* was originally stressed on the second syllable *fast* but because of shift of stress many people now pronounce it **Bel***fast*. See **stress**.

stem (dental, o-, etc.) Classification of nouns based on the form of their endings before the Old Irish period.

stress The degree of force with which a syllable is pronounced. For example, the name Antrim is stressed on the first syllable while Tyrone is stressed on the second.

subdenomination A smaller land division, usually a division of a townland.

substantive A noun.

suffix A verbal element placed at the end of a word which modifies the meaning of the word; e.g. *-less* in *senseless*.

syllable A unit of pronunciation containing one vowel sound which may be preceded or followed by a consonant or consonants; e.g. *I, my, hill,* have one syllable; *outside, table, ceiling* have two; *sympathy, understand, telephone* have three, etc.

207

syncopation   The omission of a short unstressed vowel or digraph when a syllable beginning with a vowel is added; e.g. *tiger*+*ess* becomes *tigress*.

tate   A small land unit once used in parts of Ulster, treated as equivalent to a townland, although only half the size.

termon   Irish *tearmann*, land belonging to the Church, with privilege of sanctuary (providing safety from arrest for repentant criminals), usually held for the bishop by a coarb as hereditary tenant.

terrier   A list of the names of lands held by the Church or other body.

tithes   Taxes paid to the Church. Under the native system they were shared between parish clergy and erenagh (as the tenant of the bishop), under the English administration they were payable to the local clergyman of the Established Church.

topography   The configuration of a land surface, including its relief and the position of its features.

toponymy   Place-names as a subject for study.

townland   The common term or English translation for a variety of small local land units; the smallest unit in the 19th-century Irish administrative system.

transcription   An indication by written symbols of the precise sound of an utterance.

tuogh   Irish *tuath* "tribe, tribal kingdom", a population or territorial unit.

unrounded   Articulated with the lips spread or in neutral position; see **rounded**.

velar   Articulated with the back of the tongue touching the soft palate; e.g. *c* in *cool*.

vicarage   A parish in the charge of a vicar, the deputy either for a rector who received some of the revenue but resided elsewhere, or for a monastery or cathedral or lay impropriator.

visitation   An inspection of (church) lands, usually carried out for a bishop (ecclesiastical or episcopal visitation) or for the Crown (regal visitation).

vocalization   The changing of a consonant sound into a vowel sound by widening the air passage; akin to the disappearance of *r* in Southern English pronunciation of words like *bird, worm, car*.

voiced   Sounded with resonance of the vocal cords. (A test for voicing can be made by closing the ears with the fingers and uttering a consonant sound. e.g. *ssss, zzzz, ffff, vvvv*. If a buzzing or humming sound is heard the consonant is voiced; if not it is voiceless).

voiceless   See **voiced**.

INDEX TO IRISH PLACE-NAMES
(with pronunciation guide)

The following guide to the pronunciation of Irish forms suggested in this book is only approximate. Words are to be sounded as though written in English. The following symbols have the value shown:

ă   as in *above, coma*
ā   as in *father, draught*
ċ   as in *lough, Bach*
ch as in *chip, church*
ġ   does not occur in English. To approximate this sound try gargling without water, or consider the following: *lock* is to *lough* as *log* is to *loġ*. If you cannot manage this sound just pronounce it like g in *go*.
gh as in *lough, Bach*; not as in *foghorn*
ī   as in *five, line*
ky as in *cure, McKeown*
ly at beginning of words as in *brilliant, million*
ō   as in *boar, sore*
ow as in *now, plough*

Stress is indicated by writing the vowel in the stressed syllable in bold, e.g., Arm**a**gh, Ballym**e**na, L**u**rgan.

Place-Name	Rough Guide	Page No.
Abhainn Bhuí, An	ăn óne **wee**	159
Abhainn Ghann, An	ăn óne **ġan**	158
Achadh an Tobair	aghoon **tu**bber	90
Achadh Bhile	aghoo **vi**llă	56
Achadh Cabhán	aghoo **cow**an	91
Achadh na Maolrátha	aghoo nă mw**ee**lrahă	57
Achadh na nGabhann	aghoo năng **ō**ne	58
Allt na bhFiach	alt nă **vee**agh	6
Ard Caorach	ard **kee**ragh	90
Ard Darach	ard **da**rragh	6
Bábhún, An	ă **bá**woon	64
Baile an Bhealaigh	ballin **va**lly	63
Baile an Chorraigh	ballin **ċu**rry	135
Baile an Deiseoláin	ballin **jesh**ăline	59
Baile an Dubhaltaigh	ballin **doo**lty	136
Baile an Fheadáin	ballin **ya**ddine	142
Baile an Locha	ballin **lou**ghă	93
Baile an Mhuilinn	ballin **wi**llin	79
Baile an Reanna	ballin **ra**nnă	137
Baile an Toir	ballin **ti**r	138
Baile Bláthach	ballă **blá**gh	92
Baile Bocht, An	ă ballă **bo**ċt	39
Baile Caol	ballă **kee**l	118
Baile Dubh	ballă **doo**	118

209

Place-Name	Rough Guide	Page No.
Baile Eachmhílidh	bal aċveely	140
Baile Éamainn	bal aimin	140
Baile Mhic an Reachtaí Beag	ballă vick ă raċty beg	93
Baile Mhic an Reachtaí Mór	ballă vick ă raċty more	93
Baile Mhic Dhonnchaidh	ballă vick ġonaghy	61
Baile na gCléireach	ballă nă gleyragh	72
Baile na gCreag	ballă nă grag	9
Baile na Ladhaire	ballă nă leyră	7
Baile na Muine	ballă nă mwinnă	141
Baile Ruiséil	ballă rushel	62
Baile Uí Thuathaláin	bally hoohăline	8
Barr an Fheadáin	bar ă nyadine	44
Bearn Mhín	barn veen	119
Beitheanach	beyhănagh	10
Bhascoill, An	ă waskăl	95
Bhoirinn, An	ă wirrin	65
Caiseal Fhlannagáin	kashel lanagine	14
Caol Uisce	keel ishkă	163
Carn Bán	karn bán	12
Carn Éanaigh	karn ainy	120
Carraig an Éin	karrick ăn yane	157
Carraig an Róin	karrick ă róne	157
Carraig Chró Mhadaidh	karrick ċro waddy	96
Carraig Uí Chrosáin	karrick ee ċrossine	68
Carraig Uí Mhaoilsté	karrick ee wilshtey	69
Ceathrú Mhic Ceallaigh	kyarhoo vick cally	11
Ceathrú Mhín	kyarhoo veen	67
Chabrach, An	ă ċabragh	66
Charraigeach Bhán, An	ă ċarrigagh wán	96
Cheis, An	ă ċyesh	109
Chloch Fhada, An	ă ċlogh addă	84
Chloch Mhór, An	ă ċlogh wore	158
Chros, An	ă ċross	121
Cill Bhrónaí	kill wroney	132
Cill Eoghain	kill óne	146
Cill Fiacháin	kill feeaghine	144
Cloch Ghearráin	clogh yarrine	157
Clochán Ramhar	cloghan ráwăr	14
Cluain Dalláin	cloon dalline	54
Cluainte Flís	cloonchă fleesh	72
Cnoc Bán	crock bán	158
Cnoc Bearach	crock barragh	148
Cnoc na nAirní	crock nă narnyee	102
Cnoc Sí	crock shee	158
Coill Tarbh	kăl taroo	122
Coillidh Sabháin	kălly sawine	101
Corr Chríochach	corr ċreeċagh	16

Place-Name	Rough Guide	Page No.
Lios Dubh, An	ă lyiss doo	30
Lios na Rí	lyiss nă ree	31
Lios na Srian	lyiss nă sreean	125
Lios Seaghsa	lyiss shysă	123
Liosar Buí	lyissăr bwee	31
Loch Cairlinn	lough karlin	81
Loch Eorna	lough orna	32
Lorga an Áir	lorrag ăn are	103
Lorgain Chú Chonnacht	lorragin ċoo ċonnaght	124
Lorgain Uí Cháinte	lorragin ee ċántchă	78
Maigh Eo	mwy ó	78
Maigh Ó gCanann	mwy o gannăn	150
Mónaidh Droma Bhrisc	money drumă vrishk	104
Muine Mór	mwinnă more	105
Pointe, An	ă pwintchă	160
Poll na nGrásta	pull năng rástă	44
Ráth Cruithne	ra crinhă	43
Ráth Fraoileann	ra freelăn	126
Rí, An	ă ree	40
Rian	reean	33
Rinn an Lis	rin ă lish	107
Rinn Bhán, An	ă rin wán	106
Rinn Chláir	rin ċlár	107
Rinn Mhic Giolla Ruaidh	rin vick gillă rooey	165
Ros Treabhair	ross trower	152
Ruáin, Na	nă rooine	158
Sabhall Beag	sowăl beg	34
Sabhall Mór	sowăl more	34
Seanáthán	shanahan	35
Sliabh an Charnáin	shleeoo ă ċarnine	84
Sliabh Bán	shleeoo bán	158
Sliabh Diarmada	shleeoo jeermădă	158
Sliabh Fada	shleeoo faddă	158
Sliabh Mártain	shleeoo mártin	159
Sliabh Meascán	shleeoo maskan	159
Sliabh Mhic Rúslaing	shleeoo vick rooslin	159
Sliabh Mín	shleeoo meen	159
Sliabh Míol	shleeoo meel	159
Sliabh Rua	shleeoo rooa	159
Tamhnach an Choirthe	townagh ă ċirhă	80
Tamhnaigh Bheithe	towny veyhă	155
Tuar Mór, An	ă toor more	39
Tulach na Croise	tullagh nă croshă	101
Tulaigh Mhór	tully wore	108
Tulaigh Uí Chaollaí	tully ċeelly	124
Tulaigh Uí Mhuirí	tully wirree	108
Uanlaigh	oonly	32

PLACE-NAME INDEX

Sheet numbers are given below for the OS 1:50,000 map only where the name occurs on that map. Not all the townlands discussed in this volume appear on the published 1:50,000 map and no sheet number is given for those names. The sheet numbers for the 1:10,000 series and the earlier 6-inch series, which is still important for historical research, are supplied for townlands, although not for other names. The 6-inch sheet numbers refer to the Co. Down series except where otherwise stated.

Place-Name	1:50,000	1:10,000	6 inch	Page
Ballyrussell		267, 277	51	62
Ballyvally	29	267	47, 51	63
Barnmeen	29	253	41, 47	119
Bavan	29	253, 267	47	64
Benagh	29	266, 267	47	10
Bernish Rock	29			40
Burren	29	266, 267, 276, 277	51	65
Buskhill		237, 252	40, 41	95
Cabragh	29	253, 267	47	66
Cargabane	29	237, 252	41	96
Carlingford Lough	29			81
Carmeen	29	267	47, 51	67
Carnacally	29	252	40, 41, 46, 47	11
Carnany	29	253, 267	47	120
Carnbane	29	252	22, 26 (Arm.)	12
Carneyhough		266	46, 47	12
Carnmeen		252	46	13
Carpenham	29			156
Carrickbawn Wood	29			156
Carrickcrossan	29	253, 267	47	68
Carrickmacstay	29	267, 277	51	69
Carrickrovaddy		252	40, 46	96
Carriganean	29			157
Carrigaroan	29			157
Carrogs	29	266, 277	51	71
Cash, The	29			109
Castle Enigan		252, 253	41, 47	14
Clanrye River	29			40
Cloghadda	29			84
Cloghanramer		252	46, 47	14
Cloghgarran	29			157
Cloghmore	29			158
Clonallan Glebe	29	277	51, 54	72
Clonallan Parish				54
Clonta Fleece	29	267, 277	51	72
Commons		266	46, 50, 51	15
Corcreeghy	29	252	40, 41, 46	16
Corgary	29	237, 252	40, 46	97
Craigmore Viaduct	29			43
Craignamona	29			84
Creeve		266	46, 47	16
Crenville	29			158
Croan	29	253, 267	47	74
Crobane	29	266	47	17
Crockbane	29			158
Croreagh		252, 266	47	18
Cross	29	253	41, 42, 47, 48	121

Place-Name	1:50,000	1:10,000	6 inch	Page
Greenan	29	266, 276	50, 51	28
Hawkins Bridge	29			44
Kilbroney	29	267, 277	51, 52, 54	144
Kilbroney Parish				132
Kilbroney Upper	29	267, 277	51, 52	144
Kilfeaghan	29	277, 278, 284	55	144
Kilfeaghan Upper		277, 278	55	144
Killowen				157
Killowen Mountains	29	277	54, 55	146
Killysavan	29	237	33, 40	101
Kiltarriff	29	253	41	122
Knockbarragh	29	267, 277	51	148
Knocknanarny		252	40, 46	102
Knockshee	29			158
Leckan Beg		277		158
Leckan More	29			158
Levallyclanone		277	51, 54	149
Levallyreagh		277	51	150
Lisdrumgullion		266	46 (Arm.)	29
Lisdrumliska	29	266	46, 50 (Arm.)	29
Lisduff	29	252	46	30
Lisnaree		253	41	31
Lisnashrean	29			125
Lisserboy		252	40, 41	31
Lissize	29	253	41	123
Loughorne	29	252	41	32
Lurganare	29	252	40, 46	103
Lurgancahone	29	253	41, 47	124
Lurgancanty	29	267	51	78
Maddydrumbrist		252	40	104
Mayo	29	267	47, 51	78
Mayobridge	29			83
McGaffin's Corner	29			113
McGinn's Cross	29			125
Milltown	29	266, 267	51	79
Moneymore		237, 252	40	105
Mount Mill Bridge	29			113
Moygannon	29	277	51, 54	150
Narrow Water	29	276, 277	51, 54	163
Newry Parish				3
Newtown		277	51, 52, 54	151
Newtown Upper		267, 277	51, 52	151
Ouley	29	238, 253	41	32
Point Park, The		277	54	152
Pollnagrasta	29			44
Rathfriland	29	253		126
Ringbane		252, 253	41	106